STRATEGY SUSTAINABILITY *and* MANAGEMENT ACCOUNTING

Chandana Alawattage

CGA
PUBLISHING

Wishaw, North Lanakshire, UK.

Strategy Sustainability and Management Accounting

ISBN: 978-1-9193748-0-2

CGA Publishing (author self-publishing), 96 Shankly Drive, Morningside, Wishaw, ML2 9QZ, United Kingdom

cgalawattage@hotmail.com

The cover page features an image generated by AI using prompts related to strategy, management accounting, and sustainability

to my family ...

wife Lalani

daughter Imesha

son Sajan

Preface

This book is the result of my years of teaching strategic management accounting (SMA) at two venerable liberal universities. My dual goal is to present SMA as a social science while also exploring its techno-managerial and professional essence. This approach may seem paradoxical, as it seeks to achieve two seemingly conflicting objectives within the constraints of limited teaching time.

On the one hand, in line with its professional focus, the book introduces the prevalent techno-managerial aspects of SMA. Within the confines of a ten-week course, it comprehensively explores key strategic management accounting themes. These themes range from pre-Porterian, Porterian (after Michael Porter), and post-Porterian strategy discourses, to specific topics of strategic pricing, strategic performance management, strategic management control, organisational resilience, quality costing and management, manufacturing flexibility, and strategic cost management. The book addresses the techno-managerial nuances of these strategic themes.

On the other hand, in keeping with the critical approach expected of students in liberal universities, emphasising research-led teaching and learning, this book aims to provide a social science perspective on the techno-managerial aspects of the subject. As I have explored in my classrooms and further elaborated in my other publications (e.g., Alawattage and Wickramasinghe, 2024), this social science approach to teaching SMA involves enacting the following epistemic actions: particularising, contextualising, historicising, politicising, and theorising.

1. Particularising: This refers to understanding the specific techno-managerial aspects of various SMA topics, such as strategic positioning, strategic performance management and control, organisational resilience, quality costing, and manufacturing flexibility. This foundational epistemic act enables a deeper engagement with SMA's core techno-managerial elements and sets the stage for other critical epistemic actions. Particularisation helps to learn and clarify the techno-managerial specificities that determine how management accounting techniques and frameworks are deployed in particular organisational settings in relation to strategy and sustainability.
2. Contextualising: This involves placing SMA's techno-managerial elements within the broader political-economic context of capitalism and neoliberalism to appreciate and critique their underlying political-economic logics. Through contextualising, we can understand the broader reasons why these management accounting techniques are necessary, and the politico-institutional rationales for their adoption in contemporary organisational settings.
3. Historicising: This refers to exploring and explaining the evolution of SMA's political-economic role in tandem with the historical dynamics of capitalism. It includes examining the historical specificities that have shaped current accounting calculations and rationalisations, which we learn as SMA and sustainability in this textbook.
4. Politicising: This act examines the political roles that SMA plays. It means recognising how SMA techniques and methods evolved to serve the interests of dominant groups, primarily owners of socialised private capital, and how they can be remoulded to serve interests beyond such dominant groups, including a broader agenda of sustainability. Politicising captures how management accounting techniques and frameworks implicate power dynamics such as exploitation, domination, subjugation, colonisation, decolonisation, empowerment, and justice. However, other forces, such as the need to account for sustainability, can also challenge these. In teaching SMA as a social science, it is essential to incorporate political ideologies beyond the conventional capitalist axiom of shareholder wealth maximisation, acknowledging social and ecological justice issues.

5. Theorising: This involves employing social theories as a foundation for contextualising, historicising, and politicising the techno-managerial aspects of SMA, leading to their theoretical interpretation and explanation. Theorising helps develop a deeper conceptual and critical understanding of management accounting techniques and frameworks.

'Particularising' – the development of a deep techno-managerial understanding and the professional skills required to perform management accounting functions – constitutes the core element of conventional approaches to management accounting education. This conventional approach, termed the 'practicist epistemology' of management accounting, concentrates on the mastery of practical and professional knowledge and skills, with the objective of preparing students to become effective and efficient accountants. In contrast, the other epistemic elements (i.e., contextualising, historicising, politicising, and theorising) extend this practicist epistemology into a 'liberal epistemology', in which the primary objective becomes teaching and learning management accounting as a 'social science'. Critical social science perspectives are employed to provide a broader, historicised, contextualised, politicised, and theoretically substantiated understanding of the political-economic rationalities and functions of management accounting. For a detailed comparison of the practicist and liberal doctrines of management accounting education, see Alawattage and Wickramasinghe (2024), 'Teaching strategic management accounting with sustainability'.

Many of these critical epistemic elements are enabled and enacted by incorporating a sustainability perspective into SMA. Consequently, the global sustainability agenda serves as the broader politico-ideological foundation that contextualises, historicises, politicises, theorises, and critiques SMA. Throughout this book, I explore the sustainability implications of various SMA techniques and frameworks at appropriate points. Thus, sustainability functions as the book's unifying theme.

As an overarching theme, sustainability allows us to examine and decode conventional management accounting's tendency to 'overcode'[1]

1 In Deleuze and Guattari's writings, "overcoding" refers to the representation of human activities and intentions solely through the capitalist axiomatics of capital accumulation. It seeks to impose an overarching economic singularity on the diverse range of human activities and social organisations, which can dangerously overshadow and marginalise the axioms of social and ecological justice that are central to sustainability.

organisational decisions and actions with the capitalist logic of accumulation, that is, profit maximisation – often at the expense of social and ecological justice, which the global sustainability agenda seeks to promote. In other words, integrating sustainability helps us recognise conventional management accounting's fundamental weaknesses and limitations in the broader pursuit of a sustainable future. It also allows us to envision new management accounting approaches that embed ecological and social justice imperatives into organisational decision-making.

After using the first edition of this book in my teaching and receiving valuable feedback from students and instructors, this second edition includes considerable refinements and additions. While preserving the techno-managerial aspects of the previous edition, this version further strengthens the social-science dimensions of SMA learning, particularly in relation to sustainability. Additionally, new sections have been added to enhance academic skills such as critical thinking, reasoning, and essay writing. Chapter-end exercises have been updated to support this emphasis on academic skill development. There are new case studies added at the end of the chapters.

The book is structured for a ten-session SMA course. However, it offers the flexibility to shorten the course by omitting certain topics or to extend it beyond ten sessions by exploring specific subjects in greater detail over multiple sessions. I hope this adaptability allows others to tailor the book to their programme needs.

This book represents the culmination of teaching notes I have developed for my students over many years. The transformation of these teaching notes into a book was also significantly aided by my research publications, co-authored with my research colleague and mentor, Professor Danture Wickramasinghe. I must express my gratitude to him for his invaluable support.

Chandana Alawattage

September 2025

References

Alawattage, C., & Wickramasinghe, D. (2024). Teaching strategic management accounting with sustainability. Accounting Education, 1–33. https://doi.org/10.1080/09639284.2024.2404923

Contents

List of Tables

List of Figures

CHAPTER

1 Strategic management accounting: **emergence, definitions, and domains of strategic actions**

1.1 Introduction

This opening chapter introduces key concepts and themes for a critical exploration of Strategic Management Accounting (SMA) within the global sustainability agenda. It examines how SMA emerged, what it signifies, and how it is defined, comparing it with other forms of accounting and exploring the domains where strategies are enacted.

The rise of SMA is tied to extensive political-economic and techno-managerial transformations: the neoliberalisation of politics, globalisation of economic entities, digitalisation of technologies, and virtualisation of spaces. These shifts created new competitive conditions. As political systems neoliberalised, economic entities globalised; concurrently, the methods by which people and organisations conduct their activities became digitalised and virtualised. These transformed conditions necessitated significant changes in how we conceptualise markets, manage organisational hierarchies, conduct operations, oversee labour processes, and address environmental dynamics.

These new ways of managing markets, hierarchies, labour, and environmental dynamics are collectively known as strategy or strategising. The calculative and rationalisation techniques that constitute these new approaches are now known as SMA.

This textbook critically examines the techno-managerial content and context of SMA. It offers insights into the managerial frameworks and techniques that constitute SMA and explores their political-economic and institutional rationales and implications.

To begin this critical exploration, this chapter:

1. Clarifies the contextual and epistemic dynamics underpinning SMA's emergence and evolution.
2. Defines strategy in its plurality, provides a definition of SMA, and compares SMA with other forms of accounting, including sustainability-driven SMA.
3. Explores specific domains of strategic action where strategies are enacted and enabled with multiple competitive imperatives.

The chapter is structured around three learning objectives:

1. **Evolutionary context:** Section 1.2 explains the historical conditions that led to the emergence of SMA. This historical condition is termed the 'strategic turn', whereby strategy discourses became integral to contemporary organisational management. These dynamics are categorised into two themes: contextual and epistemic.
2. **Definitions and differentiations:** Section 1.3 develops a broader understanding of 'competitive conditions'—the foundational concept for strategy formation. This discussion leads to a broader definition of strategy and SMA. We also differentiate SMA from financial accounting and conventional management accounting, extending this to see how SMA must be redefined in relation to sustainability.
3. **Domains of Strategic Actions:** Section 1.4 explores the interrelated domains or sites of strategic action where strategies are enacted. The book's key themes relate to these domains, so this objective also outlines the textbook's overall structure, relating its chapters to these domains.

1.2 The strategic turn

Since the 1980s, many managerial disciplines have been designated 'strategic', marking a 'strategic turn'. Examples include strategic management, strategic marketing, strategic human resource management, and SMA. This shift extends beyond the private sector to public and third-sector organisations, all now urged to adopt a strategic approach. Consequently, these organisations strive to be strategic, incorporating strategic plans, visions, leadership, and control.

The prefix 'strategic' elevated many subjects to a higher order of importance. Aspects of strategy are frequently emphasised as critical to success, with achievements often attributed to strategic thinking, planning, and control. Conversely, corporate failures are often linked to firms and their managers not being sufficiently strategic. Investments are directed towards enhancing strategic capabilities, with strategy consultants playing a crucial role. Strategy consultancy has become a multi-billion-dollar industry, with major accountancy firms taking a prominent role. Many books have been written on being strategic in organisational processes and managerial thinking.

Strategy now encompasses the techno-managerial, institutional, and political-economic elements that underpin how we govern organisations. It has become ingrained in our culture as a taken-for-granted belief that strategies are essential for success. Strategy discourses are integral not only to economic enterprises but also to the management of socio-political and cultural institutions. This confluence of significance in strategy discourses is what is termed the 'strategic turn'. The strategic turn, therefore, represents the political-economic, techno-managerial, and institutional transformation that propelled strategy to the forefront of managing contemporary institutions. The question then arises: what triggered this strategic turn?

Contradictions necessitate strategic thinking and formulation. In mainstream strategy discourses, these contradictions are encapsulated by the notion of 'competitive conditions', often related to the market. The transformation of competition into neoliberalised, globalised, digitalised, and virtualised conditions is what we collectively call the strategic turn. These structural transformations deepen the contradictions underpinning global sustainability, creating a risky, volatile, and unjust world where ecological and social justice issues have become paramount, necessitating a rethink of strategy and accounting in sustainability terms.

While numerous factors contributed to this transformation, for analytical simplicity, we can categorise them into three groups:

1. Contextual dynamics,
2. Epistemic dynamics, and
3. The sustainability agenda.

Contextual dynamics behind the strategic turn

Contextual dynamics are the global-scale political-economic, techno-managerial, and institutional shifts that created a new set of competitive conditions worldwide. These transformations gave rise to global consumers, markets, firms, brands, and supply chains, as well as global governance and regulatory infrastructure. They created politically neoliberal, institutionally global, technologically digital, and spatially virtual competitive conditions. These dynamics fall into four linked categories:

1. Neoliberalisation of politics,
2. Globalisation of economic entities and activities,
3. Digitalisation of technologies, and
4. Virtualisation of spaces.

Neoliberalisation of politics

Before neoliberalisation began in the 1970s, the global economy was vastly different. Nation-states adhered to political-economic doctrines of protectionism. Economies were relatively closed, and international free trade faced significant restrictions. Import/export duties, tariffs, and licensing systems governed global trade and safeguarded domestic producers. Foreign exchange mechanisms controlled capital flows, and labour markets operated with stringent immigration controls. Prevailing ideologies sought to shield the domestic sphere from global influences.

National economic policies were characterised by welfareism and state ownership. Public sector enterprises played a pivotal role, with major industries nationalised and managed through centralised planning. Extensive welfare budgets were allocated to state entities providing public services. During this period, markets were heavily regulated by state agencies. Mechanisms such as subsidies, taxes, and direct state interventions controlled market activity. The prevailing ideology did not view markets as the governing force for polity and society; instead, markets were economic spaces to be regulated, or even monopolised, by the state for the benefit of the masses. In summary, pre-neoliberal nations were protectionist, state-centric, welfare-focused, and heavily regulated.

Neoliberalisation marked a shift away from state-centric welfareism, protectionism, and regulation. Endorsed by economists like Milton Friedman and Friedrich Hayek, and backed by institutions like the World Bank and the IMF, the Reagan administration in the US and the Thatcher government in the UK initiated a significant political change away from this model, a shift other nations quickly adopted. This resulted in global changes:

1. **Economic Opening:** Economies opened to allow the international movement of goods, services, capital, and labour, facilitated by political arrangements like the European Union.
2. **Privatisation of Industries:** Industries were privatised to minimise state involvement in economic activities. Multinational corporations became globally dominant, their performance closely linked to capital markets, and stock market performance became a key indicator of corporate success.

3. **Managerial Shift:** Bureaucratic administration focused on welfare was replaced by new managerial principles emphasising shareholder value maximisation and market competition. Even public and third-sector organisations adopted private-sector doctrines like New Public Management (NPM) and value for money. Public administration was reformed to adopt a competition-based management regime.
4. **Ideological Emphasis on Markets:** Markets gained ideological prominence, becoming a dominant political institution. Neoliberal doctrine advocates for markets to regulate everything, with the state's role limited to facilitating market-based governance. Neoliberalists believe competition is the fundamental political principle of justice: whatever competition decides is deemed fair, efficient, and legitimate. Hence, market prices are conceived as fair and efficient. The standardisation of fair value accounting epitomised this ideological transformation.

In summary, neoliberalisation represents a shift from state-centric welfareism to a private-capital-centric, market-based ideology. It replaces welfareism with market austerity to enhance private capital accumulation through competition.

Neoliberal connections of SMA

Competition is the foundational condition that necessitates strategies and strategic calculations. The type of competition dictates the strategies a firm should adopt. The emergence of SMA is linked to the competitive conditions shaped by neoliberalism. The shift to neoliberal principles introduced new competitive conditions marked by open markets, multinational corporations, and the free flow of goods, services, capital, and labour. This laid the groundwork for contemporary globalised competitive conditions, which can be termed 'neoliberal competitive conditions'.

These conditions required a new set of calculations to manage markets, organisational hierarchies, and labour processes. Consequently, new tools emerged to analyse markets, assess performance, and manage operations, including Porter's five forces model, the value chain model, activity-based costing, and balanced scorecards (topics covered in forthcoming chapters). This collection of calculative techniques constitutes SMA. In essence, SMA is a phenomenon born out of the neoliberalisation of politics.

Globalisation of markets and organisational hierarchies

The second factor influencing the strategic turn is the globalisation of markets and organisational hierarchies. While neoliberalisation illuminates the politico-ideological aspect, globalisation concerns its market, institutional, and managerial dimensions. Broadly, globalisation encompasses the rise of global markets, the integration of consumers and producers through global supply chains, and the dominance of multinational firms and their brands.

Operating across global output, capital, and labour markets, organisational hierarchies have become truly globalised. While headquarters are often in cities like New York or London, factories and call centres are dispersed globally. As a result, organisational hierarchies now reflect national and cultural differences, requiring a cosmopolitan approach to management.

Globalisation also encompasses the establishment of new regulatory and epistemic institutions. Regulation and governance have evolved beyond nation-states. The emergence of global markets, firms, and supply chains necessitated a regulatory regime extending beyond national boundaries. Consequently, a new set of regulatory institutions has emerged, such as the Basel Committee on Banking Supervision. Global institutions for standardisation, including the International Accounting Standards Board and the International Organisation for Standardisation, also arose to coordinate and regulate global markets and firms. In essence, basic economic activities have become globalised, organised through global markets, corporations, and regulatory bodies.

Globalisation leads to SMA

Again, the critical link is what happens to competitive conditions. Competition necessitates strategies and strategic calculations. Globalisation ushered in a new competitive landscape characterised by global markets, consumers, firms, brands, supply chains, and regulatory frameworks. This environment requires coordinating, monitoring, and controlling activities across diverse and dispersed global sites. Consequently, it calls for a new set of accounting practices and calculations, which collectively form SMA. Examples include cloud-based accounting, big data analytics, enterprise resource planning, and supply chain management systems.

Digitalisation of technologies and virtualisation of spaces

Over the past fifty years, we have experienced an unparalleled technological revolution. The rise of the World Wide Web, mobile computing, and cloud computing has shifted our world from mechanical to digital and from physical to virtual. These advancements have revolutionised how we engage in economic activities. Computer-aided design and manufacturing are now standard, allowing flexible manufacturing and mass customisation. The integration of digitalisation and virtualisation has transformed marketplaces into platforms like Amazon and eBay. Online transactions have become the primary mode of global trade. The movement of products in global supply chains is now traceable in real-time. The internet has become a vast repository for transactions, automatically recorded in mega-databases, where each mouse click is trackable, offering new insights and challenges for managers.

Technology, competitive conditions and strategy

The competitive landscape has shifted with digitalisation and virtualisation. Competition is now virtual, digital, traceable, and analysable online in real-time. Big data analytics continuously reproduce customer and competitor profiles, making the complexities of competition visible on dashboards. Managers can analyse this intricate competition and plan for different scenarios, albeit more complex than ever. Digitalisation and virtualisation have given rise to a new set of accounting calculations providing real-time insights into market dynamics and competitive performance. These calculations, aggregated into industry averages and benchmarks, serve as the foundation for SMA.

Contextual factors summary

Neoliberalisation, globalisation, digitalisation, and virtualisation are the contextual shifts driving the 'strategic turn'. Neoliberalisation reflects the politico-ideological aspect, globalisation pertains to the transformation of economic entities, and digitalisation and virtualisation encapsulate the techno-managerial aspects. These changes have given rise to a new global order and a distinct set of competitive conditions: neoliberal, global, digital, and virtual. This evolving competition presents an intricately interconnected and volatile context for business.

This shift necessitated substantial changes in how we approach:

1. Conceptualising and navigating markets,
2. Managing organisational hierarchies,
3. Overseeing labour processes, and
4. Addressing sustainability issues arising from these transformations.

Emergent approaches to managing these areas collectively form what we now call strategy. The calculative techniques embedded in these strategic necessities constitute SMA.

Epistemic dynamics

'Episteme' refers to how we know, understand, and interpret the world. Ideological doctrines, theories, and models are the means to comprehend the world, shaping our thinking and actions. In management accounting, we rely on theories and models that influence organisational management. For instance, agency theory is often used to explain management control issues. Accounting standards form the basis for reporting. Concepts like fixed and variable costs help determine profit-maximising quantities, while models such as the balanced scorecard have become popular performance management frameworks.

These epistemic tools gain acceptance through the support of powerful epistemic institutions. Accounting standards owe their existence to the institutional infrastructure of the accountancy profession. Similarly, innovations like the balanced scorecard, championed by figures like Robert S. Kaplan, gain prominence through association with influential networks such as Harvard Business School. Management accounting is inherently epistemic and evolves within an epistemic context. This implies two interconnected dimensions in the development of knowledge: conceptual and institutional.

Epistemic dynamics – conceptual elements

The conceptual dimensions of the strategic turn involve creating and popularising models, frameworks, and theories that form the foundation of SMA. We can categorise these conceptual advancements into four domains:

1. **Strategic analysis of external environmental elements:** This includes industry, market, and competitor analysis, with models such as SWOT analysis, Porter's five forces model, and Big Data analytics. Such analyses support decisions on strategic directions, priorities, and ambitions, often encapsulated by corporate vision, mission, and objectives. They are also critical for competitive market positioning, including strategic pricing.
2. **Strategic analysis of organisational hierarchy and control apparatuses:** This focuses on management control and performance management frameworks, such as the balanced scorecard and Simon's Levers of Control framework.
3. **Calculative technologies for production systems and labour processes:** This involves an emerging set of analytical techniques for managing three key strategic imperatives at the point of production: quality, flexibility, and cost. Examples include activity-based costing, activity-based management, throughput accounting, quality costing, flexible manufacturing, enterprise resource planning, target costing, and lifecycle costing.
4. **Accounting techniques related to sustainability:** Though still developing, this addresses the growing need for techniques related to sustainability, such as carbon costing and reporting on social justice issues.

Management approach: from administration to strategy

These innovative conceptual frameworks have transformed management approaches from administrative to strategic. The tools have urged and empowered managers to recognise the neoliberal condition, asserting that competition is the fundamental doctrine of management. Managers now possess a new toolkit to analyse the competitive impact of their activities. These tools empower managers to view every situation as competitive, demanding strategic thinking. The new frameworks establish competitive benchmarks and standards that shape our understanding of competition. Consequently, every organisational scenario is interpreted as a 'competitive situation'. Individual and collective performances are continuously scrutinised and evaluated against these benchmarks, constructing and incorporating competition in all aspects of organisational life. Therefore, being strategic entails proficiency in using these new conceptual tools to excel in competitive situations.

Epistemic dynamics – institutional elements

The term 'epistemic' is also tied to institutions. Knowledge is generated and sustained through specific institutions that hold sway over societies. In pre-modern times, religious institutions governed knowledge production. In the contemporary era, 'modern' institutions have taken the lead, including universities, professional associations, global governance bodies like the World Bank and the UN, consultancy firms, and corporations. The epistemic is deeply intertwined with institutional infrastructures.

Amid the recent acceptance of strategy discourses, a noteworthy institutional development has emerged: the consultocracy. The rise of the consultancy industry underscores the swift evolution of strategy discourses.

The world before consultocracy

Consultocracy refers to the recent emergence of consultants and management gurus as a new class of intellectuals and the specific epistemic structure they have established. To grasp its significance, consultocracy must be contrasted with bureaucracy, the system it has influenced.

Bureaucracy became prevalent during modernity, replacing pre-modern aristocratic systems. A fundamental doctrine of bureaucracy was that governing power should not be centred on individual charisma or inherited power, but should be formally defined and attributed to positions in the organisational hierarchy. Bureaucracy modernises and depersonalises power, aiming for a system where actions adhere to rules, laws, and procedures, which, when associated with 'scientific management', should be scientifically derived. Bureaucratic rules, even within private organisations, should ensure governance aligns with constitutional, legal, and regulatory frameworks.

Another crucial aspect of bureaucratic governance is its focus on regulation and control, striving for stability, predictability, and uniformity to minimise risks. The expectation was that things should progress predictably. Administrators play a pivotal role in maintaining this uniformity and stability by adhering to bureaucratic rules.

The strategic turn inspired by neoliberalism introduced an epistemic critique of the bureaucratic model. Consultants and gurus emerged, critiquing bureaucracy for being rigid, excessively control-oriented, and resistant to change in a rapidly evolving competitive environment. Essentially, bureaucratic structures were faulted for their inability to adapt to the new conditions brought about by neoliberalisation, globalisation, digitalisation, and virtualisation. Administrative approaches were criticised for prioritising regulation over adaptability.

The growth of consultocracy

The 1970s and beyond marked an era of neoliberalisation, ushering in new concepts like entrepreneurship, risk-taking, and continuous improvement. The traditional bureaucratic style was considered inadequate for the new competitive conditions. A new generation of managerial roles emerged, known as change agents, strategy consultants, and strategic leaders, lauded for instigating change. There was a search for new organisational structures to replace bureaucracy, aiming to create flatter, leaner, and more flexible organisations. Terms like 'learning organisations' and 'business process re-engineering' became popular lexicons for change. Management gurus and consultancy firms played a dominant role in steering these transformations, giving rise to what we now call consultocracy, which became a vital epistemic pillar in the neoliberal management landscape.

Side note:

For a deeper exploration of the political-economic and strategic significance of the consulting industry, the following references are recommended: Kantola and Seeck (2011), McKenna (2006), United Nations (1993), and Werr and Stjernberg (2003).

In this way, management gurus and consultancy firms emerged as crucial pillars in the epistemic structure of neoliberal management. Figures like Michael E. Porter and Robert S. Kaplan became influential global intellectuals, their ideas widely adopted worldwide. Consequently, consultancy evolved into a multi-trillion-dollar industry, with renowned firms reaching multi-billion-dollar status. Their impact extended beyond the private sector, infiltrating public sector organisations globally. These consultancy giants now offer strategic vision, leadership, and change programs to organisations worldwide. The ideas from these gurus and the influence of consultocracy permeated the curricula of professional bodies and universities, giving rise to a distinct field of study known as SMA. Perhaps ironically, this textbook is a culmination of these neoliberal epistemic developments. Still, it offers a critical insight into the content and context of SMA while making you aware of its managerial and technical core.

Global sustainability agenda

The global sustainability agenda is a collective international effort to address environmental, social, and economic challenges to ensure a more just and equitable future, currently characterised by the UN Sustainable Development Goals (UN SDGs). The agenda has significant implications for management accounting as organisations increasingly integrate sustainability (including environmental, social, and governance, or ESG, considerations) into their decision-making.

The global sustainability agenda affects management accounting in several ways:

1. **Reporting and disclosure:** Management accountants are increasingly involved in collecting, measuring, and reporting sustainability-related information, such as carbon emissions and social impact. Sustainability reporting standards, like the Global Reporting Initiative (GRI), guide organisations in disclosing relevant ESG information. The International Sustainability Standards Board's (ISSB) Climate-related risk reporting standards, S1 and S2, are a clear example of how the sustainability agenda is penetrating corporate reporting.
2. **Performance Measurement:** Organisations are integrating sustainability metrics into their key performance indicators (KPIs). Management accountants help develop and track these metrics, for example, through sustainability-balanced scorecards.
3. **Costing and Resource Allocation:** Sustainability initiatives require investments, and management accountants must accurately allocate the associated costs and assess their impact. For example, activity-based costing (ABC) may be used to understand the true costs of products, including their environmental and social costs, thereby internalising 'externalities'.
4. **Risk Management and resilience:** The sustainability agenda introduces new risks related to climate change and reputational damage. Management accountants are involved in identifying, assessing, and mitigating these risks, for instance, by using scenario analysis.
5. **Regulatory Compliance:** Management accountants must stay informed about evolving sustainability regulations to ensure organisational compliance.
6. **Incentive Structures:** Accountants are involved in designing incentive structures, such as bonus schemes, that align employee behaviour with sustainability goals.
7. **Supply Chain Management:** Accountants play a role in evaluating the sus-

tainability performance of suppliers, which can impact cost structures and supply chain resilience.

8. **Integration with Strategic Planning:** Sustainability is becoming a core component of strategic planning, and management accountants contribute by ensuring goals are integrated into the overall business strategy with the necessary financial resources.

In summary, the global sustainability agenda has transformed management accounting by requiring a broader consideration of factors beyond traditional financial metrics. This shift reflects a growing recognition that sustainable business practices contribute to long-term financial success. Strategising management accounting now includes considering sustainability as a strategic priority and developing techniques to plan, monitor, and control activities toward sustainability goals.

Strategic turn summary

This section explained the circumstances that led to the 'strategic turn' in management accounting. The 'strategic turn' encompasses the broader political-economic, techno-managerial, and epistemic dynamics that form the foundation for the emergence of strategy discourses. These dynamics fall into two main categories: contextual and epistemic.

Contextual factors pertain to global transformations that created a new competitive landscape, classified under four dynamics: (a) the neoliberalisation of politics, (b) the globalisation of markets and hierarchies, (c) the digitalisation of technologies, and (d) the virtualisation of spaces. These dynamics have created a new competitive landscape, necessitating a new set of calculative techniques to analyse and understand it, which constitute SMA.

Epistemic factors involve conceptual and institutional advancements that introduced new theories, models, and practices related to strategic analyses. These are categorised into conceptual developments (new theories and techniques that populate SMA) and institutional developments (the emergence of consultocracy).

The global sustainability agenda is the third element that underpins the contemporary evolution of management accounting, with implications for how we manage markets, hierarchies, and labour processes. For a visual representation of how the strategic turn is conceptualised in this chapter, refer to Figure 1.1.

Figure 1.1: The strategic turn

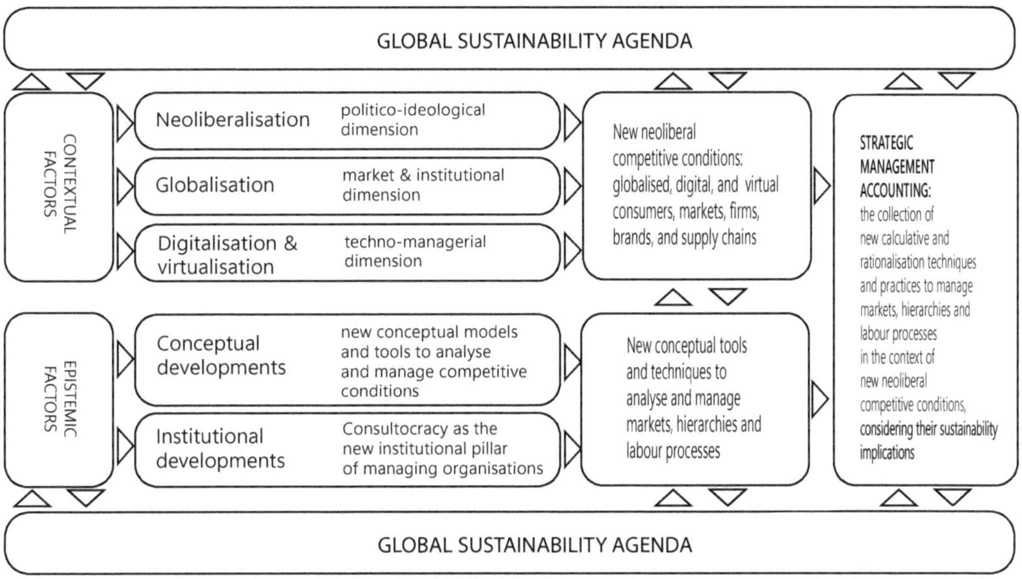

1.3 Definitions and differentiations

A meaningful definition of SMA must centre on its primary focus: strategy. The concept of strategy distinguishes SMA from traditional management accounting and becomes imperative in situations of competition or war. For business strategies, the exigencies of competition necessitate strategic approaches. Therefore, a comprehensive understanding of 'competitive conditions' forms the bedrock of our definitions of strategy and SMA.

Before its popularity in business, strategy was a concept in military science and philosophy. We will first examine the military connections of strategy discourses, as these have been a popular thread for interpreting business strategy.

Strategy discourses: military connections

Before gaining popularity in business management, strategy was primarily used in military science. Timeless classics such as Sun Tzu's Art of War and Carl von Clausewitz's On War articulated strategic concepts in a military context. The shift towards neoliberalism and intense global competition in the 1970s led to markets being considered 'battlefields', and strategic rhetoric gained traction in the business press, which often referred to military classics.

Side note: Sun Tzu's Art of War is an ancient Chinese text supposedly written in the 5th century BC and is considered one of the oldest texts on military strategies (see http://classics.mit.edu/Tzu/artwar.html). General von Clausewitz's "On War" is a European classic on military strategies, published in 1832.

Whether in military science or business management, defining strategy must be in relation to 'competitive conditions', which can be markets, industries, or battlefields. In a broader sense, strategy is the approach people adopt to engage with a particular competitive condition, positioning themselves to gain an advantage over rivals. As Mintzberg (1987) explains, strategies may be plans, such as 'strategic plans', or ploys, such as 'game plans'. Alternatively, strategies may be emergent, appearing as historically evolved patterns of action. Strategies can also represent broader perspectives on competition.

In any scenario, the meaning of strategy invariably revolves around 'positioning'—how organisations plan, employ tactics, or cultivate a standpoint to position themselves and their resources in the competitive arena. The ultimate goal is to secure victory, sustain one's position, or achieve other strategic objectives.

Positioning is a central concept, commonly interpreted in terms of engagement and deployment. As elucidated by Sun Tzu and Carl von Clausewitz, strategising involves deciding when, where, and how to deploy resources (such as military units) to interact with enemies, allies, and civilians. The strategist's role is to determine how resources should be gathered, deployed, and engaged. To accomplish this, they employ epistemic devices such as maps, scouts, and spies to understand the competitive terrain. Therefore, as a form of positioning, strategising entails determining the time-space distribution of resources to achieve specific territorial, political, economic, or cultural-symbolic goals. In military contexts, these objectives often involved inhumane aims, such as capturing land or enslaving people, frequently justified through rhetoric of emancipation.

Nevertheless, essential takeaways from military definitions of strategy include:

1. Strategy as positioning involves the time-space distribution, deployment, and engagement of resources, connecting strengths and weaknesses with opportunities and threats.
2. Strategising requires epistemic tools for understanding the time-space nature of the competitive terrain, essentially 'mapping the territory'.
3. Strategic mapping involves actively defining the competitive terrain by associating it with enemies, allies, and citizens.
4. Strategising encompasses determining ways to achieve specific short-term and long-term objectives across multiple dimensions.

Strategy translated into business contexts

A parallel emerges when these military conceptions are transposed into business contexts. Much like military commanders, corporate strategy luminaries such as Michael Porter and Henry Mintzberg endorse positioning as a pivotal component of business strategies. The essence of strategising lies in orchestrating a company's resources within a competitive terrain—aligning the firm's strengths and weaknesses with the opportunities and threats posed by prevailing competitive conditions.

To perceive business strategy as positioning, one must first grasp how the competitive terrain is conceptualised in corporate strategy discourses. Markets or industries serve as the contexts within which competition is defined. Traditionally, in neoclassical economic theory, the market is perceived as a structural determinant influencing a firm's decisions on prices and quantities. Economists commonly classify a firm's competitive environment into four structural conditions: perfect competition, imperfect competition, oligopoly, and monopoly. These conditions are presupposed to dictate a firm's ability to establish prices and quantities. In perfect competition, firms are 'price takers', whereas in other conditions, they possess varying degrees of power to influence prices. Neoclassical models offer a reactive approach to strategy, where firms respond to market demand based on their marginal costs to maximise profit. In this framework, strategy is simplified to the doctrine that prices and quantities should be determined by equating marginal cost to marginal revenue.

This neoclassical thinking underpinned traditional management accounting calculations, which were geared towards production optimisation. It was assumed that competitive conditions, reflected in demand forecasts, were a predetermined constraint. Techniques such as budgeting and cost-volume-profit analysis were employed to determine operational parameters based on this constraint. Therefore, within conventional management accounting, strategies have typically been operational or tactical, with a primary emphasis on enhancing operational efficiency. Strategising was narrowly conceptualised as achieving efficiency through established calculation methods.

Side note:

Refer to Porter (1996) for a critique of viewing strategy solely through the lens of operational effectiveness.

Epistemic dynamics associated with the 'strategic turn' significantly altered this perspective in the 1980s and 1990s. Strategy experts like Michael Porter introduced novel frameworks for analysing competitive conditions. They adopted a more comprehensive, systemic, and territorial outlook. In this new paradigm, competition was perceived as a dynamic interplay of forces, including inter-firm rivalry, the threat of new entrants and substitutes, and the bargaining power of buyers and suppliers. The concept of competition also took on a territorial dimension, where markets were analysed and categorised into distinct segments. This evolution gave rise to new analytical tools, including big-data analytics and Porter's five forces model. These tools enabled managers to recognise a 'strategic context' for their decisions, which encompasses both immediate competitive conditions and broader infrastructural and regulatory dynamics. Figure 1.2 summarises the key elements of a strategic context.

Figure 1.2: Key elements of the strategic context

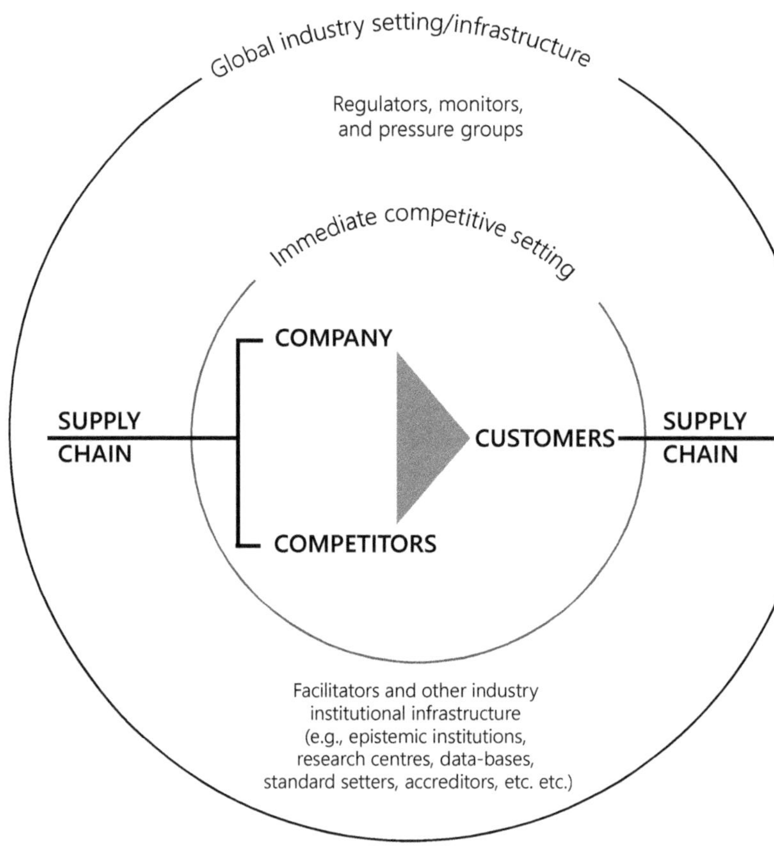

In traditional management accounting, operational decisions are primarily grounded in demand forecasts. In SMA, however, the approach shifts significantly. Competition is no longer merely acknowledged through demand forecasts; it must be meticulously profiled and mapped. Strategic maps, such as the BCG growth-share matrix, and profiling techniques like big-data analytics now form the foundation for competitive positioning decisions. Strategy entails a thoughtful placement within a competitive landscape to secure a competitive advantage. The transition from traditional management accounting to SMA is underscored by a profound change in how we conceptualise and analyse competition.

We can revisit the four pivotal points regarding military strategy and see how they translate into business contexts:

1. **Strategic positioning:** This encompasses the temporal and spatial allocation of resources, aligning strengths and weaknesses with opportunities and threats by analysing the market, industry, and broader political-economic landscape.
2. **Epistemic devices for strategising:** Effective strategising requires tools to comprehend the competitive terrain, essentially mapping the territory by analysing the market, industry, and macro-context. Conceptual tools like Porter's five-forces model and the four-corners model of competitor analysis are popular in this regard.
3. **Strategic mapping:** This involves defining the 'competitive terrain' by associating it with competitors, supply chain connections, customer profiles, and regulatory infrastructure.
4. **Setting objectives in multiple dimensions:** Strategising entails defining short- and long-term objectives across territorial, political, economic, or cultural-symbolic dimensions, such as establishing a corporate vision, mission, and KPIs. These normative elements should encompass financial, customer, internal process, and learning perspectives, as well as the social and ecological justice dimensions of sustainability.

Defining and differentiating SMA

Based on our discussion, SMA can be defined as:

> An ever-evolving set of calculative and analytical techniques used to analyse competitive conditions to gain and sustain an advantageous strategic position; such techniques enable the decision-making, implementation, and control of strategies in relation to the market, the point of production, the organisational hierarchy, and social and environmental issues.

Encapsulated in this definition are several critical points:

1. **Dynamic field of study:** SMA is dynamic, its techniques evolving in response to changing competitive conditions.

2. **Analytical focus:** The primary analytical focus of SMA is to understand the competitive conditions faced by a strategic entity. Its central aim is to appreciate the time-space nature of the terrain in which resources are deployed.
3. **Comprehensive strategic mapping:** Strategic analysis defines competitive conditions by associating the terrain with the potential actions of competitors, suppliers, customers, and others.
4. **Strategy as positioning:** Strategy entails the distribution, deployment, and engagement of resources in the most appropriate segments of the competitive terrain. SMA should empower managers to decide on the most suitable positioning to ensure competitive advantage.
5. **Strategic pluralism and uncertainties:** Strategising involves determining specific objectives across various dimensions. Hence, SMA techniques should address strategic uncertainties and the pluralistic nature of strategic goals.
6. **Domains of strategic actions:** Strategies are enacted in four interrelated domains: markets, points of production, organisational hierarchies, and social and environmental arenas.

To better understand SMA, one can compare it with conventional management accounting and financial accounting. Table 1.1 provides this comparison, including an additional column for 'sustainability-driven SMA'.

1.4 Sustainabilising strategy

Preceding discussions centred on market competition and positioning, with little substantive attention to sustainability—an indispensable dimension for contemporary organisations. Situating strategy within sustainability discourses requires acknowledging fundamental contradictions that extend beyond mere market competition. Accordingly, four foundational structural categories must be considered: economy, polity, society, and ecology.

These structural conditions are inherently contradictory, illustrating that economic pursuits of profit maximisation can compromise our shared world's social, political, and ecological dimensions. Strategic decisions within economic domains can have diverse implications for political, social, and ecological justice. This encompasses concerns such as carbon emissions, global warming, gender disparities, and modern slavery, with which companies must engage. Frameworks like the UN SDGs, ISSB's sustainability and climate-related disclosure standards (IFRS S1 and S2), and GRI reporting protocols encapsulate critical issues that companies must consider while formulating strategies.

Accordingly, contemporary strategic considerations must encompass a more expansive array of factors. Strategic attention should be paid not only to the economic doctrines of efficiency and profitability but also to higher-order principles related to the polity (freedom and sovereignty), society (solidarity and social justice), and ecology (solidity of nature through biodiversity). In this context, strategic planning must transcend market positioning for competitive advantage to encapsulate non-economic domains. Instead, it should be viewed as an endeavour to forge sustainable connections between the economy, polity, society, and ecology, realised through decisions regarding operations in markets, organisational hierarchies, and labour processes. This sustainability conception of SMA is illustrated in Figure 1.3.

Figure 1.3: Sustainablising strategy

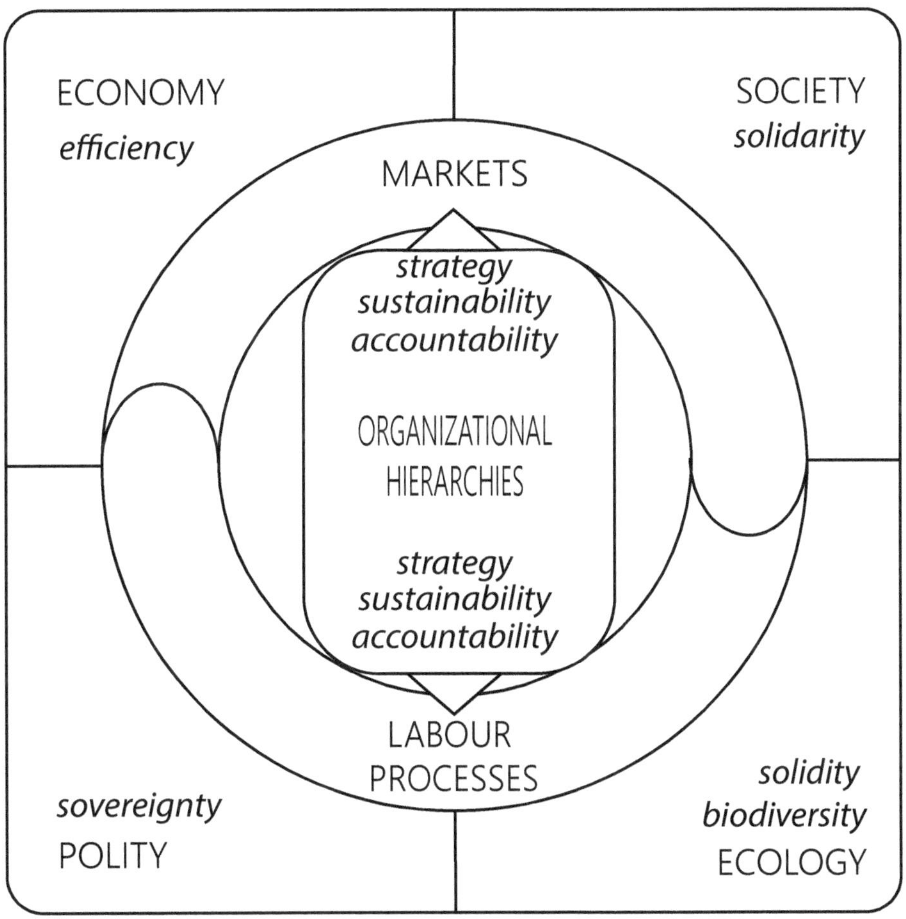

Table 1.1: Differentiating SMA

Aspect	Financial Accounting	Management Accounting	Strategic Management Accounting	Sustainability-driven Strategic Management Accounting
What do you analyse?	Financially measurable past events and transactions.	Financial impacts of operational decisions (costs, revenues, risks).	Competitive conditions the firm is facing and will face.	In addition to economic conditions, political, social, and ecological justice issues.
What is your analytical focus/aim?	Financial reporting: Providing a fair representation of financial outcomes for the period (net income, financial position, cash flows).	Operational optimisation: Analysing outcomes of short-term operational decisions on resource allocation and assessing future cash flows from investments.	Strategic positioning: Determining the company's long-term vision, mission, and strategic moves in its competitive conditions. Developing controls to ensure strategic intentions are achieved.	Sustainabilising strategic position: Considering sustainability as a critical element of strategic positioning. Incorporating ecological and social justice issues into the company's vision and integrating them into performance management systems.
Where does the data for analysis come from?	Company's internal accounting system.	Company's accounting and other operational data systems (e.g., production, marketing). Primarily internal data.	Internal data as well as external data from databases, big data analytics, market surveys, consultants, and industry reports.	Expanding data sources to understand sustainability implications, including UN SDGs and other global sustainability information.

Aspect	Financial Accounting	Management Accounting	Strategic Management Accounting	Sustainability-driven Strategic Management Accounting
What are the typical tools of analysis?	Financial statements, ratio analysis, cash flow analysis, debt analysis.	Budgeting, standard costing, variance analysis, marginal costing, cost-volume-profit analysis, discounted cash flows.	Five forces model, SWOT analysis, value chain analysis, supply chain management, big data analytics, activity-based costing, balanced scorecards.	Carbon costing, ecosystem analysis, ecological footprint analysis, UN SDG compliance analysis, GRI compliance analysis, compliance with social laws (e.g., Modern Slavery Acts).
Who is involved in the analysis and decision-making?	Financial accountants and auditors.	Management accountants and other operational managers.	Plural multidisciplinary forums of internal and external parties (e.g., strategy groups, special task forces).	Plural multidisciplinary forums of internal and external parties, including sustainability experts.
Where do the analytical principles come from?	Accounting standards (GAAPs), auditing standards, company law.	Neoclassical economics, statistics, industrial engineering, organisational sciences.	Strategic management, technology fields (big data analytics), marketing, organisational studies, industry-specific expertise, regulatory bodies, and consultancy.	Environmental sciences, UN SDGs, Global Reporting Initiative.
To whom are the accounts provided?	Mainly to shareholders.	Operational managers.	Top management and other parties involved in strategic decision-making.	Top management, other parties involved in strategic processes, and wider stakeholder groups.
What is the time orientation?	Past.	Current and short-term future (or predictable future for capital investment decisions).	Long-term uncertain and competitive future, as well as short-term strategic scenarios.	Long-term future in terms of ecological and social conditions to which the firm contributes.

In light of the sustainability imperative, one might redefine SMA as an:

> ever-evolving suite of calculative and analytical techniques oriented towards conceptualising and evaluating an organisation's competitive and contradictory conditions in enabling and enacting strategies within the realms of markets, organisational hierarchies, and labour processes, with the aim of not only competitive positioning but also addressing broader ecological and social justice issues.

1.5 Domains of strategising and the course structure

The discussion in this chapter has led us to identify several critical aspects of strategising:

1. **Contradictions and competition:** The foundation upon which strategies are conceived.
2. **Competitive advantage:** The ability to surpass competitors, achieved through a distinctive strategic position. The ultimate goal is a sustainable competitive advantage.
3. **Positioning:** An overarching plan, perspective, and coherent pattern of action a firm adopts to secure a competitive advantage.
4. **Rationalisations/calculations:** The analyses and calculations essential for comprehending and responding to competition. The frameworks and techniques employed constitute SMA.
5. **Ecological and social justice:** Effective strategising requires grounding in broader contradictions entailing social, political, and ecological justice issues, captured by global regulatory institutions such as the UN SDGs.

These five elements can bolster a company's ability to compete by reconfiguring its structures and processes. Strategising entails reinventing a firm's internal conditions to align with external competitive conditions. It is an ongoing effort to establish and sustain a viable alignment between the demands of competition and the company's capacity to meet them. This underscores the imperative of establishing alignment across various domains of strategic actions.

Strategising occurs within these interdependent domains:

1. **Strategising the market:** The company engages in strategic positioning through pricing and other marketing strategies.
2. **Strategising the labour process** (or value chain): The company ensures its productive system can generate and deliver its intended strategic position.

3. Strategising the organisational hierarchy: The company transforms its hierarchy and control systems to establish strategic connections between the market and its operations, while enhancing its resilience.
4. **Social and Environmental Strategising:** The company makes strategic decisions that contribute to the global sustainability agenda, addressing ecological and social justice issues.

The structural framework of this textbook underscores the interconnectedness of these four areas. As depicted in Figure 1.4, the book explores nine topics associated with these domains across nine subsequent chapters.

Figure 1.4: Structural logic of the course

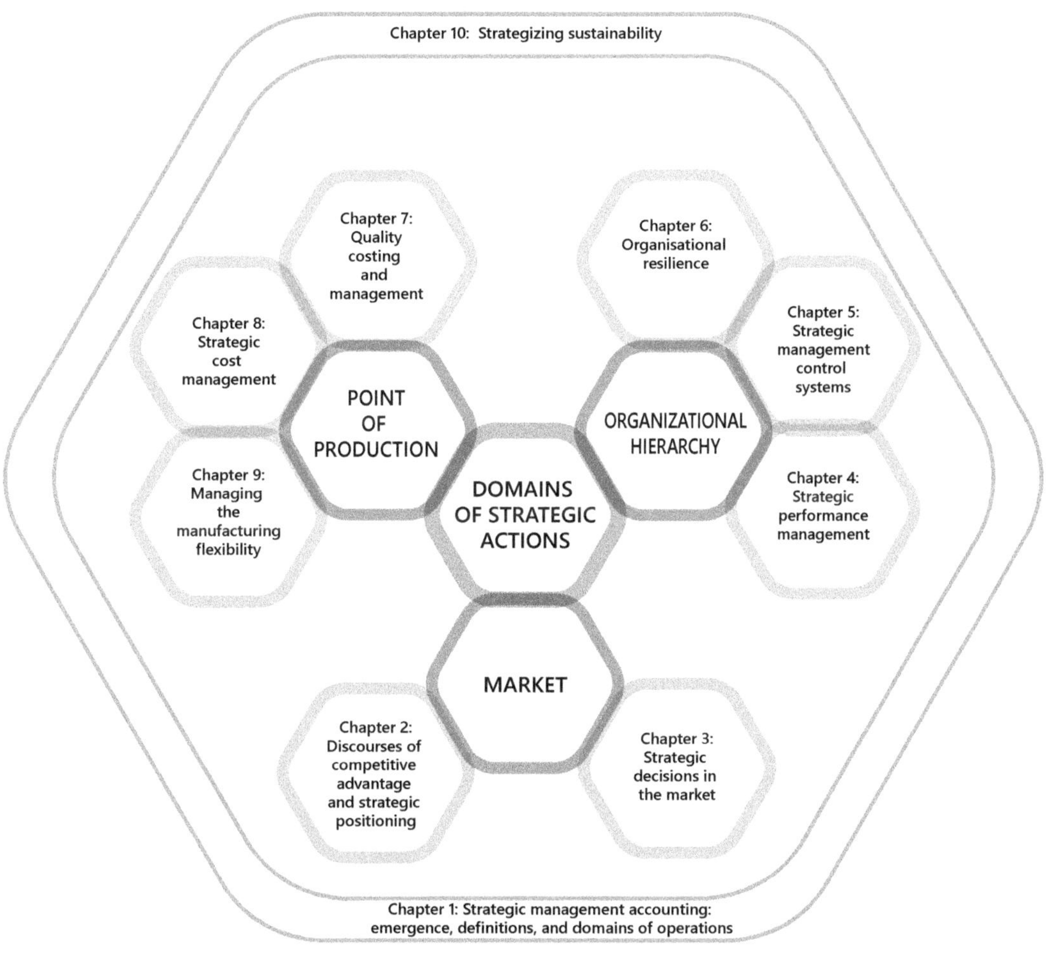

1. Chapter 1: Strategic Management Accounting - Emergence, Definitions, and Domains of Operations

   This chapter delved into the contextual conditions underpinning SMA's emergence and the foundational concepts that constitute and differentiate it.

2. Chapter 2: Reconceptualising Competition - Discourses of Competitive Advantage and Strategic Positioning

   This chapter explores how strategy discourses provide new conceptual bases for understanding contemporary organisations.

3. Chapter 3: Strategy in the Market - Strategic Pricing Decisions

   This chapter discusses how contemporary competitive conditions complicate pricing decisions, with attention to marketing elements and techniques like target and lifecycle costing.

4. Chapter 4: Strategy in the Hierarchy - Strategising Performance

   Focusing on the Balanced Scorecard (BSC), this chapter explores its new strategic focus on performance management and recent attempts to reimagine it for sustainability.

5. Chapter 5: Strategy in the Hierarchy - Strategising Management Control

   This chapter centres on management control systems, particularly Simons' Levers of Control (LOC) framework, offering a strategy-based conception of control.

6. Chapter 6: Strategy in the Hierarchy - Organisational Resilience

   Extending the strategic control theme, this chapter explores how 'organisational resilience' has entered the management control lexicon as a strategic imperative.

7. Chapter 7: Strategy at the Point of Production - Quality Management and Costing

   This chapter focuses on the strategic imperative of quality, examining how strategic notions penetrate the operational elements of managing the labour process.

8. Chapter 8: Strategy at the Point of Production - Managing Flexibility

   This chapter explores the strategic imperative of flexibility, discussing various micro-organisational and macro-political elements of manufacturing flexibility.

9. Chapter 9: Strategy at the Point of Production - Strategic Cost Management

   Exploring the strategic imperative of managing costs, this chapter focuses on both intra-organisational techniques and extra-organisational arrangements for managing costs across supply chains.

10. Chapter 10: Strategising Sustainability

    This chapter examines how the global sustainability agenda has affected management accounting, especially its performance management and control systems, with attention to contemporary ESG discourses.

Chapter summary

This chapter introduced SMA, structured around three elements. Firstly, it elucidated the contextual and epistemological backdrop of the 'strategic turn'. Contextual dynamics include: (a) the neoliberalisation of politics, (b) the globalisation of markets and hierarchies, and (c) the digitalisation and virtualisation of technologies and spaces. Regarding epistemological dynamics, the chapter explored the interplay between the strategic turn and new institutional and conceptual developments, such as new models of strategy and the rise of consultocracy.

The second section delved into basic definitions, distinguishing SMA from other forms of accounting. Drawing insights from military strategy, the understanding emerges that strategy entails positioning in competitive conditions: the temporal-spatial distribution, deployment, and engagement of resources. Consequently, strategic analyses involve mapping the competitive terrain to ascertain optimal approaches for deploying resources. This military perspective was then applied to business contexts. Key to strategic analyses are the notions of competitive conditions and competitive positioning. SMA is therefore characterised as an evolving set of techniques aimed at conceptualising and evaluating a firm's competitive and contradictory conditions, guiding decisions on strategies in relation to market competition as well as broader ecological and social justice issues.

In conclusion, four interconnected domains of strategic actions were identified: markets, organisational hierarchies, labour processes, and the social and environmental spheres. The essence of strategising lies in establishing a sustainable alignment between actions and outcomes across all these domains.

Case Study: Nike, Inc.: strategising in a neoliberal and digital world with sustainability problems

1. Introduction

Nike, Inc. exemplifies a modern multinational corporation. From its origins as a shoe distributor to its current status as a global cultural and economic powerhouse, its journey encapsulates the profound transformations in the global competitive landscape over the past five decades. The company's strategic evolution illustrates the 'strategic turn', where firms have been forced to innovate how they engage with markets, manage hierarchies, conduct operations, and oversee labour processes in response to new competitive conditions.

This case study examines how the contextual dynamics of neoliberalisation, globalisation, digitalisation, and virtualisation have shaped Nike's strategic apparatuses. Furthermore, it explores how the global sustainability agenda—crystallised in initiatives like its 'Move to Zero' campaign—has compelled the company to redefine its strategies across the primary domains of strategic action: the market, the organisational hierarchy, and the point of production. While such corporate initiatives can be questioned as greenwashing, for students of Strategic Management Accounting (SMA), Nike's story is a narrative of adaptation, crisis, and the continual reinvention of the calculative practices that underpin competitive advantage.

2. Case background: from blue ribbon sports to global hegemon

Founded in 1964 as Blue Ribbon Sports, Nike initially acted as a distributor for Japanese shoemaker Onitsuka Tiger. Its strategic pivot in the 1970s involved designing its own footwear and, crucially, outsourcing manufacturing to low-cost Asian countries. This move was a harbinger of the large-scale political-economic shifts to come. By decoupling the brand and design functions (retained in the US) from physical production, Nike became a prototype of the 'hollowed-out' corporation, a model enabled by the emerging neoliberal consensus favouring open markets and free movement of capital.

This strategy fuelled explosive growth. However, by the 1990s, Nike's globalised production network became its Achilles' heel. Widespread reports of labour abuses, including low wages, poor working conditions, and child labour in its suppliers' factories, led to global consumer boycotts and significant reputational damage. This crisis forced a strategic reckoning. The company could no longer view its supply chain as a mere operational concern; it had become a central strategic issue with profound implications for its brand and market position. This moment marked the beginning of Nike's long, complex journey to transform its business toward sustainability.

3. Nike and the 'strategic turn': responding to a new competitive terrain

Nike's history can be analysed through the contextual and epistemic dynamics that define the 'strategic turn'. The company did not merely react to these changes; it actively shaped and exploited them.

1. **Neoliberalisation and Globalisation:** Nike's business model is a direct product of the neoliberal shift towards open economies. The ability to establish vast, global supply chains allowed the company to minimise production costs and maximise shareholder value—a key tenet of the new managerial principles that replaced bureaucratic administration. This globalisation created new 'neoliberal competitive conditions', where managing a dispersed and diverse supply chain became a core strategic necessity, demanding new control systems that extended beyond its corporate boundaries, not only for cost management but also to mitigate political and regulatory risks associated with non-compliance with globalised regulations, including anti-slavery disclosure requirements.
2. **Digitalisation and Virtualisation:** In recent decades, Nike has aggressively embraced digitalisation and virtualisation. This is evident in its 'Consumer Direct Acceleration' strategy, which leverages digital platforms to build direct relationships with customers. The Nike app and e-commerce website are not just sales channels; they are vast data-gathering ecosystems. Every user interaction provides data points that are fed into big data analytics to reproduce customer and competitor profiles, allowing for sophisticated market segmentation. This digital transformation has made competition virtual, traceable, and analysable in real-time, demanding a new suite of SMA tools.
3. **The Global Sustainability Agenda:** Initially a reactive measure, sustainability has become a proactive component of Nike's strategy, articulated through its 'Move to Zero' initiative, launched in 2019. This vision sets a journey 'towards zero carbon and zero waste'. The strategy is underpinned by specific, measurable goals, including:

    a. Carbon: Reducing greenhouse gas (GHG) emissions from its owned facilities by 70% through 100% renewable electricity, while keeping supplier emissions below 2020 levels. The company also aims to reduce its GHG emissions by 0.5 million tons by increasing the use of environmentally preferred materials to 50% of its total.
    b. Waste: Diverting 100% of waste from landfills in its supply chain, with at least 80% being recycled back into manufacturing, and increasing refurbished or donated product tenfold.

c. Water: Reducing freshwater usage in textile dyeing and finishing by 25% per kilogram and restoring 13 billion litres of water by 2050.
d. Materials Innovation: Driving this strategy is a focus on new materials, such as Nike Flyleather (using at least 50% recycled leather fibres), Recycled Polyester (lowering carbon emissions by 30%), and Recycled Nylon (reducing carbon emissions by up to 50%).

While one can be suspicious of corporate ambitions to achieve zero carbon status, this reflects a recognition that contemporary strategy must address broader ecological and social justice issues. Nike publishes extensive sustainability reports, tracks its carbon footprint, and invests in low-impact materials like Flyknit. This shift means management accountants are now deeply involved in collecting, measuring, and reporting sustainability-related information, turning an 'externality' into a core performance metric.

4. Analysis through the domains of strategic action

Nike's strategic responses can be mapped onto the four interconnected domains of strategic action.

1. **Strategising the Market:** Nike's core strategy is differentiation, built on a powerful brand. Its 'positioning' is achieved through massive marketing investments and premium pricing. Increasingly, sustainability is a key part of this positioning. The 'Move to Zero' branding is now physically present on its packaging. By advertising its use of recycled materials in high-profile products, Nike attempts to align its brand with the values of a growing segment of global consumers, thereby creating a competitive advantage.
2. **Strategising the Point of Production (The Value Chain):** The 1990s crisis forced Nike to strategically re-engage with its labour processes. Today, this has evolved into a comprehensive sustainability agenda for its supply chain. Progress is evident: by 2020, 94% of its products were sourced from factories meeting the brand's definition of sustainability, and 100% of its cotton was certified organic, recycled, or sourced via the Better Cotton Initiative. However, this strategy faces challenges. The complexity of footwear manufacturing has hindered progress; in 2020, only 29% of materials in its shoes were sustainable, a 1% decrease from the previous year. This indicates that while the strategy is clear, implementation varies across product lines. In response, Nike has launched new products like the Air VaporMax 2021, made of 40% recycled content by weight, to accelerate this change.
3. **Strategising the Organisational Hierarchy:** To execute these complex

strategies, Nike's internal hierarchy and control systems had to evolve. The creation of a Chief Sustainability Officer (CSO) role institutionalised sustainability within the corporate structure. Furthermore, specific public targets—like using 100% renewable energy by 2025—necessitate sophisticated management control systems. Performance management must now incorporate and track these detailed ESG metrics, linking executive decisions directly to sustainability outcomes.

4. Social and Environmental Strategising: Nike's strategy explicitly addresses its role in tackling global challenges, such as the need to 'limit the increase in global temperature to less than 2°C above pre-industrial levels'. By setting public targets and reporting progress, Nike engages with non-market stakeholders—NGOs, governments, and the public—to maintain its 'social license to operate'. As Nike's sustainability reports demonstrate, this requires accounting practices that can measure and report on issues like carbon emissions, water restoration, and chemical usage across a global supply chain, as well as diversity and inclusion metrics.

5. The role of strategic management accounting at nike

Nike's evolution necessitates an SMA toolkit that is externally focused, forward-looking, and non-financial. At a company like Nike, SMA techniques would be crucial for:

1. Lifecycle Costing: Analysing the total cost and environmental impact of a product like the Air VaporMax 2021, from raw material sourcing to end-of-life recycling.
2. Target Costing: Integrating sustainability into the design phase by setting a target cost for a new shoe that incorporates recycled nylon (which reduces carbon emissions by up to 50%) while still achieving required profit margins.
3. Sustainability-Driven Performance Management: Developing performance measurement frameworks that track specific KPIs from the 'Move to Zero' goals, such as:

    a. Carbon & Energy: '% of renewable energy used in owned facilities' (48% in 2020 against a 2025 target of 100%).
    b. Water: '% reduction in freshwater usage per kg in textile dyeing' (against a 25% target).
    c. Materials: '% of sustainable materials in footwear' (29% in 2020, highlighting a performance gap).
    d. Waste: '% of waste diverted from landfill' (against a 100% target).
    e. Carbon Costing: Assigning an internal price to carbon emissions to

make the environmental cost of different choices visible to managers, thereby driving progress towards the 70% reduction goal in GHG emissions from owned facilities.

6. Conclusion

Nike's strategic journey illustrates a corporation adapting to complex and often contradictory pressures. Its story shows that strategy is an ongoing effort to keep pace with an evolving competitive landscape. The company has leveraged neoliberalism and digitalisation to build a formidable market position, while being forced by social pressure to confront the sustainability challenges of its globalised production model. The evidence shows Nike's commitment is serious and its progress in some areas, such as its use of sustainable cotton, is substantial. However, the case also reveals significant challenges, particularly in the 'highly complex process' of sustainable footwear manufacturing, where progress has stalled.

For management accountants, Nike's case demonstrates that their role has irrevocably shifted. They must now provide the calculations that enable a firm to navigate a competitive terrain defined not only by markets and technology but also by the urgent imperatives of social and ecological justice.

Discussion questions

1. Using the concept of the 'strategic turn', explain how the fundamental purpose and practice of management accounting at a company like Nike have changed since the 1980s.
2. This chapter identifies four 'contextual dynamics' behind the strategic turn: neoliberalisation, globalisation, digitalisation, and virtualisation. Provide a specific example of a strategic decision or initiative from Nike for each dynamic and explain how it helped the company create a competitive advantage. You should research the Nike website for further information.
3. Analyse Nike's response to its 1990s labour scandal and its evolution into the current 'Move to Zero' initiative through the lens of the three domains of strategic action: the market, the point of production, and the organisational hierarchy. How are actions in each domain interconnected?
4. Imagine you are a senior management accountant at Nike. Using the specific targets from the 'Move to Zero' initiative (e.g., 70% GHG reduction), explain which SMA techniques (e.g., Balanced Scorecards, Big Data Analytics, Quality Costing) you would prioritise and how they would help managers make decisions to close the gap between current performance and future goals. Look into the future chapters of the book for materials on such techniques.

5. This chapter notes that economic pursuits can create 'ontologically fundamental contradictions' with social and ecological goals. Using the data provided, where is the clearest evidence of this contradiction within Nike's current strategy? (Hint: compare its performance in apparel vs. footwear). How can SMA make this contradiction more transparent to decision-makers?

Chapter review questions

Select the single best answer for each of the following questions based on the information and analysis presented in Chapter 1.

1. According to the chapter, the 'strategic turn' is best conceptualised as:

    a. The widespread adoption of military terminology within corporate annual reports since the 1980s.
    b. A comprehensive transformation in political-economic, techno-managerial, and institutional spheres that elevated the importance of strategy in managing contemporary organisations.
    c. The shift from financial accounting to strategic management accounting as the primary source of information for shareholders.
    d. A managerial shift focused exclusively on the privatisation of state-owned enterprises as endorsed by the Reagan and Thatcher administrations.

2. The chapter identifies four key 'contextual dynamics' that propelled the strategic turn. Which of the following is not one of these dynamics?

    a. The neoliberalisation of politics.
    b. The stabilisation of national markets.
    c. The globalisation of economic entities.
    d. The digitalisation of technologies.

3. The rise of 'consultocracy' is presented as a key institutional element of which broader dynamic?

    a. Contextual dynamics.
    b. Neoclassical economics.
    c. Epistemic dynamics.
    d. The global sustainability agenda.

4. The chapter contrasts the pre-neoliberal era with the current one. Which of the following characteristics best describes the political-economic conditions before the onset of neoliberalisation in the 1970s?

   a. Open economies, dominance of multinational corporations, and a focus on shareholder value maximisation.
   b. Market-based governance, minimal state intervention, and the ideological prominence of competition.
   c. Protectionist doctrines, state-centric welfareism, and heavily regulated markets.
   d. Digitalised technologies, virtualised spaces, and globalised supply chains.

5. When translating strategy from its military origins to a business context, what does the chapter identify as the pivotal, central concept?

   a. Bureaucracy.
   b. Positioning.
   c. Operational effectiveness.
   d. Welfareism.

6. How does Strategic Management Accounting primarily differ from conventional management accounting with respect to its analytical focus and aim?

   a. SMA aims for operational optimisation by analysing short-term decisions, while conventional management accounting focuses on providing a fair representation of past financial events.
   b. SMA aims for strategic positioning by analysing long-term competitive conditions, while conventional management accounting aims for operational optimisation based on internal data.
   c. SMA aims to ensure compliance with accounting standards, while conventional management accounting aims to determine profit-maximising quantities by equating marginal cost and revenue.
   d. SMA aims to motivate employees through incentive structures, whereas conventional management accounting focuses on managing supply chain logistics.

7. When the chapter discusses 'sustainabilising strategy', it argues that strategic thinking must expand beyond market competition to acknowledge 'ontologically fundamental contradictions' between which four foundational categories?

   a. Customers, suppliers, new entrants, and substitutes.
   b. Vision, mission, key performance indicators, and shareholder value.
   c. Market, labour process, hierarchy, and technology.
   d. Economy, polity, society, and ecology.

8. Which of the following is identified as a calculative technique or framework specifically associated with Strategic Management Accounting, rather than conventional management accounting or financial accounting?

    a. Standard costing and variance analysis.
    b. Cost-volume-profit analysis.
    c. Porter's five forces model and the balanced scorecard.
    d. Financial statement ratio analysis.

9. In corporate expansions like Nike in the 1980s and 1990s, the business model of outsourcing manufacturing to low-cost Asian countries can be seen as a direct consequence of which two interconnected contextual dynamics?

    a. Digitalisation and virtualisation.
    b. Neoliberalisation and globalisation.
    c. The sustainability agenda and epistemic dynamics.
    d. Consultocracy and bureaucracy.

10. Corporations like Nike started to develop codes of conduct for its supply chain partners and invested in auditing its global supply chain following the 1990s labour scandals. This is a primary example of strategic action within which of the following?

    a. Market positioning.
    b. Strategising the Organisational Hierarchy.
    c. Brand development and reputation management.
    d. Strategising the Point of Production (The Value Chain).

Comprehension questions

These questions assess your comprehension of key concepts discussed in the chapter.

1. What is meant by the term 'strategic turn'? Provide a brief explanation.
2. Populate the table below with the factors underpinning the 'strategic turn'.

Factors underlying the strategic turn		Meaning of the subcategory	Collectively, how did they lead to the evolution of SMA
Major categories	Subcategories		

3. Provide a brief explanation of military connections in conceptualising business strategies.
4. Compare and briefly explain how the concept of 'competitive terrain' is conceptualised in military and business contexts.
5. Briefly explain what is meant by strategy in relation to the idea of 'competitive terrain'.
6. Characterise and differentiate SMA from conventional management accounting based on the following dimensions:
   a. What is analysed?
   b. What is the analytical focus/aim?
   c. From where is the data for analysis sourced?
   d. What are the principal tools of analysis?
   e. Who is involved in the analysis and decision-making?
   f. What is the source of the analytical principles, rules, and frameworks?
   g. To whom are the accounts provided?
   h. What is the time orientation of the analyses?
7. Briefly explain how sustainability-driven SMA may reconfigure these dimensions.
8. Enumerate fundamental contradictions that 'sustainable strategic management' must address.
9. Populate the table below in relation to the domains in which strategies are enabled and enacted.

Domains of strategic action	Strategic imperatives to deal with

Explore further

1. To familiarise yourself with sustainability issues, visit the United Nations Sustainable Development Goals website (https://sdgs.un.org/goals) and reflect on why the UN had to develop such an extensive framework to address sustainability issues on a global scale. Consider how far conventional management accounting and emerging strategy discourses might have contributed to creating our contemporary 'unsustainable' methods of managing economic enterprises.

   Develop brief notes on these issues for a classroom discussion forum.

2. The International Federation of Accountants (IFAC) issued a statement titled, 'Accounting for Sustainability: From Sustainability to Business Resilience'. In introducing this document, the IFAC declares that it 'clarifies the important role accountants can, and must, play in embracing sustainability to ensure that the organisations they serve are resilient by linking sustainability to a broader business agenda and strategy'. The document begins with a visionary statement that 'accountants will save the world'.

   Download this document from the IFAC site (www.ifac.org).

   Critically evaluate the ways in which management accounting, as a practice and body of knowledge, should change to help 'save the world'. Do you consider the parameters set by this document sufficient to achieve this goal?

Develop your critical argumentation skills

1. Write an argumentative essay on the following theme:

   'The emergence of SMA is due to a set of interconnected political-economic, institutional, techno-managerial, and epistemic dynamics, all of which created new competitive and contradictory conditions in which strategising became a necessity.'

2. Write an argumentative essay on the following theme:

   'Strategy discourses encapsulate a militaristic reconception of competition, where the time-space distribution, positioning, and deployment of resources to engage with enemies and allies are considered strategy.'

References

Alawattage, C., and D. Wickramasinghe. 2019. Strategizing Management Accounting: Liberal Origins and Neoliberal Trends. London: Routledge.

———. 2022. Strategizing management accounting: liberal origins and neoliberal trends. Accounting, Auditing & Accountability Journal 35 (2):518-546.

Kantola, A., and H. Seeck. 2011. Dissemination of management into politics: Michael Porter and the political uses of management consulting. Management Learning 42 (1):25-47.

McKenna, C. D. 2006. The World's Newest Profession: Management Consulting in the Twentieth Century: Cambridge University Press.

Mintzberg, H. 1987. The strategy concept I: five Ps for strategy. California Management Review 30 (1):11-24.

Porter, M. E. 1996. What Is Strategy? Harvard Business Review 1996 (November-December):61-78.

Tzu, S. 2009 [circa 5th century BC]. The Art of War [translated by Lionel Giles]. Translated by L. Giles. www.PaxLibrorum.com: Pax Librorum Publishing House.

United Nations. Management consulting: a survey of the industry and its largest firms. United Nations 1993 [cited. Available from https://books.google.co.uk/books?id=-81C1AAAAIAAJ.

von Clausewitz, C. 2007 [1832]. On War. Translated by M. Howard and P. Paret. Oxford: Oxford University Press.

Werr, A., and T. Stjernberg. 2003. Exploring Management Consulting Firms as Knowledge Systems. Organization Studies 24 (6):881-908.

CHAPTER

2 Reconceptualising competition: **discourses of competitive advantage and strategic positioning**

2.1 Introduction

The preceding chapter highlighted competition as the driving force behind strategies and strategic discourses. We explained how transforming global competitive conditions, driven by broader contextual and epistemic factors, reinforced the strategic imperative in managing contemporary organisations. We also noted strategy's long history in military science. This 'militaristic' concept of strategy was transposed into business management, reimagining industries and markets as competitive arenas. Strategic management accounting (SMA) emerged from this reimagining of markets as strategic arenas where firms must adopt a 'strategic' approach to thrive. We also explored how sustainability issues have entered strategic considerations.

This chapter explores the evolution of business strategy discourses within SMA over the past five decades. Two interconnected discourses are at play: one from business management disciplines (organisational theory, marketing, operations management, and strategic management); the other from industrial economics, particularly the work of Alfred Chandler and Michael Porter. Contemporary strategy discourses amalgamate these two schools of thought. SMA captures the accounting elements of this convergence.

This chapter explores the strategy concepts and tools introduced by these discourses, focusing on the techno-managerial aspects of generic strategies, corporate planning, portfolio planning, and industry analysis. The chapter also explores the political-economic and institutional conditions that necessitated these concepts and tools.

The chapter addresses the following learning objectives:

1. Explain the different ways in which competition and strategy are conceptualised in classical business policy and corporate planning models.
2. Explain how Porterian (i.e., after Michael Porter) discourses of strategy have transformed our understanding of, and approach to, the concepts of competition and strategy.
3. Explain the various modes of calculation and rationalisation introduced by these strategy discourses.
4. Explain how emerging sustainability discourses implicate these conceptions.

The chapter is structured around these learning objectives.

- Section 2.2 explores how strategy is conceived in business policy and corporate planning, discussing concepts and frameworks such as SWOT analysis, portfolio planning models, long-term goal setting, and strategic diversification.
- Section 2.3, the chapter's core, addresses learning objectives two and three. It examines how Porterian discourses redefined competitiveness and strategy as both macro-level political-economic and organisational-level managerial problems. This section examines Porterian concepts and frameworks such as competitive advantage, generic strategies, the five forces model, the four-corner model, and value chain analysis.
- Finally, Section 2.4 discusses the modes of calculation and rationalisation popularised by these strategic discourses.

2.2 From management to strategic management: organisational discourses of strategy

The rise of modern management is traceable to two institutional apparatuses of production that emerged during the Industrial Revolution: the factory and the corporation. These two elements provided the institutional impetus for modern management, notably 'scientific management'. Initially, modern management focused on organising and rationalising labour processes for mechanised, large-scale mass production. In its early phase, 'scientific management' evolved around inventions by Frederick W. Taylor and other industrial engineers. The initial focus of modern management was rationalising and systematising labour processes.

A labour process is the specific 'set of relations into which men and women enter as they confront nature, as they transform raw materials into objects of their imagination' (Burawoy, 1979, p. 15). In simpler terms, these are the 'relations in production' that constitute the point where a product or service is produced. They encompass techno-managerial and social relationships between men and women as co-workers and supervisors. They also encompass relationships between workers and the tools they use, comprising not only physical elements like tools, machinery, and raw materials, but also conceptual aspects such as rules, procedures, standards, and processes. As an engineering task, management involves defining, implementing, and controlling these relationships to enhance production efficiency. The key functions of scientific management were the division, planning, delegation, monitoring, and control of work, alongside motivating workers with appropriate incentives.

During the 'scientific management' era, management was a function directed at the factory floor to enhance operational efficiency and profitability. Marketing and market positioning were not crucial, as a ready market existed for products made as inexpensively as possible. The Fordist assembly line later emerged to streamline labour processes further, evolving 'scientific management' into Fordist mass production.

Scientific management and Fordism were strategic only to the extent that strategies were implicit and directed towards operational efficiency. There was neither an explicit discussion of strategy, nor were there texts or gurus on the subject. The implicit strategy in scientific management and Fordism was to manufacture products as inexpensively as possible through the efficient use of labour, machinery, and materials. Consequently, there were only budgets and standards, not strategic plans; only work schedules, rules, routines, and procedures, not strategies. The concept was to design and control work processes, methods, schedules, and payment schemes to synchronise labour with machinery, generating maximum efficiency through economies of scale.

Emergence of corporate planning

As capitalism transitioned from industrial to 'monopoly capitalism', managerial emphasis shifted from the factory floor to the corporate hierarchy. This occurred in the early 20th century, particularly in the US, as companies sought monopolies through mergers and acquisitions. Managing the organisation as a totality became as crucial as, if not more than, overseeing the factory floor. The pursuit of capital accumulation—sustained growth in sales and profits for an abnormal return on capital—necessitated corporate expansion into new regions, markets, and industries through mergers and acquisitions. Before and during the third wave of mergers, companies aimed to broaden their production, distribution, and market operations. This led to the emergence of multidivisional corporate conglomerates, such as DuPont and General Electric. Strategic and corporate planning thus emerged as a distinct top management expertise.

In the 1960s, early strategy discourses (e.g., Ansoff, 1965; Chandler, 1962) show that corporate strategy or planning evolved around three interrelated issues:

1. Coordination between business units in multidivisional organisational forms.
2. External environmental legitimacy.
3. Market and product diversification.

Strategy as coordinating multidivisional organisations

In his seminal work, Chandler (1962) explained that by the 1950s, US industrial organisations had become decentralised, multi-division enterprises. DuPont, General Motors, Standard Oil, and Sears Roebuck were among the influential companies Chandler analysed. These corporations were pivotal in shaping many strategic management concepts and frameworks. As depicted in Figure 2.1, these multidivisional enterprises comprised multiple businesses organised into decentralised divisions, each dedicated to a specific product, service line, or region. In contemporary strategy discourses, these are known as Strategic Business Units (SBUs). Each SBU is considered to have a unique competitive condition and autonomously handles its production, sales, distribution, and other core functions.

Figure 2.1: Multidivisional organisation form

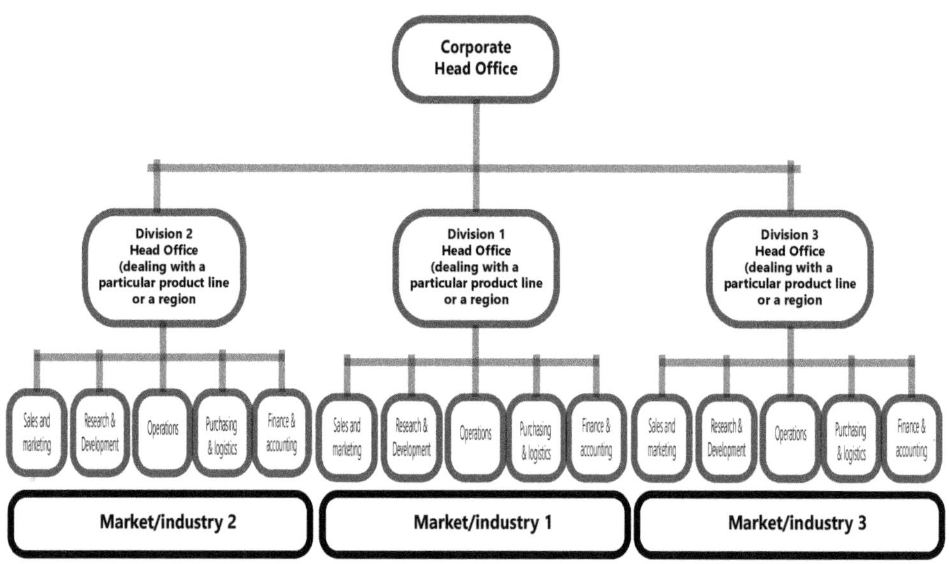

In multidivisional (M-Form) organisations, corporate planning and strategy are the predominant functions of the corporate head office, or in Chandler's term, the 'General Office'. Strategy formulation becomes the head office's primary responsibility, involving the integration and coordination of SBUs into a unified corporation. This requires institutional mechanisms to consolidate quasi-independent divisions into a cohesive 'corporation'. The objective of corporate planning is to ensure the corporation's overall growth as a collective of SBUs. Thus, the strategic imperative is to coordinate and integrate SBUs into a single corporation.

To achieve this, three interrelated functions characterise corporate planning:

1. Setting Long-term Goals: Establishing long-term goals for the corporation and its SBUs, and determining actions to achieve them.
2. Formulating Policies: Developing corporate policies to standardise and control activities across SBUs.
3. Resource Allocation: Allocating and reallocating resources among SBUs, deciding how investments should be prioritised.

The importance of these three elements is clear in Chandler's (1962, p. 13) classic definition:

> The thesis that different organisational forms result from different types of growth can be stated more precisely if the planning and carrying out of such growth is considered a strategy, and the organisation devised to administer these enlarged activities and resources, a structure. ***Strategy can be defined as the determination of the basic long-term goals and objectives of an enterprise, and the adoption of courses of action and the allocation of resources necessary for carrying out these goals.*** Decisions to expand the volume of activities, to set up distant plants and offices, to move into new economic functions, or become diversified along many lines of business involve the defining of new basic goals. New courses of action must be devised and resources allocated and reallocated in order to achieve these goals and to maintain and expand the firm's activities in the new areas in response to shifting demands, changing sources of supply, fluctuating economic conditions, new technological developments, and the actions of competitors. As the adoption of a new strategy may add new types of personnel and facilities, and alter the business horizons of the men responsible for the enterprise, it can have a profound effect on the form of its organisation.

Accounting calculations in corporate planning:

Accounting played a crucial role in corporate planning. First, accounting, particularly through consolidated financial statements, provided the calculative foundation for assessing corporate and divisional performance. Corporate planning decisions were based on these assessments. Second, during the monopoly capitalism era, corporate growth was measured by return on investment (ROI) or return on equity (ROE). This was linked to 'responsibility accounting' frameworks, where SBUs were treated as 'investment centres'. An SBU's success was judged by its ROI compared to other SBUs and head office expectations. As the primary criterion for performance management, ROI was dissected into operational sub-elements (see Figure 2.2). The DuPont Corporation pioneered this decomposition by analysing how ROI was influenced by profitability, asset utilisation, and leverage. Other performance elements, such as revenue and market share, can be linked to ROI, elucidating how a target ROI is achieved. ROI thus became the ultimate accounting indicator of corporate performance or, as Bryer (2012) termed it, the 'accounting signature of monopoly capitalism'. Long-term growth targets for the corporation and its SBUs were primarily outlined and measured through ROI.

Figure 2.2: Accounting in corporate planning - dupont system of financial analysis

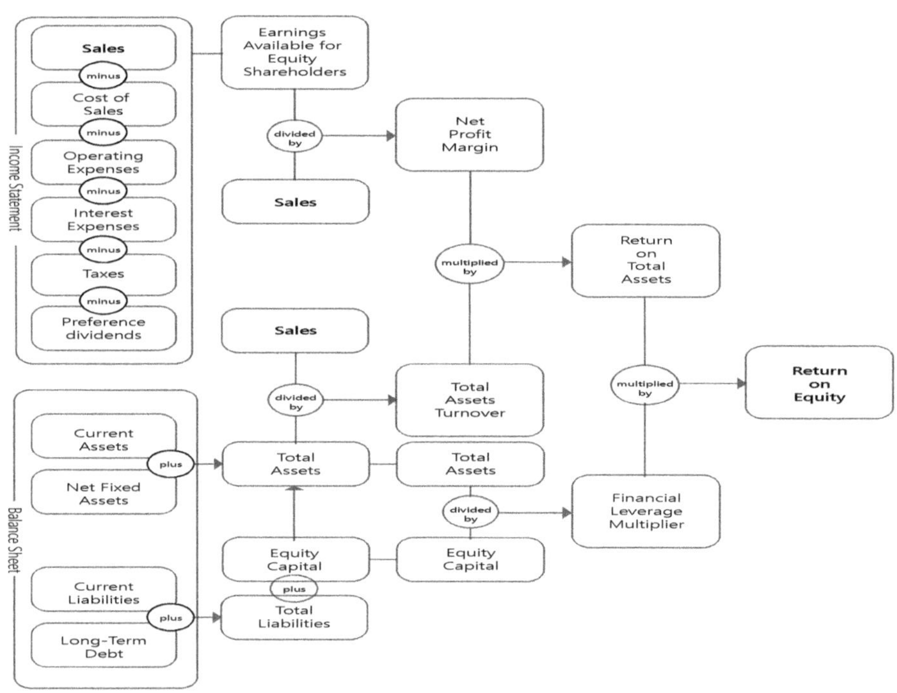

Business portfolio models in corporate planning:

Resource reallocation was a key function of corporate planning. A key consideration was which SBUs to fund for growth and which to divest as a source of corporate funds. Corporate planners in large corporations like General Electric began viewing the corporation as a portfolio of businesses. Within this framework, resource allocation decisions depend on each SBU's investment attractiveness. Corporate planning involved making strategic investment and divestment decisions across SBUs. Portfolio planning models, such as the Boston Consultancy Group's (BCG) Growth-Share Matrix and General Electric's Nine-Cell Matrix, were techniques that popularised this investment-divestment logic (see Figure 2.3).

Figure 2.3: Portfolio planning models

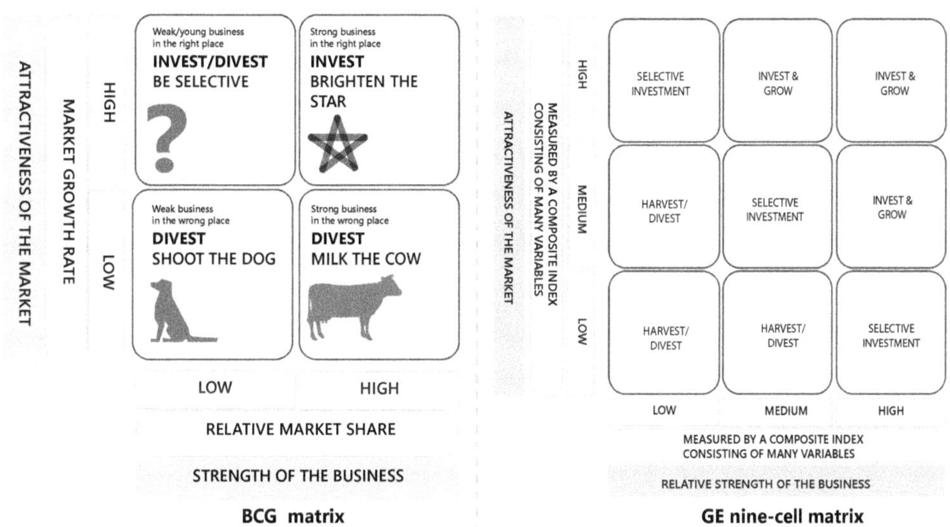

These models offer a two-dimensional 'strategic map' for evaluating SBUs based on two criteria:

1. Market Attractiveness: Assessing whether a business operates in an attractive market with growth potential. In the BCG Matrix, this was gauged by market growth rate. General Electric enhanced this by incorporating a composite index of multiple indicators. In both cases, the evaluation revolves around the business's 'location'—whether its industry is attractive enough for corporate funding.

2. **Competitive Strength:** Evaluating a business's strength relative to its competitors. The BCG Matrix uses relative market share for this assessment. General Electric again advanced this by using a composite index of business strength. The focus is on assessing if the business is robust enough to warrant corporate funding.

Viewed through these models, corporate strategy involves making investment and divestment decisions about SBUs. This entails determining the flow of corporate funding from some SBUs to others. This is often expressed through metaphors: 'killing dogs', 'milking cows', 'brightening stars', and being selective about 'question marks'. The idea is that corporate growth is achieved by reallocating capital from weaker businesses in less attractive markets to promising businesses in attractive ones. This reallocation of funds aims to maximise the corporation's cash flow and long-term ROI.

An additional framework associated with portfolio models is the product life cycle, which traces a product's life from development through introduction, growth, and maturity to decline. Investment decisions are often aligned with this cycle. This model is frequently linked with the BCG matrix: introduction is a 'question mark', growth a 'star', saturation a 'cash cow', and decline a 'dog'.

Strategy as dealing with external environmental conditions

The external environment was the second focal point for strategy discourses. In the 1970s, influenced by general systems theory, the external environment became a critical factor in corporate growth planning. Concepts of political-economic, legal, and socio-cultural legitimacy permeated business management literature. Viewing organisations as subsystems of a broader system, corporations were seen as 'environment-serving organisations' or ESOs (Ansoff, 2007). Strategic management is thus a boundary-spanning activity, aiming for optimal alignment between the organisation's internal and external environments. The following quotation from Ansoff (2007, p. 25) explains the strategic thrust and three attributes of the ESO:

> ... the commercial results realised by an ESO are largely determined by an alignment of certain attributes. [...] Part of this alignment is external, between the level of environmental turbulence and what we shall call the strategic thrust of the ESO. Another part is internal, between the strategic thrust and three attributes of the ESO: its strategic culture, its managerial capability, and its logistic capability. [...] When the attributes are properly matched, the potential performance is optimised; when they are not, the potential deteriorates

> proportionally to the mismatch. [...] The performance is also influenced by the resource commitment, the strategic budget, which the ESO makes to its strategic thrust. The theory defines for each environment a strategic budget level, called critical mass, below which the ESO cannot hope to realise a positive net commercial exchange with the environment. Above the critical mass, the ROI rises for a while as the budget is increased, but eventually levels at a maximum.

This quotation shows that despite including sociological and behavioural elements, corporate strategy was still seen as the pursuit of growth through ROI. However, unlike portfolio planning models, this perspective stressed the alignment of external environmental and internal organisational attributes. Techniques like SWOT and PEST (or PESTEL, which adds Ecological and Legal factors) analysis gained popularity for achieving this alignment.

Diversification as strategy: dealing with corporate growth

Diversification entered the managerial lexicon in the 1960s as a 'strategy' for corporate growth and improved ROI, as seen in Igor Ansoff's writings. Faced with escalating competition and expanding global markets post-World War II, companies sought to augment their ROI through product and market expansions. Ansoff's product-market matrix became a popular framework to explain diversification strategies (see Figure 2.4).

Figure 2.4: Ansoff's product-market matrix

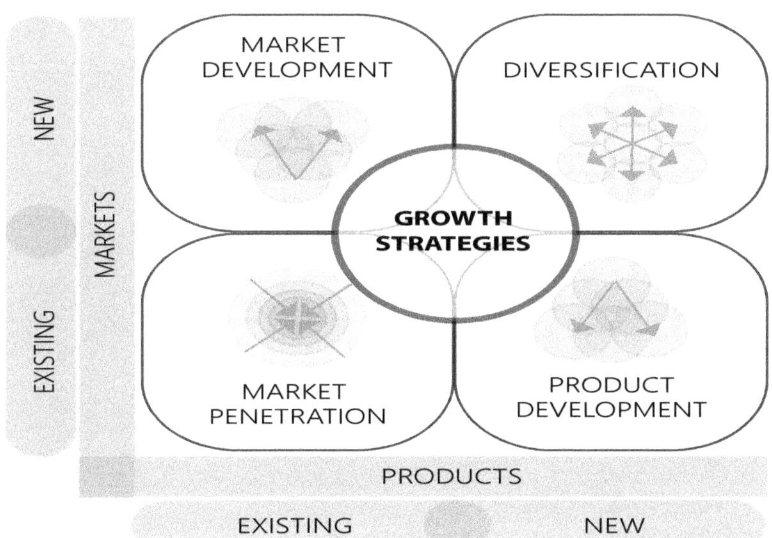

Ansoff also prioritised firm growth to maintain a robust ROI, delineating a specific path for firms. The least perilous strategy is 'market penetration', maximising profit potential in existing markets with existing products. Tactics such as new pricing, intensified sales, and targeted marketing are used. The next option is 'market development', introducing existing products to new markets. This is riskier as it entails more cost and ventures into uncharted territory. The third option, 'product development', is riskier still, requiring significant investment in research and development and production capacity. Finally, the riskiest yet potentially most rewarding option is 'diversification', where a firm enters new markets with new products, often via mergers and acquisitions.

Bringing people and cultural factors in

During the 1960s and 1970s, corporate strategy discourses were dominated by rational models. In the 1980s and 1990s, attention shifted to the behavioural and institutional aspects of strategy implementation. The emphasis was on the structural and behavioural dynamics that hindered or facilitated strategy implementation, particularly managing the change process. Consequently, change management became a prominent agenda in strategy consultancy. Books such as In Search of Excellence by Peters and Waterman (1982) and Peter Senge's The Fifth Discipline (1990) became essential readings. Concepts like mission and vision, learning organisations, corporate culture, and business process re-engineering gained widespread acceptance. McKinsey's 7S framework (see Figure 2.5) exemplifies how these dimensions were expressed. McKinsey's consultants believed corporate success depends on the totality of these seven fundamentals.

Figure 2.5: McKinsey's 7S framework as a manifestation of the structural and behavioural dynamics of strategy

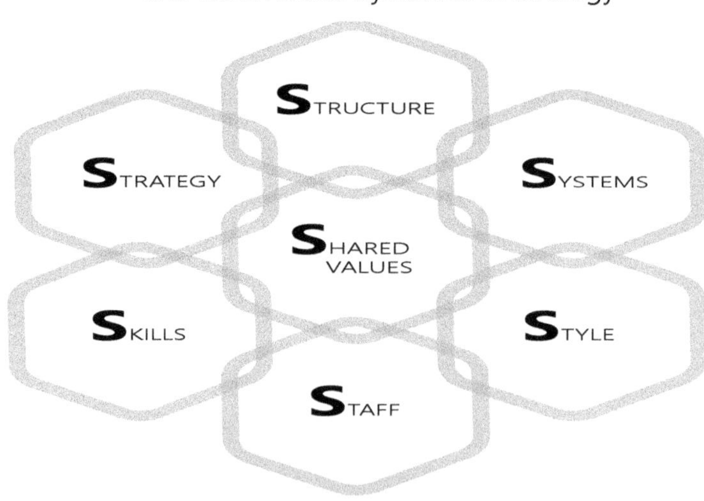

Another critical issue was integrating performance measurement with corporate strategies. Two key models gained popularity: Johnson and Kaplan's Balanced Scorecard and Simons' Levers of Control (LOC) framework. Chapters 4 and 5 will discuss these models in detail.

Summary of pre-porterian strategy discourses

This section outlined the issues from which corporate and strategic planning emerged. In the early 20th century, during the scientific management and Fordist era, the focus was on rationalising the labour process. However, as corporations expanded into M-form enterprises through mergers and acquisitions, managerial attention shifted to managing the corporation as a totality. Corporate head offices were established to manage the interconnection of SBUs. Corporate planning, or business policy, constituted the functions these head offices performed to address three interrelated issues: (1) coordinating SBU operations; (2) aligning internal and external environmental factors for legitimation and growth; and (3) sustaining growth through product and market diversification.

Various planning models emerged to address these issues. Since the late 1970s, managerial attention has shifted toward strategy implementation and change management. The institutional logic of these models relates to the key issues corporate managers faced. Table 2.1 summarises this explanation.

Table 2.1: Classical corporate planning issues and models

Issue	Strategy Models and Concepts
Coordination and consolidation of independent business divisions (SBUs)	Setting long-term goals and objectives: • Vision and mission statements • Corporate and long-term divisional objectives • Return on Investment (ROI) / Return on Equity (ROE) as a long-term objective Developing and implementing corporate and business policies: • Accounting policies • Pricing policies • Advertising policies • Investment policies (including ROI specifications) Allocating resources among divisions: • Portfolio planning models (e.g., BCG Growth-Share Matrix, GE Nine-Cell Matrix)
Creating and maintaining a strategic fit between external and internal environments	• SWOT analysis • PEST • PESTEL analysis
Sustaining corporate growth through product and market developments	• Ansoff's Product-Market Matrix of growth strategies
Strategy implementation and change management	Behavioural, cultural, institutional, and structural frameworks, including: • Management by objectives • Transformational leadership discourses • Learning organisations • Business process re-engineering • Continuous improvement • McKinsey's 7S framework

2.3 Porterian discourses of strategy

Michael Porter significantly influenced strategy discourse during neoliberal times, shaping a distinct trajectory for competitiveness and strategy formulation. This section critically examines the strategy schema he popularised.

Revising the structure-conduct-performance model

The models discussed so far emerged from management, organisational studies, and consulting. In contrast, Porter's contributions are rooted in industrial economics. In his early work, he formulated his strategy concept by revising the prevalent structure-conduct-performance model. This model explained how a firm's structural conditions determined its conduct (strategy) and collective performance. As Figure 2.6 (panel A) shows, the model conceptualises strategy as conduct: the firm's decisions on price, production quantity, capacity, quality, and so on.

Figure 2.6: Porterian revision of the structure-conduct-performance model

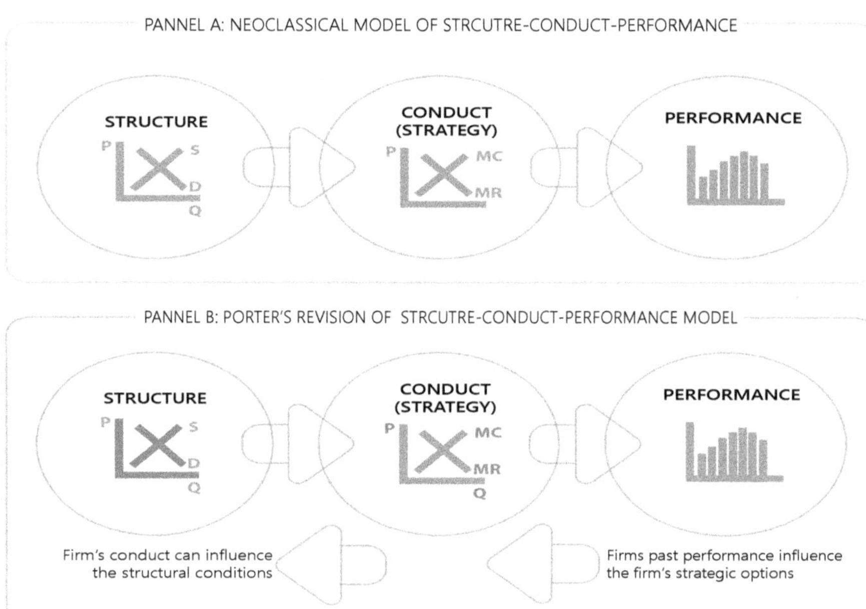

The model is deterministic, assuming a linear causality between industry structure and a firm's conduct. It posits that structural conditions determine conduct, and performance encompasses collective outcomes at the industry level, such as allocative efficiency and innovation. A fundamental flaw is its failure to grant the firm any strategic agency. The firm is seen as a passive entity conditioned by market structure.

Porter addressed this weakness. As Figure 2.6 (panel B) shows, he argued that while structural conditions (e.g., number of rivals, entry barriers, demand elasticity) influence a firm's conduct, its past performance creates strategic options to innovate and alter these conditions (Porter, 1981). Depending on its capabilities and strategy, a firm can influence structural conditions, creating opportunities to position itself for a 'competitive advantage' and abnormal returns. For Porter, strategising is this distinctive positioning within the competitive structure to gain a competitive advantage.

The notion of competitive advantage

Porter's framework begins with a foundational concept: competitive advantage. This is the ability of a firm or country to surpass competitors consistently. As an economic and managerial inquiry, it asks how a firm or nation can outperform rivals. Economists traditionally used theories of absolute advantage, comparative advantage, and factor endowment, which hinge on resource availability and opportunity costs. Porter's concept of competitive advantage offers an alternative, emphasising strategies over factor endowment and opportunity costs.

Unlike traditional economic theories, Porter contends that strategy determines the competitive advantage of both firms and nations. In The Competitive Advantage of Nations, he introduced his 'diamond model', outlining six factors influencing a nation's competitive advantage:

1. Related and supporting industries
2. Factor conditions
3. Demand conditions
4. Firms' strategy and structure of rivalry
5. The political role of the government
6. Chance

Porter identifies 'firm strategy and structure of rivalry' as the most critical factor. He argues that the effectiveness of strategies and the competitive landscape are paramount in determining national competitive advantage.

Porter introduces competitive advantage in two interconnected contexts: the macroeconomic landscape of a nation and the micro-organisational context of firms. Within the nation's political context, Porter identifies competitiveness as 'The Looming Challenge of Competitiveness', the foremost problem faced by nation-states. Porter and other Harvard academics frame this as a 'biopolitical problem' (see Alawattage and Wickramasinghe, 2019), where competitiveness becomes the primary criterion for assessing social and political elements. The political effectiveness of taxation, education, democracy, employment rights, and trade unions is thus judged by their contribution to the global competitiveness of the nation's firms. For instance, Porter (2013) argued to the US House of Representatives that the 'challenge is competitiveness, not jobs per se'.

As a national problem, competitiveness requires macroeconomic and political measurement. Over recent decades, attempts have been made to develop a 'global competitiveness index', notably the World Economic Forum's Global Competitiveness Report, in which Porter played a prominent role. By positioning competitiveness as a national problem, Porter elevates business strategy from a managerial to a political-economic concern. Acquiring and maintaining a competitive advantage is thus both a managerial challenge for the firm and a political-economic one for the nation.

Once framed as the 'most critical problem of our times', strategy gains macropolitical significance beyond its managerial use. Strategy is seen as the fundamental means to address competitiveness at both organisational and national levels. Notably, Porter argues that it is a nation's firms, not nations themselves, that compete in global markets. Therefore, enhancing a nation's competitiveness requires improving the capabilities of its firms.

Porter's generic strategies

At the firm level, Porter's framework posits two generic strategies. As depicted in Figure 2.7, a firm has two strategic options, 'cost leadership' or 'differentiation', which can be applied in a broad or narrow market context. Porter stresses that strategy involves positioning the firm's brand and products to distinguish them from competitors' offerings. Whether pursuing 'differentiation' or 'cost leadership', the objective is to distinguish the firm's offerings. If this distinction is based on cost and price, it is 'cost leadership'. If achieved by other means, it is 'differentiation'.

Value for money:

The distinction between cost leadership and differentiation can be understood using the concept of 'value for money'. This underpins a customer's decision-making and a firm's ability to reach a market segment. It can be expressed as:

Value for Money = Value/Price.

In this formula, 'value' encompasses the benefits, qualities, and features a consumer gains from a product. 'Price' is the consumer's sacrifice to own it. A firm has two approaches to enhance value for money.

Figure 2.7: Porter's framework of generic strategies

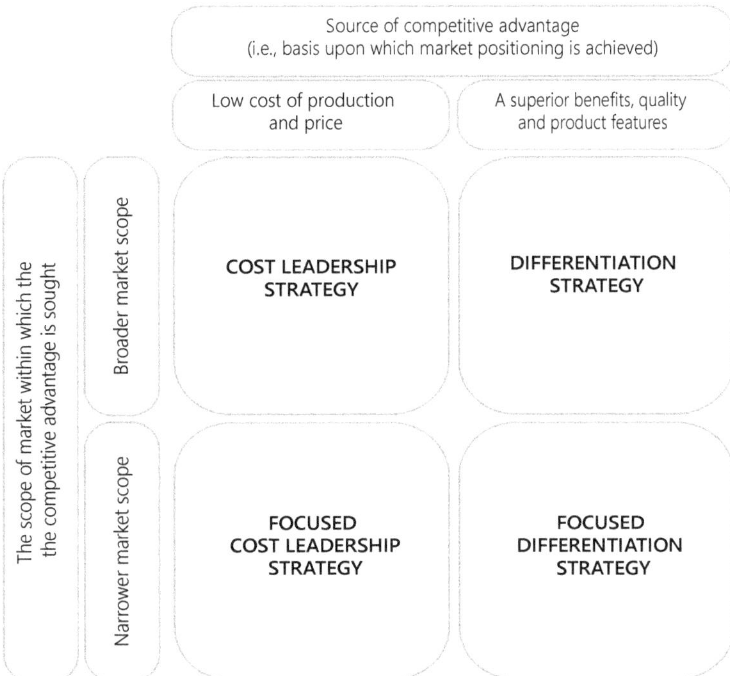

Source: based on Porter's various writings

The first, cost leadership, deals with the denominator, price. While maintaining an acceptable value, the firm focuses on reducing costs to offer the product at a lower price than competitors. The focus is on cost management to lower the price and generate higher value for money. This requires advanced cost management techniques, such as a well-coordinated supply chain and a just-in-time (JIT) inventory system. Japanese car manufacturers, especially Toyota, are classic examples. This strategy is most effective in price-sensitive markets where consumers accept a standard level of value.

The second approach, differentiation, deals with the numerator, value. The strategy is to offer superior quality, benefits, and features at a higher price, but with a greater value-for-money ratio. The value package must be greater than competitors' to justify the extra price. Products targeting 'high-end' market segments exemplify this strategy. For example, in the digital camera market, Sony follows this strategy with its A9, while Canon and Nikon offer the R5 and Z9, respectively, with superior features that justify their premium prices.

Porter's models of strategic analysis

According to Porter, decisions on generic strategy should be based on three interconnected analyses:

1. Analysis of the Structure of Rivalry – Macro-Industrial Analysis
2. Analysis of the Value Chain – Micro-Organisational Analysis
3. Analysis of the Competitor Response Profile – Competitive Context Analysis

Porter's five forces analysis:

Porter presents his Five Forces Framework for industry analysis. According to this framework, an industry's competitive intensity (the model's central point, see Figure 2.8) is determined by four structural conditions: the bargaining power of buyers, the bargaining power of suppliers, the threat of new entry, and the threat of substitutes. A firm's ability to pursue a specific generic strategy depends on how these forces influence it.

Figure 2.8: Porter's five forces analysis

Source: Porter's various writings

For instance, in a market where non-price competition dominates, the ability to pursue a 'differentiation' strategy depends on:

- Whether customers have bargaining power and use it to demand premium features and quality. In this case, a differentiation strategy has a better chance.
- Whether the firm has bargaining power over suppliers, enabling it to dictate terms regarding the quality of raw materials and components. This is crucial for a differentiation strategy.
- Whether the firm's specific quality and features are not easily imitated or substituted.

Similar conditions apply to a 'cost leadership' strategy, with the variation that:

- Customers have bargaining power to demand standard products at lower prices.
- The firm has bargaining power over suppliers to dictate prices and delivery schedules to manage costs.
- Competitors or new entrants cannot easily imitate the firm's cost advantage.

Overall, a firm's ability to pursue a strategy depends on three factors: its customers' bargaining power; its own bargaining power over suppliers regarding cost, delivery, quality, and terms; and whether competitors can easily imitate its cost or differentiation advantage.

Value chain analysis:

While the Five Forces model covers external industrial conditions, value chain analysis focuses on the internal factors a firm must establish to achieve a successful market position. The notion is that a firm's ability to pursue a strategy depends on its value chain. Here, 'value chain' denotes the interconnectedness of inbound supply, internal processes, and outbound supply to generate customer value while ensuring a satisfactory ROI.

Figure 2.9 illustrates Porter's conception of a value chain. The proposition is that differentiation and cost-leadership strategies require distinct value chain configurations. To pursue cost leadership, the value chain must be configured to minimise the cost of all activities while delivering an acceptable benefit to the customer. Core and support functions must be consistently re-evaluated to reduce costs. Similarly, for a differentiation strategy, every aspect of the value chain must be configured to consistently innovate and produce the quality, flexibility, and new features that create a distinctive market appeal.

Figure 2.9: Value chain

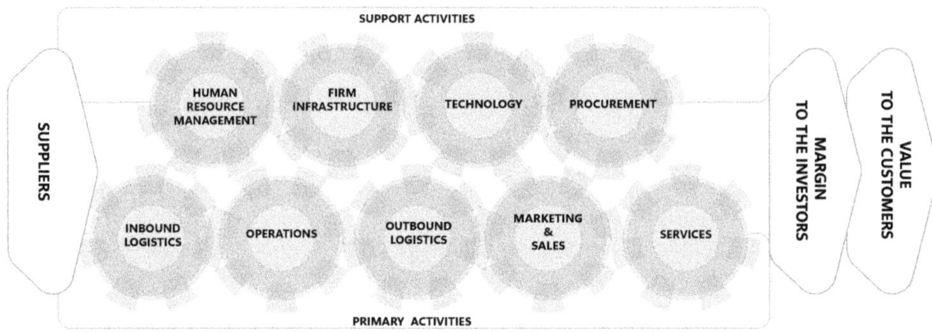

Source: Porter's various writings

Four-corner analysis:

This is Porter's third analytical model, a tool for evaluating competitors' probable strategies. It offers a more targeted analysis of potential strategic responses from key competitors than the broad Five Forces model. Its objective is to formulate a 'competitor's response profile', evaluating four interconnected elements of the competitor's future strategy (see Figure 2.10):

1. **Strategic drivers:** An examination of factors propelling the competitor, including financial and non-financial goals, vision, leadership, corporate culture, and constraints.
2. **Strategic assumptions about itself and the industry:** The competitor's perceived strengths and weaknesses, cultural values, and perceptions of industry forces.
3. **Current strategy:** The competitor's existing actions and competitive approaches, including market positioning, value creation methods, and investment areas.
4. **Capabilities:** An evaluation of the competitor's strengths and weaknesses, such as marketing skills, product quality, workforce skills, patents, and financial strength.

According to Porter, an analysis of these 'four corners' should construct the 'competitor's response profile', addressing these questions (Porter, 2004, p. 49):

1. Is the competitor content with its current position?
2. What probable moves or shifts in strategy might the competitor undertake?

3. Where is the competitor susceptible?
4. What actions are likely to trigger the most significant and effective retaliation from the competitor?

Figure 2.10: Porter's four-corners analysis

Source: Porter's various writings

Porter's grand schema of strategy in summary:

The Porterian concepts discussed so far form a 'grand schema of strategy' spanning from macro-political to micro-organisational dimensions, interconnecting various institutional facets of strategising. This schema establishes a 'biopolitical hierarchy of competitiveness' (see Alawattage and Wickramasinghe, 2019, 2022). As Figure 2.11 shows, the apex is competitive advantage, discussed as a challenge and goal for the nation-state (the biopolitical realm). It is seen as a pathological issue for the nation-state, requiring neoliberal policies that support the nation's global economic strategies. Porter's diamond model then delineates the factors influencing a nation's competitive advantage.

In Porterian discourses, particular emphasis is placed on 'firm strategy, structure, and rivalry'. This is the nexus between the macro-political (biopolitical) and the micro-organisational (anatomico-political). In the domain of organisational competitiveness, Porterian discussions have popularised four interconnected frameworks for strategic analysis: the five forces model, the model of generic strategies, the value chain model, and the four-corners model.

Figure 2.11: Porterian strategy discourses as a biopolitical hierarchy of competitiveness

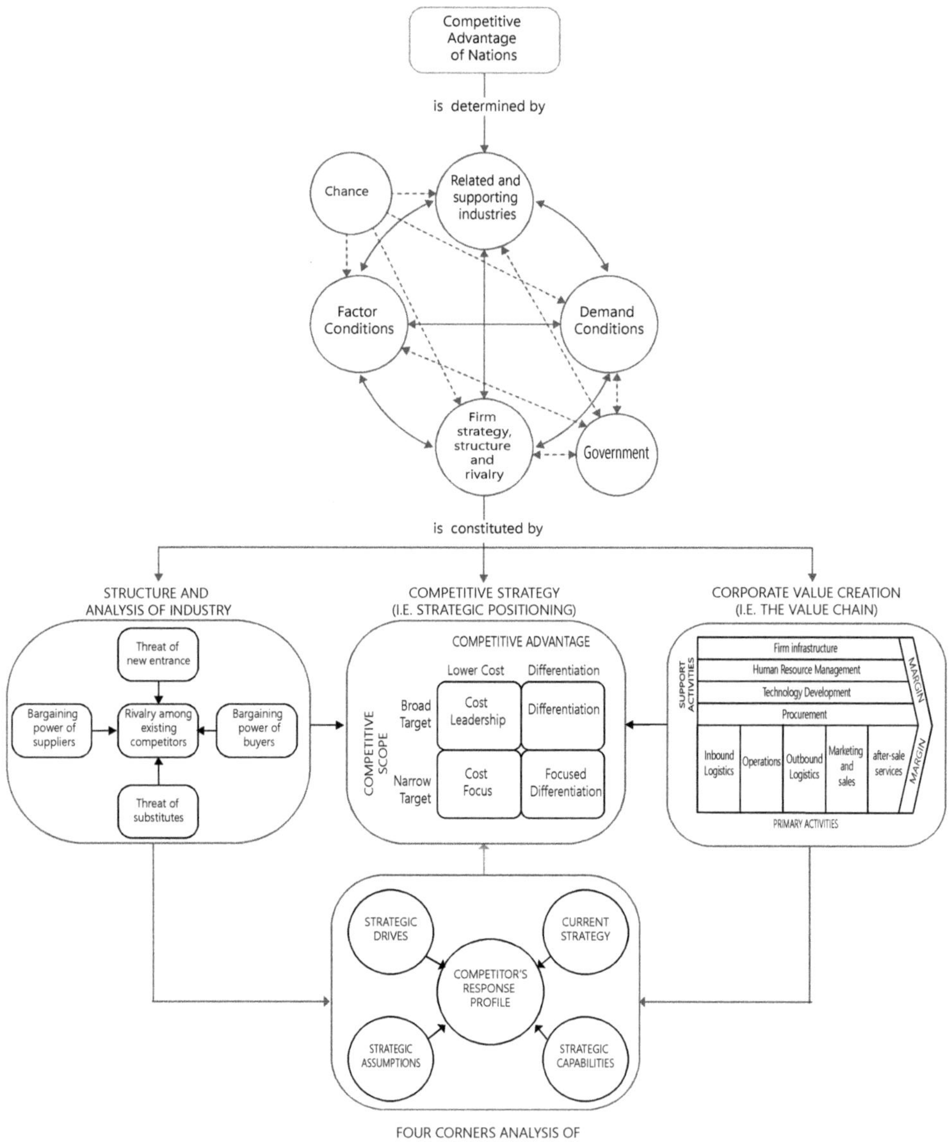

2.4 Sustainability implications

The preceding strategic discussions conspicuously overlook sustainability, i.e., ecological and social justice concerns. Strategy has been conceptualised within a narrow organisational scope, disregarding its broader social and ecological implications. However, sustainability has gained recent global recognition, particularly with the UN's Sustainable Development Goals (SDGs). Corporations are increasingly embracing the SDGs, and sustainability reporting has become a crucial aspect of corporate reporting, with companies adopting standards from the Global Reporting Initiative (GRI).

In response, strategy experts like Michael Porter are refining their frameworks to incorporate sustainability (see Porter and Kramer, 2006). However, even here, the primary focus has been on how sustainability can augment a company's strategic positioning. A close examination reveals their primary concern is not sustainability itself, but how to leverage its emerging discourses to enhance competitive positioning—the strategic instrumentality of sustainability. For example, Porter and Kramer (2006, p. 13) explain:

> Creating a social dimension to the value proposition. At the heart of any strategy is a unique value proposition: a set of needs a company can meet for its chosen customers that others cannot. The most strategic CSR [corporate social responsibility] occurs when a company adds a social dimension to its value proposition, making social impact integral to the overall strategy.

To develop a 'sustainability value proposition', Porter and Kramer (2006) adapt Porter's value chain and industry analysis frameworks to map social opportunities by identifying 'inside-out' and 'outside-in' linkages. Mapping 'inside-out linkages' involves identifying the social impacts of a firm's value-chain activities, while 'outside-in linkages' refer to the social dimensions of the firm's competitive context. They propose a revised industry analysis model to perform these mappings, which includes four dimensions: context for firm strategy and rivalry, factor (input) conditions, local demand conditions, and related and supporting industries. Table 2.2 summarises Porter and Kramer's integration of sustainability into their tools.

Table 2.2: Strategising sustainability – Porter and Kramer (2006)

Model	Model Dimensions	CSR Examples
Value-chain analysis	(inside-out linkages)	
	Inbound logistics	Transportation impacts (e.g., emissions, congestion, logging roads)
	Operations	Emissions & waste | Biodiversity & ecological impacts | Energy & water usage | Worker safety & labour relations | Hazardous materials
	Outbound logistics	Packaging use and disposal (McDonald's clamshell) | Transportation impacts
	Marketing and sales	Marketing & advertising (e.g., truthful advertising, advertising to children) | Pricing practices (e.g., price discrimination, anti-competitive pricing, pricing policy to the poor) | Consumer information | Privacy
	After-sales services	Disposal of obsolete products | Handling of consumables (e.g., motor oil, printing ink) | Customer privacy
	Procurement	Procurement & supply chain practices (e.g., bribery, child labour, conflict diamonds, pricing to farmers) | Uses of particular inputs (e.g., animal fur) | Utilisation of resources
	Technology development	Relationships with universities | Ethical research practices (e.g., animal testing, GMOs) | Product safety | Conservation of raw materials | Recycling
	Human resource management	Education & job training | Safe working conditions | Diversity & discrimination | Health care & other benefits | Compensation policies | Layoff policies
	Firm Infrastructure	Financial reporting practices | Government practices | Transparency | Use of lobbying

Chapter summary

This chapter traced the evolution of managerial discourses on strategy. While strategy has a long history in military science, it gained prominence in business management in the early 1960s. During modern management's initial phase, strategy was not an explicit concern. In the 'scientific management' era, the focus was on the point of production and the labour process. The objective was to enhance efficiency by synchronising labour with machinery, subordinating it to capital accumulation. The implicit strategy was the rationalisation of labour through deskilling and mechanisation, as seen in Taylorist and Fordist regimes.

Table 2.2: Strategising sustainability (continued)

Model	Model Dimensions	CSR Examples
Industry analysis	(outside-in linkages)	
	Context for Firm Strategy and Rivalry	Fair and open local competition | Intellectual property protection | Transparency (e.g., Extractive Industries Transparency Initiative) | Rule of law | Meritocratic incentive systems
	Factor (Input) Conditions	Availability of human resources (Marriott's job training) | Access to research institutions (Microsoft's Working Connections) | Efficient physical and administrative infrastructure | Availability of scientific and technological infrastructure (Nestlé's knowledge transfer to milk farmers) | Sustainable natural resources (GrupoNueva's water conservation) | Efficient access to capital
	Local Demand Conditions	Sophistication of local demand (e.g. appeal of social value propositions: Whole Foods' customers) | Demanding regulatory standards (California auto emissions standards) | Unusual local needs that can be served globally (Urbi's housing financing, Unilever's "bottom of the pyramid" strategy)
	Related and Supporting Industries	Availability of local suppliers (Sysco's locally grown produce; Nestlé's milk collection dairies) | Access to firms in related fields | Presence of clusters instead of isolated industries

Source: based on Porter and Kramer (2006, pp. 5-6)

However, mergers and acquisitions starting in the late 19th century created the need for strategic thinking. Corporations expanded into conglomerates, leading to the rise of multidivisional (M-form) organisations like DuPont. Managerial attention shifted from the labour process to the holistic management of the corporation. Three challenges surfaced: (a) coordinating business units, (b) establishing external environmental legitimacy, and (c) diversification for corporate growth. Corporate planning and strategy emerged to tackle these challenges.

Long-term goal-setting, corporate policies, and resource allocation became essential for coordination. Corporate planning incorporated concepts like vision and mission statements to provide overarching direction. Portfolio planning models, particularly the BCG and GE matrices, gained popularity for rationalising investment decisions. Concerning environmental legitimacy, planners viewed corporations as environment-serving organisations (ESOs) and emphasised a fit between external and internal factors. Analytical models such as SWOT and PEST were developed. Diversification was addressed through techniques like Ansoff's product-market matrix.

The behavioural school of strategy emerged in the mid-1970s, focusing on implementation and change management. Discourses such as 'in search of excellence', 'learning organisations', and business process re-engineering gained popularity.

Since the mid-1970s, with neoliberalisation and globalisation, managerial attention shifted to market positioning. Strategising in the market became more critical than managing the hierarchy. Strategy acquired a new meaning: strategy as positioning. Michael Porter's contributions became pivotal. Porter provides a schema that presents strategy and competitive advantage as both macro-political issues for the nation-state and managerial issues for the firm.

Porter revised the neoclassical structure-conduct-performance model, attributing strategic agency to the firm. He argued that a firm could influence its structural conditions through its strategies, making strategy a fundamental factor in competitive advantage. According to Porter, a firm may adopt two generic strategies: cost leadership or differentiation, in a narrow or broad market scope. The decision should stem from three analyses: (1) industry analysis (Five-Forces model); (2) analysis of internal processes (value-chain analysis); and (3) analysis of competitor responses (Four-Corner analysis).

Finally, the chapter explored how sustainability discourses have influenced strategy, particularly recent attempts to rebrand Porter's tools in light of corporate social responsibility (CSR).

Case Study: Strategic positioning and sustainability in the global automobile industry: a comparative case study of Tesla, Volkswagen, and Toyota

1.0 Introduction: a paradigm shift in mobility

The global automobile industry is undergoing its most profound transformation in over a century. The established paradigm of the internal combustion engine (ICE) and incremental innovation is being disrupted by powerful, interconnected forces. This is a paradigm shift, driven by the imperatives of electrification, autonomous driving, and connectivity, and framed by the demand for environmental sustainability. The vehicle is evolving from a mechanical product to a software-defined platform, altering competition, value creation, and corporate strategy.

This case study examines the strategic responses to this disruption by three significant players: Tesla, Inc., Volkswagen Group, and Toyota Motor Corporation. This analysis is a practical application of the concepts in Chapter 2. The chapter traces strategic thought from the pre-Porterian era's focus on internal coordination to the Porterian focus on the external competitive environment and strategic positioning. This case illustrates a further evolution where sustainability is no longer a peripheral CSR concern but is integral to strategic positioning and a primary driver in reconfiguring value chains.

To explore these dynamics, this case presents three firms with distinct strategic archetypes.

1. Tesla, Inc. represents the disruptive innovator. Founded to accelerate the world's transition to sustainable energy, its strategy is built on technological differentiation and a vertically integrated business model that challenges industry conventions.
2. Volkswagen Group (VW) is the legacy incumbent, compelled into a radical pivot by technological disruption and the 'Dieselgate' emissions scandal. Its response is a colossal bet on leveraging its scale to dominate the electric vehicle (EV) market.
3. Toyota Motor Corporation, the master of operational excellence and pioneer of hybrid technology, embodies a more cautious, risk-averse posture. Its 'multi-pathway' approach, investing in a portfolio of technologies including hybrids, plug-in hybrids, battery electric vehicles, and hydrogen fuel cells, reflects a strategic logic rooted in its Toyota Production System (TPS).

The pedagogical objectives are to enable students to:

1. apply Porter's frameworks of industry analysis and generic strategies to a dynamic and uncertain environment;
2. analyse how the sustainability imperative reconfigures corporate value chains, creating new sources of cost and value; and
3. critically compare the long-term viability of these divergent strategies, appreciating the interplay between strategy, operations, and societal demands.

2.0 The competitive arena: an industry in flux (Porter's five forces analysis)

To understand their strategic choices, we must first analyse the industry structure. Porter's Five Forces framework reveals how the transition to electric and software-defined vehicles is reshaping the industry's competitive architecture. The analysis shows a shift from a stable oligopoly to a volatile, intensely competitive environment.

2.1 Intensity of rivalry (high and intensifying)

Rivalry in the automotive sector is exceptionally high and intensifying. The industry is transitioning from a mature oligopoly to a hyper-competitive arena. This is driven by several factors. First, aggressive price wars, initiated by Tesla and followed by Chinese manufacturers, are pressuring profit margins, forcing incumbents to re-evaluate cost structures. Second, the rise of Chinese EV manufacturers like BYD, NIO, and XPeng has altered the global landscape. No longer confined to their domestic market, these firms are becoming major exporters, challenging established brands with high-quality, technologically advanced, and competitively priced vehicles.

Furthermore, the industry has extremely high fixed costs, particularly in R&D for new EV platforms, battery technology, and autonomous driving, as well as the capital required to retool factories. This high-cost structure incentivises firms to maximise production volume for economies of scale, intensifying the fight for market share. Finally, the shift to EVs appears to be weakening brand loyalty. Many consumers, especially first-time EV buyers, are willing to switch brands based on product specifications—such as range, charging speed, and technology—rather than historical allegiance. This lowers switching costs and forces firms to compete more directly on product attributes.

2.2 Threat of new entrants (moderate to high)

Historically, the automobile industry had formidable barriers to entry, including immense capital requirements, economies of scale, protected dealership networks, and brand equity. However, the transition to EVs has lowered or reconfigured some barriers. The success of Tesla demonstrates that technological innovation, a strong brand narrative, and a novel business model (direct-to-consumer sales) can overcome traditional barriers. Following this path, numerous EV start-ups and, more significantly, state-backed Chinese firms have successfully entered the industry.

Furthermore, the evolution towards the 'software-defined vehicle' creates a potential entry point for major technology companies (e.g., Apple, Google) with deep expertise in software and data ecosystems. Despite this, the threat is moderated by the persisting capital investment required for global-scale manufacturing, secure battery supply chains, and a robust sales infrastructure. While the technological barrier has shifted, the financial and logistical barriers remain substantial.

2.3 Bargaining power of suppliers (shifting and polarised)

A critical structural shift is the polarisation of supplier power. For traditional, commoditised components like seating, plastics, and chassis parts, suppliers have very low bargaining power. The massive purchasing volumes of global automakers allow them to exert significant price pressure.

In contrast, a new class of powerful suppliers has emerged in the EV era. The EV's strategic heart is its battery, and the supply chain for cells and raw materials (lithium, cobalt, nickel) is highly concentrated. A few companies, like CATL, LG Energy Solution, and Panasonic, control a majority of the market, giving them significant leverage. Similarly, as vehicles rely more on software and electronics, suppliers of critical components like semiconductors and high-performance chips (e.g., NVIDIA) are gaining immense power. These firms possess intellectual property that most automakers cannot easily replicate.

This polarisation creates a strategic challenge. Automakers can squeeze traditional suppliers but face increasing dependence on powerful technology and battery suppliers. This dynamic drives strategic moves to mitigate supplier power, such as Tesla's vertical integration into battery manufacturing, Volkswagen's creation of PowerCo, and Toyota's partnership with Panasonic.

2.4 Bargaining power of buyers (high)

The bargaining power of buyers remains high. Consumers have access to a wide array of brands and models, and online resources provide unprecedented transparency on pricing, specifications, and reviews. This strengthens their negotiating position and allows detailed comparison shopping.

Switching costs are relatively low, particularly in mass-market segments. While brand loyalty exists, attractive pricing or superior technology can persuade a buyer to switch. Automakers mitigate this power through differentiation via design, performance, or technology, and by building strong brands. Furthermore, some firms, like Tesla, create ecosystems—such as its proprietary Supercharger network—that enhance the ownership experience and create a soft lock-in effect.

2.5 Threat of substitutes (moderate and growing)

The threat of substitutes for personal vehicle ownership is moderate but growing, particularly in dense urban environments. The primary substitutes are not other cars, but different modes of mobility. The expansion of ride-sharing services like Uber and Lyft provides a convenient on-demand alternative. Simultaneously, improvements to public transport and the rise of micro-mobility solutions like e-bikes and electric scooters offer viable options for short-distance urban travel.

These substitutes directly challenge the traditional use case for a personal automobile. The future development of Vehicle-to-Everything (V2X) technologies and their integration into 'smart city' infrastructure will likely make these alternatives more seamless. As these systems become better integrated, the perceived necessity of owning a private car for all transport needs is likely to diminish.

3.0 Strategic positioning: three firms, three paths

Faced with this turbulent environment, each firm has adopted a distinct strategic position. An analysis using Porter's framework of generic strategies reveals the logic underpinning their approaches.

3.1 Tesla, Inc.: the focused technology differentiator

Tesla's strategy is a clear example of focused differentiation. It targets consumers who prioritise technology, performance, and sustainability, and differentiates its offerings on non-price attributes. Its advantage is not being the cheapest, but being perceived as the most innovative and technologically advanced choice.

This differentiation is supported by several pillars.

1. **Technology and Performance:** Tesla has established a lead in core EV technologies, particularly battery management, powertrain efficiency, and software. This translates into product advantages like superior range and acceleration. Its development of in-house capabilities in artificial intelligence and autonomous driving software (Full Self-Driving) creates a technological moat.

Force	Intensity	Key Drivers and Evidence	Strategic Implications for Automakers
Intensity of Rivalry	High and Intensifying	• Aggressive price wars initiated by Tesla and Chinese OEMs. • Rapid global expansion of Chinese brands (e.g., BYD). • High fixed costs in R&D and manufacturing driving need for scale. • Weakening brand loyalty among first-time EV buyers.	• Intense pressure on cost structures and profit margins. • Need for clear differentiation beyond price. • Imperative to build brand loyalty in the new EV context.
Threat of New Entrants	Moderate to High	• The success of Tesla and Chinese start-ups proves entry is possible. • Shift to software-defined vehicles opens door for tech giants. • High capital requirements for global manufacturing and battery supply remain a significant barrier.	• Incumbents must leverage scale and manufacturing expertise as a defence. • Need to develop strong software and ecosystem capabilities to counter tech entrants. • Constant innovation is required to maintain a lead over new players.
Bargaining Power of Suppliers	Polarised (Low/High)	• Low Power: Suppliers of commoditised, traditional parts face immense pricing pressure from OEMs. • High Power: Concentrated battery supply market (CATL, LG, Panasonic). • High Power: Critical role of specialised semiconductor and software providers.	• Necessity of strategic responses to secure critical supplies and manage costs. • Drives strategies of vertical integration (Tesla), joint ventures (VW/PowerCo), and deep partnerships (Toyota/Panasonic) for batteries and software.
Bargaining Power of Buyers	High	• Wide choice of brands and models. • High price transparency via online resources. • Low switching costs for consumers in mass-market segments.	• Pressure to offer competitive pricing and high value-for-money. • Importance of differentiation through technology, design, and brand. • Need to create customer ecosystems (e.g., charging networks) to build loyalty.
Threat of Substitutes	Moderate and Growing	• Growth of ride-sharing services (Uber, Lyft). • Expansion of public transport and micro-mobility (e-bikes, scooters) in urban areas. • Future integration of mobility services via smart city infrastructure.	• The personal car ownership model is under threat in urban centres. • Need to invest in or partner with mobility-as-a-service (MaaS) platforms. • Potential for new business models beyond simply selling vehicles.

2. Brand Image and Ecosystem: Tesla has cultivated a brand image that transcends the automobile, positioned as a high-tech, aspirational lifestyle brand. This is reinforced by a unique business model. The direct-to-consumer sales model gives Tesla complete control over pricing and the customer relationship. The proprietary Supercharger network provides a reliable fast-charging solution, creating a powerful ecosystem.
3. Vertical Integration: A key enabler is Tesla's high degree of vertical integration. By designing and manufacturing many components in-house—

from battery cells to software—Tesla maintains tight control over quality, accelerates innovation, and can adapt quickly to supply chain disruptions.

3.2 Volkswagen group: the broad-scope hybrid strategist

Volkswagen's positioning is more complex, reflecting its status as a multi-brand conglomerate. Its approach is a hybrid strategy, attempting to simultaneously pursue cost leadership in mass-market segments and differentiation in premium segments.

The cornerstone of its cost leadership ambition is the Modular Electric Drive Toolkit (MEB), a standardised platform for a wide range of mass-market EVs across the Volkswagen, SEAT/Cupra, and Škoda brands. The logic is to replicate the success of its MQB platform for ICE vehicles: by producing millions of vehicles on a shared architecture, VW aims for massive economies of scale to offer affordable EVs, with models planned below €25,000. The MEB platform is even licensed to competitors like Ford to further increase volume and establish it as an industry standard.

Simultaneously, VW pursues differentiation with its premium brands. Audi and Porsche co-developed the Premium Platform Electric (PPE), an architecture for higher-performance, luxury vehicles. While sharing technology for efficiency, these brands are positioned with distinct designs, superior performance, and powerful brand identities that command price premiums.

This hybrid strategy is a high-stakes gamble. Volkswagen faces the risk of being 'stuck in the middle': its mass-market brands may not achieve the cost structures of Chinese rivals, while its premium brands face a formidable challenge from Tesla. Success hinges on its ability to flawlessly execute its platform strategy and manage its diverse brand portfolio.

3.3 Toyota Motor Corporation: the best-cost provider

Toyota's strategy is best understood as that of a best-cost provider. This involves giving customers more value for their money by satisfying expectations on quality, features, and performance while beating their price expectations. This is rooted in its operational philosophy and cautious assessment of the energy transition.

The foundation is the legendary Toyota Production System (TPS). Its principles—including eliminating waste (muda, mura, muri), Just-in-Time (JIT) production, and continuous improvement (kaizen)—have enabled Toyota for decades to produce high-quality, reliable vehicles at a competitive cost. This provides the cost-side strength of its strategy. The value-side strength comes from its brand reputation for durability and reliability.

In the EV transition, Toyota is applying this logic through its 'multi-pathway' approach. Rather than committing exclusively to battery electric vehicles (BEVs), Toyota is investing in a diversified portfolio including its world-leading hybrids (HEVs), plug-in hybrids (PHEVs), BEVs, and hydrogen fuel cell vehicles (FCEVs). This is a deliberate choice based on the assessment that regions will decarbonise at different speeds and that customer needs and infrastructure vary too widely for a 'one-size-fits-all' BEV solution. By offering a range of reliable and affordable low-emission vehicles, particularly hybrids, Toyota aims to provide a pragmatic path to sustainability for the mass market. While criticised for tardiness in the BEV race, it is a calculated bet that the transition will be slower than competitors assume, allowing Toyota to leverage its existing strengths in the hybrid market for years.

Company	Generic Strategy	Strategic Scope	Primary Basis of Competitive Advantage	Key Supporting Activities and Capabilities
Tesla, Inc.	Focused Differentiation	Narrow (Premium EV and technology-focused segments)	Technology, Performance, Brand Image, and Customer Experience	• In-house software and AI development (FSD). • High degree of vertical integration (e.g., Gigafactories). • Direct-to-consumer sales and service model. • Proprietary Supercharger network.
Volkswagen Group	Hybrid (Cost Leadership and Differentiation)	Broad (Spanning from mass-market to luxury segments)	Economies of Scale and Multi-Brand Portfolio Management	• Standardised platform strategy (MEB for volume, PPE for premium). • Massive manufacturing footprint and purchasing power. • Extensive and distinct brand portfolio (VW, Audi, Porsche, etc.). • In-house battery development and production (PowerCo).
Toyota Motor Corp.	Best-Cost Provider	Broad (Global mass-market focus)	Operational Excellence, Quality, Reliability, and Pragmatic Technology	• Toyota Production System (TPS) for efficiency and quality. • 'Multi-pathway' technology portfolio (HEV, PHEV, BEV, FCEV). • Deeply entrenched supplier relationships and collaboration. • Unmatched brand reputation for durability and reliability.

4.0 The sustainability imperative: reconfiguring the value chain

The industry's contemporary strategic landscape requires integrating the sustainability imperative into the analysis. As outlined in Chapter 2, frameworks like Porter's value chain can be adapted to map social and environmental linkages.

For these firms, sustainability is not merely CSR; it is a fundamental force shaping their value propositions, operations, and competitive strategies.

4.1 From 'shared value' to strategic necessity: the role of sustainability in the value proposition

The role of sustainability differs markedly among the firms, revealing its integration into their core strategies.

For Tesla, sustainability is its foundational purpose. Its mission is to "accelerate the world's transition to sustainable energy". This is the central pillar of its value proposition. Customers are not just buying a car; they are buying into a vision of a post-fossil-fuel future. This provides Tesla with an authentic brand narrative that resonates with a growing market segment. Its competitive advantage is intrinsically linked to the alignment of its products with a grand societal objective.

For Volkswagen, sustainability is a catalyst for strategic transformation and reputational repair. The 'Dieselgate' scandal was an existential crisis that necessitated a radical break. The subsequent aggressive pivot to electrification and its comprehensive 'regenerate+' sustainability strategy are strategic necessities designed to rebuild trust. VW frames its commitment holistically across four dimensions: nature, people, society, and business. Here, sustainability is the engine of strategic renewal.

For Toyota, sustainability is a natural evolution of its philosophies, particularly 'Respect for the Planet'. Its approach is methodical and integrated with its operational culture. Consistent with TPS, Toyota focuses on life-cycle assessment and eliminating waste across all operations. Sustainability is framed not as a radical new direction, but as the application of its core principle of continuous improvement to pressing environmental and social challenges.

4.2 A Comparative value chain analysis: mapping sustainability linkages

Using Porter's value chain model, we can compare how each firm embeds sustainability into its activities, revealing how they operationalise their distinct strategies.

1. Inbound Logistics

   Sourcing raw materials for batteries is a critical 'outside-in' linkage: an external social and environmental issue directly affecting the firms. All three must contend with the human rights and environmental risks of mining cobalt and lithium.

Tesla addresses this through vertical integration and disintermediation. It seeks direct relationships with mining companies to gain transparency and enforce higher ethical standards.

Volkswagen leverages its purchasing power. Through its due diligence management system, it contractually obligates battery suppliers to meet specific CO_2 limits and use certified renewable power, cascading sustainability requirements down the supply chain.

Toyota relies on its deep, long-term supplier partnerships. It promulgates its 'Supplier Sustainability Guidelines', addressing human rights and environmental protection, and works collaboratively with suppliers to mitigate risks.

2. Operations

   Achieving carbon neutrality in manufacturing is a key 'inside-out' linkage, where internal activities have a direct environmental impact.

   Tesla designs its 'Gigafactories' with efficiency as a core principle. It employs AI-controlled energy management, invests in waste heat recovery, and aims to power facilities with on-site renewables.

   Volkswagen has set a goal for its global sites to be net carbon-neutral by 2040. Its primary levers are large-scale procurement of renewable electricity and its 'Zero Impact Factory' initiative, which targets reductions in energy, water, waste, and emissions.

   Toyota applies TPS principles to its factory operations. The philosophy of eliminating waste is directly applied to minimising energy, water, and raw material consumption. Toyota aims for its plants to be carbon neutral by 2035, leveraging kaizen for incremental efficiencies.

3. Outbound Logistics

   Vehicle distribution presents another sustainability challenge.

   Tesla's direct-to-consumer model provides an inherent advantage. By forgoing a vast network of third-party dealerships, it reduces the cumulative emissions and physical footprint of traditional distribution.

   Volkswagen and Toyota, with their extensive dealership networks, face the challenge of influencing their partners' environmental performance. Both have launched initiatives, like VW's 'goTOzero retail' programme, to provide guidance and incentives for dealers to invest in energy efficiency and renewables.

4. Marketing and Sales

   How sustainability is communicated reveals its strategic role.

   Tesla engages in minimal traditional marketing; the product and its mission are the message. Sustainability is inherent in the brand's identity.

   Volkswagen's marketing heavily features its EV family (the ID. series) and its sustainability goals. This is a strategic effort to reshape its public image and build a new value proposition.

   Toyota's marketing highlights the practicality and efficiency of its hybrids. It positions sustainability as an accessible, pragmatic choice for the mass market, not a radical leap into a BEV-only future.

5. Service (After-Sales)

   The end-of-life management of vehicles, particularly batteries, is a critical challenge and an opportunity for a circular economy.

   Tesla is developing in-house battery recycling capabilities. Its goal is to 'close the loop', recovering valuable raw materials and feeding them back into production, reducing its reliance on virgin mining.

   Volkswagen, through its subsidiary PowerCo, is also investing in this area, having established a pilot facility for battery recycling. This is a strategic move to secure future raw materials.

   Toyota is pursuing its 'Battery 3R' (Reduce, Rebuilt/Reuse, Recycle) strategy, primarily through partnerships with specialised firms. Its global approach aims to establish efficient collection and recycling systems.

5.0 Conclusion: the evolving nature of competitive advantage

This comparative analysis illuminates the profound strategic recalibration in the global automobile industry. Faced with a paradigm shift, each firm has charted a distinct course. Tesla has leveraged its identity as a sustainability-native innovator to pursue focused differentiation. Volkswagen has embarked on an ambitious hybrid strategy, attempting cost leadership at scale while preserving differentiation. Toyota has adopted a more cautious best-cost provider strategy, hedging its bets with a multi-pathway approach.

The case demonstrates that sustainability has transcended its peripheral CSR role to become a central element of competitive strategy. It is the essence of Tesla's value proposition. It is the catalyst for strategic renewal at Volkswagen. And for Toyota, it is a guiding principle for operational efficiency. The reconfiguration of the value chain for sustainability is no longer optional but a strategic necessity, influencing everything from procurement to end-of-life management.

Value Chain Activity	Tesla, Inc.	Volkswagen Group	Toyota Motor Corporation
Inbound Logistics	Vertical integration and direct sourcing from mines to control ethical/environmental standards.	Focus on securing a long-term supply of battery raw materials. Raw materials due diligence system for 18 high-risk materials. Contractual requirements for suppliers on CO_2 emissions and renewable energy use in battery production.	Long-term supplier partnerships governed by 'Supplier Sustainability Guidelines'. Collaborative approach to risk management in the supply chain for human rights and the environment.
Operations	'Gigafactory' design principle: AI-controlled energy management, on-site renewables, waste heat recovery. Goal of 100% waste diversion from landfill.	'Zero Impact Factory' initiative targeting reductions in energy, water, waste, and emissions. Goal of net carbon-neutral production sites by 2040 and 100% renewable electricity procurement by 2030.	Application of the Toyota Production System (TPS) to eliminate waste in energy, water, and materials. Goal of carbon-neutral manufacturing plants by 2035. Focus on continuous improvement (kaizen) for resource efficiency.
Outbound Logistics	The direct-to-consumer sales model eliminates the environmental footprint of a traditional dealership network.	'goTOzero retail' programme to support and incentivise decarbonisation of the independent dealership network.	Works with dealers and distributors to implement global environmental policies and reduce CO_2 emissions at sales and service points.
Marketing & Sales	Sustainability is inherent to the brand mission; minimal traditional marketing needed to convey this value proposition.	Marketing heavily promotes the EV transition and 'regenerate+' strategy to rebuild trust and create a new brand identity.	Marketing focuses on the pragmatic benefits of hybrids (reliability, efficiency), positioning sustainability as an accessible choice for the mass market.
Service (After-Sales)	Developing in-house 'closed-loop' battery recycling to recover and reuse raw materials.	Investment in proprietary battery recycling pilot plant via PowerCo subsidiary to control the end-of-life value chain.	'Battery 3R' (Reduce, Rebuilt/Reuse, Recycle) strategy implemented through global partnerships. Focus on establishing safe and efficient regional collection systems.

This reality offers possibilities for applying Porter's foundational frameworks to understand how strategies evolve. The logic of analysing industry structure, choosing a defensible position, and optimising the value chain remains relevant. However, the content of these frameworks has changed. A Five Forces analysis is incomplete without considering the power of battery suppliers or the threat from shared mobility. An analysis of generic strategies must account for how a low-carbon value proposition can be a powerful differentiator. Value chain analysis must move beyond financial cost to incorporate the costs of carbon and the value of resource circularity.

The divergent paths of these three giants leave critical questions for the future that will define the competitive landscape for decades. Will Tesla's first-mover advantage prove insurmountable, or will it be eroded by the scale of incumbents like Volkswagen? Can Volkswagen successfully manage the complexity of its hybrid strategy? And is Toyota's cautious approach a prudent hedge against uncertainty, or a strategic blunder that will leave it far behind? The long-term success of each firm will likely depend not just on its technology or manufacturing, but on how deeply it integrates sustainability into its competitive advantage.

6.0 Seminar questions and discussion points

This section provides questions to guide classroom discussion, moving from applying concepts to critically evaluating corporate strategies.

Application Questions

1. Using the data and analysis in the case and the framework from Chapter 2, conduct a similar analysis for an emerging Chinese firm such as BYD, SAIC Motor, FAW Group, Geely Group, or Changan. Find relevant data from their websites and other secondary sources.

    a. Map the competitive strategies of Tesla, Volkswagen, and Toyota onto Porter's generic strategies matrix against the Chinese company you analysed.
    b. Select one primary activity (e.g., Operations) and one support activity (e.g., Procurement) from the value chain model. For each, compare and contrast your Chinese company case with how Tesla, Volkswagen, and Toyota are reconfiguring their processes to address sustainability.

Critical evaluation questions

2. Chapter 2 discusses the 'strategic instrumentality of sustainability discourses', suggesting firms may adopt sustainability initiatives primarily for competitive advantage. To what extent do you believe each firm's strategy is driven by genuine commitment versus competitive advantage? Does the motivation matter if the outcomes are positive? Discuss.

3. Critically evaluate Toyota's 'multi-pathway' strategy. Is it a prudent, risk-managed approach that leverages its core competencies, or is the company failing to commit to the dominant BEV trajectory and risking obsolescence?
4. Volkswagen's strategy relies on leveraging scale through its MEB platform. What are the primary risks associated with this strategy? Consider risks related to technology, market acceptance, operational complexity, and brand differentiation.
5. Tesla's high degree of vertical integration is a key enabler of its differentiation strategy. What are the primary advantages and disadvantages of this approach compared to the more collaborative, network-based models of Volkswagen and Toyota? Consider innovation speed, cost, risk, and flexibility.

Management Accounting Linkage

6. Imagine you are a senior management accountant at one of these three companies. The board has asked you to develop key performance indicators (KPIs) to monitor the success of the sustainability initiatives in the value chain analysis. Propose three financial and three non-financial KPIs, and explain how they would help manage the strategy.

Chapter review questions

Section A: Foundations of strategic management: from operational efficiency to corporate planning

1. During the early era of 'scientific management' and Fordism, how was the concept of 'strategy' best characterised?

   a. As an explicit, top-down process of five-year corporate planning and market positioning.
   b. As a focus on marketing and brand differentiation to capture emerging consumer markets.
   c. As an implicit set of practices directed towards operational efficiency through the rationalisation of the labour process.
   d. As a series of mergers and acquisitions designed to achieve monopoly status.

2. According to the chapter's analysis, which of the following represents the primary institutional driver that necessitated the emergence of 'corporate planning' as a distinct managerial function?

   a. The invention of new production technologies during the Industrial Revolution.

b. The rise of the multidivisional (M-form) corporate structure resulting from growth via mergers and acquisitions.
c. Increased pressure from trade unions for better working conditions and wages.
d. The development of general systems theory, which highlighted the importance of the external environment.

3. As defined by Alfred Chandler (1962), 'strategy' encompasses three core elements. Which of the following is NOT one of those elements?

   a. The determination of the basic long-term goals and objectives of an enterprise.
   b. The allocation and reallocation of resources necessary for carrying out goals.
   c. The adoption of specific courses of action to achieve established long-term goals and objectives.
   d. The production of quarterly earnings reports.

4. The chapter describes Return on Investment (ROI) as the 'accounting signature of monopoly capitalism'. Why did this specific metric become the pre-eminent tool for corporate planning within M-form organisations?

   a. Because it was the only metric capable of measuring the efficiency of the labour process on the factory floor.
   b. Because it provided the corporate head office with a standardised financial mechanism to govern disparate Strategic Business Units (SBUs) 'at a distance', treating them as comparable 'investment centres'.
   c. Because it was mandated by government regulators as the primary indicator of corporate performance.
   d. Because it directly measured customer satisfaction and brand loyalty, which were the main concerns of corporate planners.

5. The Boston Consulting Group (BCG) Growth-Share Matrix and the General Electric (GE) Nine-Cell Matrix are both portfolio planning models. What is the key distinction in the criteria they use to evaluate SBUs?

   a. The BCG matrix uses market growth rate and relative market share, whereas the GE matrix uses a composite index for industry attractiveness and a composite index for business strength.
   b. The BCG matrix focuses on financial metrics like ROI, whereas the GE matrix focuses on non-financial metrics like employee morale.
   c. The BCG matrix is used for diversification strategies, whereas the GE matrix is used for market penetration strategies.
   d. The BCG matrix evaluates SBUs as 'dogs' and 'stars', whereas the GE matrix evaluates them based on the product life cycle.

6. Ansoff's Product-Market Matrix outlines four primary strategies for corporate growth. A company that decides to offer its existing products in a new geographical region is pursuing which of these strategies?

    a. Market Penetration
    b. Product Development
    c. Diversification
    d. Market Development

Section B: Analysing the competitive environment: the Porterian framework

7. How did Michael Porter's revision of the Structure-Conduct-Performance (SCP) model fundamentally alter the understanding of a firm's role in its industry?

    a. It reinforced the neoclassical view that firms are passive entities whose strategies are determined entirely by market structure.
    b. It introduced the idea that a firm's performance could influence its conduct, but that industry structure remained an unchangeable external factor.
    c. It attributed 'strategic agency' to the firm, proposing that a firm's strategies and past performance could actively alter the structural conditions of its industry.
    d. It replaced the concept of 'conduct' with 'corporate culture' as the primary link between industry structure and firm performance.

8. The chapter suggests that Porter elevates the issue of competitiveness to a 'biopolitical problem'. What is the core implication of this framing?

    a. That business strategy should be concerned primarily with the biological and ecological impacts of its operations.
    b. That the central function of the state and its public policies (e.g., education, taxation, regulation) should be to enhance the global competitiveness of the nation's firms.
    c. That firms should be managed like political campaigns, with a focus on public relations and lobbying.
    d. That national competitiveness is determined solely by a country's endowment of natural resources, a concept central to biopolitics.

9. The concept of 'value for money', expressed as Value/Price, is used to explain Porter's generic strategies. Which statement accurately describes the primary focus of the differentiation and cost leadership strategies within this equation?

    a. A differentiation strategy focuses on minimising the 'Price' denominator, while a cost leadership strategy focuses on maximising the 'Value' numerator.

b. Both strategies focus exclusively on minimising the 'Price' denominator to attract the largest possible customer base.
c. A cost leadership strategy focuses on minimising the 'Price' denominator for an acceptable level of value, while a differentiation strategy focuses on maximising the 'Value' numerator to justify a premium price.
d. Both strategies focus exclusively on maximising the 'Value' numerator, as price is considered irrelevant in modern competition.

10. A firm operating in an industry characterised by powerful buyers who are highly price-sensitive, a low threat of new entrants, and intense rivalry among existing competitors would, according to Porter's interconnected frameworks, most logically:

    a. Adopt a differentiation strategy and configure its value chain around radical product innovation and premium branding.
    b. Adopt a cost leadership strategy and configure its value chain to achieve maximum operational efficiency and cost reduction in all activities.
    c. Adopt a focused differentiation strategy, targeting a niche market that is not price-sensitive.
    d. Exit the industry, as the structural conditions make sustained profitability impossible for any firm.

11. According to Porter's Four-Corner Analysis, which of the following elements would be most important to be examined to understand a competitor's 'strategic drivers'?

    a. The competitor's perceived strengths and weaknesses and its assumptions about the industry.
    b. The competitor's current market positioning and the specific value creation methods it employs.
    c. The financial goals, corporate culture, and leadership style of the competitor's top management team.
    d. The competitor's marketing skills, patents, and financial strength.

Section C: Strategy, Society, and Sustainability

12. The chapter discusses the 'strategic instrumentality of sustainability discourses'. What does this concept mean?

    a. That corporations are primarily motivated by a genuine desire to solve social and ecological problems, using strategy as the instrument to do so.

b. That sustainability is viewed not as an end in itself, but as a means to enhance a firm's competitive advantage and value proposition.
c. That the only effective way to achieve sustainability is through government regulation, rendering corporate strategy instrumental but secondary.
d. That financial instruments, such as green bonds, are the most important tools for promoting sustainable business practices.

13. Porter and Kramer (2006) propose using the Value Chain and a revised industry analysis model to map a firm's social opportunities. How do they distinguish between 'inside-out' and 'outside-in' linkages?

    a. 'Inside-out' linkages refer to global sustainability standards, while 'outside-in' linkages refer to a firm's internal ethical code.
    b. 'Inside-out' linkages refer to the social dimensions of the competitive context, while 'outside-in' linkages refer to the social impacts of the firm's value chain activities.
    c. 'Inside-out' linkages refer to the positive and negative social impacts of a firm's own value chain activities, while 'outside-in' linkages refer to the social dimensions of the external competitive context that affect the firm.
    d. 'Inside-out' linkages refer to employee relations, while 'outside-in' linkages refer to customer relations.

14. According to the analysis of Porter and Kramer's work, what is the primary objective of adding a 'social dimension to the value proposition'?

    a. To minimise all negative social and environmental impacts of the firm's operations, irrespective of the financial cost.
    b. To comply with the minimum legal requirements for corporate social responsibility reporting in a given jurisdiction.
    c. To create 'shared value' by identifying social issues that can be addressed in a way that also enhances the firm's competitive positioning and advantage.
    d. To replace the pursuit of profit with the pursuit of social justice as the corporation's sole purpose.

Section D: Synoptic Assessment: Tracing the Evolution of Strategic Thought

15. Match each Strategic Framework/Concept from Column 1 with its corresponding Primary Managerial Issue (Column 2), Key Analytical Focus (Column 3), and Dominant Performance Metric (Column 4).

Column 1: Strategic Framework/Concept	Column 2: Primary Managerial Issue	Column 3: Key Analytical Focus	Column 4: Dominant Performance Metric
1. BCG Growth-Share Matrix	A. Gaining a defensible position against competitors	i. The industry and its structural forces	W. Long-term Growth Rate
2. Porter's Five Forces Analysis	B. Coordinating a portfolio of disparate businesses	ii. The firm's internal configuration of activities	X. Relative Market Share
3. Value Chain Analysis	C. Sustaining corporate growth through expansion	iii. The portfolio of Strategic Business Units (SBUs)	Y. Return on Investment (ROI)
4. Ansoff's Product-Market Matrix	D. Building capabilities to support a generic strategy	iv. Existing vs. new products and markets	Z. Customer Value Proposition

Select the correct combination of matches:

a. 1-B-iii-Y, 2-A-i-Z, 3-D-ii-X, 4-C-iv-W
b. 1-B-iii-X, 2-A-i-Y, 3-D-ii-Z, 4-C-iv-W
c. 1-C-iv-W, 2-D-ii-Z, 3-A-i-X, 4-B-iii-Y
d. 1-D-i-Y, 2-C-iii-W, 3-B-iv-Z, 4-A-ii-X

16. Based on the chapter's narrative of the evolution of strategic thought, which of the following characteristics accurately describe the pre-Porterian era of corporate and strategic planning? (Select all that apply)

a. An external focus on market positioning and competitive advantage.
b. A primary concern with managing the internal hierarchy and achieving co-ordination across divisions.
c. The dominance of financial growth metrics, such as Return on Investment (ROI), as the ultimate measure of success.
d. The attribution of significant strategic agency to the firm to alter its industry structure.
e. e) An emphasis on achieving a 'strategic fit' between the organisation and its external environment for legitimacy and survival.

f. f) A view of strategy as a political-economic instrument for enhancing national competitiveness.

Comprehension questions

1. What was the implicit strategic focus of managing modern organisations during the eras of scientific management and Fordism?
2. Briefly explain the contextual and historical conditions underpinning the emergence of 'corporate planning'.
3. List the three interrelated issues that 'corporate planning' aimed to address.
4. What is a multidivisional firm? What are the critical managerial functionalities of the corporate head office (or the General Office, as Chandler identified it) in a multidivisional firm?
5. Explain the key elements of Chandler's definition of strategy.
6. Coordination between business units (SBUs) is a crucial function to be carried out under corporate planning. List and explain three managerial functions that fall under this coordination role of the corporate head office.
7. Briefly explain which accounting techniques were mobilised, and in which ways, to aid the corporate planning function of coordinating and consolidating SBU performance.
8. What is a portfolio planning model? Use the examples of the BCG growth-share matrix and the GE nine-cell matrix to explain. Also, focus on the fundamental criteria upon which resource allocations among SBUs were decided with such models.
9. Dealing with the external environment is also considered a key function of strategic management. Explain the concept of 'environment-serving organisations'. How do you explain strategic management in relation to this function?
10. What are the key strategic analysis frameworks that deal with this external environmental dimension of strategising?
11. Briefly explain how Ansoff's product-market matrix identifies different strategies for corporate growth.
12. Using McKinsey's 7S framework as an example, explain the key behavioural and cultural dimensions that strategy formulation and implementation must consider.
13. What is the structure-conduct-performance model? Explain how Michael Porter revised this model and enabled a new economic understanding of a firm's strategic agency and capabilities.
14. Briefly explain the notion of competitive advantage and how it occupies a central position in Porterian strategy discourses.

15. What are the key factors affecting a nation's competitive advantage? Explain using Porter's diamond model.
16. What are the two fundamental competitive strategies that Porter conceptualised? In which ways can they be operationalised in relation to the scope of their deployment?
17. Explain how Porter's generic strategies can be related to the concept of value for money.
18. Porter provides three frameworks to analyse competitive conditions. List them.
19. Briefly explain Porter's five forces model and how it can be related to the choice of cost-leadership or differentiation strategies.
20. Briefly explain Porter's value chain model and how it can be related to the choice between cost-leadership and differentiation strategies.
21. Explain the key parameters according to which a competitor's response profile can be analysed. Use Porter's four-corner analysis as a guide.
22. Explain Porter and Kramer's ideas for strategising sustainability.

Explore further

1. Visit the website of a large multidivisional corporation where you can find a good deal of information on the company's strategic choices and declarations. Carefully study the website information and make notes on the following:

   a. The means through which the company communicates its strategic intents, especially its long-term directions and guiding principles.
   b. Its major strategic business units and the competitive market conditions within which they operate.
   c. Study its history and try to identify the manner in which it diversified its business over time.
   d. Select one of its key products or product lines and determine whether it adopts a differentiation or a cost leadership strategy.
   e. Analyse whether and how its higher-order strategic statements (e.g., vision and mission statements, long-term goals, guiding principles) capture sustainability.
   f. In which ways do the UN SDGs appear in its website information?
   g. What specific programmes is the company implementing to achieve the UN SDGs?

2. Visit the websites of the IMD World Competitiveness Centre (https://www.imd.org) and the World Economic Forum (https://www.weforum.org). These two organisations publish policy views and rankings related to national competitiveness.

   a. Read carefully how they conceptualise and measure the idea of 'competitiveness'.
   b. Try to see how their conceptualisation is based on Porterian ideas of a nation's competitive advantage.
   c. Look into the key themes that they prioritise over time.
   d. Based on the changes in the thematic structure of their reports, can you think of how the notion of competitiveness is evolving?
   e. Analyse the extent to which, and the ways in which, the UN SDGs appear in these competitiveness themes.

3. Visit the OECD Competition Assessment Toolkit website (https://www.oecd.org/daf/competition/assessment-toolkit.htm). You can download three volumes there: Volume 1 - Principles, Volume 2 - Guidance, and Volume 3 – Operational Manual.

   a. Read Volume 1 and explain the purpose of this competition assessment toolkit.
   b. What level of competition does this toolkit try to assess (organisational, industry/market, or national)?
   c. Why does the OECD think that competition needs to be assured through regulation?
   d. Explain the conditions under which this competitiveness assessment toolkit is to be used.
   e. Drawing on other relevant materials on neoliberalism (e.g., Harvey, 2005; Alawattage and Wickramasinghe, 2022), can you think of how this competition assessment toolkit operationalises neoliberalism? Write a brief note on the neoliberal conditionality of this toolkit.

Develop your critical argumentation skills.

1. Compose an argumentative essay on the theme:

   'The evolution of strategy discourses, frameworks, and techniques, from Alfred Chandler to Michael Porter and beyond, signifies the emerging managerial and institutional challenges posed by transformations in organisational structures, competitive landscapes, and environmental conditions'. Utilising the strategy frameworks discussed in this chapter, explain the specific managerial challenges these frameworks evolved to tackle.
2. Draft an argumentative essay on the theme:

   'The popularity of Porter's strategy discourse can be ascribed to its conceptualisation and integration of competitiveness and competitive advantage across an analytical spectrum that encompasses macro-political to micro-organisational dynamics of strategising and policy-making'. When building this argument, focus on how Porter's various models and concepts interconnect through diverse layers of managerial and policy analysis.
3. Construct an argumentative essay on the theme:

   'Owing to their hyper-capitalistic nature, contemporary strategy discourses and frameworks exhibit a limited capacity to provide genuinely effective approaches for addressing the pressing sustainability issues of our times'. Explain this assertion with particular reference to Porter's recent endeavour to incorporate sustainability into his strategic frameworks.

References

Alawattage, C., and D. Wickramasinghe. (2019). Strategising Management Accounting: Liberal Origins and Neoliberal Trends. London: Routledge.

Alawattage, C., and D. Wickramasinghe. (2022). 'Strategising management accounting: liberal origins and neoliberal trends'. Accounting, Auditing & Accountability Journal, 35(2), pp. 518-546.

Ansoff, I. (1965). Corporate Strategy: An Analytical Approach to Business Policy for Growth and Expansion. New York: McGraw-Hill.

Ansoff, I. (2007). Strategic Management. Basingstoke: Palgrave Macmillan.

Bryer, R. (2012). 'Americanism and financial accounting theory – Part 1: Was America born capitalist?'. Critical Perspectives on Accounting, 23(7–8), pp. 511-555.

Burawoy, M. (1979). Manufacturing Consent: Changes in the Labour Process Under Monopoly Capitalism. Chicago, IL: University of Chicago Press.

Chandler, A. D. (1962). Strategy and Structure: Chapters in the History of the Industrial Enterprise. Cambridge, MA: M.I.T. Press.

Gaughan, P. A. (2007). Mergers, Acquisitions, and Corporate Restructurings. 4th ed. Hoboken, NJ: Wiley.

Peters, T. J., and R. H. Waterman. (1982). In Search of Excellence: Lessons from America's Best-run Companies. New York: Harper & Row.

Porter, M. E. (1981). 'The Contributions of Industrial Organisation to Strategic Management'. The Academy of Management Review, 6(4), pp. 609-620.

Porter, M. E. (2004). Competitive Strategy: Techniques for Analysing Industries and Competitors. London: Simon & Schuster.

Porter, M. E., and M. R. Kramer. (2006). 'Strategy and society: the link between competitive advantage and corporate social responsibility'. Harvard Business Review, December, pp. 1-15.

Senge, P. M. (1990). The Fifth Discipline: The Art and Practice of the Learning Organization. New York: Doubleday/Currency.

CHAPTER

3 Strategy in the market: **strategic pricing decisions**

3.1 Introduction

As discussed in previous chapters, a firm has three interconnected domains of strategic action: the market, the point of production, and the organisational hierarchy. From a positioning perspective, the market is arguably the most significant of these. Prevailing strategy discourses (e.g., Porter, 1985, 1996) suggest that business strategy fundamentally revolves around the firm's competitive market positioning. Strategy, therefore, entails creating and maintaining a competitive position to gain an advantage. To achieve this, a firm may adopt cost leadership or differentiation strategies within a narrow or broad market scope. In executing these strategies, pricing is a critical strategic consideration.

Pricing's strategic centrality arises from two interrelated factors. Firstly, it is inextricably linked to the 'value for money' equation, where price is the denominator, underscoring its pivotal role in the firm's value proposition. Price is a crucial variable through which customers assess the value a brand or product provides. Pricing is therefore the strategic calculation through which firms enact their competitive market positioning.

Side note:

value for money = value/price

Secondly, pricing is financially fundamental, as it is the sole variable in the marketing mix that generates revenue. It is therefore essential for ensuring adequate profits and a sufficient return on investment. This creates a critical tension: the price must both capture market dynamics to enable a strategic market position and allow the firm to earn sufficient profits. This dual role makes pricing a crucial element of strategic decision-making.

Viewing pricing as a critical strategic decision for market positioning, this chapter is structured around three main themes, which also serve as its learning objectives.

1. Firstly, the chapter examines how pricing is conceptualised in neoclassical economics and conventional management accounting, establishing a traditional framework for comparison.
2. Secondly, it examines the processes and dynamics of strategic pricing, emphasising its practice as an element of competitive positioning alongside market segmentation, targeting, and positioning.
3. Thirdly, the chapter delves into three important related topics: lifecycle costing, target costing, and dynamic pricing.

Upon completing this chapter, you should be able to explain and critique neoclassical economics and accounting pricing models, elucidate the strategic pricing process, and detail target costing, lifecycle costing, and dynamic pricing as strategic techniques.

3.2 The neoclassical economics model of pricing

One of the most widely discussed pricing models is the neoclassical economic model, typically covered in introductory economics courses. This section may therefore serve as a review. However, refreshing the neoclassical model is crucial, as it provides a comparative basis against which strategic pricing can be better understood.

The neoclassical model assumes the firm's primary objective is to maximise profit. Hence, the profit maximisation rule is the criterion for deciding a product's optimal price. Mathematically, the profit function is the objective function to be maximised. Given that profit comprises revenue and costs, the profit maximisation objective is operationalised through a mathematical proposition: at the point of profit maximisation, marginal revenue must equal marginal cost (MR=MC). In other words, the additional revenue from producing and selling one more unit should equal the additional cost incurred. This proposition is explained by the numerical example below and illustrated in Figure 3.1.

A numerical example of the neoclassical economic model of pricing

Demand function: $p = 100 - 5q$, where p is the price and q is the quantity produced (in millions of units).

Total cost function: $TC = 100 + 0.05q^3 - 0.25q^2 + 5q$, where TC is the total cost and q is the quantity produced.

Given these functions, the requirement is to calculate the profit-maximising price and quantity.

The profit function is $\pi = TR - TC$, where TR is total revenue.

Given that $TR = p \times q$, the TR function is derived by multiplying the demand function by q:

$TR = (100-5q)q$

$TR=100q-5q^2$

Profit is maximised when MR=MC. Marginal revenue (MR) and marginal cost (MC) are derived by differentiating the TR and TC functions, respectively.

$MR = dq/dTR = 100-10q$ (i.e., first differentiation of TR function)

$MC = dq/dTC = 0.15q^2-0.5q+5$ (i.e., first differentiation of TC function)

Equating MR to MC:

$100-10q = 0.15q^2-0.5q+5$

Solving this equation yields a quantity (q) of approximately 8.7822 million units.

Substituting this value of q into the demand function gives the price (p):

$p = 100-5(8.7822) = 56.09$

With these values, we can calculate the total revenue, total cost, and maximum profit:

Total revenue: 8.7822×56.09=£492.62 million

Total cost: 100+0.05(8.7822)3−0.25(8.7822)2+5(8.7822)=£158.50 million

Maximum profit: 492.62−158.50=£334.12 million

According to this model, the demand curve approximates and integrates the market into the decision-making framework. The market is where a firm strategically positions its products, forming a complex nexus of consumer behaviour and marketing strategies. In the neoclassical model, however, the demand function singularly represents this market, conceptualising demand as the causal link between price and quantity. Assuming other factors remain constant (ceteris paribus), the quantity a firm can sell decreases as its price increases. The demand curve illustrates the potential price-quantity combinations available, which determine total revenue (TR=p×q). The marginal revenue curve is also derived from the demand curve, as MR=dqdTR.

Figure 3.1: The neoclassical economic model of pricing

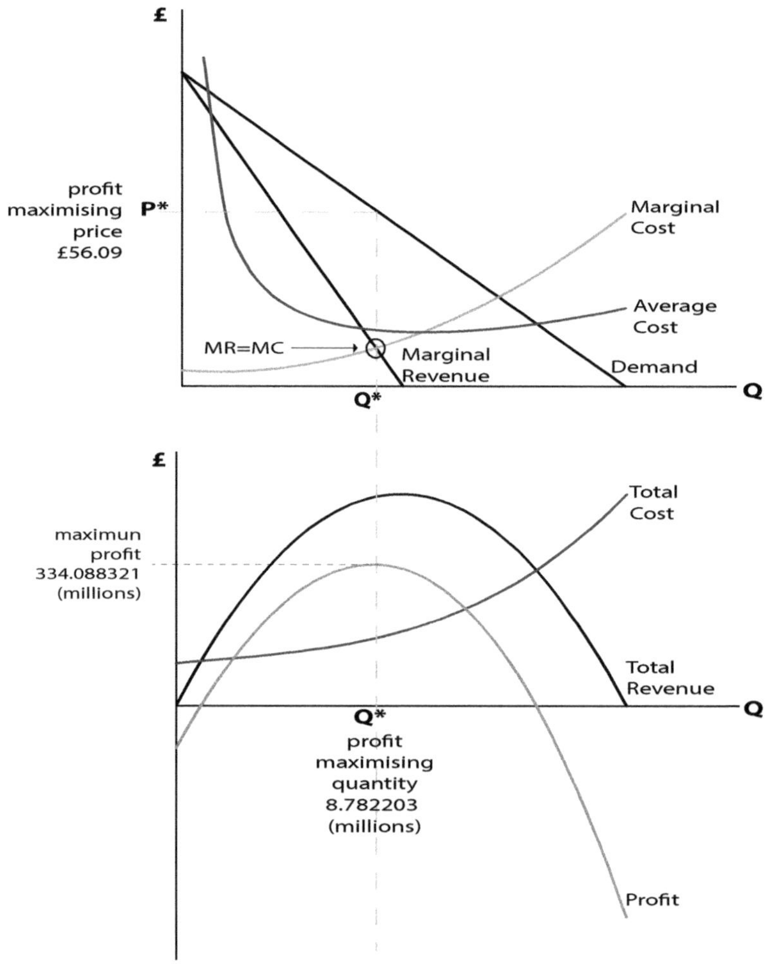

The demand curve, however, only considers the revenue side of the profit-driven formula. The other facet is the point of production, where costs are incurred. Cost curves are thus used to represent the point of production in determining the optimal price and quantity, which occurs where marginal cost equals marginal revenue.

Despite its theoretical elegance, the neoclassical model offers a narrow and problematic understanding of how firms establish prices. The following points outline its fundamental limitations.

1. **Problematic assumption of profit maximisation.** The assumption of profit maximisation is questionable in practice. Managers do not typically aim for absolute profit maximisation; rather, they strive to achieve specific profit targets outlined in budgets and incentive plans. The formal application of 'maximisation' logic is not commonly observed. Depending on a firm's market position, variables such as sales growth, market share, and strategic objectives like market penetration often take precedence. For instance, firms may incur losses during a product's introductory period by setting low introductory prices. Even in a product's mature stages, firms may be content with achieving a target profit and a satisfactory return on investment, rather than maximising profit.
2. **Limited market conceptualisation.** The neoclassical model integrates the market exclusively through the demand curve, envisioning it solely as a causal link between price and quantity. This reflects a limited understanding of the competitive landscape. From a strategic standpoint, the competitive landscape is far more intricate. A strategic conceptualisation must consider the firm's strengths and weaknesses, its competitive positioning goals, competitors' strengths and weaknesses, and their potential strategic moves. It should also consider customer profiles (demographic, political, economic, legal, cultural), supply chain dynamics, and the broader regulatory infrastructure. The competitive landscape for pricing is considerably more complex than this economic model can accommodate.
3. **Limited strategic agency attributed to the firm.** According to the neoclassical model, the firm has limited or no strategic agency. Aligned with the structure-conduct-performance model, neoclassical economics assumes structural determinism. Demand is regarded as a condition determined by market structure, and the firm merely determines its price based on the price-quantity relationship dictated by that demand. Demand is perceived as a structural imposition, and the firm's only option is to adjust its price-quantity combination according to the rule MR=MC. As explored in the previous chapter, Michael Porter's revision attributes strategic agency to the firm, arguing that firms can shape and reshape markets through their strategies. The neoclassical model does not acknowledge such strategic agency.
4. **Isolation of the pricing decision.** The neoclassical model perceives pricing as an independent, singular decision. Strategically, however, pricing is just one element of a 'marketing mix' that firms manage to achieve a competitive position. As a critical variable, pricing cannot be isolated from other marketing variables: product, place (distribution), and promotion. All these decisions collectively determine the firm's competitive market position.

In summary, the neoclassical model uses 'marginal analysis' to maximise profit where marginal revenue equals marginal cost. Critically, this model is contested for its problematic assumptions, its limited market conceptualisation, the restricted agency it attributes to firms, and its isolated consideration of pricing.

3.3 The accounting model of pricing

The second model is the conventional accounting model, commonly known as cost-plus pricing. This model determines the price by adding a desired profit margin to a product's full cost. The primary accounting challenge is calculating the full cost, which comprises direct costs and overheads.

Calculating direct costs—direct labour, materials, and expenses attributable to a cost object—is relatively straightforward, as operational information systems typically provide the necessary data. The greater challenge lies in overhead allocation and absorption: computing the portion of overheads attributable to a given cost unit. Numerous overheads are incurred throughout the organisation, and their relative significance has increased significantly over recent decades. The unit price must encompass a share of all these costs.

For this purpose, traditional absorption costing techniques may be used, with bases such as direct labour hours or prime cost. Alternatively, a firm may use activity-based costing (ABC), a more refined method of tracing overheads. In ABC, the activities performed in producing a cost unit are deemed the most accurate 'cost drivers'. Overheads are therefore absorbed based on such activities, rather than on arbitrary bases. Consequently, overheads are allocated to cost units based on the set of activities that underpin cost incurrence.

Proponents of ABC argue that activities provide a superior basis for capturing 'cost incidence' and accurately tracing overheads. In other words, activities are the real drivers of costs; hence, tracing costs based on activities provides a more precise cost estimation that can be used to manage the activities themselves. The following numerical example and Figure 3.2 illustrate the cost-plus model using an ABC approach.

A numerical example of cost-plus pricing (activity-based costing)

1. Basic data for product a (budget period)

Item	Value/Quantity
Direct materials cost	£2,250
Direct labour cost	£3,000
Direct expenses	£1,500
Budgeted production units	400
Direct labour hours	90
Number of setups	6
Number of orders	8
Machine hours	180
Kilowatt-hours	90

2. Organisational overhead data (budget period)

Overhead Item	Expected Cost	Relevant Activity Driver	Expected Activity Volume
Setup costs	£150,000	Number of setups	1,200
Ordering costs	£40,000	Number of orders	10,000
Maintenance	£200,000	Machine hours	16,000
Power	£20,000	Kilowatt-hours	100,000
Total	£410,000		

3. Cost and Price Calculations

The required profit margin is 30% on cost.

Step 1: Calculate activity cost driver rates

Overhead Item	Expected Cost	Expected Activity Volume	Activity Cost Driver Rate
Setup costs	£150,000	1,200 setups	£125.00 per setup
Ordering costs	£40,000	10,000 orders	£4.00 per order
Maintenance	£200,000	16,000 machine hours	£12.50 per machine hour
Power	£20,000	100,000 kWh	£0.20 per kWh

Step 2: Allocate overheads to product a

Overhead Item	Activity Driver Rate	Activity Volume for Product A	Total Overhead Attributed
Setup costs	£125.00 per setup	6 setups	£750.00
Ordering costs	£4.00 per order	8 orders	£32.00
Maintenance	£12.50 per machine hour	180 machine hours	£2,250.00
Power	£0.20 per kWh	90 kWh	£18.00
Total Overhead Cost for Product A			£3,050.00

Step 3: Calculate total cost and selling price per unit

Cost Component	Calculation	Per Unit Cost
Total Direct Costs		
Direct materials	£2,250 / 400 units	£5.63
Direct labour	£3,000 / 400 units	£7.50
Direct expenses	£1,500 / 400 units	£3.75
Subtotal: Direct Cost per Unit		£16.88
Overhead Cost per Unit	£3,050 / 400 units	£7.63
Total Cost per Unit	£16.88 + £7.63	£24.51
PLUS: Profit Margin (30% of cost)	30% of £24.51	£7.35
Selling Price per Unit	£24.51 + £7.35	£31.86

The cost-plus model is straightforward and has been widely used for decades. Corporate information systems are often configured to support it. However, from a strategic perspective, this model has several fundamental weaknesses.

1. **Market consideration absent.** The model lacks any consideration for the market, the ultimate arena for strategy. It does not help determine a price that captures market dynamics. A sound strategic approach should analyse the competitive terrain, including rivalry, the threat of new entrants and substitutes, and the bargaining power of suppliers and customers. This pricing model fails to consider such factors.
2. **Production-driven 'push' strategy.** Cost-plus pricing is inherently production-driven, embodying a 'push' strategy where pricing originates from the factory floor. The calculated cost, plus a required profit margin, is then 'pushed' onto customers. These costs, however, merely represent the accounting value of resources consumed, not strategic targets. This can

Figure 3.2: The accounting model of pricing

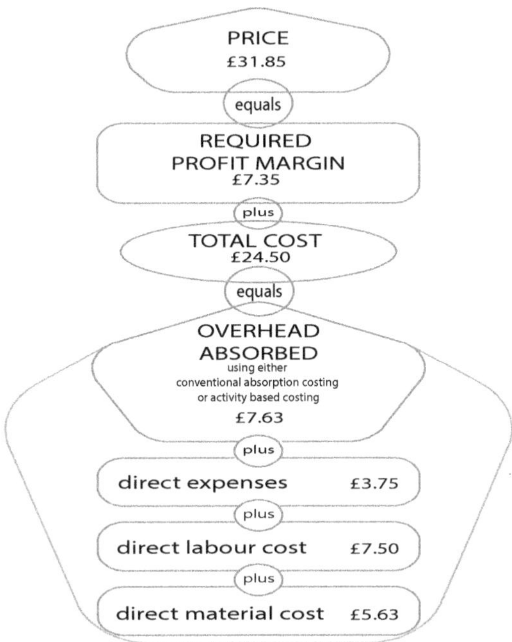

render the product uncompetitive. This strategy is effective only where the firm holds high monopoly power. In a competitive market, the firm must adopt a 'pull' strategy, starting from a market-aligned price and working backwards to manage costs. This ensures the firm can deliver the product at the market-driven price while achieving its desired profit, making a Target Costing system (see section 3.6) crucial.

3. **Firms' inefficiencies are passed on to customers.** Accounting costs can encompass a firm's inefficiencies, including wastage and suboptimal capacity utilisation. Cost-plus pricing incorporates these into the price. Furthermore, by calculating the profit margin as a percentage of cost, the model allows the firm to profit from its own inefficiencies. This not only makes the firm less competitive but also raises moral and economic concerns about transferring inefficiencies to others for a profit.
4. **Incompatibility with highly competitive conditions.** The cost-plus model may falter in highly competitive conditions where: (a) customers are price-sensitive and wield significant bargaining power; (b) competitors can manage costs more effectively; or (c) the company is pursuing a 'cost leadership' strategy.

In summary, the cost-plus pricing model exhibits fundamental weaknesses when confronted with modern market dynamics.

3.4 Strategic pricing: pricing for competitive positioning

The neoclassical and accounting models assume a paradigm of mass production and mass marketing, envisioning the market as an undifferentiated expanse of demand. This perspective aims to create a universal marketing package appealing to all consumers. During the early stages of industrial capitalism, particularly at the zenith of the Ford Motor Company, mass production was standard. The focus was on achieving economies of scale to offer products at the lowest possible cost, epitomised by Henry Ford's statement, 'Any customer can have a car painted any colour that he wants so long as it is black'. This reflected his vision:

> 'I will build a motor car for the great multitude... it will be constructed of the best materials, by the best men to be hired, after the simplest designs that modern engineering can devise. But it will be so low in price that no man making a good salary will be unable to own one'. (Ford, in Crowther & Ford, 2015, p. 73)

While such a strategy thrived in the near-monopoly conditions of the time, contemporary markets—shaped by neoliberalism, globalisation, and digitalisation—are highly fragmented. They necessitate more than a mass marketing strategy. As explored previously, achieving a 'competitive advantage' requires 'strategic positioning'. Therefore, in the current landscape, a market-driven positioning strategy is imperative. Such an approach encompasses market segmentation, targeting, and positioning—in short, STP marketing. Figure 3.3 illustrates the key elements of this approach.

Figure 3.3: Market segmentation, targeting, and positioning

Segmentation

Segmentation revolves around the idea that distinct customer groups require unique strategies. Each category has specific demands. Segmentation, therefore, is the analytical process of profiling the market to identify strategically crucial bases for dividing it into different customer categories, each requiring different positioning strategies.

The first step is to identify potential segmentation bases that differentiate market segments, using market surveys and big data analytics. The critical question is to identify which forms of segmentation necessitate different marketing mix: different pricing, product characteristics, distribution channels, and promotional themes. There are four key sets of variables upon which the market can be segmented (see Figure 3.4).

Side note

The marketing mix encompasses product, price, place (distribution), and promotion (advertising, sales promotions, publicity, personal selling), often abbreviated as the 4Ps.

1. **Geographic segmentation** involves considering geographic differences such as legal standards, cultural disparities (e.g., Asia vs. Europe), urban vs. rural distinctions, climate, and population density.
2. **Demographic segmentation** is vital when variables like age, gender, ethnicity, religion, and family life cycle demand differences in product design, pricing, distribution, and promotion.
3. **Psychographic segmentation** relates to differences in consumers' psychological or trait characteristics, such as risk aversion, lifestyle, colour or taste preferences, and the AIO concept (activities, interests, and opinions).
4. **Behavioural segmentation** focuses on different purchasing patterns, considering factors such as:

    a. Benefit orientation (specific benefits sought from the product),
    b. Occasion orientation (e.g., one-off vs. repeated purchases),
    c. Usage orientation (e.g., heavy, moderate, or minor usage),
    d. Loyalty orientation (customer retention rate).

These segmentation bases are not mutually exclusive; they can be combined to create, for example, geodemographic segmentations, which are increasingly popular due to the availability of large databases and big data analytics.

Figure 3.4: Bases of market segmentation

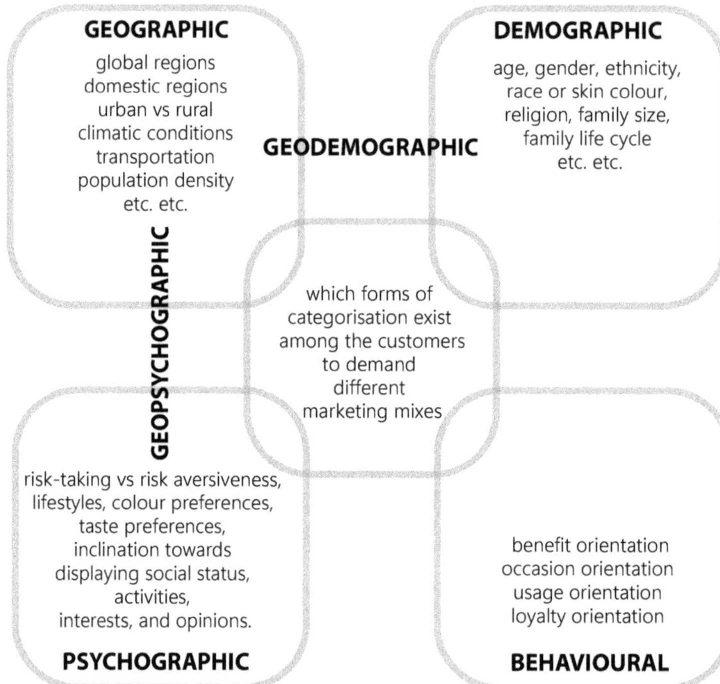

Market segment profile

The analytical outcome of segmentation is the development of detailed market segment profiles. These profiles provide a comparative view of each segment against a selected set of variables. Table 3.1 provides a possible template for developing such profiles.

Targeting

Once market segment profiles are developed, appropriate segments should be selected for targeting. In deciding which segments to target, the firm needs to assess the following criteria:

1. Is the segment **substantial** enough for the company's strategic objectives?
2. Is the segment uniquely **identifiable** in the differences it demands in the marketing mix?
3. Is the segment **reachable** by the company?
4. Is the segment **profitable** (a determination relying on management accounting)?

Table 3.1: Market segment profiling

	Semgment 1	Segment 2	Segment 3
KEY MEASURES			
Segment size			
Segment growth			
Proportion of market			
CONSUMER BEHAVIOUR			
Main consumer needs			
Usage level			
Level of brand loyalty			
Price sensitivity			
Product involvement			
Retailer preferences			
DESCRIPTION			
Geographic spread			
Demographic description			
Psychographic description			
COMPETITION/COMMUNICATION			
Main competitive offerings			
Main media choices			

5. Is the segment **responsive** to the firm's new offerings?

Depending on these assessments, targeting could range from single-segment concentration to full market coverage with different marketing mixes for each segment.

Positioning

Positioning is the strategic act of creating a specific perception of the product or brand in the minds of customers within a target segment. While it involves using various marketing tools, its ultimate objective is a cognitive-psychological outcome: to associate the brand with a distinct 'position' in the customer's mind. Positioning can be explained by answering three questions:

1. **Where do you position?** In the mind of the customer. The brand must cater to the specific needs of the targeted segment.
2. **What do you position?** An idea, concept, image, or benefit to define the brand. A brand is 'a name, term, sign, symbol, or design, or a combination of them, intended to identify the goods or services of one seller... and to differentiate them from those of competitors' (American Marketing Association).
3. **How do you position?** Creatively using all elements of the marketing mix (the 4Ps): product, price, promotion, and place.

The strategic role of pricing in STP

The accounting and economic models consider pricing a singular decision based only on revenue and cost. In contrast, within the STP framework, pricing decisions are interdependent with other marketing mix decisions. All elements should be treated as components of a total marketing package, directed towards the specific positioning propositions the firm is trying to achieve.

For example, if a firm is pursuing superior differentiation in a segment with a high-quality product, premium distribution channels, and a premium promotional campaign, its pricing should reflect this with relatively high prices. In such a strategy, price may not be the most critical variable; the focus is on superior product quality. In contrast, if the firm's strategy is 'cost leadership' for a standard product, pricing should manifest this with a competitive price tag. There must be a clear connection between price and the quality proposition. Figure 3.5 illustrates possible positioning concepts arising from this connection.

Figure 3.5: Value propositions between product price and quality

Nevertheless, price is a special element in the marketing mix because it is the only variable that generates revenue. The financial viability of any positioning strategy depends on the price's capacity to generate sufficient revenue to guarantee the desired return on investment. To that end, accounting calculations remain critical in assessing segment profitability and the financial implications of different positioning strategies.

Other pricing considerations and techniques: fine-tuning the pricing strategy

Once a price or price range is identified for each segment, it needs to be adapted and communicated to create cognitive appeal. To that end, firms often adopt 'psychological pricing'. This involves the subtle use of the price tag to encourage a purchasing decision and includes the following techniques.

Psychological pricing

1. Charm pricing: Using prices ending in 9, for example, £1.99 instead of £2.00. The idea is that the customer sees the '1' first and perceives the price as closer to £1.00. However, the prevalence of this practice has created an opposite effect in some contexts, where prices ending in 9 connote a 'value price' and prices ending in 0 connote a 'prestigious price'.
2. Artificial time constraints: Associating a time-limited special value with the price, for example, 'today only'.
3. Innumeracy: Framing an offer to seem more appealing, for example, 'buy one, get one free' rather than '50% off two items'.
4. Price appearance: Making the price 'appear small'. This is often used on menus in high-end restaurants, where prices are stated in a small font without a currency sign (e.g., '12' instead of '£12.00').

Market skimming vs. penetration pricing.

These two techniques are useful when a new product is introduced. They represent opposing approaches to product introduction.

Market skimming is suitable where:

1. the market is vertically stratified with layers of different purchasing power, where the top layers are relatively price-insensitive; and
2. the product is new and innovative and can command a higher price initially. A market skimming strategy first 'skims' the top layer with a high price and then gradually drops the price to 'skim' lower layers. This aligns with Porter's idea of 'differentiation'.

Market penetration, on the other hand, is more suitable when the market is 'flat' and saturated with competitive offers, and the product is generic. In such cases, firms may offer the product at a relatively low introductory price to capture the largest possible market share. This aligns with Porter's idea of 'cost leadership'.

3.5 Lifecycle costing

The economic and accounting models discussed earlier adopt a short-term perspective, mainly capturing costs incurred during a specific accounting period. In contrast, lifecycle costing introduces a long-term viewpoint. The concept is straightforward: when calculating a product's cost and determining its price, all costs incurred or anticipated throughout the product's entire lifecycle must be considered. In accounting literature, lifecycle costing is addressed for two distinct purposes: asset management and product costing.

Lifecycle costing in asset management

The asset management perspective evaluates the total lifecycle cost of owning and using a specific asset. This is the viewpoint of a product user or purchaser. For instance, when using lifecycle costing to decide on purchasing a car, considerations should encompass:

1. Purchase price,
2. Interest or borrowing costs during its useful life,
3. Estimated running costs (fuel, repairs, insurance, tax) over the intended usage period,
4. Its disposal or sales value at the end of its useful life.

In line with EU public procurement directives (e.g., Directive 2014/24/EU), lifecycle costing has become a crucial element in the procurement procedures of public authorities, where it is used to assess the 'most economically advantageous tender' (MEAT). According to the European Commission, all costs incurred throughout a product's lifecycle should be considered. The lifecycle cost of an asset includes:

1. Purchase price and all associated costs (delivery, installation),
2. Operating costs, including energy, spares, and maintenance,
3. End-of-life costs (decommissioning) or residual value.

The European Commission also provides guidelines on when the 'cost of externalities' (e.g., greenhouse gas emissions) may be included. The adoption of lifecycle costing in asset procurement is intended to encourage savings on energy, maintenance, and disposal costs.

Lifecycle costing in product costing

As a product costing technique, lifecycle costing adopts the seller's perspective to determine a product's selling price, considering all its associated lifecycle costs. From a production standpoint, the lifecycle can be categorised into three phases:

4. **Pre-production Phase:** Costs incurred involve research and development (R&D), market surveys, product design, prototyping, technology licensing, and supply chain development.
5. **Production or Operational Phase:** This phase encompasses the actual production, distribution, and selling of the product. All variable and fixed costs associated with these activities should be considered over all accounting periods in which the product is produced and sold.
6. **Disposal and Decommissioning Phase:** This marks the end of the lifecycle and involves estimated disposal and decommissioning costs.

Lifecycle costing is most effective for products with a definite lifecycle, such as high-tech products that require periodic replacement. For products like Coca-Cola, it has limited utility. The concept can be expressed with the following formula:

$$\textit{average cost per unit} = \frac{\textit{total cost incurred and estimated to be incurred during the entire life cycle of the product}}{\textit{total number of units to be sold during the entire lifecycle of the product}}$$

$$\textit{Price} = \textit{average cost per unit} + \textit{required profit margin per unit.}$$

A mini case study illustrating lifecycle costing is provided in the appendix. Table 3.2 offers a simplified example.

The price calculated using this method is an average for the entire lifecycle, establishing a long-term target. The price can then be adjusted according to specific market conditions. For instance, a lower penetration price may be set during the introductory phase, or a higher skimming price may be used if market conditions permit, provided the average lifecycle price is still attained.

As a cost management technique, lifecycle costing requires a long-term perspective on activities from pre-production to post-production. It offers a more comprehensive understanding of long-term cost management and can have positive sustainability effects by compelling management to consider future resource usage and disposal costs. A significant challenge, however, is that its accuracy depends

Table 3.2: Lifecycle costing example

This product is expected to be replaced after three operating years, and management requires a 35% profit margin on cost.

	pre-production	operating years			post-production	total
		1st	2nd	3rd		
Estimated sales (units)		50,000	60,000	40,000		150,000
Costs						
Research and development	£200,000	£25,000	£10,000			£235,000
Licensing and other preparatory costs	£25,000					£25,000
Variable cost per unit		£300	£325	£350		
Total variable cost = per unit VC * estimated sales		£15,000,000	£19,500,000	£14,000,000		£48,500,000
Fixed overheads attributable to the product		£5,000,000	£5,500,000	£6,000,000		£16,500,000
product decommissioning and disposal costs					£30,000	£30,000
After-sales service commitment costs not included in the three operating years					£50,000	£50,000
TOTAL LIFECYCLE COST						£65,340,000
AVERAGE LIFECYCLE COST PER UNIT = TOTAL COST (i.e. 65,340,000)/TOTAL UNITS (i.e. 150,000)						£435.60
Required profit margin per unit (35%)						£152.46
AVERAGE LIFECYCLE PRICE PER UNIT = AVERAGE COST + REQUIRED PROFIT MARGIN						£588.06

heavily on estimates of future activities. It also necessitates a multidisciplinary approach to facilitate collaborative information-sharing across the organisation.

3.6 Target costing

Pioneered by Japanese companies like Toyota, target costing is a market-driven approach to pricing and cost management. The costing methodologies discussed thus far, including lifecycle costing, embody a 'push strategy', where costs are determined based on resource consumption and then passed on to customers with a profit margin.

In contrast, target costing embodies a 'pull strategy', initiating the process from a market perspective. It begins by evaluating the market to establish a competitive price that customers are willing to pay. This market-dictated price serves as the starting point. The firm then works backwards, deducting the desired profit margin to calculate the cost at which the product must be produced. The target costing formula is:

Target Cost = Target Price – Target Profit Margin

This approach is distinct from the conventional formula, 'Cost + Profit Margin = Price', as it shifts from a 'push' to a 'pull' strategy, aligning production with market demands.

Crucially, target costing is not merely a product costing technique but an overarching managerial approach to strategically manage costs. Originating in the 1970s, it gained popularity in the 1980s and 1990s as a pivotal component of Japanese management systems. It forms an integral part of a comprehensive management package, alongside methodologies such as total quality management (TQM) and continuous improvement (kaizen). According to Cooper and Slagmulder (1997), target costing, coupled with value engineering, establishes a strategic link between the price, quality, and functionality of a firm's market offerings.

Our discussion here is built around three interconnected themes:

1. the Survival Zone,
2. the Triangle of Target Costing, and
3. the Target Costing Process.

The concept of the survival zone

As a framework for value engineering and cost management, target costing should be grounded in a delineation of the 'survival zone' for the company (Cooper & Slagmulder, 1997). The survival zone, or 'triangle of survival', represents the competitive realm within which a firm must operate; straying beyond it may imperil its viability. This concept delineates the competitive landscape in terms of three interconnected variables: price, quality, and product functionalities. As illustrated in Figure 3.6, the survival zone is demarcated by upper and lower limits for each variable.

1. **Price:** There is a maximum allowable price, above which a product may lack competitive viability, and a minimum allowable price, below which it is financially unviable.
2. **Functionalities:** This pertains to a product's specific capabilities. There is a technically and financially viable upper limit to the functionalities a product can incorporate, and a 'must-have' set of functionalities as a lower limit.
3. **Quality:** This refers to how proficiently the product executes its functionalities. There is a minimum allowable quality, below which a product is not competitive, and a maximum feasible quality that is technically and financially viable.

Figure 3.6: The survival zone

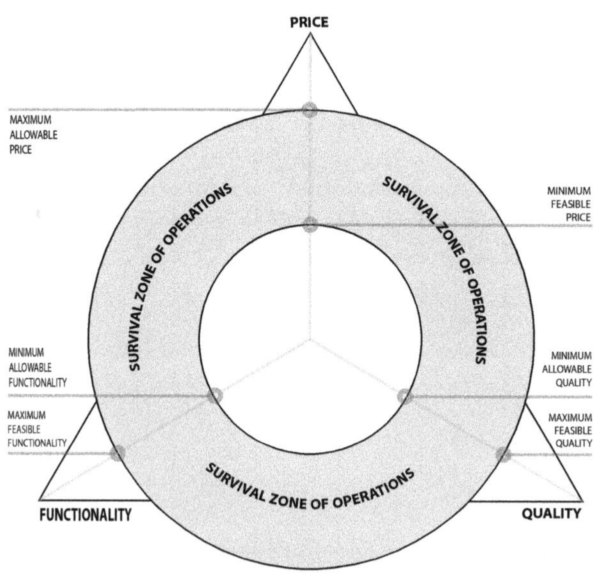

Source: Adapted from Cooper and Slagmulder (1997, p. 5).

The triangle of target costing

While the survival zone defines the sphere of operation, a firm's success within this zone depends on how it connects three critical actors: customers, suppliers, and product designers. The target costing triangle conceptualises these interconnections. As depicted in Figure 3.7, the network of interactions among these actors determines the cost elements a target costing system should address, constituting the firm's profit management regime.

Figure 3.7: The target costing triangle

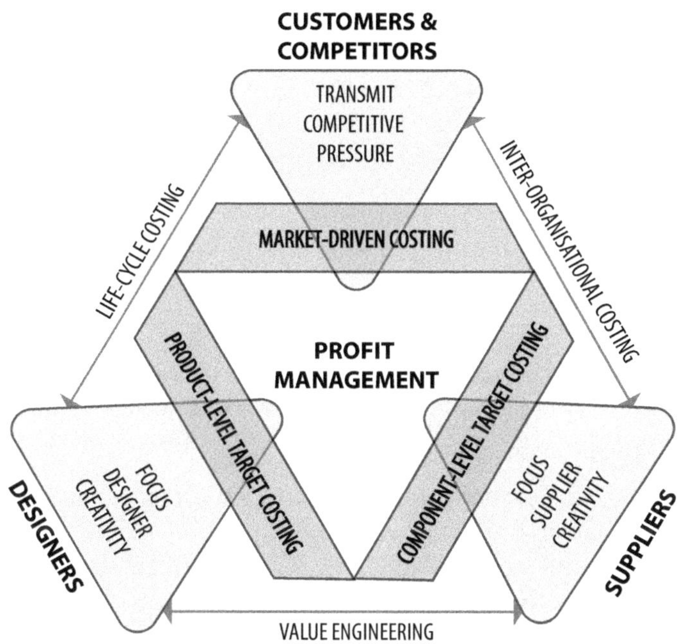

Source: Adapted from Cooper and Slagmulder (1997, p. 9).

Target costing can be understood as a system of profit management that integrates customers, suppliers, and product designers through a series of costing and value engineering processes. Accordingly, it comprises the following key elements:

1. **Market-driven target costing** transmits customer requirements and competitive pressures as specific cost targets to suppliers and designers.
2. **Inter-organisational target costing** across the supply chain intensifies competitive pressure on suppliers, requiring them to be innovative in meeting cost requirements.

3. **Lifecycle costing** connects customers with product designers and ensures that target profit margins consider upfront investments and future costs over the product's life.
4. **Component-level target costing** operates between the company and its suppliers to stimulate supplier creativity in meeting quality requirements at specified target costs.
5. **Product-level target costing** stimulates designers' creativity, demanding that they meet product quality and functionality targets at specified costs.
6. **Value engineering** complements target costing to create strategic optimality between product quality, functionalities, and price.

Viewed through this set of relationships, target costing is 'a structured approach to determining the lifecycle cost at which a proposed product with specified functionality and quality must be produced to generate the desired level of profitability over its life cycle when sold at its anticipated selling price' (Cooper & Slagmulder, 1997, p. 10).

The target costing process

Target costing is a meticulous procedure that determines, oversees, and enhances functional, component, and activity-level target costs. The process commences with establishing a competitive market price and extends to the points of production. Figure 3.8 illustrates the process.

The process initiates with the **target price**, which requires a thorough analysis of product requirements, technology, and the market to ascertain how the firm can operate within the survival zone. Once the target price is determined, deducting the **target profit** margin reveals the **target unit cost**. This requires a financial analysis of how the target profit aligns with financial expectations.

Next, the target cost must be compared with the **current cost**, calculated using techniques such as lifecycle and activity-based costing. This comparison highlights the **cost differential** that needs to be managed. This differential is then allocated to its sub-elements:

1. **Functional-level target costs** encompass measures to reduce overheads associated with functional departments.
2. **Component-level target costs** pertain to specific cost targets for product components, involving cost management activities with suppliers.
3. **Activity-level target costs** are the most fundamental, relating to cost and time targets for distinct activities, often operationalised through activity-based management.

Figure 3.8: The target costing process

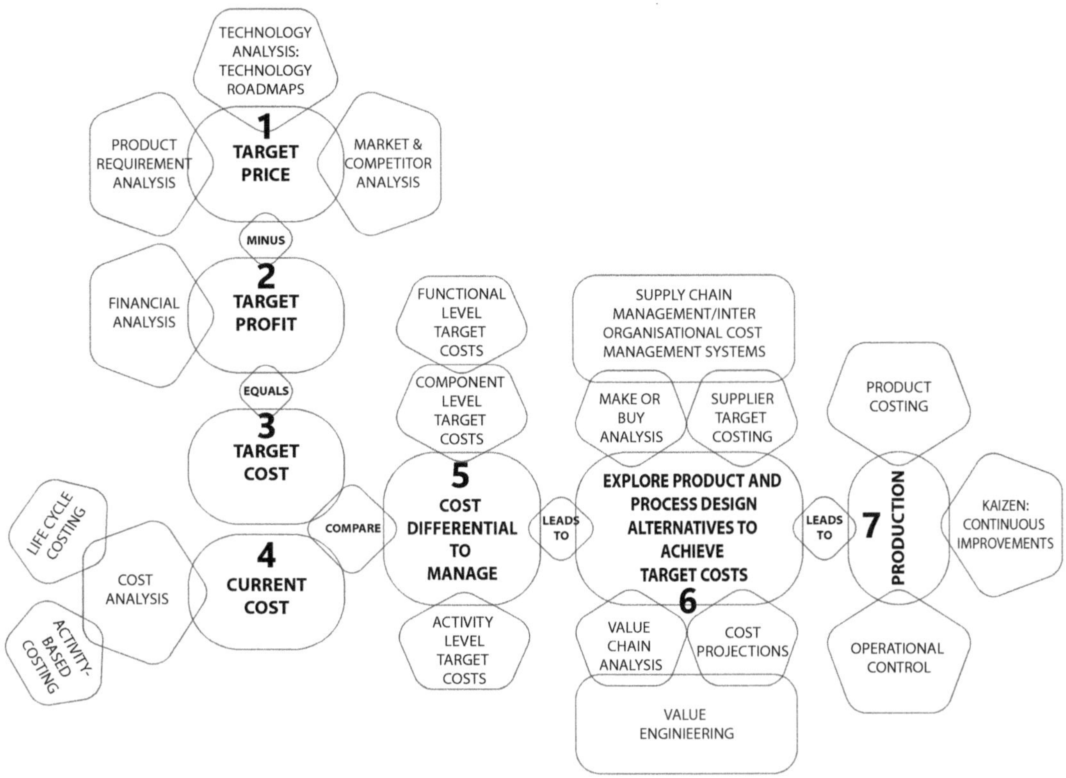

Identifying these targets leads to exploring product and process design alternatives, such as supply chain management (make-or-buy decisions) and value engineering. The final step is actual production, which requires continuous evaluation through product costing, monitoring via production control, and improvement through **continuous improvement** systems (kaizen).

Sustainability implications of target costing

The sustainability implications of target costing are paradoxical. On one hand, the collaborations inherent in the system can incorporate growing market demands for sustainable product features, potentially facilitating market pressures for more energy-efficient and environmentally friendly products. Heightened customer awareness can redefine the 'survival zone', compelling firms to integrate new ecological features. Furthermore, using lifecycle costing can help identify and address sustainability issues such as energy usage and carbon emissions.

On the other hand, target costing transmits intense market pressure down the supply chain, from influential customers to vulnerable labourers, often in peripheral economies. The system can exert unequivocal pressure to continuously reduce costs. This pressure can cascade down the supply chain, its impact intensifying until it falls most severely on low-wage labourers. In such contexts, the relentless drive for cost reduction can contribute to exploitative labour practices, a phenomenon documented in research on global supply chains (e.g., Neu et al., 2014; Christ et al., 2019). As Burawoy (1983, p. 588) notes, 'despotic regulation of the labour process is constituted by the economic whip of the market ... anarchy in the market leads to despotism in the factory'. Such despotism can manifest in practices akin to modern slavery, a burgeoning research area (e.g., Crane, 2013; Christ & Burritt, 2021). These practices have become a significant social injustice issue, prompting governments in the UK and Australia to enact anti-modern slavery laws.

3.7 Dynamic pricing

Dynamic pricing is a strategy that adjusts the prices of products or services based on real-time data. Determining factors can include market demand, competitive conditions, customer behaviour, and a firm's inventory levels. This approach can help businesses optimise revenue and outperform competitors. However, implementing it demands a robust data infrastructure, supported by advanced analytics and algorithms.

In economic terms, the following are preconditions for deploying dynamic pricing, which is essentially a technologically enabled form of price discrimination:

1. The firm must have bargaining power over buyers.
2. There must be consumer segments with different elasticities of demand.
3. The firm must have the techno-managerial capacity to gauge how demand fluctuates.
4. There must be minimal possibilities for resale between buyers.

More than anything, however, contemporary dynamic pricing is a manifestation of technological innovation. It revolves around technology enabling firms to practise automated and continuous price discrimination using real-time data and algorithms. In its contemporary form, dynamic pricing is a technologically-driven strategy where prices are adjusted automatically based on data-driven analyses. Examples include:

1. Airlines use dynamic pricing to set fares based on demand, seasonality, and competition.

2. E-commerce platforms like Amazon adjust prices based on a customer's purchase history and browsing patterns.
3. Ride-sharing services like Uber use 'surge pricing' to adjust fares based on demand and supply.
4. Sports teams set ticket prices based on team performance, the opponent, and seat location.

While powerful, dynamic pricing comes with significant challenges:

- Customer perception: It can negatively impact customers' perception of fairness, leading to frustration if they feel charged arbitrarily high prices.
- Competition: It may increase competition and trigger price wars, necessitating constant monitoring of competitor prices.
- Complexity and cost: Implementation requires large amounts of data and sophisticated technology, which can be complex and costly.
- Legal and ethical issues: Businesses may face legal and ethical issues such as antitrust laws, illegal price discrimination, or price gouging.

Chapter Summary

This chapter has delved into the neoclassical economic model, conventional accounting models, and the contemporary approach of strategic pricing. The neoclassical model employs 'marginal analysis' to determine the profit-maximising price. It was critiqued for its narrow understanding of market dynamics and its problematic assumptions about firm behaviour. The accounting model adopts a cost-plus approach and was critiqued for neglecting market dynamics and promoting an inwardly focused 'push strategy'.

Strategic pricing was presented as an intricate process involving market segmentation, targeting, and positioning (STP), requiring close integration with other marketing mix decisions. Segmentation identifies market stratifications that necessitate distinct positioning strategies. Four key sets of segmentation variables—geographic, demographic, psychographic, and behavioural—were discussed. The outcome is the development of segment profiles, which facilitate a comparative understanding of different market segments. Based on this, a firm can decide which segments to target, with selection criteria including whether a segment is substantial, identifiable, reachable, profitable, and responsive. Positioning involves strategically shaping perceptions of the product in customers' minds through the coordinated use of the marketing mix.

Lifecycle costing was discussed as a strategic technique applicable from two perspectives. As an asset management technique, it considers the total cost of owning and using a product. As a product costing technique, it calculates the average lifecycle cost by considering all costs associated with the pre-production, production, and post-production phases.

The chapter also explored target costing as a comprehensive, market-driven cost and profit management system. In contrast to the 'push' strategies of traditional models, target costing employs a 'pull' strategy built around three themes: the survival zone, the target costing triangle, and the target costing process. It integrates customers, suppliers, and designers through techniques such as lifecycle costing and value engineering. Despite its advantages, target costing was shown to have paradoxical implications for sustainability, offering potential for environmental improvements but also risking the transmission of intense cost pressure down the supply chain.

Finally, dynamic pricing was introduced as a technology-driven strategy that adjusts prices in real time, offering potential for revenue optimisation but also posing challenges related to customer perception, complexity, and ethics.

Case Study: Patagonia – pricing a proposition to save our home planet

Introduction: the activist company

In the contemporary business landscape, few brands have cultivated an identity as distinct as Patagonia. More than a purveyor of outdoor apparel, Patagonia has positioned itself as a corporate activist, defined by an uncompromising purpose: 'We're in business to save our home planet'. This statement is not a peripheral slogan but the foundational principle permeating every facet of the organisation's strategy. This integration of sustainability and activism into its core identity makes Patagonia a compelling subject for academic inquiry. The company's considerable commercial success, with a valuation estimated at $3 billion and annual revenues exceeding $1 billion, demonstrates that its unconventional model is highly profitable, challenging long-held assumptions about corporate objectives.

This case study explores a central strategic paradox: Patagonia has achieved remarkable success through a strategy that often appears 'anti-marketing' and is explicitly rooted in an anti-consumerist ethos. This is famously encapsulated in its 2011 'Don't Buy This Jacket' advertising campaign, which urged consumers to consider the environmental costs of consumption. Such a stance directly confronts the growth-oriented logic of conventional business models, creating a fascinating tension between its commercial imperatives and its planetary mission.

This paradox is not a sign of strategic incoherence but the very source of the brand's authenticity and market power. The mission statement functions as the primary filter for all strategic decisions. Actions difficult to justify through a traditional return on investment (ROI) analysis, such as donating 100% of its Black Friday sales to environmental causes or its unique ownership structure where 'earth is its only shareholder', become logical extensions of its identity.

This case study analyses how Patagonia's commitment to sustainability shapes its strategic pricing, market positioning, and underlying management accounting practices. It serves as a real-world counter-narrative to the traditional pricing models discussed in this chapter. Patagonia offers a compelling illustration of a market-driven, value-led approach where price is not merely a financial variable but a powerful signal of a complex value proposition encompassing product quality, durability, and profound ethical and environmental commitments. By examining Patagonia, students can explore the interplay between a firm's mission, market strategy, and accounting systems in an era where sustainability is a central strategic imperative.

Market segmentation and targeting – the conscious consumer

The success of any market-driven strategy hinges on a sophisticated understanding of the market through segmentation, targeting, and positioning (STP). Patagonia's approach is exemplary, demonstrating how a deep alignment with a specific customer segment's values can create a formidable competitive advantage. The company's strategy moves beyond simplistic categorisations to build a brand that resonates on a profound psychographic level with a community of 'conscious consumers'.

Profiling Patagonia's target market

Patagonia's customer base is a multi-faceted profile where psychographic and behavioural variables are the primary drivers.

1. Psychographic Segmentation: This is the cornerstone of Patagonia's strategy. The core customer is defined not by what they do, but by what they believe. They are environmentalists, social activists, and ethically-minded consumers who view their purchasing decisions as an extension of their values. This segment rejects the 'fast fashion' model, prioritising minimalism, authenticity, and long-term value. They are not passive consumers but active participants in a lifestyle that values experiences over possessions and seeks to minimise personal environmental impact.
2. Behavioural Segmentation: The psychographic profile translates directly into distinct purchasing behaviours. This segment exhibits exceptionally high brand loyalty, rooted in shared values. They are 'conscious buyers' who value product durability, functionality, and repairability, actively participating in programmes like Worn Wear, which encourages the repair and reuse of garments. Their purchasing decisions are deliberate and researched, reflecting a value-driven calculus where a product's ethical and environmental credentials are as important as its physical performance.
3. Demographic Segmentation: While secondary, the demographic profile is distinct. The core age range is 25 to 45, encompassing educated millennials and Gen Xers. These consumers are often college-educated, with a greater awareness of complex issues like supply chain ethics. They generally fall into the middle to upper-middle income bracket (household incomes often exceeding $75,000 per year), which provides the disposable income to invest in premium-priced products that align with their ethical commitments.
4. Geographic Segmentation: Patagonia's target market is concentrated in areas where environmental consciousness is a strong cultural norm. This includes progressive states in the United States, such as California and

Colorado, as well as major urban centres like San Francisco and Denver, where a lifestyle of outdoor activity and social activism is prevalent.

Targeting strategy: a community of shared values

Patagonia's targeting strategy eschews mass-market appeals in favour of cultivating a deep relationship with its core segment. The objective is not simply to sell products but to build a community unified by a shared commitment to environmental and social responsibility. The company's marketing and activism act as a powerful filtering mechanism. By taking bold stances – such as suing the federal government to protect national monuments – Patagonia attracts individuals who share its worldview while deterring those who do not.

This approach creates a self-selected customer base that is inherently less sensitive to price and more focused on value alignment. The investment in community-building, through initiatives like 1% for the Planet, can be viewed as a form of strategic risk management. By fostering a loyal community, Patagonia insulates itself from price-based competition. This customer base is more resilient during economic downturns; they may reduce consumption, but their investment in the brand makes them far less likely to switch to a cheaper alternative. The notable increase in sales following the 'Don't Buy This Jacket' campaign provides strong evidence for this resilience. This loyal community, therefore, acts as a strategic asset, stabilising long-term revenue.

Section 2: Positioning and the marketing mix – weaving sustainability into the 4Ps

Having targeted its core customer segment, Patagonia's next challenge is to create a distinct position in their minds. For Patagonia, that position is 'authentic sustainability'. This is not achieved through slogans alone but is meticulously constructed through an integrated marketing mix, where every element of the 4Ps (Product, Price, Promotion, and Place) serves as tangible evidence of the brand's promise.

Positioning: owning 'authentic sustainability'

Applying the 'what, where, how' framework for positioning:

- Where do you position? In the mind of the conscious consumer, who is sceptical of corporate greenwashing and seeks genuine alignment between a company's claims and its actions.
- What do you position? The idea of authentic, radical, and uncompromising environmental and social responsibility. This is not about being 'slightly greener' than competitors but about fundamentally reimagining the role of business in society.

Table 1: Patagonia's segmentation, targeting, and positioning (stp) strategy

<table>
<thead>
<tr><th>Segmentation Variable</th><th>Profile of Patagonia's Target Segment</th><th>Targeting Approach</th><th>Positioning Statement</th></tr>
</thead>
<tbody>
<tr><td>Psychographic</td><td>Values environmentalism, activism, authenticity, and minimalism; rejects fast fashion; sees consumption as an expression of identity and a tool for change.</td><td>Builds a community around shared values; uses activism, storytelling, and educational content as primary engagement tools to foster deep, long-term relationships.</td><td rowspan="4">For the conscious consumer and outdoor activist, Patagonia is the apparel brand that delivers uncompromising performance and durability while actively working to save our home planet.</td></tr>
<tr><td>Behavioural</td><td>Exhibits high brand loyalty; values product durability and repairability over novelty; participates in circular economy models (e.g., repair, reuse); makes deliberate, value-driven purchasing decisions.</td><td>Reinforces desired behaviours through programmes like Worn Wear and free repair services; discourages impulse buying through 'anti-marketing' campaigns.</td></tr>
<tr><td>Demographic</td><td>Ages 25-45; educated (college degree or higher); middle to upper-middle income (household income >$75,000); appeals to both men and women, with strong loyalty among millennial and Gen Z women.</td><td>Focuses communication on platforms and themes that resonate with an educated, socially aware audience; premium pricing aligns with the segment's financial capacity.</td></tr>
<tr><td>Geographic</td><td>Concentrated in environmentally progressive regions (e.g., US West Coast, Western Europe) and urban centres with a strong outdoor and activist culture.</td><td>Establishes retail stores as community hubs for local activism and events; tailors store offerings to reflect local environments and activities (e.g., surf gear in coastal towns).</td></tr>
</tbody>
</table>

- How do you position? Through a coherent and self-reinforcing marketing mix where every component is a proof point of the core mission. This creates a formidable barrier to imitation, as a competitor cannot simply copy one element (like an advertisement) without the substance of the others to back it up.

This creates a formidable barrier to imitation. A rival might attempt to replicate Patagonia's provocative advertising (Promotion), but without a product genuinely engineered for longevity (Product), the campaign would be exposed as inauthentic. To develop such a product would require massive investment, which would necessitate a premium price point (Price). And to command that premium, the competitor would need the decades of credibility Patagonia has built through its mission-driven retail presence (Place). Thus, the marketing mix functions as a coherent evidentiary system.

A deconstructed marketing mix (the 4Ps)

- **Product:** The product itself is the most powerful manifestation of Patagonia's brand promise. It is the tangible proof that the company's commitment to sustainability is not just rhetoric.
- **Core Attributes:** The defining features of Patagonia's products are durability, multifunctionality, and repairability. These are deliberately positioned as primary environmental attributes, offering a direct challenge to the planned obsolescence model that drives much of the apparel industry. The company's Ironclad Guarantee, which promises to repair, replace, or refund any product that does not perform to satisfaction, underscores this commitment to longevity.
- **Sustainable Materials:** Patagonia has been a pioneer in the research, development, and adoption of high-cost, low-impact materials. This includes being an early adopter of organic cotton to avoid the devastating environmental impact of pesticides used in conventional cotton farming. Today, its material portfolio is a showcase of sustainable innovation, featuring Regenerative Organic Certified® cotton, which prioritises soil health; extensive use of recycled materials like polyester, nylon, down, and wool; and novel materials like NetPlus®, which is derived from 100% recycled fishing nets, directly addressing a major source of ocean plastic pollution. In Fiscal Year 2024, 73% of its apparel materials were from recycled sources, while only 16% were virgin petroleum-based.
- **Promotion:** Patagonia's promotional strategy is famously unconventional, often described as 'anti-marketing' because its primary goal is to build credibility and reinforce values rather than to drive short-term sales.
- **Iconic Campaigns:** The 'Don't Buy This Jacket' campaign is the quintessential example. By transparently detailing the environmental cost of producing one of its own products – requiring 135 litres of water and generating 20 pounds of carbon dioxide – the campaign educated consumers about the impact of their consumption and solidified Patagonia's position as a trustworthy, mission-driven brand. The subsequent 'Buy Less, Demand More' campaign furthered this ethos, encouraging consumers to demand higher standards of sustainability and labour ethics from the entire industry.
- **Content Marketing and Storytelling:** Rather than relying on traditional product advertising, Patagonia invests heavily in content marketing that educates and engages its community. This includes producing high-quality documentary films (such as Worn Wear Stories, which celebrates the longevity of its products), publishing books, and maintaining blogs and online platforms that focus on environmental activism and storytelling. This approach positions the brand as a thought leader and a hub for the environmental move-

ment, fostering a much deeper connection with its audience than transactional marketing ever could.

- **Price:** Patagonia's products command a significant price premium, a fact that is central to its strategic positioning and business model. This is not simply premium pricing based on perceived quality but can be more accurately described as 'value-reflective pricing'.
- **Justification of the Premium:** The high price internalises numerous costs that competitors often externalise or avoid altogether. This includes: the substantial investment in R&D for innovative, sustainable materials; the payment of Fair Trade premiums to factory workers to improve their livelihoods; the commitment to donate 1% of all sales to environmental non-profits through 1% for the Planet; and the fundamental cost of designing and manufacturing a product for maximum durability and longevity, not for disposability.
- **Connection to Value Proposition:** As illustrated in Figure 3.5 of Chapter 3, Patagonia firmly occupies the 'High Quality / High Price' quadrant. However, it has successfully expanded the definition of 'quality' beyond mere technical performance to encompass a rich tapestry of ethical, environmental, and social values. The price is a signal of this expanded value proposition, and its target customers understand and willingly pay for this comprehensive value.
- **Place (Distribution):** Patagonia's distribution channels are strategically designed to be more than just points of sale; they are extensions of the brand identity and crucial touchpoints for community engagement.
- **Curated Retail Environments:** Patagonia's physical stores are intentionally designed as community hubs. They host film screenings, guest speakers, and workshops focused on environmental activism and outdoor skills, transforming the retail space into a gathering place for like-minded individuals. Furthermore, the product assortment is often tailored to the local environment and community needs – for instance, featuring more surf equipment in coastal California stores and more snow gear in Colorado.
- **Direct-to-Consumer (DTC) Focus:** A robust e-commerce platform and direct sales channels are critical to Patagonia's strategy. This DTC focus allows the company to maintain complete control over its brand narrative, customer data, and the overall customer experience, avoiding the brand dilution that can occur through third-party retailers. It also facilitates a direct line of communication for its activism and educational content.

Section 3: Strategic management accounting – beyond conventional costing

Patagonia's unique positioning necessitates an approach to management accounting that transcends conventional models. The company's mission is fundamentally incompatible with frameworks built solely around profit maximisation. Instead, Patagonia's practices reflect a sophisticated application of strategic management accounting, where accounting serves to operationalise its ethical commitments.

A critique of traditional models in practice

Patagonia's business model is a practical rejection of the assumptions of both neoclassical and traditional accounting pricing models.

1. Rejecting Neoclassical Economics: The neoclassical model, which posits profit maximisation as the primary objective, is wholly inadequate to explain Patagonia's behaviour. The company's decision-making is guided by purpose maximisation. This was made clear in 2022 when the Chouinard family transferred 100% of the company's ownership to two new entities, the Patagonia Purpose Trust and the Holdfast Collective. This structure legally mandates that any profit not reinvested back into the business must be distributed as a dividend to fight the climate crisis. This act is the ultimate repudiation of shareholder profit maximisation. For Patagonia, profit is a vital means to fund its environmental mission, not the end goal.
2. Rejecting Cost-Plus Pricing: Similarly, the conventional accounting model of cost-plus pricing (Price = Cost + Profit Margin) is antithetical to Patagonia's approach. Its prices are not determined by starting with internal costs. Instead, its prices are 'pulled' from the market, reflecting the value its target segment places on the brand's ethical proposition. The company's high costs—driven by sustainable materials and Fair Trade premiums—are a deliberate consequence of its strategic commitment, reversing the logic of the traditional cost-plus formula.

Lifecycle costing embodied

Patagonia's business philosophy is a powerful, real-world manifestation of the principles of lifecycle costing, extending the concept beyond mere financial calculation to encompass the full environmental and social lifecycle of its products.

- Pre-production Phase: This phase is characterised by significant, long-term investment in research and development aimed at creating and sourcing innovative, low-impact materials and processes. This includes funding agricultural transitions to Regenerative Organic Certified® practices and developing new recycling technologies, costs that are incurred years before a product generates revenue but are essential to the brand's value proposition.
- Production Phase: The costs in this phase are intentionally elevated to reflect the company's values. Material costs are higher due to the use of recycled and organic inputs. Labour costs are also higher, as Patagonia pays premiums to its suppliers who are Fair Trade Certified, ensuring that a portion of

the product's cost is returned directly to workers to improve their wages and community facilities.

- Post-production Phase (The '4 R's'): Patagonia's commitment extends far beyond the point of sale. The company strategically manages the product's end-of-life through its comprehensive '4 R's' programme: Reduce, Repair, Reuse, and Recycle. The Worn Wear programme, which facilitates the trade-in and resale of used gear, and the company's extensive repair services (the largest garment repair facility in North America) represent significant operational costs. However, these are not viewed as mere expenses but as strategic investments that reinforce product longevity, reduce waste, and build profound customer loyalty. This turns a potential waste stream and environmental liability into a value-generating, brand-affirming ecosystem.

A 'pull' strategy for a better world: target costing reimagined

Viewed through the lens of target costing, Patagonia's model exemplifies a sophisticated 'pull strategy'. However, it adapts the framework to serve its dual mission of commercial viability and social responsibility.

The Process:

- Target Price: The process begins with the market. The target price is what Patagonia's psychographically defined market segment is willing to pay for a product that delivers superior performance, extreme durability, and, crucially, verifiable environmental and ethical integrity.
- Target Profit: The target profit is the margin required to ensure the company's long-term financial health, fund its continuous innovation, and generate the dividends that now flow entirely to its environmental mission.
- Target Cost: The resulting allowable cost, calculated as Target Price - Target Profit, becomes the strategic challenge for Patagonia's product designers, material scientists, and supply chain partners. The goal is to engineer a product that meets this cost target while upholding the brand's uncompromising quality and sustainability standards.

A critical aspect of this interpretation is how Patagonia addresses the potential dark side of target costing. As Chapter 3 warns, the relentless pressure to meet a target cost can be transmitted down the supply chain, leading to exploitative labour practices and "despotism in the factory ". Patagonia's 'Responsible Purchasing Practices' (RPP) programme is a direct and explicit management system designed to counteract this very risk. The RPP framework institutionalises collaboration with suppliers, mandating fair payment terms, realistic lead times, and a shared responsibility for social and environmental outcomes. This represents a conscious attempt to re-engineer the target costing dynamic – to achieve demanding cost and quality goals without externalising the social costs onto the most vulnerable workers in the supply chain.

This application of management accounting frameworks suggests a significant evolution in their purpose. Where lifecycle costing traditionally serves to minimise total financial cost, Patagonia's model is reoriented to minimise total environmental and social harm, accepting higher financial outlays to achieve this. Similarly, where target costing is often a mechanism for exerting downward price pressure, Patagonia's framework attempts to achieve cost targets without compromising worker welfare. This re-frames management accounting from a purely technical, value-neutral discipline into one with profound moral and social dimensions, used not just for financial control but as a framework for enacting ethical commitments.

Section 4: performance and paradox – the financials of a mission-driven business

A central question for any business model, however noble its mission, is its ability to deliver sustainable performance. In Patagonia's case, performance must be assessed through a dual lens: its financial viability and its effectiveness in fulfilling its environmental and social objectives. The company presents a compelling, though not uncritical, case that purpose and profit are not mutually exclusive but can be mutually reinforcing. This section examines Patagonia's financial and non-financial performance, while also addressing the inherent paradoxes and critiques that arise from being a large, for-profit entity dedicated to an anti-consumerist mission.

Quantifying the 'return on purpose'

Patagonia's financial track record provides strong evidence that its sustainability-led strategy is commercially successful. The company has demonstrated robust and consistent revenue growth, with sales reportedly quadrupling over the decade leading up to 2019 to exceed $1 billion annually. Its overall valuation is estimated to be around $3 billion. Perhaps the most striking evidence of the financial power of its brand positioning was the aftermath of its 2011 'Don't Buy This Jacket' campaign. In a seemingly paradoxical outcome, the company's revenues grew by approximately 30% to $543 million in 2012, demonstrating that its message of conscious consumption resonated deeply with its target market and translated into increased loyalty and sales.

Table 2: Key sustainability performance indicators (financial & non-financial)

Performance Area	Key Metric	FY23 Data	FY24 Data
Financial Giving	Cumulative 1% for the Planet Donations (since 1985)	$212,000,000	$226,000,000
	Fair Trade Premiums Paid to Workers (since 2014)	$26,184,897	$32,262,384
Material Sourcing	% of Apparel Materials from Recycled Sources	73%	73%
	% of Products Made without PFC/PFAS Chemicals	86%	97%
Energy	% of Global Owned/Operated Electricity from Renewable Sources	61%	98%
Labour Practices	% of Products Made in a Fair Trade Certified™ Factory	87%	88%
	Factory Workers Earning a Fair Trade Premium	86,696	82,815
Circularity	Number of Garments Repaired Worldwide	153,506	145,446
	Metric Tons of Recycled Fishing Nets Used (NetPlus)	1,419	2,000

Note: Data is extracted from Patagonia's Annual Benefit Corporation Report for Fiscal Years 2023 and 2024.

This financial success is mirrored by its strong non-financial performance, which is rigorously tracked and independently verified through its status as a Certified B Corporation. The B Corp framework assesses a company's social and environmental performance across multiple domains. In its 2023 recertification, Patagonia achieved a global B Corp score of 166, a significant increase from its previous scores and far exceeding the median score of 50.9 for ordinary businesses and the minimum passing score of 80. This high score is substantiated by a wide range of key performance indicators that quantify its commitment to its mission.

The inherent contradiction: critiques and greenwashing allegations

Despite its impressive performance metrics and widespread acclaim, Patagonia is not immune to criticism. Its position as a large, profitable, global corporation dedicated to sustainability creates inherent tensions that lead to credible allegations of paradox and greenwashing.

1. **The Scale Paradox:** The most fundamental critique is that a billion-dollar company, regardless of its intentions, is an engine of consumption. Its global

supply chain, manufacturing processes, and international shipping all contribute to a significant carbon footprint and resource depletion. Critics argue that the very act of producing and selling new products, even durable and recycled ones, is fundamentally at odds with a message of reducing consumption. The company's growth, in this view, inevitably contributes to the environmental problems it claims to be solving.

2. **The Labour Critique:** While Patagonia is a leader in implementing Fair Trade standards, it has faced criticism for not yet achieving a verifiable living wage for all workers across its entire complex global supply chain. This highlights the immense difficulty of ensuring social equity within the prevailing structures of global capitalism, where pressure to manage costs remains a reality. For some critics, anything less than a guaranteed living wage for every worker represents a compromise of its ethical positioning, suggesting that the company's profitability is still, in part, built on the low wages endemic to the apparel industry.
3. **The 'Greenwashing' Charge:** Patagonia has also faced specific accusations of greenwashing, where its marketing messages are seen as exaggerating its positive impact. A notable instance occurred in France, where an advertising ethics jury upheld a complaint against the company for a press release that claimed its clothing made from recycled materials "protect the oceans". The jury ruled that this message was disproportionate and could mislead the public, arguing that while the practice helps reduce pollution, it does not in itself "protect" the oceans. This case illustrates the fine line between communicating genuine efforts and making claims that overstate their effect.

Patagonia's defence and the nature of 'imperfect' progress

In response to these critiques, Patagonia's leaders have consistently adopted a stance of transparency and humility. They are often the first to admit the company's imperfections and the unavoidable environmental and social impacts associated with manufacturing and selling products. Their defence is not a claim of environmental purity but a commitment to a continuous journey of harm reduction. Initiatives like the 'Footprint Chronicles' on their website, which trace the supply chain and environmental impact of individual products, are designed to provide a high degree of transparency. The company frames its work not as having found all the answers, but as being relentlessly committed to asking the hard questions and striving for better solutions, positioning itself as a work-in-progress rather than a finished model of sustainability.

Conclusion: key learnings and discussion points

Synthesis of the case

Patagonia provides a powerful case study in the integration of sustainability into business strategy, with profound implications for pricing and management accounting. It demonstrates that a market-driven 'pull' strategy, rooted in a deep understanding of a segment's values, can successfully support a premium price point and deliver exceptional financial performance. The company's success is built on constructing a complex value proposition where the price reflects a bundle of tangible benefits (durability) and intangible attributes (environmental stewardship, social ethics).

The case serves as a living critique of traditional accounting and economic models. Patagonia's purpose-maximisation objective and 'value-reflective' pricing cannot be explained by frameworks that assume profit maximisation. Furthermore, it offers a practical illustration of how strategic management accounting techniques can be adapted. Lifecycle costing is expanded from a tool for financial optimisation to a framework for managing total environmental and social impact. Target costing is reimagined, pairing the market-driven 'pull' for a competitive price with a programme designed to mitigate negative social externalities. Patagonia challenges students to see management accounting not as a static set of procedures, but as a dynamic tool that can serve a broader strategic and ethical mission.

Comprehensive discussion questions for students

Connecting to theory:

1. Using the critiques from Chapter 3, explain why Patagonia's pricing strategy cannot be adequately explained by the neoclassical economic model or the conventional cost-plus accounting model.
2. How does Patagonia's '4 R's' philosophy represent a practical application of the 'product costing' perspective of lifecycle costing? What costs are being managed at the pre-production, production, and post-production phases?
3. Analyse Patagonia's business model using the 'Target Costing Triangle' (Figure 3.7). Who are the key actors, and how does Patagonia's approach attempt to manage the potential negative social consequences of target costing?

Strategic and financial analysis:

4. Deconstruct the value proposition of a Patagonia jacket (referencing Figure 3.5). What tangible and intangible benefits are customers paying for? How does this justify its premium price compared to a competitor?

5. Patagonia's revenue grew significantly after its 'Don't Buy This Jacket' campaign. From a strategic pricing and positioning perspective, explain this paradoxical outcome.
6. Examine the KPIs in Table 2. As a management accountant for Patagonia, how would you argue that investments in sustainability generate a positive financial return? What are the challenges in measuring this 'Return on Purpose'?

Critical thinking and ethical debate:

7. Critically evaluate the 'greenwashing' allegations against Patagonia. Is it possible for a billion-dollar global company to be genuinely sustainable, or is 'sustainable consumption' an oxymoron?
8. The chapter warns that target costing can lead to 'despotism in the factory'. Despite its 'Responsible Purchasing Practices', critics point to a lack of a universal living wage in Patagonia's supply chain. Does this invalidate their ethical positioning?
9. In 2022, the Chouinard family transferred ownership of the company to a trust, making 'earth its only shareholder'. What are the strategic and accounting implications of a structure where all profit is legally mandated for environmental causes? How does this alter the concept of 'performance'?
10. If you were a competitor, how would you attempt to compete with Patagonia? What are the biggest barriers to imitating its business model?

Chapter review questions

Part I: Traditional Pricing Models: Principles and Critiques

1. According to the neoclassical economic model of pricing, a firm achieves profit maximisation where:
   a. Total revenue is maximised and total cost is minimised.
   b. The selling price is set at the highest point on the demand curve.
   c. Marginal revenue equals marginal cost (MR=MC).
   d. Average cost per unit is at its lowest point.
2. A primary critique of the neoclassical economic model from a strategic management perspective is that it:
   a. Fails to provide a mathematically rigorous formula for calculating the optimal price.
   b. Assumes firms operate with limited strategic agency, passively reacting to market structures.
   c. Overemphasises the role of overhead costs in determining the final selling price.
   d. Cannot be applied in markets that are not perfectly competitive.
3. In the conventional accounting model of cost-plus pricing, the most significant technical challenge is typically:
   a. Accurately forecasting the total number of units to be sold.
   b. Calculating direct material and direct labour costs with precision.
   c. Determining the appropriate profit margin to add to the full cost.
   d. The allocation and absorption of organisational overheads to specific cost units.
4. The cost-plus pricing model can create a perverse incentive structure because:
   a. a. It requires complex information systems that are costly to maintain.
   b. b. By calculating profit as a percentage of cost, it can financially reward internal inefficiencies.
   c. c. It legally prevents a firm from pricing below its full cost.
   d. d. Its focus on historical costs makes it unsuitable for industries with high technological change.

Part II: The Strategic pricing framework: segmentation, targeting, and positioning (STP)

5. A new company is launching a range of premium, ethically sourced, organic food products. Its marketing communications emphasise a healthy, environmentally conscious lifestyle. Which would be the most relevant primary basis for segmenting its market?

   a. Geographic, based on urban versus rural population density.
   b. b. Demographic, based on age and family size.
   c. c. Psychographic, based on consumer lifestyles, activities, interests, and opinions (AIO).
   d. d. Behavioural, based on occasion orientation.

6. According to the chapter, which of the following lists best represents the key criteria for selecting a target segment?

   a. a. The segment must be historical, global, predictable, and aligned with the company's mission.
   b. b. The segment must be substantial, identifiable, reachable, profitable, and responsive.
   c. c. The segment must be homogenous, easily divisible, and accessible through mass media.
   d. d. The segment must be temporary, defined by competitors, and require minimal marketing expenditure.

7. A luxury watchmaker has developed a new timepiece using rare materials (Product), plans to sell it exclusively through high-end boutiques (Place), and promote it in elite lifestyle magazines (Promotion). Which pricing strategy would be inconsistent with its overall positioning?

   a. Setting a premium price to signal exclusivity.
   b. Using market skimming by launching with a very high price.
   c. Adopting a market penetration strategy with a low introductory price.
   d. Employing psychological pricing where the price ends in '000' to connote prestige.

Part III: Advanced costing for strategic pricing

8. When used as an asset management technique, lifecycle costing is adopted from the viewpoint of the:

   a. Producer, to calculate the total cost of bringing a product to market.
   b. Regulator, to ensure the firm is not engaging in anti-competitive pricing.

   c. Purchaser, to evaluate the total cost of owning, operating, and disposing of an asset.
   d. Competitor, to estimate the cost structure of a rival's product.

9. A firm is considering a significant upfront investment in sustainable materials. This would increase pre-production costs but substantially reduce end-of-life disposal costs for customers. Which costing technique provides the most suitable framework for justifying this strategic investment?

   a. Activity-based costing.
   b. Cost-plus pricing.
   c. Lifecycle costing.
   d. Neoclassical marginal analysis.

10. Target costing represents a fundamental shift from traditional approaches. Its logic is best described as a:

    a. 'Push' strategy, where internal costs are calculated and then 'pushed' onto the market.
    b. 'Pull' strategy, where a competitive market price is the starting point from which the 'target cost' is derived.
    c. 'Standstill' strategy, where costs are locked in at the design phase.
    d. 'Cost-averaging' strategy, where costs are averaged across all products.

11. As conceptualised by Cooper and Slagmulder (1997), the 'survival zone' is defined by the interplay of which three critical variables?

    a. Market share, return on investment, and cost of capital.
    b. Price, product quality, and product functionalities.
    c. Supplier power, customer power, and competitive rivalry.
    d. Direct costs, overhead costs, and administrative costs.

12. Within the 'target costing triangle', the system that facilitates intense collaboration with component manufacturers is referred to as:

    a. Market-driven costing.
    b. Value engineering.
    c. Inter-organisational costing.
    d. Product-level target costing.

13. Under a target costing regime, the majority of cost reduction is achieved during which phase?

    a. During the manufacturing process, through continuous improvement (kaizen).

b. During the post-production phase, by minimising warranty costs.
c. During the pre-production phase, through proactive value engineering and product design.
d. During the distribution phase, by optimising logistics.

Part IV: Contemporary Pricing Strategies and Broader Implications

14. A primary reason a firm might choose not to implement a sophisticated dynamic pricing system is the significant risk of:

    a. Violating patent laws held by competitors.
    b. Facing technical challenges related to data storage.
    c. Damaging brand equity due to negative customer perceptions of fairness.
    d. Incurring excessively high R&D costs to develop the software.

15. The sustainability implications of target costing are described as paradoxical because the system can:

    a. Simultaneously increase a product's energy efficiency while reducing its recyclability.
    b. Promote sustainable materials while also transmitting cost-reduction pressures that may lead to exploitative labour practices.
    c. Reduce carbon emissions during production but increase emissions during transportation.
    d. Help firms comply with environmental regulations in one country but circumvent them in another.

Comprehension questions

1. Provide a brief explanation of the neoclassical economic model of pricing.
2. What are the primary weaknesses of the neoclassical economic model of pricing?
3. Briefly outline the conventional accounting model of pricing.
4. Identify the most challenging element of the conventional accounting model of pricing, and discuss how activity-based costing improves this aspect.
5. Enumerate the critical weaknesses of the conventional accounting model of pricing.
6. Explain strategic positioning as the primary objective of strategic pricing.
7. List the three critical elements of strategic pricing.
8. Briefly describe the four principal bases for segmenting a market, with examples.
9. Enumerate the key parameters for developing a market segmentation profile.
10. List the criteria for selecting a market segment for targeting.

11. Explain the concept of 'positioning' using the questions of what, where, and how.
12. In relation to the 'value proposition', explain the strategic role of price.
13. Illustrate the use of 'psychological pricing' with specific examples.
14. Differentiate between market penetration and market skimming pricing.
15. Distinguish the use of lifecycle costing as an asset management technique and as a product costing technique.
16. As a product costing technique, provide the generic formula for calculating lifecycle cost and price.
17. Differentiate target costing from conventional costing techniques.
18. Briefly explain the concept of a survival zone.
19. Outline the target costing triangle, emphasising:

    a. key parties integrated,
    b. key strategic capabilities developed, and
    c. specific systems that facilitate integration.

20. Briefly explain the key stages of the target costing process.
21. Briefly explain the practice of dynamic pricing, paying special attention to the centrality of technology.

Explore further

1. Investigate the product development, promotion, and pricing strategies in the toothpaste market, considering:

    a. segmentation based on benefits sought (e.g., whitening, sensitivity),
    b. the design of promotions based on these themes, and
    c. the manifestation of segmentation variables in product design.

2. Visit the European Commission website pages on lifecycle costing and Green Public Procurement (GPP), exploring:

    a. guiding principles,
    b. conditions under which it is mandated,
    c. prescribed administrative procedures, and
    d. its contribution to the global sustainability agenda.

3. Read Robin Cooper and Regine Slagmulder's book, ***Target Costing and Value Engineering***, to explore case studies on the techno-managerial core of target costing.
4. Read the report 'Discrimination, Artificial Intelligence and Algorithms' published by the Council of Europe (Borgesius, 2018).

Summarise the key ethical and legal challenges of using AI in business decisions, including dynamic pricing.

Develop your critical argumentation skills

1. Craft an argumentative essay on each of the following themes:

   'Contemporary competitive conditions demand a more sophisticated and market-driven approach to pricing than what neoclassical economic and accounting models offer.'

   'Target costing is not merely a technique for determining product costs but a comprehensive profit management system connecting customers, product designers, and suppliers.'

   'Concerning sustainability, target costing can address certain issues positively but may also contribute to social injustice, including despotic labour controls and modern slavery.'

2. Write an exploratory essay articulating the techno-managerial and legal-ethical issues of using dynamic pricing.

Mini case study

GreenGig Product Development and Pricing Strategy: An Illustrative Case Study in Lifecycle Costing

This hypothetical case elucidates concepts such as limiting factor analysis, lifecycle costing, and target return pricing.

ABC Plc, a high-tech chemical company, has historically relied on patent rights for its market success. These rights confer a temporary monopoly, shaping a culture that emphasises significant investment in R&D. R&D expenses, a substantial element of corporate overheads, have risen notably. Despite the cost, this has positioned ABC Plc as a profitable industry leader. With a global presence, ABC Plc employs approximately 60,000 people. Its recent financial performance indicated a 20% increase in pre-tax profits, representing 35% of turnover.

The strategic challenge for ABC Plc is sustaining R&D to launch new products as older patents expire. Approximately 30% of revenue has been derived from one product over the last four years. As its underlying technology loses its edge, sales are expected to decline sharply. To address this, a new product, GreenGig, has completed development and is poised for global marketing. Product testing has demonstrated it is 200% more technically efficient than the best competitor product (GifChem), providing a superior competitive advantage.

The retail market price of a one-litre can of GifChem is £12.00. It is understood that GifChem's bought-in cost for the retailer is £9.00 per can. GreenGig's total activity costs (excluding R&D and other overheads) of taking the product to the retailer are estimated to be £3.00 per litre. However, the new product must be sold in 1.5-litre cans, as the recommended use quantity is 1.5 times larger than that of GifChem.

Availability of shelf space is a critical limiting factor for most retailers. The shelf area occupied by each can of GifChem is 18 square centimetres, while that of GreenGig is 24 square centimetres. The holding cost for the retailer is estimated as £0.40 per can for GifChem and £0.50 per can for GreenGig. Market analysis indicates that the average weekly sales volume for retail outlets stocking both products will be 120 cans of GreenGig and 20 cans of GifChem, provided that GreenGig offers retailers a better contribution per unit of limited shelf space.

ABC Plc has invested £20 million in R&D for GreenGig, with an additional £5 million committed for further refinement over the next five years. Annual marketing and other overhead costs attributable to the product are estimated at £4 million. None of these costs have been absorbed into the £3.00 per litre variable cost.

The Marketing Director has proposed two alternative strategic directions: a 'supreme value' strategy and a 'supreme quality' strategy. Under the **supreme value strategy**, the GreenGig retail price will be in the range of £12 to £15 per 1.5-litre can. The marketing mix will convey that customers get superior quality for a competitive price. The **supreme quality strategy** will set the retail price much higher (in the range of £15 to £18 per 1.5-litre can). The marketing mix will convey that the product is costly but extremely superior.

Demand and market share forecasts under each strategy are as follows:

	Supreme Value Strategy	Supreme Quality Strategy
	Sales (Litres)	Sales (Litres)
Year 1	800,000	700,000
Year 2	1,200,000	1,100,000
Year 3	1,500,000	1,300,000
Year 4	1,400,000	1,300,000
Year 5	1,000,000	900,000
Year 6	50,000	30,000
Total for six years	5,950,000	5,330,000

Required:

1. Explain the company's strategic scenario using relevant concepts, such as the product life cycle and the BCG growth-share matrix.
2. Explain the two strategic options using Porter's framework of generic strategies.
3. Calculate the minimum contribution per can that GreenGig must offer the retailer to ensure that retailers prefer shelving GreenGig over GifChem. (Hint: carry out a limiting factor analysis using shelf space as the limiting factor).
4. The company requires a 30% return on investment over the total expenditures on the product over its six-year lifespan. The company wishes to replace the product in year six and anticipates no decommissioning costs. Calculate the minimum average selling price per litre for each strategy required to meet this target rate of return. The company management does not wish to consider the time value of money. (Hint: use lifecycle costing combined with target return pricing).
5. Based on your calculations, which strategy should the company adopt for GreenGig? Justify your answer.

References

Ahmed, S., M. A. Islam, and J. S. Islam. (2023, forthcoming). ***Modern slavery in the tea supply chain: Interdisciplinary insights and the role of accounting.*** Abingdon: Routledge.

Borgesius, F. Z. (2018). ***Discrimination, artificial intelligence and algorithms.*** Strasbourg: Directorate General of Democracy - Council of Europe.

Burawoy, M. (1983). Between the Labor Process and the State: The Changing Face of Factory Regimes Under Advanced Capitalism. *American Sociological Review, 48*(5), 587-605.

Christ, K. L., and Burritt, R. L. (2021). Accounting for modern slavery risk in the time of COVID-19: challenges and opportunities. *Accounting, Auditing & **Accountability** Journal, 34*(6), 1484-1501.

Christ, K. L., Burritt, R. L., and Schaltegger, S. (2020). Accounting for work conditions from modern slavery to decent work. *Accounting, Auditing & Accountability Journal, 33*(7), 1481-1504.

Christ, K. L., Rao, K. K., and Burritt, R. L. (2019). Accounting for modern slavery: an analysis of Australian listed company disclosures. *Accounting, Auditing & Accountability Journal, 32*(3), 836-865.

Cooper, R., and Slagmulder, R. (1997). ***Target costing and value engineering.*** Portland: Productivity Press.

Crane, A. (2013). Modern Slavery as A Management Practice: Exploring the Conditions and Capabilities for Human Exploitation. *The Academy of Management Review, 38*(1), 49-69.

Crane, A., LeBaron, G., Phung, K., Behbahani, L., and Allain, J. (2022). Confronting the Business Models of Modern Slavery. *Journal of Management Inquiry, 31*(3), 264-285.

Crowther, S., and Ford, H. (2015). *My Life and Work.* Mansfield Centre: Martino Publishing.

Islam, M. A., and Van Staden, C. J. (2022). Modern Slavery Disclosure Regulation and Global Supply Chains: Insights from Stakeholder Narratives on the UK Modern Slavery Act. *Journal of Business Ethics, 180*(2), 455-479.

Neu, D., Rahaman, A. S., and Everett, J. (2014). Accounting and Sweatshops: Enabling Coordination and Control in Low-Price Apparel Production Chains. *Contemporary Accounting Research, 31*(2), 322-346.

New, S. J. (2015). Modern slavery and the supply chain: the limits of corporate social responsibility? *Supply Chain Management: An International Journal, 20*(6), 697-707.

Porter, M. E. (1985). *Competitive Advantage: Creating and Sustaining Superior Performance.* New York: The Free Press.

CHAPTER

4

Strategy in the hierarchy: **strategising performance**

4.1 Introduction

As previous chapters emphasised, firms enact strategies within three interconnected domains: markets, organisational hierarchies, and labour processes. Those chapters explored the market and industrial dynamics of strategising, focusing on competitive positioning and related calculative practices such as lifecycle costing, target costing, and dynamic pricing.

The next three chapters examine how strategies unfold within organisational hierarchies to link markets with labour processes through performance management and management control. This chapter examines performance management; the next two address strategising management control and organisational resilience. Performance management, management control, and organisational resilience are inseparable, overlapping themes of strategising. For analytical clarity, they are addressed in separate chapters, allowing a focused examination of specific management accounting frameworks.

This chapter examines performance management by addressing two fundamental questions: what is performance, and how is it managed? The answers depend on the approach taken: traditional or strategic. This chapter is structured around three themes:

1. The traditional approach to managing performance: This section explores the philosophies, concepts, and techniques of the traditional approach. Understanding this approach provides a basis for comparison with strategic approaches, highlighting the weaknesses the latter seeks to rectify.

2. A strategic approach to managing performance: This section explores the philosophies, concepts, and techniques of the strategic approach, primarily based on the Balanced Scorecard (BSC) framework. It examines how this approach addresses the perceived weaknesses of the traditional model and also examines potential drawbacks.
3. Sustainability implications of performance management: Finally, the chapter examines how contemporary strategic approaches to performance management address broader social and ecological justice issues.

Upon completing this chapter, readers should have a critical understanding of traditional and strategic performance management and their sustainability implications.

4.2 Conceptualising performance

To understand performance management, we must first define performance. Performing differs from simply doing, acting, or producing. We engage in many activities: reading, studying, singing, dancing, and running. In the workplace, employees perform tasks ranging from writing and cleaning to specialised duties like data entry, order processing, and machine operation. They also engage in managerial and clerical activities, such as creating reports and making decisions. These activities are integral to work but do not necessarily constitute performance.

For actions to become performance, they or their outcomes must be goal-directed and subject to observation, evaluation, and judgment. One might sing or dance alone; this is not performing. If these actions occur on a television programme like ***Britain's Got Talent*** to win a prize, they become performances: they are goal-directed and subject to evaluation. In university, students read, attend lectures, and study; examinations transform these actions into performances. Assessed and graded classroom presentations are performances. Similarly, when managerial decisions and their outcomes are assessed and ranked, they become performance outcomes.

Thus, *performances are goal-directed actions, behaviours, and outcomes subject to observation, evaluation, and judgment.* These evaluations lead to accreditations, rankings, financial and non-financial rewards, and punishments. Performance is thus the basis for distributing status, opportunities, resources, and power.

Performance is context-specific. How actions, behaviours, and their outcomes are conceptualised, evaluated, and rewarded depends on the specific political, legal, and socio-cultural context. Therefore, expected performance is also context-specific. Performance management sets context-specific parameters for how individual or collective actions, personal attributes (such as skills and knowledge), and their outcomes are directed, assessed, and rewarded. University marking schemes, for example, specify how student performance is assessed and rewarded. Similarly, corporate performance management systems should specify how individual, departmental, and corporate performances relate to organisational goals and are measured and rewarded.

The context-specificity of performance management arises from:

1. **The entity being managed:** This can range from individuals and groups to corporations, nations, and transnational bodies like the UN, World Bank, and IMF.
2. **The nature of observation:** Performance can be assessed through objective measures (e.g., units produced, task completion speed) or subjective narratives.
3. **The basis of legitimacy:** The authority to evaluate performance may be legal, institutional, economic, political, or cultural-religious.

With these variations, performance signifies how an entity contributes to a larger schema or set of higher-order principles. These principles include, for example, productivity, efficiency, profitability, quality, competitiveness, innovation, corporate vision, well-being, sustainability, and global peace. These principles define the schema towards which performance is directed. Performance, then, is the extent and manner of one's contribution to these principles. Performance management assesses how an entity contributes to a relevant set of higher-order principles. In a corporate setting, these principles are communicated through the mission, vision, goals, and key performance indicators (KPIs).

Performance is a hybrid of the actual and the expected. Performance is what people produce from their actions, which is then assessed against predetermined expectations embedded, for example, in goals, targets, standards, and regulations. These institutionalise the expectations of dominant organisational actors. Performance is the degree to which one's actions meet these institutionalised expectations. As Figure 4.1 illustrates, performance management seeks to enhance the overlap between the actual and the desired.

Figure 4.1: Key elements of performance

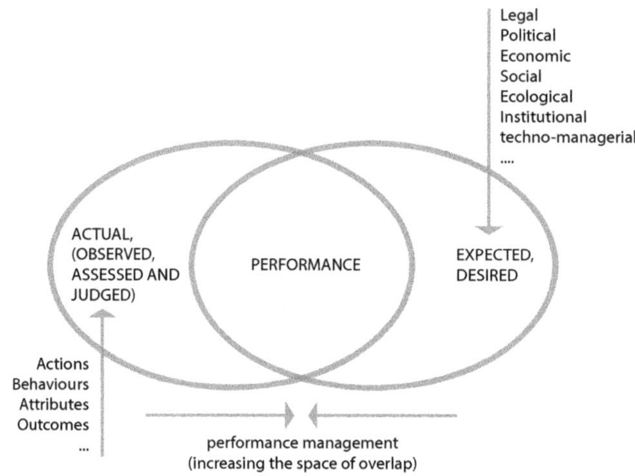

4.3 The traditional approach to performance management: responsibility accounting

The traditional approach to performance management is based on 'responsibility accounting'. Developed over centuries in Western organisations, responsibility accounting institutionalises accounting calculations in performance management by translating techno-managerial centres of performance into accountability centres. For instance, a machine workshop managed by engineers is redefined as an accountability centre for which specific accounting calculations are prescribed to assess performance.

The philosophy behind responsibility accounting has three main points:

1. **Hierarchy of Accountability Centres:** To manage performance, different sites of organisational activity are redefined as specific types of responsibility centres: cost, revenue, profit, and investment. This ensures their performance becomes the responsibility of their managers. These centres are hierarchically organised, from cost centres at the bottom to investment centres at the top.
2. **Accounting Calculations:** Each centre's performance is defined by a specific set of accounting calculations, hierarchically arranged in line with the responsibility centres. These calculations, commonly managed through budgeting, standard costing, variance analysis, and ratio analysis, enable managers to assess whether investment centres achieve required returns and how other centres contribute.

3. **Concept of Controllability:** The manager of each centre should be held accountable only for performance under their direct control. Uncontrollable variances in cost, revenue, profit, and investment returns should be excluded when assessing a manager's performance.

Figure 4.2 and Table 4.1 summarise the accountability hierarchy that responsibility accounting constructs. Return on investment (ROI) occupies the pinnacle as the dominant higher-order principle, reflecting a capitalist logic of accumulation where all other centres are directed towards this end.

Figure 4.2: Accountability hierarchy in responsibility accounting

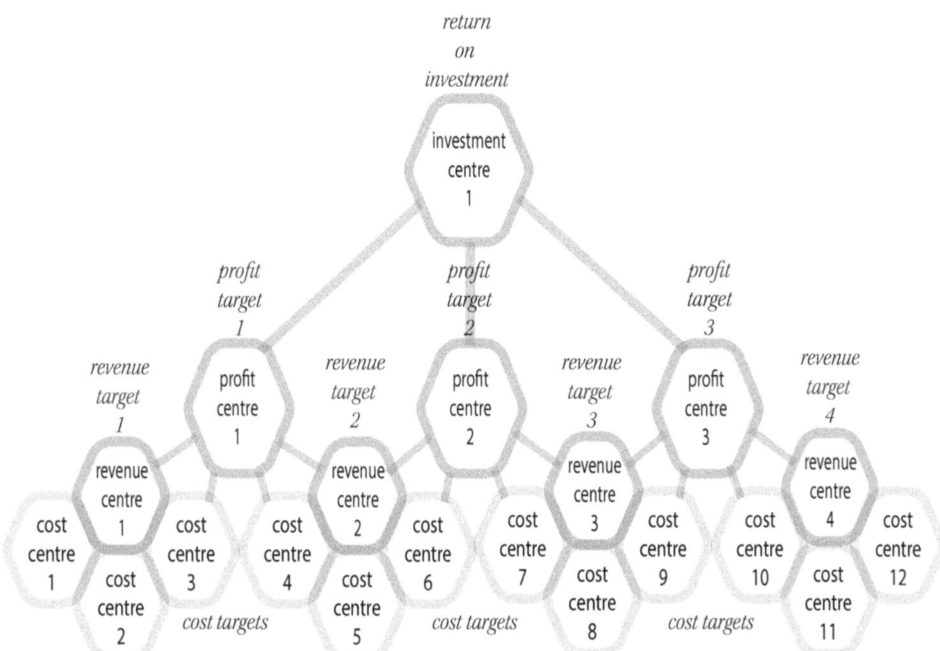

From operational to accounting logic

Organisational hierarchies are operational or techno-managerial before they become financial and accounting; they are techno-managerial arrangements for the division of work and supervision. In an automobile company, for example, work is divided based on engineering, administrative, and marketing functions, with divisions managed by experts in those operations. Similarly, a university's hierarchy is primarily academic, organised by disciplines and headed by experts in those fields. A hospital's hierarchy encompasses medical and administrative divisions.

Table 4.1: Responsibility accounting – accountability centres

Hierarchical element	Accountability focus	Popular techniques and measures
Cost centres	Performance is conceptualised and assessed through various cost measures. Often operates at the bottom of the operational hierarchy, performing basic activities that drive costs. In manufacturing, examples are workshops or machine centres.	Operational budgeting (material and labour usage, production). Enterprise resource planning schedules. Inventory control techniques. Standard costing and variance analysis.
Revenue centres	Performance is conceptualised and measured through various revenue measures. Represents departments responsible for selling and distributing goods or services. These centres connect to cost centres involved in production.	Operational budgeting (sales budget and variances). Sales growth rates. Market share statistics.
Profit centres	Performance is conceptualised and measured through various profit and profitability measures. Profit centres consolidate cost and revenue centres, making a manager responsible for their combined outcomes. They direct relevant cost and revenue centres to meet profit targets.	Master budgeting (budgeted profit and loss, balance sheet, cash flow). Profit variances. Profit margins (gross and net profit ratios).
Investment centres	Performances are measured through various investment efficiency criteria. These represent top-level management responsible for investment decisions for a set of profit centres, such as SBU managers and the board of directors.	Assessments of investment efficiency: Return on investment. Stock market performance. Costs of capital, discounted cash flows, internal rate of return, payback period. Return on total assets. Total assets turnover.

Responsibility accounting systems superimpose a financial logic and hierarchy over these non-accounting structures. They require that the non-accounting operational logic of running an organisation (e.g., production efficiency, innovation, patient care, research excellence, teaching excellence) is translated into financial measures so the company can be managed with the financial logic of return on investment. In this way, responsibility accounting imposes an accounting logic for managing organisations, assessing techno-managerial outcomes through accounting numbers.

Techniques and structure of responsibility accounting

This accounting logic is implemented through conventional management accounting techniques: budgeting, standard costing, and variance analysis, often supplemented by ratio analysis frameworks like the DuPont system. Collectively, these techniques institutionalise a hierarchical system of performance management by:

1. Establishing a system of planning where organisational activities are planned based on their contribution to profits and ROI. Budgeting is the fundamental tool, creating a hierarchy of calculations from operational budgets to master budgets.
2. Establishing a comparative basis against which actual performance is evaluated. Standard costing and variance analysis are critical here. Cost standards provide the basis for cost targets, serving as benchmarks. Variance analysis highlights deviations from the standard, enabling corrective action.
3. Conceptualising and operationalising capital accumulation as the primary purpose of the enterprise. These techniques make all other techno-managerial and social purposes secondary to capital accumulation.

As Figure 4.3 illustrates, these techniques create a hierarchy of accounting measures where profitability, especially ROI, occupies the pinnacle.

In a broader context, responsibility accounting is the traditional framework for performance management where performance is evaluated chiefly through financial metrics allocated to cost, revenue, profit, and investment centres. Standard costing, variance analysis, and budgeting are the primary planning and control techniques. Ratio analysis frameworks, such as the DuPont system, break down ROI to scrutinise how various accounting measures contribute to capital accumulation. The principles of responsibility accounting are outlined in Table 4.2.

Weaknesses of responsibility accounting

This traditional regime has faced various critiques with the advent of strategic discourses. The key issues are:

1. Responsibility accounting fosters excessively centralised organisations, often dominated by accountants who lack techno-managerial expertise.
2. Its emphasis on budgets and cost standards creates a rigid and inflexible accountability regime.
3. Operational inefficiencies arise because managers often incorporate 'budgetary slack' into their targets, overestimating costs and underestimating revenue to create a safety net.

Figure 4.3: Logic of responsibility accounting: a techno-managerial hierarchy of capital accumulation

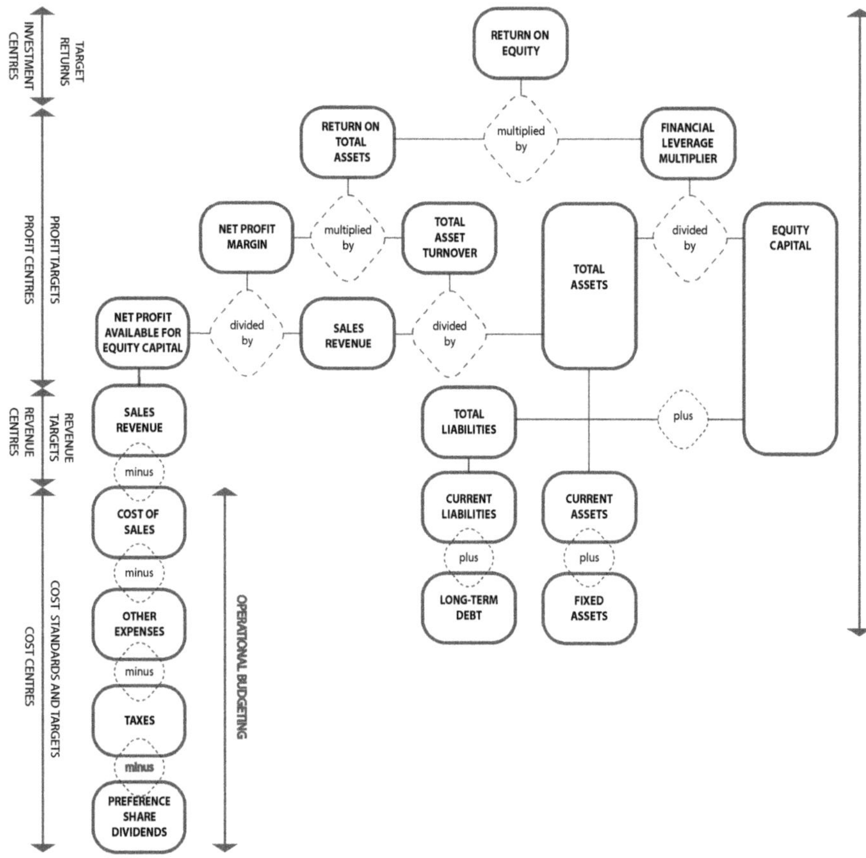

4. Because budgeting is the primary planning technique, managers often rely on incremental values from the previous period without adequately considering internal and external factors.
5. Most importantly, as argued by strategists like Robert Kaplan, responsibility accounting suffers from a lack of balance and strategic connection, which the next section will discuss.

4.4 Strategic performance management

In response to the strategic shift discussed in Chapter 1, performance management systems have developed significantly over recent decades. They aim to 'strategise' performance management by

1. imparting strategic meaning to performance and

Table 4.2: Responsibility accounting regimes of performance management: key themes

Theme	Description
Logic	Enhances operational efficiency as measured by accounting indicators. ROI is the ultimate measure of performance, with all other measures assessed on their contribution to it.
Structure	Redefines operational centres as cost, revenue, profit, and investment centres to construct a hierarchy of financial performance culminating in ROI.
Process	Defines standards and budgetary targets as the basis for assessing performance. Uses variance and ratio analysis to assess the degree to which targets are met.
Tools and Techniques	Primarily budgeting, standard costing, variance analysis, and the DuPont system, supported by other techniques such as CVP analysis and inventory control.

2. diversifying performance management beyond the narrow financial focus of conventional systems.

The most significant innovation in this regard is the 'Balanced Scorecard' (BSC) system, popularised by Kaplan and Norton (see Kaplan 2008; Kaplan and Norton 1993, 1996a, 1996b, 2000). This section explores the logic, concepts, and tools of strategic performance management, primarily based on the BSC.

While Kaplan and Norton's BSC is often hailed as the pioneer of multidimensional performance management, the concept is not new. As Cooper et al. (2017) explain, their positioning and networking were crucial to its global popularisation. However, many organisations had long recognised the multidimensional nature of corporate performance. Notably, the French performance management system, the ***tableau de bord***, introduced the concept of a 'dashboard' as early as the 1930s (see Bessire and Baker 2005; Bourguignon et al. 2004).

The logic of strategic performance management

As originally conceived by Kaplan and Norton, the logic of strategic performance management aims to rectify the narrow operational and financial focus of responsibility accounting. This is achieved by:

1. **Balancing** financial and non-financial dimensions of performance: Strategic performance management systems integrate multiple, strategically critical dimensions beyond conventional financial measures.

2. **Linking** the performance management system to corporate strategies: This is done by creating a 'cascading system of scorecards' that connects operational performance with strategic goals.

Balancing and cascading are the two pivotal actions underpinning Kaplan and Norton's BSC approach. Unlike the conventional focus on operational efficiency, strategic approaches broaden analytical attention to the multiple dimensions of strategic success. Strategic performance management entails establishing a system that encourages understanding the multiplicity of strategic priorities/objectives and their interconnections, devising strategies to contribute to these objectives, and assessing success in achieving strategic objectives.

Scorecards as fundamental building blocks

Scorecards are the fundamental building blocks of Kaplan and Norton's approach. Designed to replace budgets, scorecards are prepared for all managerial levels, from a corporate scorecard to individual scorecards. A key distinction is that budgets capture only financial dimensions, whereas scorecards provide an open template to incorporate multiple performance dimensions.

Scorecards are promoted as a flexible, simple, yet powerful tool for:

1. Identifying multiple dimensions for assessing performance, allowing managers to think beyond financial metrics.
2. Linking operational actions with corporate strategies and communicating these down the hierarchy.
3. Identifying how departments, groups, and individuals can contribute to corporate strategies through objectives related to their own operations.

Scorecards operate as a means of 'cascading' corporate objectives downward. Kaplan and Norton (1996b, 81) provide an example:

> The exploration group of a large oil company developed a technique to enable and encourage individuals to set goals for themselves that were consistent with the organisation's. It created a small, foldup personal scorecard that people could carry in their shirt pockets or wallets. ... The scorecard contains three levels of information. The first describes corporate objectives, measures, and targets. The second leaves room for translating corporate targets into targets for each business unit. For the third level, the company asks both individuals and teams to articulate which of their own objectives would be consistent with the business unit and corporate objectives, as well as what initiatives they would take to achieve their objectives. It also

asks them to define up to five performance measures for their objectives and to set targets for each measure. The personal scorecard helps to communicate corporate and business unit objectives to the people and teams performing the work, enabling them to translate the objectives into meaningful tasks and targets for themselves. It also lets them keep that information close at hand – in their pockets.

Proponents suggest scorecards should operate as a techno-managerial tool connecting individuals' and groups' daily operations to the corporation. Each scorecard embeds a hierarchical connection between the local and the corporate, incorporating the possibility of conceptualising performance in multiple dimensions, as Figure 4.4 illustrates.

Figure 4.4: Scorecards as a tool for strategic connections

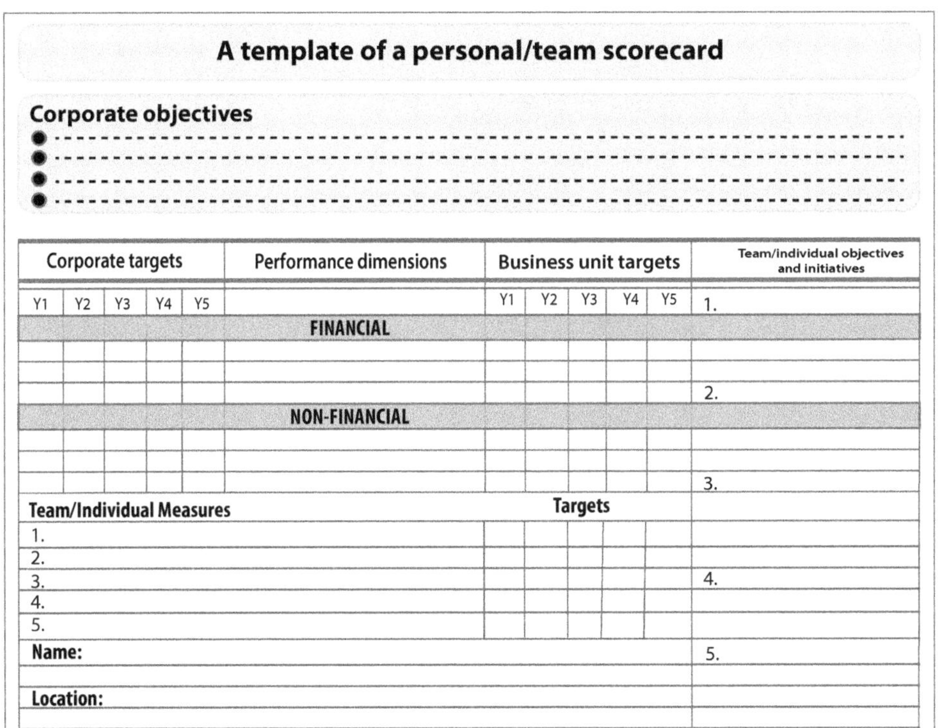

A template of a personal/team scorecard

Corporate objectives

Corporate targets					Performance dimensions	Business unit targets					Team/individual objectives and initiatives
Y1	Y2	Y3	Y4	Y5		Y1	Y2	Y3	Y4	Y5	1.
					FINANCIAL						
											2.
					NON-FINANCIAL						
											3.
Team/Individual Measures						Targets					
1.											
2.											
3.											4.
4.											
5.											
Name:											5.
Location:											

Source: based on Kaplan and Norton's various writings

If effectively mobilised, this template can wield significant influence by compelling organisational actors to consider measures imposed from above and determine how their actions can contribute. Scorecards offer a more flexible and personalised managerial space than budgets. However, they still embody a strong top-down approach; an individual's performance must always be framed within the parameters of higher-order strategies.

Strategic performance management as balancing

The BSC's popularity can be attributed to its proponents' claims that it can rectify the narrow financial focus of conventional management accounting by incorporating strategically critical non-financial dimensions. This is the 'balancing' aspect: achieving equilibrium between financial and non-financial measures.

For this purpose, Kaplan and Norton propose a framework for defining corporate performance in four key dimensions, each requiring separate 'key performance indicators' (KPIs). As Figure 4.5 illustrates, these four areas are identified as critical strategic questions, which Kaplan and Norton believe should clarify an organisation's strategic posture. The BSC is a strategic system because these questions and the resulting measures enhance the organisation's capacity to realise its strategies.

For Kaplan and Norton (1993, 1996a, 1996b, 2000), developing a strategic performance management system starts with organisational strategy, especially the corporate vision and mission. Using these as higher-order principles, they identify four 'critical performance dimensions' (financial, customer, internal business processes, and learning and growth), in which critical success factors must be identified. Critical success factors are the specific conditions firms must achieve to answer the four strategic questions successfully. For instance, a target ROI could be a critical success factor in the financial dimension. Similarly, value for money, quality management, and functional excellence can be critical success factors in the customer, internal business process, and learning and growth perspectives, respectively. These critical dimensions and success factors should then be incorporated into scorecards as measurements, targets, and initiatives.

Strategic performance management as cascading scorecards

The second strategising act the BSC promotes is linking operational actions with corporate strategies through the downward cascading of scorecards. Drawing on 'successful cases' from their consultancy, Kaplan and Norton propose a top-down approach to developing a chain of scorecards, from the corporate level to individual managers. They conceptualise this process into four key managerial processes:

Figure 4.5: BSC's redefinition of corporate performance in multiple dimensions

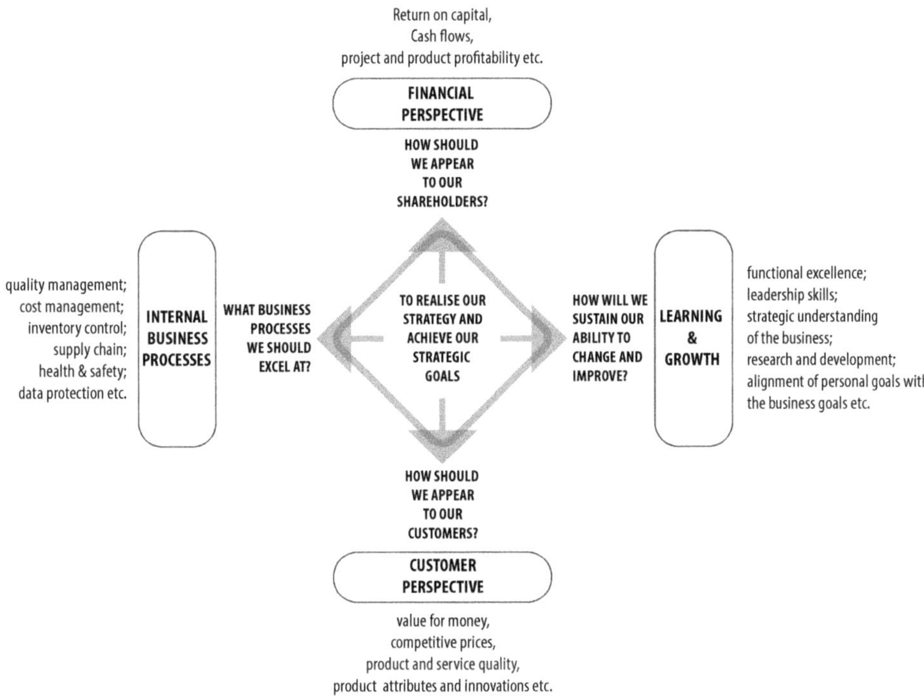

Source: based on Kaplan and Norton's various writings

1. **Translating the vision:** Building consensus around the organisation's vision and strategy, expressing them as "an integrated set of objectives and measures, agreed upon by all senior executives, that describe the long-term drivers of success" (Kaplan and Norton 1996b, 76).
2. **Communicating and linking:** Communicating the corporate strategy throughout the organisation and linking it to departmental and individual objectives. For Kaplan and Norton (1996b, 76), the "scorecard gives managers a way of ensuring that all levels of the organisation understand the long-term strategy and that both departmental and individual objectives are aligned with it".
3. **Business planning:** Integrating the financial and non-financial aspects of planning. It involves rationalising investment by eliminating non-strategic projects and initiating change management programmes, often supported by consultants.

4. **Feedback and learning:** This is what Kaplan and Norton call "strategic learning"—the processes through which managers evaluate strategy in light of recent performance. Strategy reviews based on scorecards allow managers to reflect on whether they are achieving their objectives.

A careful reading of Kaplan and Norton's writings reveals that implementation is difficult and time-consuming, often taking more than 24 months initially. It then demands continuous monitoring, frequently with expensive external consultants. Based on their consultancy, Kaplan and Norton (1996b) outlined a 10-step implementation process over 24 months. For brevity, these steps and their connection to the four key processes are illustrated in Figure 4.6.

Figure 4.6: Processes and steps of implementing BSC - its hierarchical cascading

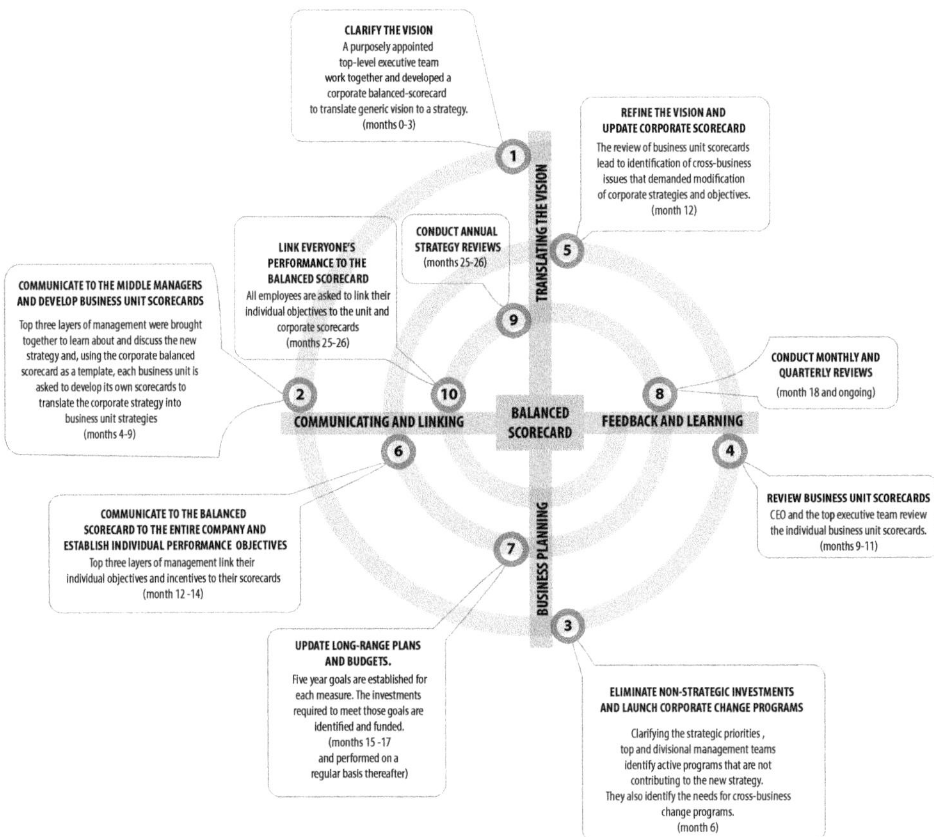

Source: based on Kaplan and Norton's various publications

Causalities in the BSC

Proponents of the BSC assume a specific set of causalities. Kaplan and Norton (1993, 1996a, 1996b, 2000) clarify that the non-financial dimensions (learning and growth, internal business processes, customer) are not a random assortment of variables but represent a fundamental set of causal relationships. They assert that, once carefully mapped, these dimensions can propel the organisation towards enhanced shareholder value. Consequently, the BSC should demonstrate causality between outcome measures and the performance drivers leading to those outcomes. For instance, they explain:

The Balanced Scorecard, unlike ad hoc performance measurement systems, argue Kaplan and Norton, articulates the 'theory of the business'. By having an explicit set of linkages among the scorecard measures, managers can test informally, if not statistically, the business theory's hypothesised causal chain of strategic initiatives, performance drivers, and outcomes (Kaplan and Norton 1996a, 261).

Their fundamental assumption is that learning and growth should improve internal business processes, which in turn give the company better capabilities to satisfy customers. This sequence, they argue, should ultimately lead to improved shareholder value. Tracing these causalities through relevant performance measures constitutes "creating strategy maps" (Kaplan and Norton 2000). The operational details are organisation-specific, but Figure 4.7 provides a generic conception.

BSC relationships: causality or finality? – Norreklit's critique

As mentioned, causal relationships among performance dimensions are analysed in a company-specific manner. According to Kaplan and Norton's discussions on 'strategy mapping', strategising involves establishing connections between the variables captured by the scorecards. These presumed causal relationships are intended to make the BSC more than an ad-hoc collection of measures; they transform it into a feed-forward control system where non-financial measures sequentially drive financial measures towards shareholder value optimisation (see Norreklit 2000).

While Kaplan and Norton describe the interconnections as 'causalities', Norreklit (2000, 2003) questions whether the BSC framework contains causal relationships. For her, there are fundamental issues with the presumed causalities, and she advances her critique on three interrelated grounds.

1. **Neglect of time dimensions:** Causal connections are often bound by a time lag between cause and effect. The BSC encompasses a problem-

Figure 4.7: Causalities presumed in BSC – mapping the strategic connections

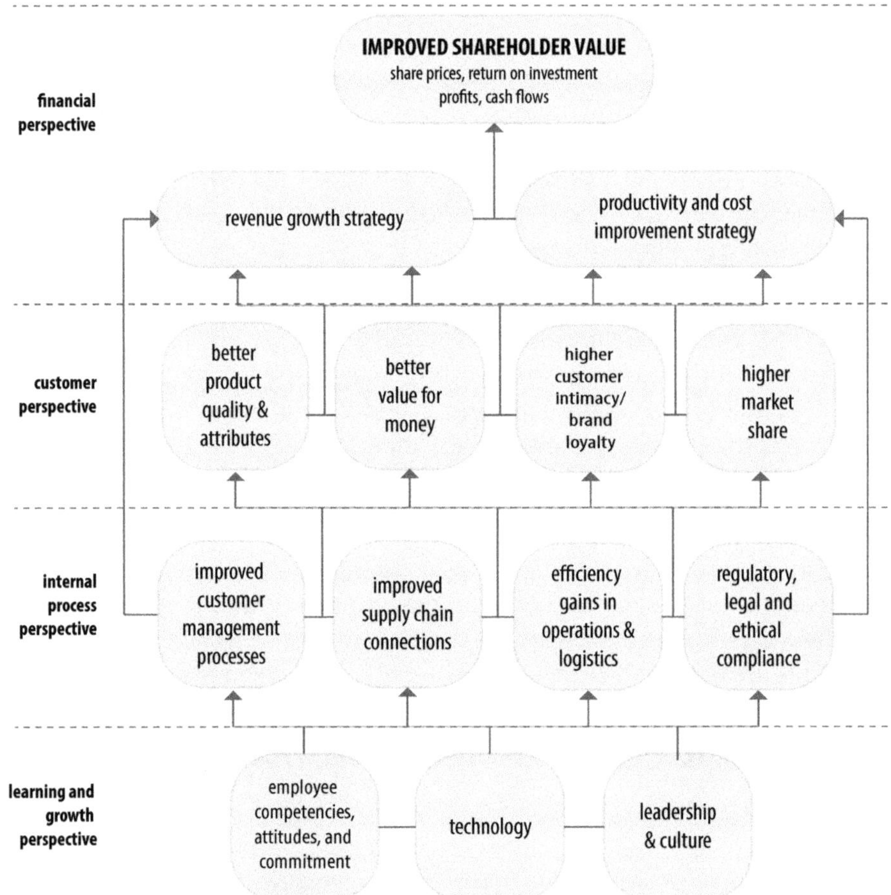

Source: based on Kaplan and Norton's various writings

atic causal connection because it does not sufficiently capture this time lag, especially between non-financial and financial outcomes. Kaplan and Norton's minimal discussions on time dimensions constitute only 'static' descriptions of causality. For example, their 'strategic mapping' manifests a space of timeless connections. Norreklit (2000, 71) argues:

> the effect of the measures will occur at different points of time because the effects of the different areas involve different time scales. While the introduction of more efficient processes may yield more satisfied customers within a period of 3 months, innovation may not affect the financial results until a few years

have passed. ... One argument for not measuring at different points of time could be that the time lag between an effort and its effect is very short. If this is the case, however, then the balanced scorecard ceases to be relevant since the full consequences of a company's actions would appear from its accounting figures.

2. **Problematic relationship between measures:** Norreklit argues that the relationship between the measures is ambiguously explained. On one hand, Kaplan and Norton assume a linear causal relationship from learning and growth to financial outcomes. This implies that a higher ROI will occur if other measures are achieved. In this sense, non-financial measures are independent variables that should produce financial outcomes. On the other hand, Kaplan and Norton's explanations demand the use of accounting calculus to decide ***whether*** and ***how*** a firm should invest in such non-financial measures. In that sense, the accounting calculus precedes the non-financial measures. Norreklit also argues there is no empirically testable guarantee that satisfied customers will lead to higher financial returns.
3. **Interdependence of the four perspectives:** For Norreklit, instead of a linear causal connection, there is an interdependency—a possible circular relationship—among the BSC measures.

Considering these issues, Norreklit (2000) argues that the connections described by Kaplan and Norton are 'finality relationships' rather than 'causal relationships'. In contrast to causal connections, which are underpinned by empirical conditions, finality relationships are logical and normative connections reflecting what people desire or believe should occur. According to Norreklit (2000, 76), finality relationships delineate how human actions and desires interrelate. They are shaped by the belief that a specific action is the most effective means to an end. A reciprocal relationship exists between ends and means; each means is one of several that can be employed, and each may have other consequences. For instance, a favourable financial outcome may be attained by marketing a product at an 'introductory price' to secure a larger market share. While this might initially result in a suboptimal return, it could create opportunities to raise prices later. This is not causality but a 'possible' outcome under specific conditions.

Conceptualising such finalities as 'causal relations' may have imparted a 'scientific appearance' to the BSC discourse and established the notion that it possesses an underlying scientific "theory of the business" (Kaplan and Norton 1996a, 261). Consequently, reframing the BSC's relationships as finalities could significantly impact its academic credibility. It is illustrative to quote Norreklit (2000, 77) here to comprehend this problem of posing a finality as a causality for 'scientific appearance':

> There are indeed indications that Kaplan and Norton want to refer to finality and not to causality. In one of Kaplan and Norton's figures, the arrows point in both directions ..., indicating assumed finality. Nevertheless, in both text and figures, an assumption of causality plays a dominant role... Giving up the assumption that cause-and-effect relationships are involved has major consequences for their entire argumentation... Finality is fundamentally different from cause-and-effect relationships. The consequence of assuming finality is that the relationships among the various perspectives become more ambiguous and less simple – complexity increases and many of the techniques suggested for the balanced scorecard will be impracticable. Furthermore, if Kaplan and Norton are assuming finality instead of causality, then the balanced scorecard is no different from many other approaches. Altogether, the power of the instrument... will be greatly reduced. (Norreklit 2000, 77)

Other Weaknesses of the BSC

Besides the issue of causality, the BSC approach is often criticised for the following reasons:

1. The implementation of the BSC is a highly autocratic, top-down process. It commences with corporate scorecards, which are then cascaded throughout the hierarchy.
2. It assumes a rather apolitical, resistance-free organisation where the wisdom of top management is unquestionably accepted by lower levels.
3. The implementation demands a substantial investment, which often fails to justify the managerial benefits it creates. The process is lengthy, during which conditions may change, leading many BSC projects to be abandoned.
4. Once implemented, the BSC system can become rigid, as altering scorecards necessitates rerunning expensive redesign processes.

Reimagining the BSC for sustainability

Numerous attempts have been made to redesign the BSC to address ecological and social justice issues (e.g., Figge et al. 2002; Hansen and Schaltegger 2016; Kalender and Vayvay 2016; Kaplan and McMillan 2021). These efforts encompass two interconnected approaches:

1. Incorporating specific sustainability measures within the existing four dimensions.
2. Introducing a new perspective to integrate sustainability more formally.

As the originator of the BSC, Kaplan's paper with a colleague is a good example of how the framework is "reimagined for the ESG era" (Kaplan and McMillan 2021). The rationale derives from their corporate experiments, beginning with their 2018 Harvard Business Review paper, "Inclusive Growth: Profitable Strategies for Tackling Poverty and Inequality" (Kaplan et al. 2018). Their central message is that successful corporate strategies for sustainability require creating "inclusive, sustainable, and profit-generating ecosystems" (Kaplan et al. 2018, 5). To achieve this, they recommend three strategies.

1. The first involves pursuing systemic, multi-sector opportunities. They recommend companies surpass the conventional corporate social responsibility (CSR) budgeting approach and seek opportunities that generate economic benefits for themselves while fostering socioeconomic gains for others. They critique the conventional CSR approach, arguing that:

   > such programs typically benefit a relatively small number of people and don't fundamentally change the community's socioeconomic conditions... they are generally funded from a sustainability budget, not embedded in the company's local business strategy... The traditional corporate sustainability approach ultimately has a limited impact because it is positioned as a social or an environmental program, not a profit-generating one (Kaplan et al. 2018, 5).

   This critique contains the implicit corporatist argument that profit is a prerequisite for sustainability. This point will be revisited later.

2. The second strategy involves mobilising complementary partners as "catalysts," such as civil society organisations (CSOs) and global development institutions, to provide access to and legitimacy within the 'new inclusive ecosystem'. Such a catalyst could be an NGO or a consulting company like Palladium, with which Kaplan and his co-authors are affiliated. The ideology is explicit:

   > Without the involvement of a profit-seeking corporation, no program is likely to go far. For an industrial ecosystem to be sustainable, it must be credible to businesses searching for

> competitive advantage and able to scale up. Governments are attracted to public-private partnerships... because they can harness the resources and innovation capabilities of profit-seeking companies (Kaplan et al. 2018, 6).

This point will also be revisited in the following critique.

3. Their third strategy involves acquiring seed and scale-up financing. Paradoxically, Kaplan and his colleagues acknowledge the incapacity, or rather the unwillingness, of corporate capitalism to address sustainability when they state that "few companies are prepared to finance this type of risky investment, especially with their limited sustainability and CSR budgets. Corporate investment funds favor safe projects with short payback periods, not projects that require disrupting an existing equilibrium..." (Kaplan et al. 2018, 6). Their strategy is to help corporations tap into the growing "pool of impact investment," which Ananya Roy (2010) calls "poverty capital"—finance for poverty alleviation sourced from development agencies, philanthropic donations, and national budgets of less developed countries. Kaplan and colleagues aim to tap into this poverty capital to develop their "new ecosystem." This is similar to the advice of C. K. Prahalad (2005) on seeking "the fortune at the bottom of the pyramid."
4. The fourth principle involves implementing a new measurement and governance system, which entails reimagining the BSC. Kaplan and colleagues (2021) assert that the BSC can be "reimagined for the ESG era" by:

    a. **Redefining the company's long-term strategic intent** to incorporate Environmental, Social, and Governance (ESG) elements, particularly alignment with the "new inclusive ecosystem."
    b. **Introducing a new layer of a "triple bottom line perspective"** or "positive impact outcomes" atop the financial perspective. This introduces a new causality from the financial to the triple bottom line perspective, suggesting sustainability is achievable only through profits for private capital.
    c. **Embedding sustainability concerns into the lower levels of the BSC**, either as a separate perspective or as measures integrated into the internal process and learning and growth perspectives. In the Amanco example, Kaplan and colleagues incorporate a "social and environmental perspective" between the internal process and learning and growth perspectives.

Reimagining the bsc as capitalist managerial capture: a political-economy critique

Kaplan and colleagues' attempt to "reimagine the BSC for the ESG era" embodies what critical accounting scholars term capitalistic "managerial capture" (e.g., Alawattage et al. 2022; Baker 2010; O'Dwyer 2003; Owen et al. 2000). Managerial capture involves processes through which wider socio-political issues are "recast in ways that pose no moral or emotional challenge to the dominant logic of shareholder [wealth] maximisation" (Baker 2010, 847). Thus, as their writings demonstrate, the pursuit of profit is framed as a necessary condition for addressing the ecological and social justice issues created by shareholder capitalism.

Embedded in this overarching capitalistic managerial capture, Kaplan and colleagues' reimagined BSC faces several but fundamental political-economic issues:

1. Its sustainability connection is built on a problematic assumption of causality (or 'finality'). It assumes that capitalistic economic value creation will necessarily lead to social and ecological sustainability. This demonstrates an ignorance or neglect of history. Any sensible understanding of economic history would acknowledge that colonial and modern industrial capitalism played a significant role in creating an unsustainable world. According to natural scientists, the 'Capitalocene' has been a fundamental historical movement underpinning global unsustainability through the profit-driven destruction of ecological and social balances (see Haraway 2015; Moore 2015). The term Capitalocene describes the current historical epoch in which capitalism has become the dominant force shaping the world and its ecosystems, arguing the current crisis is a direct result of the capitalist system.
2. Kaplan and colleagues' notion of an 'ecosystem' is narrow and misconceived. In a sustainability context, an ecosystem should encompass the fundamental contradictions between the economy, polity, society, and ecology. Intentionally or not, they appear to misuse the term 'ecosystem' for what is essentially an economic system or a new supply chain. Upon critical examination, their "new ecosystem" is little more than a set of 'profitable' connections with the poor through 'catalysts' so that corporations can tap into "poverty capital."
3. The empirical picture of inclusive capitalism they portray is problematic when considering realities in the global south. As discussed in critical scholarship (e.g., Alawattage et al. 2019; Roy 2010), ground realities are worsening. Consider the microfinance industry. Initially launched as a social movement to assist poor women, it has evolved into a highly profitable global industry, creating corporate opportunities to seek "fortunes at

the bottom of the pyramid" (Prahalad, 2005). Since this transformation, microfinance has become a social disaster in many countries, leading to a higher rate of suicides among indebted poor women in rural villages. These women face perpetual indebtedness, with institutions lending at rates of 5% to 10% per month. This situation results in microfinance companies perpetually collecting most of their income as interest, as the women cannot repay the loan principals and are trapped in cycles of interest payments. Although these women are now 'included' in the formal market economy, they are paying insanely high interest rates and reproducing their poverty. Nevertheless, because they have taken loans, they are statistically reported in glossy industry reports as new entrepreneurs.

1. In the 'new ecosystem' advocated by Kaplan and his colleagues, the poor are not offered fixed-income jobs but the "opportunity to become entrepreneurs" via high-interest loans. Unlike wage workers, they must bear the risks of running a business and pay significantly higher interest rates than corporations would. Most of the income they generate goes to corporations as interest. In assuming this business and financial risk, these individuals produce cheap raw materials for global companies. Therefore, in this new ecosystem, poor labourers are transformed into entrepreneurs to bear the risks that capital should otherwise bear. Corporations can earn a return for which someone else bears the real risk (see Alawattage et al. 2019). The strategy for this is termed "inclusive growth" and "reimagining the BSC for the ESG era"; the underlying theme is tapping into "poverty capital." In effect, it resembles 'poverty capitalism' rather than inclusive capitalism.

Chapter summary

This chapter explored performance management within traditional and strategic frameworks. It began by defining performance as goal-directed behaviour and outcomes subject to observation, evaluation, and reward or punishment.

The traditional approach is responsibility accounting, whose operational philosophy comprises a hierarchy of accountability centres, accounting calculations to measure their performance, and the principle of controllability. Responsibility accounting structures organisations into cost, revenue, profit, and investment centres. Aligned with this hierarchy, accounting techniques are employed to measure performance, linked to return on investment. Budgeting, standard costing, and variance analysis are crucial techniques. Despite its widespread use, responsibility accounting is criticised for its financial overemphasis (imbalance) and operational overemphasis (lack of strategic connection).

Kaplan and Norton's Balanced Scorecard (BSC) emerged as a solution. The BSC is a strategic performance management system because it 'balances' financial and non-financial measures and 'links' operations with strategy. The foundational elements are 'scorecards,' which combine objectives, measures, indicators, and initiatives. Balancing occurs through four performance dimensions: learning and growth, internal business processes, customer, and financial. Linking is achieved by cascading scorecards from the top down.

The BSC assumes a set of underlying causalities: that non-financial performance leads to financial performance. For Hanna Norreklit, however, this assumed causality is a major weakness, resembling 'finalities' more than 'causalities.'

Recent endeavours by Kaplan and colleagues aim to reimagine the BSC for the ESG era, envisioning an "inclusive, sustainable, and profit-generating ecosystem." Their strategies, framed within the discourse of inclusive capitalism, constitute a neoliberal ideology suggesting sustainability can only be achieved through profit-seeking ventures. This perspective is subject to a political-economy critique, highlighting issues such as "managerial capture" and a strategic neglect of the historical dynamics underlying unsustainability.

Case Study: Unilever's growth action plan: a case study in strategic performance management and sustainability

Introduction

Unilever PLC is a titan in the global fast-moving consumer goods (FMCG) sector, with a portfolio of over 400 brands and products used by 3.4 billion people daily in 190 countries. The organisation's history is one of continuous adaptation, culminating in its most recent strategy, the "Growth Action Plan 2030" (GAP2030). As mentioned in its 2024 annual report, this plan aims to transform Unilever into a "consistently higher performing business" by focusing on core brands and markets, excelling in execution, and accelerating key capabilities. Crucially, Unilever presents this strategy not merely as a vehicle for financial growth but as a framework for responsible and sustainable value creation. The GAP2030 explicitly embeds a sustainability agenda built on four pillars: Climate, Nature, Plastics, and Livelihoods, positioning the company as a leader in a "new era for sustainable business leadership".

However, this carefully articulated ambition exists in stark tension with persistent and compelling external critique. While Unilever reports progress against its sustainability targets, regulatory bodies, non-governmental organisations (NGOs), and investigative reports have documented significant failures in the company's environmental and social performance. These include formal investigations into 'greenwashing' by the UK's Competition and Markets Authority (CMA), damning evidence of the company's contribution to the global plastics crisis, and concerning findings regarding labour rights and deforestation within its complex global supply chains.

This case study explores this profound disconnect. The central problem is not simple corporate hypocrisy but a fundamental challenge of strategic performance management. It poses a critical question for advanced accounting students: ***how can an organisation with a sophisticated, multi-dimensional strategy, seemingly aligned with modern frameworks like the Balanced Scorecard, produce outcomes so contrary to its stated goals?*** The case challenges students to move beyond the technical application of performance management tools to a critical diagnosis of their implementation, exploring how systems of measurement and reward can succeed in driving financial performance while failing to govern, and at times exacerbating, critical sustainability issues. By examining the gap between Unilever's strategic intent and its operational reality, this case provides a rich, real-world context for applying the theoretical concepts of strategic performance management, its limitations, and its complex relationship with the demands of social and ecological justice.

Unilever's strategic ambition: the growth action plan

Unilever's GAP2030 is a deliberate strategic response to a period of acknowledged underperformance in growth, productivity, and returns. Launched to reclaim competitive advantage, the GAP2030 is structured around three imperatives: Focus, Excel, and Accelerate. This framework is intended to simplify the organisation, concentrate resources for maximum impact, and build the capabilities necessary to win in a changing global market.

The Pillars of Growth: Focusing for Financial Performance

The foundational principle of GAP2030 is a strategic narrowing of focus, designed to channel investment towards parts of the business with the highest potential for profitable growth. This manifests in two primary ways:

1. **Focus on Power Brands:** Unilever has identified 30 "Power Brands"—including Dove, Knorr, Hellmann's, and Domestos—that account for over 75% of turnover. The strategy dictates that these brands will receive prioritised support in investment, innovation, and execution.
2. **Focus on Top Markets:** The GAP2030 implements a geographic focus on 24 top markets, representing approximately 85% of group turnover. This allows the company to concentrate resources in high-potential regions.

This dual focus creates a clear hierarchy of accountability, mirroring the logic of traditional responsibility accounting where performance is managed through discrete profit or investment centres. The success of a brand manager for Dove in a top market, for instance, can be clearly measured within this structure.

Supporting this approach are the 'Excel' and 'Accelerate' imperatives. 'Excel' aims to drive competitiveness through five demand-creation drivers:

1. achieving "unmissable brand superiority,"
2. scaling multi-year innovations,
3. driving premiumisation,
4. mastering social-first demand generation, and
5. leading in high-growth channels. '

Accelerate' focuses on building future-fit capabilities, including leveraging technology, creating a lean supply chain, driving net productivity, and embedding scaled Artificial Intelligence (AI). Together, these elements form a comprehensive plan to enhance operational efficiency and market share.

Measuring financial success: the language of shareholder value

Ultimately, the performance of GAP2030 is communicated to investors through key financial indicators. These metrics represent the tangible outcomes of the strategy and are the primary basis for evaluating managerial performance from a shareholder perspective. They form the core of the 'Financial' perspective in any strategic performance management framework.

The principal financial Key Performance Indicators (KPIs) used by Unilever include:

1. Underlying Sales Growth (USG): A measure of turnover increase, excluding acquisitions, disposals, and currency fluctuations, reflecting organic growth.
2. Underlying Volume Growth (UVG): Measures the change in the quantity of products sold, providing insight into consumer demand independent of price changes.
3. Underlying Operating Margin (UOM): A measure of profitability reflecting underlying operating profit as a percentage of turnover, indicating operational efficiency.
4. Underlying Earnings Per Share (EPS): Represents the portion of a company's underlying profit allocated to each share, a key indicator of shareholder value.

These metrics provide a clear, quantifiable language for assessing corporate performance. As shown in Table 1, Unilever's 2024 results demonstrated progress on these fronts, with positive volume growth and a significant expansion in gross margin, which the company attributed to the early successes of GAP2030. This financial performance provides the context against which the organisation's sustainability ambitions must be evaluated.

Table 1: Unilever key financial performance indicators (2023-2024)

Financial Metric	2023	2024
Turnover (€bn)	€59.6	€60.8
Underlying Sales Growth (%)	9.0%	4.2%
Underlying Volume Growth (%)	-1.1%	2.9%
Underlying Operating Margin (%)	16.7%	18.4%
Underlying EPS (€)	€2.60	€2.98

Source: Compiled from Unilever Full Year Results Announcements

The sustainability agenda: four pillars of responsible growth

Unilever has long cultivated a reputation as a corporate leader in sustainability, a commitment it claims is a "strategic imperative" integrated into its Growth Action Plan. The company's public narrative posits that long-term financial success is linked to responsible social and environmental stewardship. This commitment is operationalised through a sustainability agenda structured around four pillars, each supported by specific targets.

Articulating the Corporate Commitment

The four pillars of Unilever's sustainability strategy represent its prioritised areas of impact:

1. Climate: A commitment to decarbonise the business in line with the 1.5°C goal of the Paris Agreement, addressing emissions from its operations and value chain.
2. Nature: A focus on protecting and regenerating ecosystems, particularly through eliminating deforestation from its key commodity supply chains and promoting regenerative agriculture.
3. Plastics: An agenda to tackle plastic pollution by moving towards a circular economy, focusing on reducing virgin plastic use and ensuring packaging is designed for reuse or recycling.
4. Livelihoods: A commitment to enhance the lives of people in its value chain, focusing on ensuring workers are paid a living wage and supporting smallholder farmers and SMEs.

These pillars form the non-financial dimensions of Unilever's strategic performance framework. Their successful achievement is presented as integral to the overall success of GAP2030.

Quantifying the Commitment: Targets and KPIs

To translate these commitments into measurable objectives, Unilever has established 15 near- and medium-term goals. These targets serve as the KPIs for the sustainability agenda. A strategic performance management system appears to be in operation, incorporating these non-financial metrics alongside financial ones. Table 2 summarises the headline targets for each pillar, providing a snapshot of the company's stated ambitions and reported progress.

Table 2: Unilever's sustainability pillars: headline targets and reported progress (as of year-end 2024)

Sustainability Pillar	Key Target(s)	Reported 2024 Status/KPI
Climate	100% absolute reduction in Scope 1 & 2 GHG emissions by 2030 (vs. 2015 baseline). 42% absolute reduction in Scope 3 energy & industrial GHG emissions by 2030 (vs. 2021 baseline). 30.3% absolute reduction in Scope 3 forest, land & agriculture (FLAG) GHG emissions by 2030 (vs. 2021 baseline).	72% reduction in Scope 1 & 2 emissions achieved. 8% reduction in Scope 3 energy & industrial emissions. 14% reduction in Scope 3 FLAG emissions.
Nature	Achieve a deforestation-free supply chain for key commodities (palm oil, paper, tea, soy, cocoa) by 2024. Implement regenerative agriculture practices on 1 million hectares by 2030.	97% of order volumes for key commodities verified as deforestation-free. 130,000 hectares covered by regenerative agriculture projects.
Plastics	Reduce virgin plastic footprint by 30% by 2026 and 40% by 2028 (vs. 2019 baseline). 100% of plastic packaging to be reusable, recyclable, or compostable (RRC) by 2030 (rigid) and 2035 (flexible).	23% reduction in virgin plastic use achieved. 57% of plastic packaging is RRC (76% rigid, 13% flexible). 21% of global plastic portfolio is from recycled content.
Livelihoods	Ensure everyone who directly provides goods and services to Unilever will earn at least a living wage by 2030. Help 2.5 million SMEs in the retail value chain grow their business through digital platforms.	Living wage paid to all direct employees since 2020. Living Wage Promise launched for suppliers. 2.58 million SMEs reached through digital platforms.

Source: Compiled from Unilever Sustainability Hub, Annual Reports, and Climate Transition Action Plan

Performance in practice: critiques and contradictions

While Unilever's strategic framework and reported KPIs paint a picture of steady progress, evidence from external sources presents a starkly different reality. This section details the major critiques that challenge Unilever's performance narrative, highlighting the disconnect between its stated strategy and operational outcomes. These contradictions form the central problem for a performance management diagnosis.

The plastics predicament: a crisis of packaging

The most acute contradiction in Unilever's sustainability performance lies in its approach to plastic packaging. The company's goals of reducing virgin plastic use and moving to a circular economy are undermined by its extensive reliance on single-use plastic sachets.

The scale of this issue is staggering. According to a 2023 Greenpeace report, Unilever is on track to sell 53 billion plastic sachets annually, or approximately 1,700 every second. This practice is prevalent in Global South countries, where sachets provide an affordable way for low-income consumers to purchase small quantities of products. However, these sachets are typically made of multi-layered, composite plastics that are technically difficult and economically unviable to recycle. This has led a senior Unilever executive to describe them as "evil because you cannot recycle [them]".

The environmental consequences are severe. In countries with inadequate waste management infrastructure, these sachets become a pervasive form of pollution, clogging waterways, exacerbating flooding, and breaking down into microplastics. In Indonesia, sachet waste reportedly constitutes 16% of all plastic pollution, and a brand audit in Bali identified Unilever as the largest source of this waste stream (Greenpeace, 2023). The practice of burning this plastic waste also releases toxic chemicals, posing health risks to local communities.

The stark contrast between Unilever's circular economy ambitions and the polluting reality of its sachet business is summarised in Table 3. This gap suggests a performance management system that fails to translate a high-level corporate goal into operational practice, likely because the financial incentives of maintaining market share in emerging markets override the non-financial sustainability objective.

Table 3: The plastics paradox - stated goals vs. reported reality (greenpeace reports)

Dimension	Stated Goal / Ambition	Critique / Reported Reality
Virgin Plastic Reduction	"Reduce virgin plastic footprint by 30% by 2026".	"On track to sell 53 billion plastic sachets in 2023". Sachet production increased by 40% from 2010 to 2023.
Circular Economy	"100% of plastic packaging to be reusable, recyclable or compostable".	"Sachets are 'evil because you cannot recycle them'" (Unilever executive quote). Sachet waste makes up 16% of all plastic waste in Indonesia.

Allegations of greenwashing: the challenge of credibility

The credibility of Unilever's sustainability claims has been formally challenged by regulators. In December 2023, the UK's Competition and Markets Authority (CMA) launched a formal investigation into Unilever over concerns that the company was engaging in 'greenwashing'—making environmental claims that could mislead consumers. According to its press release, the CMA's concerns included:

1. Vague and Broad Claims: Using ambiguous terms such as "grown sustainably" on packaging without clear, verifiable definitions.
2. Exaggerated 'Natural' Claims: Presenting ingredients in a way that may overstate how 'natural' a product is.
3. Misleading Imagery: Using colours and icons, such as green leaves, that create an impression that a product is more environmentally friendly than it is.
4. Unclear Recyclability Statements: Failing to specify whether recyclability claims apply to the entire product or only part of its packaging.

Unilever expressed that it was "surprised and disappointed" by the announcement and stated its commitment to responsible claims. The CMA closed its investigation in late 2024, noting its decision was based on factors including "changes Unilever has made to claims on some of its products" and the wider impact of the CMA's programme of work. While the closure prevented a formal ruling, the investigation itself highlights a significant performance issue: the communication of sustainability efforts was deemed potentially misleading by a national regulator, undermining the trustworthiness of the company's non-financial performance reporting.

Labour in the value chain: the human cost

Unilever's Livelihoods pillar commits the company to ensuring a living wage for workers in its value chain by 2030. However, NGO reports have consistently highlighted a gap between this policy and the reality for many workers, particularly in agricultural supply chains of the Global South.

A landmark 2013 Oxfam report, conducted with Unilever's cooperation, analysed labour conditions in the company's Vietnam operations. The study found that while wages in Unilever's factory exceeded the legal minimum, they fell short of a calculated living wage, with workers reporting their pay was insufficient to make savings or support dependents. The situation was more severe in the supply chain, where some workers engaged in excessive overtime—well beyond legal limits—simply to cover their monthly expenses. The report also identified the widespread use of precarious contract labour, with lower wages, fewer benefits, and little job security.

These are not merely historical issues. More recent reports by NGOs have pointed to the persistence of poor working conditions on tea plantations in South Asia. Furthermore, in 2020, serious allegations of sexual harassment were reported on Unilever's Kenyan tea plantations, echoing similar claims from a decade prior and raising questions about the effectiveness of the company's grievance mechanisms.

The complexity of managing these issues is further illustrated by the company's palm oil supply chain. Despite a commitment to achieve a "deforestation-free" supply chain, research has continued to link Unilever to mills that source palm fruit from plantations involved in deforestation in Indonesia. This demonstrates the immense challenge of enforcing performance standards through vast, opaque global supply chains, where the drive for low-cost raw materials can undermine sustainability and human rights goals. The persistence of these issues suggests the performance management system may not adequately incentivise procurement managers to prioritise suppliers with higher labour and environmental standards, especially if doing so would increase costs.

The performance management challenge

Unilever presents a paradigmatic case for studying strategic performance management. The organisation has articulated a sophisticated, multi-dimensional strategy that appears to align with the principles of a framework like the Balanced Scorecard. It balances traditional financial objectives (Growth Action Plan 2030) with a comprehensive set of non-financial, sustainability-oriented goals (the Four Pillars). It communicates these goals through specific, quantifiable KPIs. Yet, the evidence reveals a persistent gap between this espoused strategy and the firm's actual performance on key environmental and social dimensions. This highlights the challenges of 'cascading' strategic intentions downwards, especially across a global supply chain.

This disconnect is the central puzzle of the case. It is not enough to label the company as hypocritical; the task is to diagnose the systemic failures within its performance management system that allow such a divergence. Your task, as an advanced accounting student acting as a strategic management consultant, is to analyse the root causes of this failure. Using the theoretical frameworks from this chapter, you must deconstruct the Unilever case to understand why its strategic control systems appear ineffective in governing its sustainability agenda. Your analysis should draw upon key concepts, including the limitations of responsibility accounting, the principles of balancing and cascading, Norreklit's critique of causality versus finality, and the political-economy concept of managerial capture. By applying these theoretical lenses to the empirical data of the Unilever case, you can develop a nuanced understanding of the profound challenges of strategising performance when sustainability is a fundamental concern.

Discussion questions

1. **Traditional vs. Strategic Systems:** Critique Unilever's performance management challenges through the lens of traditional responsibility accounting. How might a narrow focus on financial metrics within its 'Power Brand' and 'Top Market' structure (which function as profit or investment centres) contribute to the environmental and social issues identified (e.g., plastic sachets to drive volume, or pressure on suppliers to reduce costs)?
2. **BSC Design:** Based on Unilever's stated Growth Action Plan and its Four Sustainability Pillars, design a high-level Balanced Scorecard for the company. Propose specific, measurable objectives and KPIs for each of the four perspectives (Financial, Customer, Internal Business Process, Learning & Growth) that explicitly integrate the company's sustainability goals. For example, under the 'Internal Business Process' perspective, what KPI could directly address the plastic sachet problem?
3. **Reimagining the BSC for Sustainability:** The chapter discusses two approaches for a "Sustainable BSC": (a) integrating sustainability measures within the existing four perspectives, or (b) adding a fifth 'Sustainability' perspective. Critically evaluate these two approaches in the context of Unilever. Which would be more effective for addressing the deep-seated issues of plastic pollution and supply chain labour rights? Justify your choice with examples from the case.
4. **Causality vs. Finality:** Apply Hanna Norreklit's critique of the BSC's presumed causalities to the framework you proposed in Question 2. Consider the link between achieving a living wage in the supply chain (a Livelihoods goal) and enhancing shareholder value (a Financial goal). Is this a scientifically verifiable *causal* relationship or a normative *finality* relationship (i.e., a desired outcome)? Discuss the managerial implications of this distinction for Unilever. What happens to the power of the BSC if its linkages are based on hope rather than proven cause-and-effect?
5. **Political-Economy Critique:** The chapter introduces "managerial capture," where socio-political issues are reframed to pose no challenge to the dominant logic of profit maximisation. To what extent do Unilever's sustainability initiatives, when viewed against the critiques from Greenpeace and Oxfam, exemplify this concept? Construct a reasoned argument, using evidence from the case, as to whether Unilever's approach constitutes genuine strategic change or a form of "poverty capitalism" that manages reputational risk without fundamentally altering its core business model.

Chapter review questions

Section 1: Foundational concepts of performance management

1. According to the chapter's definition, which scenario best exemplifies the transformation of an 'action' into a 'performance'?

   a. A factory worker assembles 100 units per hour as part of their daily routine.
   b. A university lecturer delivers a series of lectures over a semester.
   c. A junior analyst prepares a detailed financial report that is subsequently reviewed and graded by their manager as part of an annual appraisal.
   d. An employee voluntarily sings a song at an informal office gathering.

2. The chapter defines performance as a 'hybrid of the actual and the expected'. What is the primary function of performance management in this context?

   a. To exclusively document the actual outcomes of employees' actions.
   b. To establish institutionalised expectations, such as targets, without reference to actual results.
   c. To minimise the deviation between actual outcomes and institutionalised expectations by making actions goal-directed and subject to evaluation.
   d. To replace all expected targets with historical benchmarks.

3. The text states that performance is directed towards 'higher-order principles'. In a corporate setting, which is the most accurate example of such a principle?

   a. The number of units produced in a specific cost centre.
   b. The monthly sales revenue of the London office.
   c. The organisation's strategic goal of achieving market leadership through innovation.
   d. The completion of a mandatory employee training module.

4. The chapter argues that performance is 'context-specific'. Which factor is identified as a primary determinant of this context-specificity?

   a. The universal applicability of financial metrics.
   b. The basis of legitimacy upon which an entity's actions can be subjected to observation and judgment.
   c. The consistency of performance measures regardless of the entity being assessed.
   d. The exclusive reliance on objective data for all performance evaluations.

5. Which statement most accurately captures the distinction between 'doing' and 'performing'?

   a. 'Performing' involves a greater level of skill than 'doing'.
   b. 'Doing' refers to individual activities, whereas 'performing' refers exclusively to group activities.
   c. 'Performing' is distinguished from 'doing' by the presence of a goal and the application of observation, evaluation, and judgment.
   d. 'Doing' relates to operational tasks, while 'performing' relates only to managerial tasks.

Section 2: The traditional approach: responsibility accounting

6. The operational philosophy of responsibility accounting is based on three main points. Which of the following is NOT one of these?

   a. The redefinition of organisational sites into a hierarchy of accountability centres.
   b. The principle that managers should only be held accountable for outcomes under their direct control.
   c. The integration of non-financial, strategic objectives into the primary evaluation framework.
   d. The use of specific accounting calculations to assess the performance of each accountability centre.

7. Within the accountability hierarchy of responsibility accounting, what is the primary function of an 'investment centre'?

   a. To manage operational costs to meet budgeted targets.
   b. To maximise sales volume and market share.
   c. To be accountable for both revenues and costs for a business unit, focusing on profitability.
   d. To be accountable for the efficient use of capital and to achieve a target return on assets.

8. The chapter explains that responsibility accounting 'superimposes a financial logic' over an organisation's operational structure. What is the ultimate purpose of this transformation?

   a. To empower operational managers with greater autonomy.
   b. To ensure diverse techno-managerial activities are translated into accounting measures to facilitate management based on the logic of ROI.
   c. To prioritise non-financial goals over financial targets.
   d. To create separate hierarchies for financial and operational management.

9. A production manager is evaluated on a cost variance report showing a significant adverse material price variance caused by a sudden global supply chain disruption. According to the 'concept of controllability', how should this be treated?

    a. The manager should be held fully accountable for all variances.
    b. The variance should be excluded from the manager's assessment because factors outside their control caused it.
    c. The manager should be praised for managing other costs effectively.
    d. The budget should be retroactively adjusted to eliminate the variance.

10. According to the chapter, what are the two most fundamental weaknesses of responsibility accounting that strategic systems like the BSC were designed to rectify?

    a. Its excessive reliance on qualitative data and its failure to enforce budgetary discipline.
    b. Its tendency to encourage budgetary slack and its overly decentralised structure.
    c. Its lack of balance due to a narrow financial focus and its lack of strategic connection.
    d. Its high implementation cost and incompatibility with standard costing.

11. The accountability hierarchy in responsibility accounting is described as reflecting a 'capitalist logic of accumulation'. Which feature most directly embodies this logic?

    a. The use of standard costing to control inputs.
    b. The focus on market share within revenue centres.
    c. The placement of Return on Investment (ROI) at the pinnacle of the performance hierarchy.
    d. The application of the controllability principle.

Section 3: The strategic approach: Kaplan and Norton's balanced scorecard

12. Kaplan and Norton's Balanced Scorecard (BSC) is a strategic performance management system. Its two pivotal actions are best described as:

    a. Costing and controlling: focusing on minimising costs and controlling variances.
    b. Budgeting and forecasting: creating financial plans and predicting revenues.
    c. Auditing and reporting: ensuring compliance and reporting historical results.
    d. Balancing and linking: integrating financial and non-financial measures and connecting operations to corporate strategy.

13. Within the BSC framework, what is the primary strategic role of the 'Learning and Growth' perspective?

    a. To report on quarterly earnings and shareholder returns.
    b. To measure customer satisfaction and market share.
    c. To identify key internal processes that must be optimised.
    d. To identify the capabilities, skills, and systems needed to support long-term strategic objectives and drive improvements in other perspectives.

14. A large oil company creates a 'personal scorecard' for its teams, containing corporate objectives, unit targets, and space for individuals to define their own objectives. This practice is a primary example of which BSC process?

    a. The 'balancing' of financial and non-financial measures.
    b. The 'cascading' of scorecards to link individual actions with corporate strategy.
    c. The application of the 'controllability principle'.
    d. The calculation of 'Return on Investment'.

15. The BSC framework is built upon a hypothesised set of causal relationships. Which sequence best represents this presumed causality?

    a. Improved financial performance leads to greater customer satisfaction, allowing investment in better processes and training.
    b. Investments in learning and growth lead to improved internal processes, which enhance customer value, ultimately driving superior financial results.
    c. A focus on customer satisfaction is the sole driver of performance, which dictates financial results, processes, and skills.
    d. Optimising internal processes is the starting point, which directly leads to improved financial returns.

16. How does a 'scorecard' in the BSC framework fundamentally differ from a traditional budget?

    a. A scorecard is prepared monthly, whereas a budget is always annual.
    b. A scorecard is exclusively qualitative, while a budget is exclusively quantitative.
    c. A scorecard provides a flexible template for multiple performance dimensions, whereas a budget captures only financial dimensions.
    d. A scorecard is a bottom-up process, whereas a budget is strictly top-down.

Section 4: Critical analysis of the balanced scorecard

17. Hanna Norreklit critiques the BSC's 'causal relationships', arguing they are better described as 'finality relationships'. Which statement best illustrates a 'finality relationship'?

    a. 'Empirical data shows a 5% increase in our training budget has consistently resulted in a 3% reduction in product defects within six months'.
    b. 'We believe that by investing in a new CRM system to improve customer service, we will achieve our goal of becoming the market leader in customer loyalty'.
    c. 'The laws of physics dictate that increasing the process temperature by 10 degrees will increase the yield by 15%'.
    d. 'A statistical analysis demonstrates a direct, time-lagged correlation between employee satisfaction and quarterly sales'.

18. Which is a key element of Norreklit's critique regarding the BSC's presumed causalities?

    a. The model places too much emphasis on the time lag between cause and effect.
    b. The model fails to sufficiently account for the time lag between non-financial actions and their financial outcomes, presenting a static map of connections.
    c. The model's causal links have been empirically proven to be universally applicable.
    d. The model correctly identifies that the four perspectives are entirely independent.

19. According to the chapter, what is the most significant consequence of accepting Norreklit's argument that the BSC's relationships are based on finality rather than causality?

    a. It strengthens the BSC's practical utility by making it more flexible.
    b. It has no significant impact, as the distinction is purely academic.
    c. It undermines the BSC's claim to be a scientific 'theory of the business', suggesting its power derives more from its rhetorical ability to create consensus than from objective validity.
    d. It proves that traditional responsibility accounting is a superior system.

20. Besides its causal logic, the chapter identifies other weaknesses of the BSC. Which is a common criticism of its implementation?

    a. It is an excessively democratic and bottom-up process that lacks strategic focus.

b. It is a highly autocratic, top-down process that assumes the wisdom of top management will be accepted without resistance.
c. It is a rapid and low-cost implementation that often fails to secure managerial buy-in.
d. It results in an overly flexible system, creating confusion.

Section 5: Reimagining the BSC for the ESG Era: proposals and critiques

21. Kaplan and colleagues propose 'reimagining the BSC for the ESG era' to create 'inclusive, sustainable, and profit-generating ecosystems'. What is the fundamental premise of their approach?

    a. Sustainability initiatives must be pursued regardless of their financial impact.
    b. Profit is a prerequisite for corporate sustainability, and ESG goals should be pursued through opportunities that generate economic benefits.
    c. The primary goal is to maximise social and ecological benefits, with profitability being a secondary outcome.
    d. True sustainability requires dismantling corporate structures.

22. The chapter introduces 'managerial capture' to critique the reimagined BSC. Which scenario best exemplifies this concept?

    a. A company's management is prosecuted for using competitors' trade secrets.
    b. A social movement successfully lobbies a corporation to abandon a profitable but harmful product line.
    c. A corporation reframes the complex challenge of climate change as a manageable business opportunity for selling 'green' products, ensuring the profit-maximisation model remains unchallenged.
    d. An activist group takes over a company's annual general meeting.

23. The political-economy critique of Kaplan and colleagues' proposal argues their notion of an 'ecosystem' is misconceived. What is the basis for this critique?

    a. The proposed ecosystem is too focused on ecological preservation.
    b. The proposed ecosystem is essentially a new supply chain designed to create profitable connections with the poor, rather than a holistic system addressing contradictions between the economy, society, and ecology.
    c. The proposed ecosystem relies too heavily on government regulation.
    d. The proposed ecosystem is not scientifically rigorous.

24. The critique suggests the 'inclusive growth' model can devolve into 'poverty capitalism'. What is the key mechanism?

    a. Providing stable, well-paying jobs in developing countries.
    b. Shifting business and financial risks to the poor by framing them as 'entrepreneurs' who take on high-interest loans, while corporations extract value as interest.
    c. Donating a large portion of corporate profits to philanthropic foundations.
    d. Forcing corporations to pay higher prices for raw materials from small-scale producers.

25. What is the fundamental ideological conflict between Kaplan's 'reimagined BSC' and the political-economy critique?

    a. The conflict is over which KPIs are best for measuring environmental impact.
    b. Kaplan's approach seeks to absorb the challenge of sustainability into the existing capitalist framework by making it profitable, while the critique argues this approach neutralises the challenge, perpetuating the system's core problems.
    c. Kaplan's approach prioritises the 'Social' aspect of ESG, whereas the critique argues the 'Environmental' aspect is more important.
    d. The conflict is about the timeline for implementation, with Kaplan advocating gradual change and the critique demanding radical transformation.

Comprehension questions

1. How would you define performance in generic terms?
2. Enumerate three factors that underlie the context specificity of performance.
3. Elaborate on the role that 'higher-order principles' play in defining performance.
4. Define performance management in generic terms.
5. Responsibility accounting is the traditional approach to performance management. Briefly elucidate the three elements of its operational philosophy.
6. Briefly explain the hierarchy of accountability centres in a responsibility accounting system. Offer examples of performance measures for these centres.
7. Clarify how accounting transforms a non-accounting hierarchy into an accounting hierarchy. You may use examples of budgeting systems or the DuPont system.
8. Draft a concise note on the techniques and structure of responsibility accounting.

9. Summarise the key features of responsibility accounting under the themes:
   a. Logic,
   b. Structure,
   c. Process, and
   d. Tools/Techniques.
10. Define a strategic performance management system.
11. Enumerate the key weaknesses of responsibility accounting. Which of these does the BSC attempt to rectify?
12. List and elucidate the performance measurement dimensions advocated by the BSC.
13. Explain the process the BSC deploys to link operational performance with corporate strategies.
14. Outline the role that scorecards play in the managerial acts of balancing and linking.
15. Describe the process suggested by Kaplan and Norton for implementing a BSC project.
16. Expound on the causal connections that the BSC upholds.
17. Elaborate on Hanna Norreklit's critique of the causalities assumed by Kaplan and Norton's BSC.
18. How do you differentiate between causality and finality?
19. List the major weaknesses of the BSC as a system of performance management.
20. Briefly discuss the key propositions of Kaplan and his colleagues' attempt to reimagine the BSC for the ESG era.
21. Briefly explain the notion of 'managerial capture.' Using this concept, explain the political-ideological issues of Kaplan and colleagues' neoliberal reimagination of sustainability.

Explore further

1. Select a large for-profit corporation and visit its website to explore the following:
   a. How has the company communicated its long-term strategic ambitions?
   b. What performance dimensions are captured in its strategic statements?
   c. How does the company assess its achievement in those areas? What indicators are used in its corporate performance reviews?

2. Select a public organisation (e.g., the National Health Service) and explore its website.

   Examine how its performance dimensions and targets are communicated to the public.

   Pay special attention to the key performance indicators (KPIs) it highlights.

3. Visit the UN SDGs website and explore the 17 Sustainable Development Goals.

   Then, assess a for-profit organisation's corporate reports to see the extent to which and the manner in which UN SDGs are incorporated into its strategic statements.

Develop your critical argumentation skills

1. Write an argumentative essay on the following theme:

   > "From Kaplan and Norton's BSC perspective, strategising performance management involves the managerial acts of balancing and linking."

   Explain why balancing and linking are strategically important and how they are carried out with scorecards.

2. Write an argumentative essay on the following theme:

   > "Kaplan and colleagues' project of reimagining the Balanced Scorecard for the ESG era creates more problems than solutions for sustainability."

   With a thorough reading of their recent articles, and connecting them to the critical literature on managerial capture, critically assess the arguments that Kaplan and his colleagues propose.

Mini case study: a balanced scorecard for an NGO

Sarvodaya is among the largest and oldest non-governmental organisations (NGOs) operating in a less developed country. With over 60 years of history, it is a large people's organisation with a network spanning 15,000 villages. The organisation has mobilised over 100,000 youth for peacebuilding and rural development, its core focus. Engaging in a diverse range of activities, it aims to address the developmental needs of rural villages nationwide.

The organisation operates one of the country's largest microfinance organisations, with a cumulative loan portfolio exceeding one billion LKR. It administers a significant welfare programme for over 1,000 orphaned children, underage mothers, and elders. Additionally, Sarvodaya oversees 4,335 pre-schools, benefitting more than 98,000 children. Apart from profits from its microfinance operations, Sarvodaya receives development funding from international donors such as UNICEF, the World Bank, and the UN. A major recurrent grant is slated for review in three years. To enhance its case during renewal discussions, the finance director has decided to present a balanced scorecard demonstrating the NGO's performance. Accordingly, he intends to advocate for adopting a balanced scorecard at the upcoming Board of Directors meeting.

As the senior management accountant, you have been tasked with assisting him. Given that many board members—including philanthropists, politicians, religious leaders, and senior government officers—may be unfamiliar with the BSC concept, it is crucial to provide a comprehensive briefing.

REQUIRED

1. Briefing on the concept of a balanced scorecard: For the benefit of the Management Board, outline the concept of a balanced scorecard, emphasising its utility for the NGO compared to a conventional budgeting-based system.
2. Development process and examples of measures: Discuss the process for developing a balanced scorecard for the NGO and provide examples of measures that could be incorporated.
3. Addressing concerns about suitability: A colleague has raised a concern that the BSC was primarily developed for for-profit organisations and is built upon causality leading to financial perspectives. Clarify how the BSC is adaptable to a not-for-profit organisation like Sarvodaya, highlighting its relevance in measuring and improving performance in the non-profit sector.

References

Alawattage, C., C. Graham, and D. Wickramasinghe. 2019. Microaccountability and biopolitics: Microfinance in a Sri Lankan village. Accounting, Organisations and Society 72:38-60.

Alawattage, C., C. Jayathileka, R. Hitibandara, and S. Withanage. 2022. Moral economy, performative materialism, and political rhetorics of sustainability accounting. Critical Perspectives on Accounting :102507.

Baker, M. 2010. Re-conceiving managerial capture. Accounting, Auditing & Accountability Journal 23 (7):847-867.

Bessire, D., and C. R. Baker. 2005. The French Tableau de bord and the American Balanced Scorecard: a critical analysis. Critical Perspectives on Accounting 16 (6):645-664.

Bourguignon, A., V. Malleret, and H. Norreklit. 2004. The American balanced scorecard versus the French tableau de bord: the ideological dimension. Management Accounting Research 15 (2):107-134.

Brett, J. A. 2006. "We Sacrifice and Eat Less": The Structural Complexities of Microfinance Participation. Human Organization 65 (1):8-19.

Cooper, D. J., M. Ezzamel, and S. Q. Qu. 2017. Popularising a Management Accounting Idea: The Case of the Balanced Scorecard. Contemporary Accounting Research 34 (2):991-1025.

Fernando, J. L. 2011. The Political Economy of NGOs: State Formation in Sri Lanka and Bangladesh. Pluto Press.

Figge, F., T. Hahn, S. Schaltegger, and M. Wagner. 2002. The Sustainability Balanced Scorecard – linking sustainability management to business strategy. Business Strategy and the Environment 11 (5):269-284.

Hansen, E. G., and S. Schaltegger. 2016. The Sustainability Balanced Scorecard: A Systematic Review of Architectures. Journal of Business Ethics 133 (2):193-221.

Haraway, D. 2015. Anthropocene, Capitalocene, Plantationocene, Chthulucene: Making Kin. Environmental Humanities 6 (1):159-165.

Jacobs, K., M. Habib, N. Musyoki, and C. Jubb. 2012. Empowering or oppressing: the case of microfinance institutions. In Handbook of Accounting and Development, edited by T. Hopper, M. Tsamenyi, S. Uddin and D. Wickramasinghe, 162-181. Cheltenham: Edward Elgar Publishing.

Kalender, Z. T., and Ö. Vayvay. 2016. The Fifth Pillar of the Balanced Scorecard: Sustainability. Procedia - Social and Behavioral Sciences 235:76-83.

Kaplan, R. S. 2008. Conceptual Foundations of the Balanced Scorecard. In Handbooks of Management Accounting Research, edited by C. S. Chapman, A. G. Hopwood and M. D. Shields, 1253-1269. Elsevier.

Kaplan, R. S., and D. McMillan. 2021. Reimagining the Balanced Scorecard for the ESG Era. Harvard Business Review, May-June.

Kaplan, R. S., and D. P. Norton. 1993. Putting the Balanced Scorecard to Work. Harvard Business Review, September-October:134-147.

———. 1996a. The Balanced Scorecard: Translating Strategy into Action. Boston, MA: Harvard Business School Press.

———. 1996b. Using the Balanced Scorecard as a Strategic Management System. Harvard Business Review, January-February:75-85.

———. 2000. Having Trouble with Your Strategy? Then Map It. Harvard Business Review, September-October:172-180.

Kaplan, R. S., G. Serafeim, and E. Tugendhat. 2018. Inclusive growth: profitable strategies for tackling poverty and inequality. Harvard Business Review, January-February:116-123.

Moore, J. 2015. Capitalism in the Web of Life: Ecology and the Accumulation of Capital. Verso.

Norreklit, H. 2000. The balance on the balanced scorecard a critical analysis of some of its assumptions. Management Accounting Research 11 (1):65-88.

———. 2003. The Balanced Scorecard: what is the score? A rhetorical analysis of the Balanced Scorecard. Accounting, Organisations and Society 28 (6):591-619.

O'Dwyer, B. 2003. Conceptions of corporate social responsibility: the nature of managerial capture. Accounting, Auditing & Accountability Journal 16 (4):523-557.

Owen, D. L., T. A. Swift, C. Humphrey, and M. Bowerman. 2000. The new social audits: accountability, managerial capture or the agenda of social champions? European Accounting Review 9 (1):81-98.

Prahalad, C. K. 2005. The Fortune at the Bottom of the Pyramid: Eradicating Poverty Through Profits. New Jersey: Wharton School Publishing.

Roy, A. 2010. Poverty Capital: Microfinance and the Making of Development. Taylor & Francis.

Weber, H. 2006. The global political economy of microfinance and poverty reduction: locating local 'livelihoods' in political analysis. In Microfinance: Perils and Prospects, edited by J. L. Fernando. London: Routledge.

CHAPTER

5 Strategy in the hierarchy: **strategising management control**

5.1 Introduction

To recapitulate the overarching thematic structure of this textbook, it is important to recall that strategies are implemented across three interconnected domains of strategic action: the market, the organisational hierarchy, and the point of production. As elucidated in the initial three chapters, the market is the arena in which strategic positioning is implemented. Three forthcoming chapters will delve into how the point of production facilitates and executes these market positioning strategies by producing what the market demands, encompassing three critical strategic imperatives: quality, cost, and flexibility.

The organisational hierarchy provides the institutional and administrative infrastructure to manage the strategic linkage between the market and the point of production. It also ensures that the organisation complies with the ethical, legal, and regulatory obligations imposed by its external environment. Within this context, three strategic themes associated with the organisational hierarchy are delineated: performance management, management control, and organisational resilience. The preceding chapter addressed strategic performance management, while the current chapter focuses on strategic management control. The subsequent chapter will then explore organisational resilience as a further extension of these discussions.

The chapter is structured around the following key themes.

1. First, section 5.2 will examine the generic meaning of 'control' and the fundamental conditions that necessitate different forms of control. The discussion will primarily address the conventional conceptualisation of

control in the management accounting literature, before notions of strategic management control began to influence the field. This section begins with a brief discussion of how agency theory, a popular theoretical framework in mainstream accounting research, frames our understanding of management control.

Then, as systems theory-based conceptions of management control laid the initial conceptual groundwork for the subsequent development of strategic management control frameworks, this section will specifically highlight the various ways systems theory underpins our comprehension of management control.

After reading this section, you should be able to elucidate the conditions that necessitate control and the different conceptual frames according to which control is conceptualised in conventional management accounting literature.

2. Second, in section 5.3, using Simons' Levers of Control (LOC) framework, we will explore strategic management control dynamics, systems, and processes. The LOC framework enables us to understand how management control underpins broader strategic considerations, such as defining an organisation's beliefs and core values, establishing boundaries for risk-taking, managing critical performance variables through diagnostic control systems, and addressing strategic uncertainties through interactive control systems. This section will also address the possibilities and challenges of utilising the LOC framework for sustainability. After reading this section, you should be able to explain the key propositions of strategic management control using Simons' LOC framework and assess how this framework can be applied to promote sustainability.
3. Finally, section 5.4 concludes the chapter with a summary.

5.2 Understanding the fundamentals of management control

The conceptualisation of management controls manifests in various forms, often delineated by dichotomies such as operational versus strategic, bureaucratic versus cultural, external versus internal, and cybernetic versus non-cybernetic controls (see Berry et al., 2005). Despite variations in their manifestation, all control issues stem from a fundamental ontological condition: the existence of contradictions. Control is necessitated and defined by these conflicting conditions.

How control is conceptualised and how control systems, processes, and procedures are designed and implemented depend on the specific contradictory conditions to which these controls are linked. For instance, control may be necessitated by transnational contradictions between nations involving conflicting political, ideological, and economic interests. In such instances, various global governance and control mechanisms, such as international treaties and global governance institutions like the UN and EU, play a crucial role in mitigating potential crises.

Similarly, contradictions may arise between organisations, such as parties involved in market transactions or supply chain arrangements. In such cases, laws, regulations, and contracts are essential control mechanisms to maintain order. Alternatively, contradictions may be intra-organisational, occurring between different levels or departments that emphasise divergent managerial priorities. In such cases, various management control techniques, including budgets, policies, and procedures, may constitute control practices to foster coordination.

Contradictions can also be interpersonal, requiring specific human resource policies and ethical codes of conduct. Alternatively, they may be intra-personal, necessitating various 'self-control' or psychological control mechanisms. In an overall sense, control may thus involve the regulation of actions and outcomes, the mitigation of risks, compliance with norms, or the domination of one party by another. The specific form that control takes depends on the manner in which the control situation—the contradictory condition—manifests and is conceptualised. Therefore, the theoretical framing of these conditions is critical to understanding and interpreting control.

Let us consider two prevalent theoretical frameworks to observe how contradictory conditions, and hence management control, are conceptualised differently in the management accounting literature: agency theory and systems theory.

Agency theory conception of management control

In its various iterations, such as the principal-agent model, transaction cost theory, and the Rochester model, agency theory incorporates neoclassical economic perspectives on management control (see Baiman, 1990, 2006). It conceptualises management control as the means by which an organisation addresses potential inefficiencies and losses arising from the 'agency problem'. This problem, central to the theory, represents a contradiction between two parties in a contract or transaction.

In the principal-agent model, the firm is viewed as a series of hierarchically arranged agency relationships where the principal hires an agent to delegate responsibilities under a mutually agreed-upon contract. This contract outlines compensation arrangements, accountabilities, information systems, and the allocation of duties and ownership rights. Examples of such relationships include those

Side note: the discussion here focuses on the generic principal-agent model; for nuanced differences between agency theory variants, see Baiman (1990, 2006).

between owners (principals) and managers (agents), superior managers (principals) and subordinates (agents), and clients (principals) and service providers (agents). These agency relationships can exist within an organisation (intra-organisational) or between firms (inter-organisational). Organisational hierarchies and inter-firm arrangements, such as franchising and subcontracting, are examples of agency relationships.

The 'contract', whether explicit or implicit, serves as the primary control tool regulating the relationship between the agent and principal. It outlines specific objectives, duties, responsibilities, and authorities delegated to the agent, alongside compensation and information arrangements. Various managerial techniques, such as management by objectives, budgeting, responsibility accounting, and balanced scorecards, constitute complementary methods of contractual arrangement between agents (employees) and the principal (the firm). Such arrangements define the agency relationships and construct the organisation as a 'nexus of contracts' (Fama, 1980; Fama and Jensen, 1983).

Any agency relationship is inherently contradictory because, as agency theorists assume, agents are self-interested, and their interests are not naturally aligned with the principal's interest in profit maximisation. A self-interested agent is assumed to be work-averse and risk-averse and possesses private information about their own actions and work, which the principal cannot costlessly access. This contradictory condition is identified as the 'agency problem': the possibility that the agent's self-interested, risk-averse, and work-averse behaviour, coupled with information asymmetry, can undermine corporate goals.

According to agency theorists, it is this problem that necessitates management control. If self-interest is 'nature', then 'controls' are necessary to align agents' behaviour with corporate goals. Such controls define the nature of agency relationships within economic enterprises. Responsibility accounting systems involving budgeting, standard costing, and balanced scorecards, for example, may define the parameters within which agency relationships are controlled so that possible efficiency losses are minimised and shareholders' wealth is maximised.

From an agency theory perspective, the management control challenge is to design a 'performance and compensation contract' that incentivises agents to exert effort to maximise the principal's profit. Wages and rents represent opposing forms of compensation, and a combination of both is likely to maximise the principal's payoff. A wage-only contract, where the principal pays a fixed wage irrespective of the agent's effort, provides no monetary incentive for the agent to exert greater effort. In that case, the principal bears the total risk of the business. Conversely, in a total rent contract, where the principal rents out the business for a fixed payment, the agent bears the total business risk. Although a rent contract motivates the agent to perform better, their performance brings no additional gains for the principal. As such, a particular combination of wage and rent compensation is most likely to maximise the principal's payoff.

Figure 5.1 illustrates the agency theory conception of optimal performance-compensation contracting.

Figure 5.1: Agency theory conception of optimal performance-compensation contracting

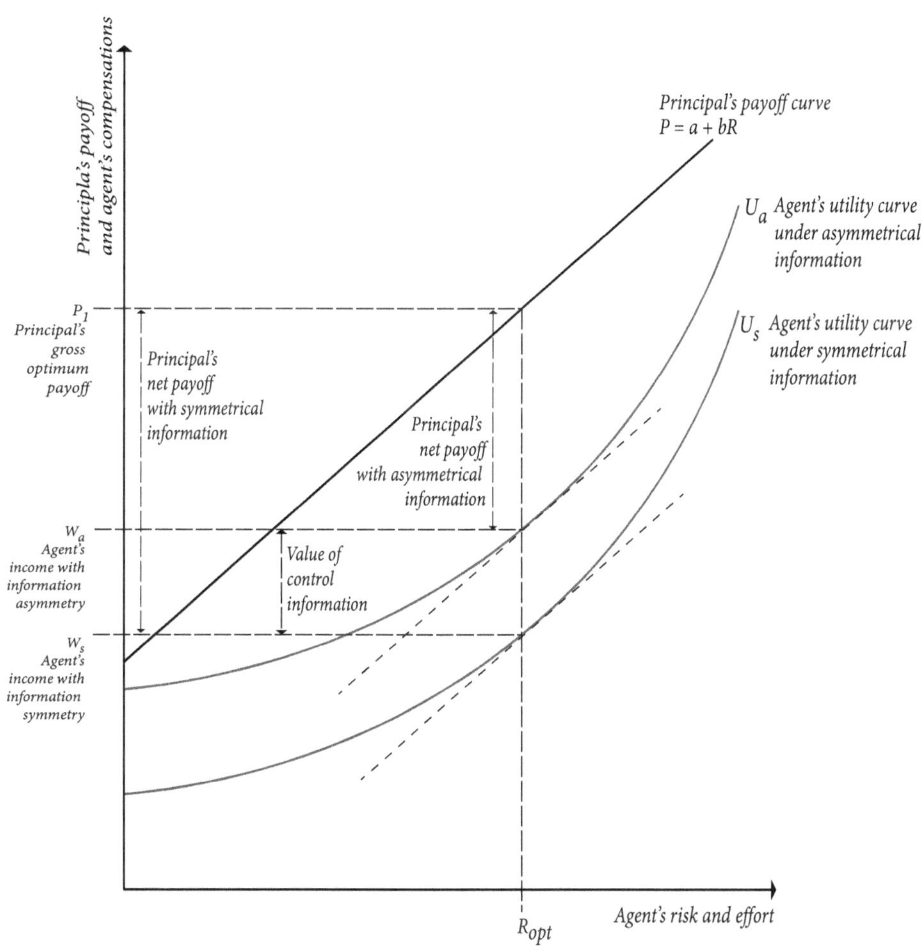

Reading Figure 5.1: The key components of Figure 5.1 are as follows:

- The vertical axis signifies the dependent variables: the principal's payoff (P) and the agent's compensation (W).
- The horizontal axis denotes the independent variables: the risks undertaken and effort exerted by the agent (R).
- The principal's payoff is determined by the agent's risk and effort, encapsulated in the linear function P=a+bR, where:
- P represents the principal's payoff (profit before deducting payments for the agent).
- 'a' represents the principal's payoff when the agent assumes no risks (equivalent to compensation under a fixed-wage contract).
- 'b' signifies the marginal contribution of the agent's additional risk and effort to the principal's payoff.
- R denotes the level of risk and effort the agent undertakes.
- The agent's risk-return preference, or utility, is denoted by U and is illustrated through indifference curves (Ua and Us). These curves portray different risk-return combinations for the agent. Ua and Us represent possibilities for agents with or without private information (i.e., information asymmetry).
- The principal's net payoff is the difference between their gross payoff (the P curve) and the agent's utility curve (U) at any given level of risk assumed by the agent. As depicted, the net payoff is maximised at Ropt.
- Two utility curves are displayed: one for information asymmetry (Ua) and one for information symmetry (Us). A condition of information symmetry opens the agent's private information to the principal, prompting the agent to accept the Ropt level of risk for a lower wage (Ws) compared to what they could obtain under information asymmetry (Wa). Consequently, the principal attains greater profit with information symmetry (P1–Ws) than with information asymmetry (P1–Wa).
- From the principal's standpoint, the solution under information symmetry is the 'first-best' solution, while the solution under information asymmetry is the 'second-best' solution. The difference signifies the value of control information, which makes the agency relationship symmetrical and the agent's behaviour more predictable. From an agency theory perspective, the value of control information lies in enhancing the principal's wealth maximisation prospects. In Figure 5.1, the economic value of control information equates to the difference between Wa and Ws. According to agency theory, a firm should not expend more resources than this value to obtain accounting and control information.

Systems theory conception of management control

Systems theory is a more dominant and extensive framework in the management control literature than the neoclassical economic concepts discussed previously. Noteworthy works, such as Berry et al.'s (2005) Management Control: Theories, Issues and Performance and Anthony et al.'s (2014) Management Control Systems, are fundamentally expositions of management control based on systems theory. Even recent innovations in strategic management control, such as Simons' Levers of Control, are essentially conceptions of management control rooted in systems theory.

The foundation of these systems theory-based conceptualisations is the acknowledgement that any organisation functions as an open system. An open system is an assembly of interacting and interdependent components that engage with its environment to achieve a common set of goals. By recognising organisations as open systems, the core challenges addressed by management control become systemic contradictions, which exist not only among various subsystems but also in the interactions between the organisation and its external environment. Consequently, systems theory-based perspectives on management control encompass a broader spectrum of dynamics than agency theory's problem-based understanding.

Taking a broader view, a systems theory-based conceptualisation of management control encompasses three interconnected perspectives: a cybernetic perspective, a hierarchical perspective, and an environmental perspective.

Cybernetic perspectives on management control

The cybernetic approach envisions the organisational system as a programmable input-conversion-output process, subject to regulation through feedback information. Cybernetic controls may target inputs, conversion processes, or outputs, representing three modes of control: feedback (output-driven), concurrent (process-driven), and feedforward (input-driven). As depicted in Figure 5.2, their controllability hinges on four necessary conditions:

1. Objectives for the system being controlled.
2. A means of measuring results along the dimensions defined by the objectives. Such measurements often encapsulate three generic dimensions:
    a. *effectiveness*, the extent to which a system achieves its intended transformation;
    b. *efficiency*, the extent to which this is achieved with minimal use of resources; and

   c. *efficacy*, the extent to which the system contributes to the purpose of a higher-order system of which it is a part.

3. A predictive model of the system being controlled.
4. A choice of relevant corrective actions available to controllers.

Figure 5.2: Cybernetic model of management control

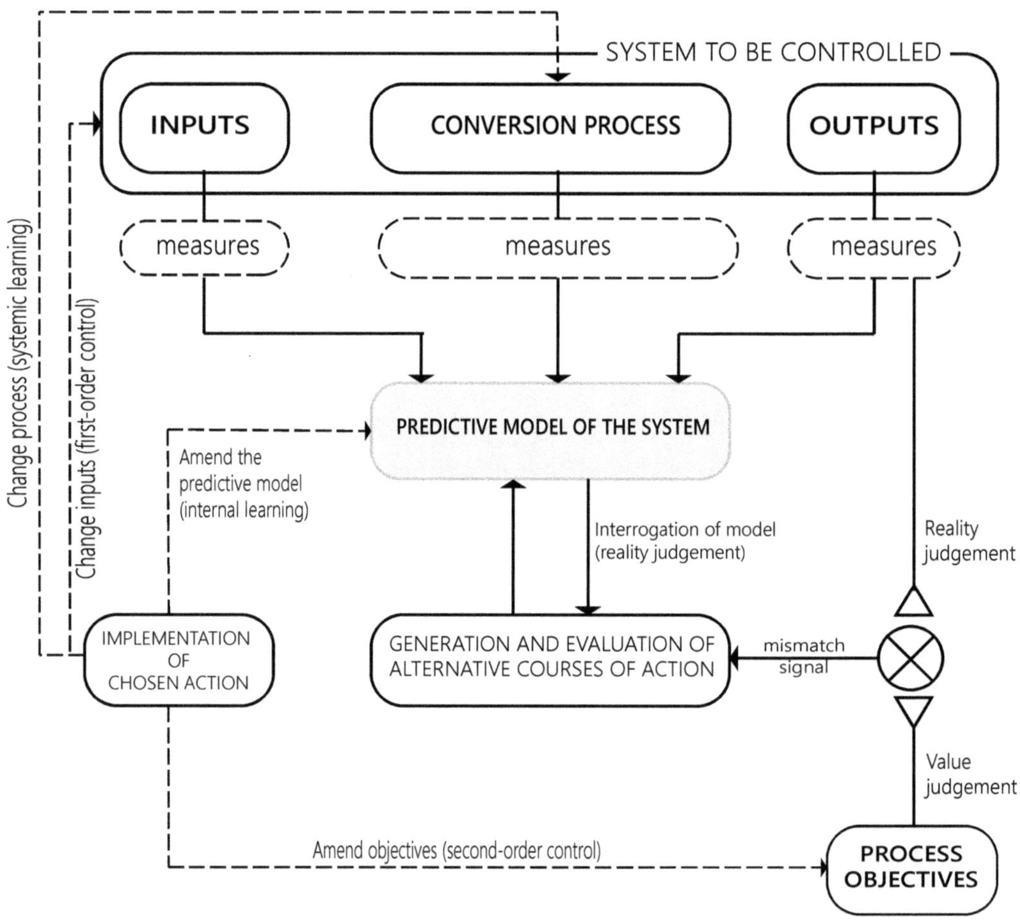

Source: Adapted from Otley and Berry (1980, p. 236)

Cybernetics emphasises the inherent interdependence of control and communication. As Baecker (2001, p. 59) highlights, 'control cannot be discussed without referencing communication. Every control act is inherently a communicative act'. Echoing this, Otley and Berry (1980, p. 236) assert that 'control can only exist when knowledge of outcomes is available'. The predictive model serves as the controlling component that executes this communicative function. It is the conduit through which the targeted system is conceptualised, measured, and understood. As Otley and Berry (1980, p. 236) elucidate, 'In the absence or malfunction of such a model, control becomes unattainable'.

The predictive model is pivotal as the performer of three essential cybernetic functions: ***detector***, ***comparator***, and ***effector***, all of which are communicative functionalities. In essence, the predictive model within a cybernetic system serves as the central epistemic tool or the conceptual framework according to which the system to be controlled is conceived, designed, and controlled in terms of inputs, conversion process, and outputs. It spells out the underlying processual logic according to which detection, comparison, and execution of corrective actions are to be designed and implemented. It establishes the performance measures pertaining to inputs, conversion processes, and outputs; it establishes data collection and testing methodologies according to which actual performances are monitored, recorded, and evaluated; it establishes the comparative benchmarks and standards against which actual performances are compared for corrective actions.

Various forms of recording, counting, accounting, seeing, and understanding constitute the detection. The control system effectively detects the actual system status through counting, accounting, costing, testing, and various other modes of seeing, recording, and understanding. Hence, for an effective cybernetic control system to operate, there needs to be an effective system that captures and meaningfully records system inputs, conversion processes, and their outputs/outcomes. Transaction processing systems, including bookkeeping, constitute the basic element of the detector functionality of a control system. Such systems of detection interrogate the system to formulate reality judgments as to how it operates and performs.

Reality judgment then leads to the second functionality of cybernetic control: the comparator. This involves comparing the reality judgment on the actual system performance with the predetermined process objectives to formulate a value judgment. A classic illustration of this process is found in standard costing and variance analysis. Substantial variances between actual performance and standards (objectives) trigger the effector—the process of implementing corrective actions. This encompasses generating and evaluating alternative courses of action, selecting the optimal one, and implementing it. Such corrective actions may be directed towards changing input (i.e., first-order control), amendments to the process objectives (i.e., second-order control), amendments to the predictive model of the process (i.e., internal learning), changes to the productive process (i.e, systemic learning) or any combination thereof.

So, this is the essence of the cybernetic conception of management control, and you should recognise that it is rather technical and mainly captures control of techno-operational processes.

Beyond cybernetics

Not all control systems can be distilled into a cybernetic framework. Acknowledging this, Hofstede (1981) devised a typology of management control that recognises both cybernetic and non-cybernetic attributes. Hofstede's typology is grounded in four key questions:

1. Are the objectives unambiguous?
2. Are the outputs measurable?
3. Are the effects of interventions known?
4. Is the activity repetitive?

Based on these characteristics, Hofstede identified six types of management control, as summarised in Table 5.1.

Table 5.1: Beyond cybernetics: Hofstede's control typology

Control Type	Objectives Unambiguous?	Outputs Measurable?	Effects of Interventions Known?	Activity Repetitive?	Cybernetic vs. Non-Cybernetic Features
Routine	Yes	Yes	Yes	Yes	A perfect cybernetic system; control is routinised.
Expert	Yes	Yes	Yes	No	Cybernetic, but control is entrusted to experts.
Trial and Error	Yes	Yes	No	No	Cybernetic, but control methods are learned through trial and error.
Intuitive	Yes	No, but surrogates found	No	No	Non-cybernetic; management control is an art.
Judgmental	Yes, or ambiguity resolvable	No	No	No	Non-cybernetic; control is a matter of subjective judgment.
Political	No	No	No	No	Non-cybernetic; control is political, depending on power, negotiation, and compromise.

Source: Based on Hofstede (1981)

As summarised in Table 5.1 and elaborated in the upcoming sections, strategic management control is distinctly 'political', involving negotiations among conflicting political-economic, social, and ecological values. This complexity is particularly pronounced in the emerging global sustainability agenda, where management control must reconcile contradictions between the economy, polity, society, and ecology

Dermer (1988) critiques the cybernetic conceptualisation, arguing that it obscures a deeper understanding of control. He states:

> Conventional thinking about order has been dominated by two concepts: strategy and cybernetics... According to this view, management controls the organisation from outside, setting the thermostat as it were, observing results, and resetting as necessary. Organisational order is thus seen as the creation of management, strategy and cybernetics as the tools it uses. (Dermer, 1988, p. 25)

For Dermer, control can be non-cybernetic; organisations can self-govern through underlying assumptions and principles. There is a need to revise the cybernetic conceptualisation, particularly concerning 'multi-rationality' and 'pluralism' (Dermer, 1988; Dermer and Lucas, 1986).

Hierarchical perspectives and structural functionalism in management control

Aligned with systems theory, hierarchical perspectives emphasise

a. the distribution of authority and responsibility and
b. the functional division of organisational goals.

These perspectives view management control as the process of achieving coordination among organisational subsystems, which often have conflicting objectives, such as hard (technical) and soft (socio-psychological) systems.

Contradictions between these subsystems have led to studies that Burrell and Morgan (1979) termed 'socio-technical system theories' and 'theories of bureaucratic dysfunctions'. The core argument of these studies is that organisational systems comprise interdependent subsystems with contradictory objectives, which requires a compromise to achieve an optimal balance. This plurality in objectives is often expressed in frameworks like Kaplan and Norton's Balanced Scorecard. Accordingly, the functional division and hierarchical ordering of organisational systems constitute the institutional basis of management control.

Underlying these perspectives is the concept of 'functional imperatives'. As the prominent systems theorist Talcott Parsons (Parsons and Smelser, 2005, p. 16) articulated in his AGIL schema, 'Any social system is subject to four independent functional imperatives or "problems" which must be met adequately if equilibrium and/or continuing existence of the system is to be maintained'. These are:

1. Adaptation (A): Establishing a viable fit between the system and its environment.
2. Goal attainment (G): Defining and mobilising resources to attain system goals.
3. Integration (I): Maintaining coordination between subsystems and inhibiting deviancy.
4. Latency or pattern maintenance (L): Motivating actors and subsystems to maintain expected performance levels.

These imperatives form the basis of 'structural functionalism', which underpins much of the systems theory-based understanding of management control. Two key propositions are central:

a. the importance of relationships among parts and their environment, and
b. the functional roles that parts perform to maintain a productive totality.

Seminal works in performance management and management control, particularly by Simons (1995), Otley (1999), and Ferreira and Otley (2009), distinctly reflect structural functionalism. In this view, management control refers to the processes implemented to regulate and sustain a social system. Managers must configure the organisation into a ***cohesive structure of units***, unified through ***vertical and horizontal relationships*** established via the division of work and delegation of objectives, authorities, responsibilities, accountabilities, and information flows.

The *functional purpose* of management control is to ensure the organisation's continuity and growth. This continuity is upheld through the processes inherent in the organisational life involving accountants, other managers, employees, and regulators. According to Ferreira and Otley (2009), these processes encompass analysis, planning, measurement, control, rewarding, and facilitating organisational learning and change. Their collective focus is on sustaining and growing the organisation by efficiently and effectively achieving goals and objectives—such as profits, customer satisfaction, employee well-being, and environmental friendliness—imposed by the external environment.

Robert Anthony (1965) posited the necessity for three interconnected organisational processes: operational control, management control, and strategic planning. This framework has been widely embraced in management accounting.

1. At the top, strategic planning processes formulate long-term directions and define the organisation's relationship with its environment. This addresses the challenge of Adaptation (A).
2. In the middle, management control processes ensure the implementation of strategic decisions. These serve the imperatives of Goal attainment (G) and Integration (I).
3. At the bottom, operational control systems ensure routine activities are carried out efficiently. This handles the functional imperative of Latency (L), focusing on the routinisation of tasks.

Table 5.2 summarises how structural functionalism underpins this classical understanding of management control systems.

Table 5.2: Parsons' structural functionalism and the classical theory of management control systems

Control Function/ Hierarchy	Functional Imperatives Addressed	Calculative Practices
Strategic Planning	Adaptation (A): Establishing relations between the system and its external environment.	SWOT analysis, industry analysis, market analysis, value chain analysis, capital investment decisions, corporate planning.
Management Control	Goal attainment (G): Defining system goals and mobilising resources. Integration (I): Inhibiting deviancy and maintaining coordination.	Budgeting, standard costing and variance analysis, financial statement analysis, Balanced Scorecards, transfer pricing, performance management.
Operational Control	Latency (L): Programming and routinisation of tasks; providing motivation.	Production scheduling, inventory management, quality control, internal checks and balances, record keeping.

Environmental perspectives on management control

The third perspective under systems theory is the environmental perspective. This focuses on how organisations navigate external pressures by adjusting their internal subsystems. The environment is perceived as a complex supra-system. As Pfeffer and Salancik (2003, pp. 2-3) elaborate:

Problems arise not merely because organisations are dependent on their environment, but because this environment is not dependable. Environments can change, new organisations enter and exit, and the supply of resources becomes more or less scarce.

To address this complexity, managers often categorise the environment into distinct spheres where different stakeholders operate. The interests of these stakeholders are identified as 'functional imperatives', and organisations structure themselves functionally to address them. Figure 5.3 provides a conceptual schema illustrating this relationship.

Figure 5.3: The Environment as a supra-system of external control

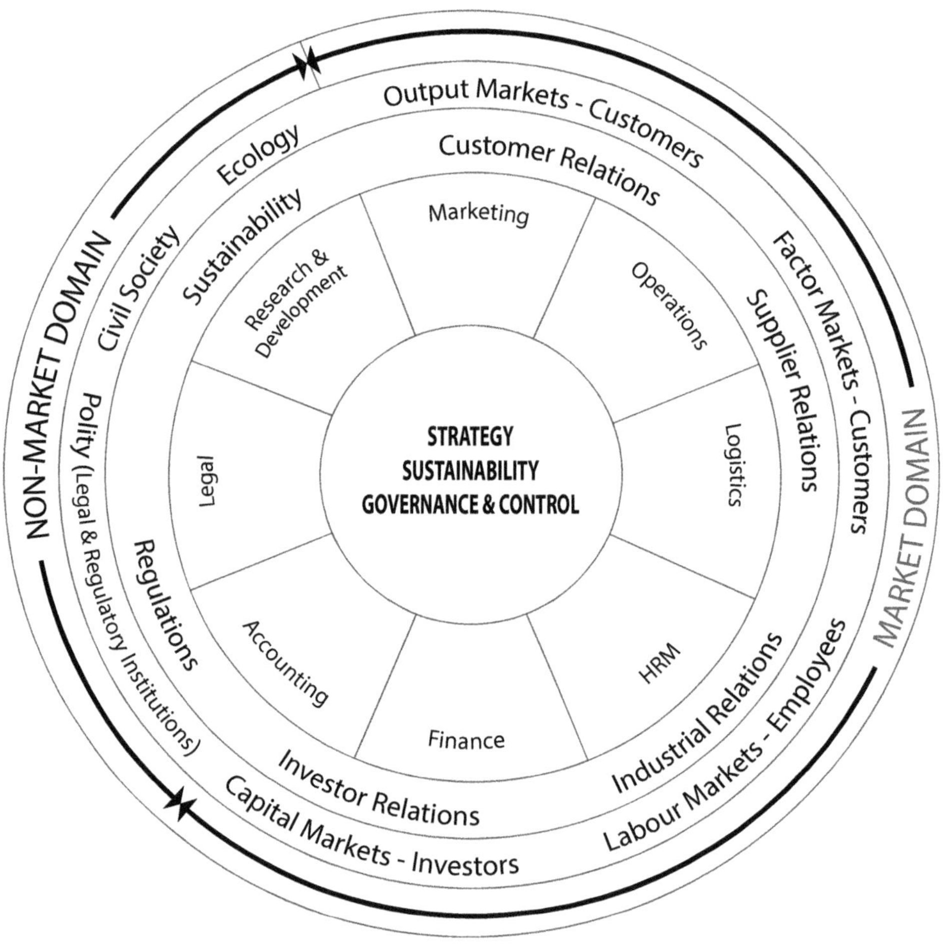

Analysing Figure 5.3, stakeholders are categorised into market (customers, employees, suppliers, investors) and non-market (political, civil, societal, ecological) domains. Organisations often structure their internal management in alignment

with this external environment, with specialised divisions (e.g., marketing, operations, HRM, finance) managing stakeholder interests. At the core, top management functions related to corporate strategy and governance must integrate all these aspects to ensure the organisation's survival and growth.

5.3 Strategic management control: levers of control

Recent advancements in strategic management control build upon systems theory-based concepts. Two notable developments aim to integrate management control with corporate strategy. The first is the strategic performance management movement, spearheaded by Kaplan and Norton's Balanced Scorecard, which links operations with strategy through 'cascading'. The second involves the strategic management control ideas popularised by Robert Simons' Levers of Control (LOC) framework, which focuses on a broader spectrum of strategic dynamics. This section delves into the fundamental principles of the LOC framework.

Simons' conception of strategic contradictions

According to Simons (1995), conventional 'command and control' methods are inadequate for today's dynamic business environment. He argues that 'command-and-control techniques no longer suffice in competitive environments where creativity and employee initiative are critical to business success' (Simons, 1995, p. 3). Consequently, Simons introduces his concept of 'levers of control', proposing that:

> A new theory of control that recognises the need to balance competing demands is required. Inherent tensions must be controlled, tensions between freedom and constraint, between empowerment and accountability, between top-down direction and bottom-up creativity, between experimentation and efficiency. (Simons, 1995, p. 4)

For Simons, therefore, the core managerial challenge is not to choose one force over another but to manage the tension between them. The goal is to create a dynamic equilibrium by integrating these opposing forces within the organisation. Organisations face the strategic imperative of balancing systemic tensions arising from the opposing dynamics of:

1. value creation (flexibility, innovation, entrepreneurship) on one hand, and
2. regulation and control (measurement, standardisation, risk minimisation) on the other.

In this context, Simons argues that the functional role of strategy and control is to address the systemic imperative of balancing these tensions.

Levers of control

Simons' framework revolves around the central concept of strategy. Drawing on Mintzberg (1987), Simons defines strategy in four interconnected ways: as plans, patterns of action, competitive positions, and overarching perspectives. This allows him to link these different forms of strategy with four distinct 'levers of control' that organisations should establish to address four strategically vital systemic imperatives (see Figure 5.4).

Figure 5.4: Simons' Levers of Control Framework

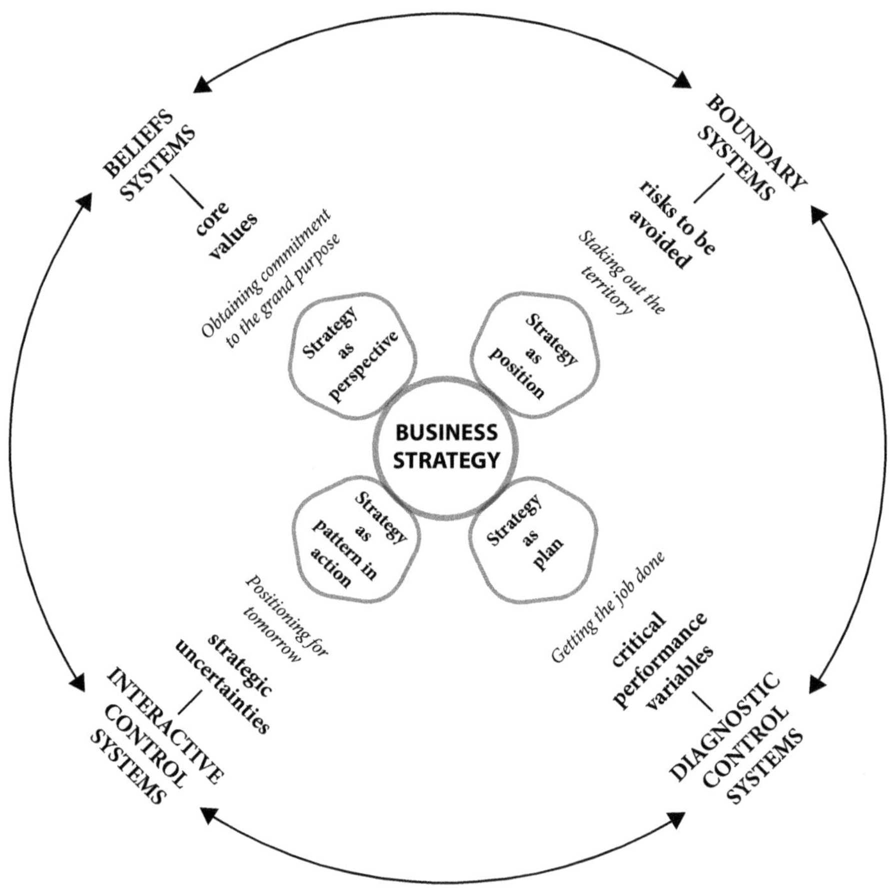

Source: Simons' various publications.

According to Simons, the LOC are specific control subsystems that organisations should implement to oversee four key strategic imperatives: core values, risks to be avoided, strategic uncertainties, and critical performance variables. These imperatives are managed through four LOCs: belief systems, boundary systems, interactive control systems, and diagnostic control systems.

1. Defining Organisational Core Values, Purposes, and Directions

   Organisations must consistently redefine their core values and purpose in response to evolving environments. This aspect of strategy, which Simons terms a 'perspective', represents the collective commitment sought by top management. To manage this, Simons proposes the use of belief systems. These are explicit organisational statements, such as vision and mission, that articulate fundamental values and purpose. Belief systems aim to inspire and guide members to discover new ways of creating value.

2. Mitigating Risks through Boundary Systems

   Avoiding risks involves defining the acceptable scope of activities, a strategic imperative managed through boundary systems. These systems counterbalance the expansionary tendencies of belief systems. Boundary systems operate in two ways. First, they set operational boundaries, framing strategic limits for business areas the organisation should avoid. This emphasises strategic positioning. Second, they establish conduct boundaries by imposing codes of business conduct. These codes draw from societal laws, the organisation's belief system, and professional associations. While belief systems encourage opportunity-seeking, boundary systems act as a restrictive mechanism.

   According to Simons, these two mechanisms—belief systems and boundary systems—collaborate to generate forces of 'yin and yang': 'The warm, positive, inspirational beliefs are a foil to dark, cold constraints. The result is a dynamic tension between commitment and punishment. Senior managers drive both processes'.

3. Managing Performance and Implementing Strategies

   Managing critical performance variables and implementing intended strategies is a crucial organisational function. According to Simons, this imperative relies on diagnostic control systems. These systems are feedback mechanisms integral to ensuring predictable goal attainment and form the foundation of traditional management control. Diagnostic control systems involve three essential functions:

   a. Defining key performance dimensions and variables to measure intended outcomes.

b. Measuring actual outcomes against predefined standards and objectives.
c. Implementing corrective actions to address deviations.

It is important to note that this lever of control specifically addresses the 'intended strategy', or strategy as a plan. Its functional role is to coordinate and monitor the implementation of this strategy. This concept aligns with the earlier-discussed notion of cybernetic control and encompasses apparatuses such as the Balanced Scorecard.

4. Managing Strategic Uncertainties and Adapting to Competitive Environments

   Strategic uncertainties are environmental factors that could render the current strategy ineffective. These uncertainties necessitate that the firm either abandons or modifies its original strategy, leading to what Mintzberg terms an 'emergent strategy'. This adaptive capacity involves asking the right questions about factors that could invalidate the current strategy.

   According to Simons, the imperative of managing strategic uncertainties is addressed by interactive control systems. An interactive control system is not a distinct type, but rather any control system that managers use interactively. When used to activate search and dialogue, a control system becomes interactive. It can focus on strategic uncertainties, stimulate debate, and encourage information gathering beyond routine channels. Interactive control systems, therefore, serve as a mechanism for organisational learning, challenging existing strategies to develop emergent strategies that enhance adaptation. The emerging discourse on organisational resilience, the theme of the next chapter, has now captured this aspect of control.

In summary, Simons' LOC framework provides a systems theory-based logic for managing organisational control and strategy. It views an organisation as a social system striving for dynamic equilibrium by addressing tensions arising from various functional imperatives. This framework aligns with Parsons' AGIL model. Adaptation (A) is integrated into belief and interactive systems. Goal attainment (G) and Integration (I) are central to diagnostic control systems, while Latency (L) is the fundamental objective of boundary and diagnostic systems.

Levers of control and integration of sustainability

Simons' LOC framework is highly adaptable and can encompass diverse control dimensions. It proves valuable as a model for viewing sustainability as a strategic challenge, necessitating transformations in an organisation's value systems, belief systems, and control systems. Arjaliès and Mundy (2013), for example, provide an analysis of how the LOC framework can be used to analyse the ways in which sustainability issues permeate organisational control structures, drawing on data from France's largest listed companies.

1. Belief Systems for Communicating CSR Core Values

   Arjaliès and Mundy's research reveals the use of formal statements, such as CSR strategic plans, 'values' charts', and mission statements, to convey the integration of CSR into organisations' core values.

2. Boundary Systems for Risk Management

   The findings highlight that companies refer to external laws, regulations, and reporting protocols (e.g., NRE, GRI) when establishing the limits within which their actions should operate. This involves defining acceptable behaviours and strategic priorities, particularly across supply chains.

3. Interactive Control Systems for Managing Strategic Uncertainties

   Integrating sustainability involves revealing and debating emergent strategies. Regular and formal discussions between CSR teams, senior management, and operational managers are popular for integrating CSR imperatives with operational requirements, facilitating the exchange of best practices.

4. Diagnostic Processes for Managing Critical Performance Variables

   While other levers set strategic parameters, the diagnostic lever demands that firms translate them into specific key performance variables. Arjaliès and Mundy's study emphasises the role of environmental management systems (EMS), standardised reporting (e.g., GRI), and competitive benchmarking in this process.

In a broad sense, Arjaliès and Mundy's study indicates that companies are making commendable efforts to incorporate sustainability into their control systems. This emphasises the strategic importance of integrating sustainability into the core business strategy. However, a critical-political examination of their data reveals the challenges managers face in addressing sustainability within control mechanisms designed primarily to prioritise capital accumulation.

Side Note:

It is crucial to note that Simons' LOC differs from Kaplan and Norton's BSC in that it does not offer a specific set of tools. Instead, the LOC framework helps managers comprehend how various control elements fit into a broader schema of strategising that considers both performance and compliance (see Tessier and Otley, 2012).

The data provided by Arjaliès and Mundy imply that sustainability and corporate social responsibility (CSR) have become crucial considerations primarily for mitigating potential profit losses arising from regulatory non-compliance. This suggests corporate sustainability endeavours are underpinned by a 'mitigative motive'. Even positive innovations often originate from a 'profit motive': the belief that strategising for sustainability can and should increase profits. Similar to the discussion in the previous chapter on the Balanced Scorecard, there appears to be a notable 'managerial capture of sustainability'. This 'managerial capture' refers to the leveraging of sustainability to enhance capital accumulation, without fundamentally transforming the ideological purpose for which such organisations and their managerial frameworks exist.

Critical accounting scholars, such as Milne (1996), emphasise that genuine sustainability can only be achieved by acknowledging the political necessity of prioritising social and ecological justice over capitalistic motives of accumulation.

Therefore, for a critical understanding, corporate sustainability efforts need to be recontextualised beyond the institutional control apparatuses of capital. It is important to note that frameworks like the LOC and BSC are tailored for profit-seeking, capitalistic organisations and are fundamentally 'organisation-centric'. They analyse how the environment affects the organisation, concentrating on economic value creation. These frameworks are inward-looking and lack the analytical capacity to adopt an 'environmental-centric' perspective. As Milne (1996) and others (e.g., Gray, 2010; Gray and Bebbington, 2001) explain, achieving true sustainability demands an environmental-centric approach to accountability rather than narrow, organisation-centric approaches that can only see sustainability as an instrument to expand the fundamentally exploitative 'capitalocene' (Haraway, 2015).

Chapter summary

As a site of strategic action, the organisational hierarchy encompasses three interrelated themes: performance management, management control, and organisational resilience. This chapter has delved into strategic control.

Contradictions and conflicts serve as the fundamental conditions for control. Consequently, the way we conceptualise these contradictory situations forms the epistemological basis for understanding and designing management control systems.

Agency theory and systems theory are the prominent theoretical frameworks that underpin the classical understanding of management control. Agency theory, rooted in neoclassical economics, focuses on optimising agency relationships through contracts to minimise inefficiencies associated with the agency problem. In contrast, systems theory-based conceptions address broader system contradictions and encompass multiple perspectives: a cybernetic perspective emphasising operational control, a hierarchical perspective emphasising the division of work, and an environmental perspective emphasising the interplay between the organisation and its environment. Structural functionalism underlies these systems theory-based conceptions.

Simons' LOC framework extends classical systems theory, recognising contemporary strategic imperatives. This framework acknowledges the tension between value creation and regulation, expressed through four control levers:

1. Belief systems define strategy as a perspective.
2. Boundary systems operationalise strategy as a position.
3. Diagnostic control systems treat strategy as a plan.
4. Interactive control systems view strategy as patterns in action.

By implementing these levers, strategic control aims to balance the dynamics of value creation with those of regulation. Referencing pertinent literature, the chapter also discussed the adaptability of the LOC framework for integrating sustainability. This integration positions sustainability as a strategic imperative requiring deliberate planning and control. However, a critical analysis reveals the difficulties in addressing sustainability within control mechanisms designed to uphold capital accumulation. It appears that sustainability and CSR have become critical considerations primarily for mitigating potential losses to corporate profits. Achieving true sustainability demands an environmental-centric approach to accountability rather than narrow, organisation-centric approaches that view sustainability as an instrument for further profit-centric expansion.

Case study: Strategising sustainability at BHP - balancing profit, people, and planet through the levers of control

Part 1: Introduction – a titan at a crossroads

BHP Group Limited stands as a titan of the global economy. As one of the world's foremost diversified natural resources companies, its operations in mining and processing essential commodities—including iron ore, copper, nickel, and metallurgical coal—are deeply embedded in the supply chains that underpin modern industrial life. The scale of its economic influence is immense; in the 2024 financial year alone, BHP reported a total economic contribution of US$ 49.2 billion, including including US$11.2 billion in payments to governments and US$ 22.1 billion in supplier spending. The materials it extracts are not merely commodities; they are foundational components for urbanisation, infrastructure, and, increasingly, the technologies required for a global transition towards a lower-carbon economy.

Yet, this central role in global development places BHP at the heart of a profound and defining contradiction of our time. As outlined in the conceptual framing of management control, control systems are fundamentally necessitated and defined by the existence of strategic and structural conditions. For BHP, this contradiction is not an abstract theoretical problem but the central operational and strategic reality of its existence. The company's core business model—the extraction of finite resources from the earth—is inherently disruptive to ecosystems and communities. The history of the mining industry, including BHP's own, is replete with examples of severe environmental degradation and social harm, from the early health impacts of lead mining in Broken Hill to the pollution of the Ok Tedi River in Papua New Guinea. Mining activities inevitably generate vast quantities of waste, consume significant water resources in often water-scarce regions, and can irrevocably alter landscapes, creating a direct and unavoidable tension between the pursuit of economic value and the preservation of socio-ecological well-being.

This case study delves into the complex world of strategic management control at BHP, examining the systems, processes, and logics the company deploys to navigate this fundamental contradiction. It seeks to understand how a global mining corporation attempts to 'strategise' its approach to sustainability, balancing the powerful and persistent imperative for financial performance against the escalating demands of society, polity, and ecology. The analysis is structured around Robert Simons' Levers of Control (LOC) framework, a model that conceptualises strategic control not as a monolithic command-and-control function, but as a dynamic interplay of four distinct yet interconnected levers: belief systems, boundary systems, diagnostic control systems, and interactive control systems.

By deconstructing BHP's management control architecture through this lens, this case study will explore how the company defines its core values and purpose (belief systems), establishes the formal rules and risks to be avoided (boundary systems), measures and monitors its performance against a plurality of competing objectives (diagnostic control systems), and responds to strategic shocks and uncertainties (interactive control systems). The analysis will culminate in a critical evaluation of BHP's approach, probing the extent to which sustainability is genuinely integrated into its strategic core versus being subject to a 'managerial capture', where socio-ecological goals are ultimately subordinated to the overriding logic of capital accumulation. The very existence of a corporation like BHP, whose business model simultaneously creates economic value and generates profound socio-ecological risk, makes it a compelling and critical subject for understanding the role of management control in one of the most challenging and contradictory arenas of modern business. Its control systems are not merely technical instruments for ensuring efficiency; they are deeply political tools designed to manage an inherent conflict and, in doing so, to secure and maintain the company's 'social licence to operate' in a world increasingly sceptical of its claims.

Part 2: The belief system – 'to build a better world'

At the apex of any strategic management control framework lies the belief system, which Simons defines as the explicit set of organisational definitions that senior managers communicate to articulate core values, purpose, and direction. This lever is designed to be inspirational, providing a 'strategy as a perspective' that encourages employees to seek new opportunities and commit to a collective vision. At BHP, this belief system is crafted and communicated through a clear hierarchy of statements that frame its corporate identity and strategic intent.

The cornerstone of this system is the company's official Purpose: '***To bring people and resources together to build a better world***'. This statement is notable for its aspirational and societal focus. It deliberately eschews more traditional corporate objectives, such as maximising shareholder wealth, in favour of a broader, more altruistic mission. This purpose is underpinned by a set of three core Values: '***Do what's right***', which speaks to integrity and safety; '***Seek better ways***', which encourages innovation and learning; and '***Make a difference***', which places accountability for creating value on every individual.

These higher-order principles are translated into a more concrete strategic vision. BHP's strategy statement declares: 'We will responsibly manage the most resilient long-term portfolio of assets... and will grow value... Through our differentiated approach to social value, we will be a trusted partner who creates value for all stakeholders'. The repeated emphasis on 'responsibility', 'social value', and 'all stakeholders' signals a conscious effort to define the company's role beyond the narrow confines of economic extraction. This narrative is further reinforced by positioning BHP's products as indispensable to solving the world's most pressing challenges. The company consistently argues that its commodities are essential for sustainable global development and, critically, for the energy transition itself. As its public messaging suggests, windmills, electric vehicles, and batteries are not made of wood; they require the very steel, copper, and nickel that BHP produces. This framing allows BHP to position itself not as a legacy extractive enterprise, but as a vital enabler of a more sustainable, lower-carbon future.

From a management control perspective, this belief system performs a crucial strategic function. It attempts to resolve the inherent contradiction between BHP's economic activities and its ecological impact at a rhetorical and ideological level. The language is deliberately value-laden, shifting the narrative focus away from the negative externalities of mining (the process) and towards the positive societal benefits of its products (the end-use). By defining its purpose as 'building a better world', BHP constructs a powerful legitimating story in which its economic success is not in conflict with, but is in fact integral to, achieving broader socio-ecological goals.

This narrative acts as a pre-emptive defence against criticism and serves to align the motivations of employees, investors, and other stakeholders with a vision that appears to reconcile profit with planet. It provides a 'value perspective' that can inspire innovation in areas like operational efficiency and safety, which have clear links to both financial and sustainability outcomes. However, the very elegance of this rhetorical solution raises critical questions that the subsequent analysis of BHP's other control levers must address.

1. Does this inspirational vision translate into tangible constraints on behaviour?
2. Is it reflected in the metrics that are most closely monitored?
3. And what happens when the ambition to 'build a better world' collides with the pressures of a volatile global commodities market?

The belief system provides the official story; the boundary, diagnostic, and interactive systems reveal how that story is operationalised, constrained, and, at times, contradicted.

Part 3: The boundary system – codifying conduct and containing risk

While belief systems provide the inspirational, expansive force in an organisation, boundary systems serve as the necessary counterbalance. According to Simons, they are the formal rules and proscriptions that define the acceptable domain of strategic and operational activity, establishing the risks to be avoided. At BHP, these boundaries are codified in a comprehensive architecture of policies, standards, and frameworks designed to contain risk and ensure compliance across its global operations. This system acts as a protective ring, intended to ensure that the entrepreneurial energy unleashed by the belief system does not lead the company into untenable legal, ethical, or reputational territory.

The most visible component of this architecture is BHP's *Code of Conduct*, a document that applies to all employees, contractors, and partners. It translates the high-level values of the belief system into more specific behavioural expectations. Crucially, it includes a section on the duty to 'Care for people and planet', which explicitly requires employees to respect human rights and demonstrate environmental responsibility. The Code is not merely a set of guidelines; it is a mandatory standard. It stipulates that where local laws are less strict than BHP's own requirements, the company's higher standard must prevail, establishing a global baseline for conduct. This is reinforced by a formal 'speak up' policy and whistleblower channels, which function as an internal enforcement mechanism to monitor and report breaches of these established boundaries.

Underpinning the Code of Conduct is a more technical and systematic boundary control: the Group-wide Risk Framework. This framework institutionalises the process of risk management, providing a single, consolidated methodology for identifying, assessing, and controlling all risks, including those related to sustainability. The framework mandates that all potential impacts—including those on health and safety, the environment, communities, and human rights—must be considered when assessing the materiality of a risk. This process is designed to ensure that sustainability considerations are embedded in all business activities. For specific high-risk areas, this general framework is supplemented by mandatory minimum performance requirements, such as those for tailings storage facilities, biodiversity, and water management. A key principle embedded in these standards is the application of the 'mitigation hierarchy', which prescribes a sequence of actions: first, to avoid environmental impacts where possible; second, to minimise them; and third, to rehabilitate affected areas.

However, a critical analysis of this boundary system reveals a fundamental orientation that has profound implications for its effectiveness. The entire apparatus is constructed from an 'organisational-centric' perspective. The language and logic of the Risk Framework are focused on identifying and managing risks to BHP. Risks are assessed based on their potential to cause adverse consequences to the company's 'legal, reputational or financial standing'. The objective of the control process is to treat risks and bring them 'within appetite', meaning to a level that is deemed acceptable for the continued operation and success of the business.

This framing is subtle but crucial. It conceptualises socio-ecological harm not as an absolute wrong to be prevented, but as a business threat to be managed. The primary goal is not the elimination of harm to the environment or society for its own sake, but the mitigation of the risk that this harm poses to the company. This distinction creates a critical vulnerability in the control system. It allows for a calculus where the perceived probability of a negative event and the potential financial cost to the company can be weighed against the cost of implementing more robust, preventative controls. If a catastrophic risk is deemed to have a very low probability, or if the cost of truly effective controls is seen as prohibitive to economic performance, the boundary system may permit activities that carry an unacceptably high potential for external harm. This organisational-centric logic, which prioritises the continuity of the business by managing external pressures, sets the stage for understanding how, despite a sophisticated and comprehensive set of formal boundaries, a catastrophic control failure like the Samarco dam disaster could occur.

Part 4: The diagnostic system – the metrics of a modern miner

Diagnostic control systems are the formal information systems that managers use to monitor organisational outcomes and correct deviations from pre-set standards of performance. They are the feedback-oriented, cybernetic heart of traditional management control, designed to ensure the predictable achievement of goals set out in the intended strategy. At BHP, the diagnostic system is a complex tapestry of financial and non-financial metrics, meticulously tracked and reported, which collectively provide a quantified picture of the company's performance. This system reveals the multiple, and often conflicting, variables that leadership must monitor to satisfy its diverse range of stakeholders.

The primacy of the economic imperative is evident in the headline financial metrics prominently featured in BHP's annual reporting. For the 2024 financial year, the company reported a profit from operations of US17.5 billion and an underlying attributable profit of US13.7 billion. This performance translated directly into shareholder returns, with total dividends amounting to US$7.4 billion. These figures are not merely outcomes; they are powerful drivers of behaviour, representing the core objective of a publicly-listed, capital-intensive enterprise. They are the ultimate diagnostic check on the company's ability to generate value for its owners, and analyst reports closely track these metrics against market expectations and commodity price fluctuations.

Simultaneously, in line with its belief system and the demands of its social licence to operate, BHP's diagnostic controls encompass a growing array of sustainability key performance indicators (KPIs). These metrics are designed to measure progress against the company's public commitments to environmental and social goals. The FY2024 reports highlight several key achievements in this domain: a 32% reduction in operational greenhouse gas (GHG) emissions (Scopes 1 and 2) against an FY2020 baseline; female workforce participation reaching 37.1%; a record US$609 million in procurement spend with Indigenous businesses; and 83,000 hectares of land being managed under 'nature-positive' practices. These indicators are disclosed in detail through a suite of public documents, including the main Annual Report, a dedicated Sustainability Report, and a Climate Transition Action Plan, which serve as the primary communication channels for this part of the diagnostic system.

The influence of external rating agencies further complicates this diagnostic landscape. Companies like Sustainalytics and S&P Global conduct their own assessments, providing ESG scores that investors increasingly scrutinise. BHP's Sustainalytics ESG Risk Rating of 27.5 places it in the 'Medium Risk' category, while its S&P Global ESG Score is 37. These external ratings act as another layer of diagnostic control, offering a benchmark against industry peers and signalling areas of perceived risk or underperformance to the investment community.

The following table provides a snapshot of this multi-faceted diagnostic system, placing key financial and sustainability metrics side-by-side. This juxtaposition makes the abstract concept of contradiction tangible, illustrating the competing objectives that BHP's management must simultaneously monitor and balance.

Table 1: BHP's key performance indicators – a diagnostic snapshot (fy2024)

Metric Category	Specific Metric	FY2024 Performance
Financial	Profit from Operations	US$17.5 billion
	Underlying Attributable Profit	US$13.7 billion
	Total Dividends to Shareholders	US$7.4 billion
Environmental	Operational GHG Emissions Reduction (vs FY2020)	32%
	Area Under Nature-Positive Management	83,000 hectares
Social	Female Workforce Participation	37.1%
	Indigenous Procurement Spend	US$609 million
External ESG Rating	Sustainalytics ESG Risk Rating	27.5 (Medium)
	S&P Global ESG Score	37

This diagnostic array provides a concrete basis for critical discussion. It forces the question of which metrics carry the most weight in strategic decision-making. In situations where a trade-off is required, does the imperative to maintain dividend payments outweigh the imperative to accelerate investment in GHG abatement? How does the company balance the cost of sourcing from local Indigenous suppliers against potentially cheaper alternatives? The existence of these parallel sets of metrics is a testament to the complex environment in which BHP operates. However, it also creates the conditions for 'managerial capture', where the non-financial sustainability metrics, while diligently reported, may be managed in a way that ensures they do not fundamentally compromise the achievement of the dominant financial objectives. The catastrophic events at the Samarco mine provide a stark illustration of what can happen when this balancing act fails and the diagnostic focus on production and cost overwhelms the controls meant to ensure safety and stability.

Part 5: A system under stress – the samarco dam disaster

On 5 November 2015, the Fundão tailings dam, part of an iron ore mining complex in Mariana, Brazil, suffered a catastrophic failure. The dam was operated by Samarco Mineração S.A., a joint venture co-owned by BHP and the Brazilian mining giant Vale. The collapse represents one of the most devastating industrial and environmental disasters in recent history and serves as a brutal case study in the failure of management control systems. It vividly illustrates the real-world consequences when the inherent contradictions within a high-risk industry are inadequately managed, and when boundary and diagnostic systems fail to contain existential threats.

The immediate aftermath of the collapse was a tragedy of immense proportions, starkly revealing the violent collision of economic, social, and ecological spheres. An estimated 44 million cubic metres of iron ore tailings—a toxic sludge of waste material—were unleashed in a torrent that obliterated the village of Bento Rodrigues downstream. The disaster claimed 19 lives, left hundreds of people homeless, and inflicted deep and lasting psychological trauma on the survivors and surrounding communities. This was the devastating societal cost.

The ecological cost was equally staggering. The mudflow surged into the Doce River system, one of Brazil's most important watersheds, and travelled over 600 kilometres to the Atlantic Ocean. It wiped out entire fish populations, destroyed thousands of hectares of protected riparian forest, and contaminated the water supply for hundreds of thousands of people with harmful heavy metals like arsenic and mercury. The event was widely described as the worst environmental disaster in Brazil's history, leaving a legacy of ecological destruction that will take decades, if not centuries, to remediate.

The economic consequences for the companies involved were severe. The disaster triggered billions of dollars in fines, compensation claims, and cleanup costs. In August 2016, BHP announced a record annual loss of US$6.4 billion, a figure directly impacted by the financial provisions made for the Samarco failure. The event erased billions in shareholder value and mired both BHP and Vale in complex, multi-jurisdictional legal battles that continue to this day.

Crucially, subsequent investigations revealed that this was not an unforeseeable 'accident' but a preventable failure rooted in systemic weaknesses in management control. Multiple reports and prosecutorial allegations indicated that Samarco had been warned about the dam's instability. Evidence pointed to known design and drainage flaws, and engineers had reportedly raised concerns about the structure's integrity prior to the collapse. Federal prosecutors in Brazil went further, filing charges against executives and alleging that the company had prioritised production increases and cost-cutting measures over safety. This claim was supported by a corporate risk assessment, conducted by Samarco itself six months before the disaster, which accurately predicted the potential for up to 20 deaths and catastrophic environmental damage in a worst-case failure scenario. Despite this internal diagnostic warning, prosecutors argued that the necessary preventative actions were not taken. Compounding these failures, key monitoring devices designed to measure water pressure and stability at the dam were reportedly non-functional at the time of the breach.

The Samarco disaster is therefore a textbook case of a control system breakdown where the diagnostic lever focused on economic efficiency (monitoring production targets and costs) was allowed to override the boundary lever (enforcing safety protocols and containing known risks). A direct conflict existed between the imperative to produce iron ore profitably in a declining commodity market and the imperative to operate a high-hazard facility safely. The evidence strongly suggests that in this conflict, the economic imperative prevailed. The formal boundary systems—the engineering specifications, the safety procedures, the risk assessments—were rendered ineffective because the diagnostic systems monitoring them were either ignored or non-operational. This demonstrates the hierarchical nature of control levers in practice; they are not always in a state of balanced tension. When one imperative, such as short-term financial performance, is given ultimate priority, it can systematically erode and disable the controls designed to manage other critical risks, leading to a complete and catastrophic system failure that reverberates across economic, social, and ecological domains.

Part 6: The interactive system – responding to strategic uncertainty

The collapse of the Samarco dam was more than a tragic operational failure; it was a profound strategic shock that fundamentally invalidated BHP's and the entire mining industry's existing assumptions about tailings dam risk management. This crisis created a state of acute strategic uncertainty, forcing the company into a reactive process of search, dialogue, and organisational learning that exemplifies the function of an interactive control system. While diagnostic systems are designed to manage expected variables and boundary systems to contain known risks, interactive systems are the mechanisms through which an organisation grapples with the unknown and adapts its strategy in the face of emergent threats. At BHP, the response to Samarco triggered just such a process, leading to significant and lasting changes in its governance, standards, and technology.

The immediate aftermath of the disaster necessitated a massive interactive response focused on crisis management. This involved intense engagement with governments, communities, and emergency services, leading to the provision of emergency relief, financial assistance, and, ultimately, the establishment of the Renova Foundation in 2016. This foundation, created through an agreement between the companies and Brazilian authorities, was tasked with the long-term, multi-billion-dollar effort of remediation and compensation, becoming the institutional vehicle for managing the disaster's complex socio-economic fallout. This phase was characterised by constant dialogue and negotiation with a wide range of stakeholders under intense public scrutiny.

Beyond the immediate crisis, the strategic uncertainty posed by the disaster—namely, the realisation that their existing control systems were insufficient to prevent such a catastrophe—compelled a systemic review of BHP's entire approach to tailings management. This internal, interactive process involved a comprehensive global review of all of the company's operated tailings dams. A key outcome of this review was a fundamental shift in risk assessment methodology. The company began conducting new dam break studies that modelled the potential impact of a hypothetical worst-case failure, regardless of its perceived probability. This represented a significant learning moment: the focus shifted from managing the likelihood of failure to managing the consequences, acknowledging that low-probability, high-consequence events required a different control logic.

This internal learning process was mirrored by an industry-wide interactive dialogue. The Samarco disaster, followed by the equally tragic Brumadinho dam collapse in Brazil in 2019 (involving a Vale-owned facility), forced a global reckoning with tailings dam safety. This led to a landmark collaborative effort between the International Council on Mining and Metals (ICMM), the United Nations Environment Programme (UNEP), and the Principles for Responsible Investment (PRI). The outcome was the creation of the Global Industry Standard on Tailings Management (GISTM) in 2020, the first-ever global standard for tailings facilities. BHP's participation in and adoption of this new standard represent a fundamental change to its boundary systems, driven by the interactive learning process initiated by the disaster.

Finally, the crisis catalysed technological innovation. The challenge of restarting the Samarco operation safely—a key strategic goal for the joint venture partners—required a new technical solution. The restart, which began in late 2020, was predicated on the adoption of new filtration and dry stacking technologies. This allows 80% of the tailings to be dewatered and stacked as a semi-solid material, with the remainder deposited in a secure, confined pit, thereby eliminating the need for a conventional upstream tailings dam of the type that failed. This represents a systemic change to the core production process itself, an emergent strategy born directly from the failure of the old one.

The entire post-Samarco episode demonstrates that interactive control systems, while crucial for adaptation and learning, are often triggered by failure rather than proactive foresight. The intense process of search, dialogue, and strategic re-evaluation was activated only after the existing diagnostic and boundary systems were proven to be fatally flawed. This raises a critical question for the theory and practice of management control: How can organisations create truly proactive interactive systems that anticipate and address such strategic uncertainties before they manifest as catastrophes? The Samarco response shows that organisations can learn and adapt, but it also highlights the immense challenge of fostering forward-looking interactive controls, particularly when dealing with risks where the short-term economic incentives strongly favour maintaining a potentially dangerous status quo.

Part 7: The political contradiction – climate commitments vs. lobbying realities

The management of sustainability extends beyond operational risks and into the realm of politics and public policy. Here, the contradictions inherent in BHP's position become particularly acute, revealing a sophisticated and multi-layered application of its control systems. This is where management control most clearly demonstrates its 'political' nature, as described by Hofstede, involving negotiation, the management of conflicting interests, and the exercise of power to shape the external environment. At BHP, a significant tension exists between its public-facing belief system on climate change and its documented history of direct and indirect lobbying, a conflict that highlights the dynamic interplay between the company's levers of control.

On one hand, BHP's belief system projects the image of a progressive and proactive corporate citizen on climate change. The company publicly states its support for the goals of the Paris Agreement, which aim to limit global warming to well below 2°C and pursue efforts towards 1.5°C. It has set a long-term goal to achieve net-zero operational emissions by 2050 and has established a medium-term target to reduce these emissions by at least 30% by 2030 from an FY2020 baseline. This narrative is central to its strategic positioning, framing its portfolio of 'future-facing commodities' like copper and nickel as essential for the global energy transition. This public stance is a critical component of its strategy to maintain legitimacy with an increasingly climate-conscious public and, perhaps more importantly, with the powerful institutional investors who prioritise ESG performance.

On the other hand, this pro-climate belief system is contradicted by a pattern of political engagement that appears to undermine the very policy frameworks needed to achieve the Paris goals. Criticism from watchdog organisations like the Australasian Centre for Corporate Responsibility (ACCR) and Market Forces has consistently highlighted BHP's membership in and funding of industry associations that have actively lobbied against robust climate action. These associations, such as the Minerals Council of Australia (MCA) and the Australian Petroleum Production and Exploration Association (APPEA), have been accused of demanding government subsidies for fossil fuels, pushing for an aggressive deregulation agenda, and opposing policies like Australia's carbon pricing mechanism—a position BHP itself also took. Reports from organisations like InfluenceMap have detailed the vast sums spent by the fossil fuel industry and its proxies on lobbying to delay, weaken, or block climate policies, creating a political environment hostile to rapid decarbonisation.

BHP is not a passive observer in this dynamic. While it has occasionally taken a divergent public stance, such as issuing an ultimatum to the MCA to stop lobbying for new coal-fired power stations, its continued membership and financial support for these groups are seen by critics as a tacit endorsement of their broader anti-climate agenda. BHP's own direct advocacy has also drawn criticism, for instance, for advocating for the use of international carbon offsets and arguing against the imposition of best-practice emissions performance requirements on new facilities in Australia.

The company's formal control mechanism for managing this contradiction is its process of periodically reviewing its industry association memberships for alignment with its own Climate Policy Principles. In its most recent review, BHP concluded that none of its material industry associations were in a state of misalignment, a finding that critics contend is not credible given the public record of these groups' advocacy.

This apparent hypocrisy can be understood as a highly strategic, multi-level deployment of control. The belief system is used for external legitimation, managing reputational risk and satisfying the diagnostic queries of ESG investors. It creates a public narrative of climate leadership. Simultaneously, the interactive system—in the form of political engagement and lobbying, both direct and indirect—is used to actively shape the company's future boundary systems (i.e., government laws and regulations). The goal of this interactive engagement is to slow the pace of policy change and prevent the imposition of stringent regulations that could threaten the profitability and long-term viability of its core assets, particularly those related to fossil fuels. This demonstrates the intensely political nature of strategic control. It is not a neutral, technical process of internal management but a dynamic exercise of power aimed at shaping the external rules of the game to favour the organisation's enduring economic objectives. This is perhaps the clearest example of 'managerial capture' in action: sustainability is embraced at the level of belief and diagnostic reporting, while the underlying political and economic structures that favour the status quo are defended through interactive political engagement.

Part 8: Synthesis and critical analysis – the 'managerial capture' of sustainability at BHP

An integrated analysis of BHP's strategic management controls, viewed through the lens of Simons' four levers, reveals a sophisticated, dynamic, and deeply contradictory system. While the company has made demonstrable efforts to embed sustainability into its formal control architecture, the evidence presented in this case study points towards a clear conclusion: BHP's approach exemplifies the 'managerial capture' of sustainability. This concept, which critical accounting scholars have long discussed, describes a situation where sustainability is integrated into corporate strategy and control systems not as a genuine end towards which corporate investments and actions are truly directed, but primarily as a means to mitigate risks, enhance reputation, and secure the long-term capital accumulation process. At BHP, the levers of control do not operate in a balanced equilibrium; they function as a hierarchical system where socio-ecological imperatives are consistently managed and subordinated within a dominant economic logic.

1. The belief system serves as the public face of this strategy. It constructs an inspirational and legitimating narrative of 'building a better world', reframing BHP's extractive business as a solution to global challenges like the energy transition. This powerful perspective is designed to align stakeholders and foster a positive corporate image, creating a reservoir of social capital.
2. The diagnostic system provides the data to support this narrative. By tracking and reporting on a range of sustainability KPIs—from GHG

emissions reductions to Indigenous procurement spend—BHP demonstrates a commitment to transparency and accountability. However, the catastrophic failure at Samarco and the ongoing contradictions in its climate lobbying suggest that these non-financial metrics, while important for reporting, do not hold the same decision-making weight as the core financial indicators that drive shareholder returns.

3. The boundary system, codified in the Code of Conduct and the Risk Framework, is designed to contain the negative externalities of the business. Yet its fundamentally 'organisational-centric' focus on managing risk to the company proved tragically insufficient at Samarco. The disaster revealed that when the pressure from the economic diagnostic system (the need for production and cost control) became intense, it could overwhelm and effectively disable the safety boundaries, with devastating consequences for society and the environment.
4. Finally, the interactive system demonstrates how the company learns and adapts, but also how it actively shapes its environment to protect its core interests. It is reactive in the face of strategic shocks, as seen in the post-Samarco overhaul of tailings dam standards, where learning was triggered by disaster. It is proactive in the political arena, where lobbying is used to influence future regulatory boundaries, slowing the pace of climate policy to protect the economic value of its assets.

When synthesised, this analysis reveals a control system where the 'yin and yang' dynamic proposed by Simons is not a balance of equals. The expansive, value-creating 'yang' of economic growth and profit maximisation consistently contains, shapes, and directs the constraining, regulatory 'yin' of sustainability. The belief and diagnostic systems provide a public performance of sustainability, creating a veneer of responsibility that is crucial for maintaining the company's social licence to operate. Beneath this surface, however, the boundary and interactive systems work to ensure that these sustainability commitments do not fundamentally threaten the economic engine of the corporation. The boundary system failed when it came into direct conflict with production pressures, and the interactive system actively works to prevent future boundaries (in the form of stringent climate regulation) from being imposed externally.

This is the essence of managerial capture. Sustainability is not a core value that redefines the purpose of the organisation; it is a strategic variable to be managed. BHP's control systems are a masterful example of this. They are designed to answer the question: 'How can we manage the risks and opportunities of sustainability to ensure the long-term success and profitability of BHP?' They are not, and cannot be, designed to answer the more fundamental, 'environmental-centric' question posed by critical scholars: 'How must BHP's business model and purpose fundamentally change to ensure a sustainable planet?'. This ultimate limitation, embedded in the very structure of the corporate form and its control systems, represents the central challenge in the quest for genuine corporate sustainability.

Part 9: Discussion questions for the seminar

1. Using Simons' Levers of Control framework, how does BHP attempt to manage the fundamental contradiction between its extractive business model and its stated purpose to 'build a better world'?
2. Analyse the Samarco dam disaster as a failure of management control. Which of Simons' levers failed most catastrophically, and how did the diagnostic and boundary systems interact to produce this outcome?
3. BHP's response to the Samarco disaster involved a global review of its dams and the adoption of new industry standards. To what extent can this be seen as an effective 'interactive control system' at work? What are the limitations of such a reactive approach to strategic uncertainty?
4. Critically evaluate the tension between BHP's stated belief system regarding climate change and its documented lobbying activities. How does this reflect the 'political' nature of management control?
5. Based on the evidence in this case, construct an argument for or against the proposition that BHP's sustainability strategy is an example of the phenomenon that critical accounting scholars identify as 'managerial capture'.
6. There is a difference between 'organisational-centric' and 'environmental-centric' approaches to sustainability. Characterise BHP's management control systems using this dichotomy. What would an 'environmental-centric' control system look like for a company like BHP, and is it achievable within its current business model?
7. How do the contradictions among economy (e.g., shareholder returns), society (e.g., community safety, human rights), polity (e.g., lobbying, regulation), and ecology (e.g., climate impact, water use) manifest in BHP's strategic control challenges? Provide specific examples from the case.

Chapter review questions

Section 1: Questions on the Theoretical Foundations of Management Control

1.1 The ontology of control and the agency theory perspective

1. Which of the following can be considered the fundamental ontological condition from which all control issues are said to stem?

   a. The scarcity of organisational resources.
   b. The existence of contradictions and conflicting conditions.
   c. The separation of ownership and management.
   d. The complexity of the external business environment.

2. Agency theory conceptualises management control as a mechanism designed primarily to address which of the following?

   a. The systemic contradictions between an organisation and its environment.
   b. The functional imperatives of adaptation, goal attainment, integration, and latency.
   c. The potential inefficiencies and losses arising from the agency problem.
   d. The political negotiations required to manage strategic uncertainties.

3. Which of the following sets of assumptions about an agent's behaviour is central to the agency theory conception of the 'agency problem'?

   a. Altruistic, effort-seeking, risk-neutral, and fully transparent.
   b. Self-interested, work-averse, risk-averse, and possessing private information.
   c. Collaborative, group-oriented, risk-seeking, and communicative.
   d. Rational, efficiency-focused, risk-neutral, and loyal to the principal.

4. Within the neoclassical economic perspective of agency theory, what serves as the primary control tool for regulating the relationship between a principal and an agent?

   a. The organisation's code of ethical conduct.
   b. The informal psychological contract between the parties.
   c. The explicit or implicit contract outlining compensation, duties, and information arrangements.
   d. The cybernetic feedback system measuring the agent's performance.

5. Referring to the agency theory conception of optimal performance-compensation contracting, what does the difference between the principal's profit under information symmetry and information asymmetry represent?

a. The total rent paid to the agent.
b. The agency costs borne by the agent.
c. The economic value of control information.
d. The agent's risk-return preference.

6. Why is the optimum contract solution under information symmetry referred to as the 'first-best' solution from the principal's perspective?

a. Because the agent undertakes the maximum possible level of risk.
b. Because the principal bears zero business risk.
c. Because it eliminates the need for a formal compensation contract.
d. Because the principal can achieve the optimal level of agent effort for a lower level of compensation than what is possible under information asymmetry.

1.2 The systems theory perspective: cybernetics and structural functionalism

7. The systems theory-based understanding of management control is founded on the conceptualisation of an organisation as which of the following?

a. A nexus of contracts between self-interested individuals.
b. A political arena for negotiation and compromise.
c. A closed system insulated from external environmental pressures.
d. An open system of interacting and interdependent components engaged with its environment.

8. According to the cybernetic model of management control, which of the following is NOT one of the four necessary conditions for controllability?

a. A set of unambiguous objectives for the system being controlled.
b. A means of measuring results along the dimensions defined by the objectives.
c. A system of political negotiation to resolve conflicting values.
d. A predictive model of the system and a choice of relevant corrective actions.

9. In a standard costing system, the process of calculating variances by comparing actual costs to standard costs exemplifies which function of the cybernetic predictive model?

a. The detector function.
b. The comparator function.
c. The effector function.
d. The feedforward function.

10. A manager adjusts the raw material input mix in a production process after a variance report indicates an unfavourable material price variance. This action is an example of which cybernetic function?

    a. The detector function.
    b. The comparator function.
    c. The effector function.
    d. The efficacy measurement function.

11. According to Talcott Parsons' AGIL schema, which functional imperative is concerned with maintaining coordination between an organisation's subsystems and inhibiting deviancy?

    a. Adaptation (A).
    b. Goal attainment (G).
    c. Integration (I).
    d. Latency (L).

12. Robert Anthony's classical classification of management control systems can be mapped directly onto Parsons' structural functionalism. Which control function primarily addresses the imperatives of Goal attainment (G) and Integration (I)?

    a. Strategic Planning.
    b. Management Control.
    c. Operational Control.
    d. Environmental Scanning.

13. The use of SWOT analysis, industry analysis, and capital investment appraisal to formulate an organisation's long-term direction is an example of which control function, and addresses which of Parsons' functional imperatives?

    a. Operational Control; Latency (L).
    b. Management Control; Integration (I).
    c. Strategic Planning; Adaptation (A).
    d. Environmental Control; Goal attainment (G).

1.3 Beyond cybernetics: environmental and political dimensions of control

14. In Hofstede's (1981) typology of management control, a situation characterised by unambiguous objectives, measurable outputs, known effects of interventions, but non-repetitive activity would be classified as which type of control?

a. Routine control.
b. Expert control.
c. Trial and Error control.
d. Intuitive control.

15. According to Hofstede's typology, a control situation where objectives are ambiguous and outputs are not measurable, necessitating reliance on power, negotiation, and compromise, is best described as:

a. Judgmental control.
b. Intuitive control.
c. Political control.
d. Trial and Error control.

16. Dermer's (1988) critique of the cybernetic conceptualisation of control suggests that it is limiting because:

a. It fails to account for the technical efficiency of operational processes.
b. It overemphasises the importance of financial performance measures.
c. It obscures the possibility that entities to be controlled can self-control through underlying assumptions and principles.
d. It cannot be applied to not-for-profit or public sector activities.

17. The environmental perspective on management control, posits that internal organisational configurations often mirror external pressures. The creation of distinct marketing, human resources, and finance departments is a direct response to which of the following?

a. The need to fulfil the functional imperatives of the AGIL schema.
b. The demands and interests of specific market and non-market stakeholder groups.
c. The requirements of the cybernetic control model for clear objectives and measurement.
d. The assumptions of agency theory regarding self-interested behaviour.

Section 2: Questions on strategising control with the levers of control framework

2.1 The core dynamics of the LOC framework

18. What is the fundamental strategic contradiction or tension that Robert Simons' Levers of Control (LOC) framework is designed to help managers balance?

a. The tension between short-term profitability and long-term shareholder value.
b. The tension between the interests of the principal and the interests of the agent.
c. The tension between the forces of value creation and the forces of regulation and control.
d. The tension between market-based strategies and production-based strategies.

19. Simons' LOC framework links four distinct levers of control to four different definitions of strategy. Which lever is associated with managing 'strategy as a position' by defining the acceptable scope of activities?

a. Belief systems.
b. Boundary systems.
c. Diagnostic control systems.
d. Interactive control systems.

20. Which of the following levers of control is primarily concerned with implementing the 'intended strategy' and ensuring predictable goal attainment through feedback mechanisms like the Balanced Scorecard?

a. Belief systems.
b. Boundary systems.
c. Diagnostic control systems.
d. Interactive control systems.

21. Simons describes the relationship between belief systems and boundary systems as generating forces of 'yin and yang'. What does this dynamic tension represent?

a. The conflict between emergent and intended strategies.
b. The balance between positive, inspirational values and restrictive, risk-mitigating constraints.
c. The trade-off between financial and non-financial performance measures.
d. The interplay between internal learning and external adaptation.

22. An interactive control system is distinguished not by its specific form but by its use. What is the primary purpose of using a control system interactively?

a. To monitor the implementation of the intended strategy and correct deviations.
b. To enforce codes of business conduct and define operational boundaries.
c. To communicate core values and inspire employees to create value.

d. To address strategic uncertainties, stimulate debate, and foster organisational learning.

2.2 Application and Critical Evaluation of the LOC Framework

23. According to the research by Arjaliès and Mundy (2013), using formal statements such as a CSR strategic plan or a 'values chart' to communicate an organisation's commitment to sustainability is an application of which lever of control?

    a. Belief systems.
    b. Boundary systems.
    c. Diagnostic control systems.
    d. Interactive control systems.

24. When a company establishes its sustainability policies by referencing external laws, regulations, and reporting protocols like the Global Reporting Initiative (GRI), it is primarily utilising which lever of control for risk management?

    a. Belief systems.
    b. Boundary systems.
    c. Diagnostic control systems.
    d. Interactive control systems.

25. The chapter introduces the concept of the 'managerial capture of sustainability'. What does this term refer to?

    a. The process by which managers successfully integrate sustainability into all four levers of control.
    b. The leveraging of sustainability to enhance capital accumulation without fundamentally changing the organisation's profit-centric purpose.
    c. The failure of managers to understand the strategic importance of social and ecological issues.
    d. The capture of managers by external stakeholder groups demanding greater social and environmental accountability.

26. The critique that corporate sustainability efforts are often underpinned by a 'mitigative motive' suggests that these actions are primarily driven by:

    a. A genuine desire to achieve social and ecological justice.
    b. The belief that sustainability can be a source of competitive advantage and increased profits.
    c. The need to avoid potential profit losses arising from regulatory non-compliance or reputational damage.

d. The pressure from employees to create a more ethical and purposeful workplace.

27. Critical accounting scholars argue that frameworks like the LOC and BSC are fundamentally 'organisation-centric'. What is the key limitation of this perspective for achieving genuine sustainability?

    a. They focus too heavily on internal processes and ignore the external environment.
    b. They are too complex for managers to implement effectively across large organisations.
    c. They lack the analytical capacity to adopt an 'environmental-centric' perspective that prioritises ecological health over corporate goals.
    d. They are primarily designed for manufacturing companies and are not applicable to service-based industries.

Section 3: Integrative and application-based questions

3.1 Comparative and synthesis questions

28. How does the conceptualisation of 'contradiction' that necessitates control in agency theory differ most significantly from the 'contradiction' addressed by Simons' LOC framework?

    a. Agency theory focuses on interpersonal contradictions, while the LOC framework focuses on intra-personal contradictions.
    b. Agency theory frames contradiction as a technical problem of information asymmetry, while the LOC framework frames it as a strategic tension between value creation and regulation.
    c. Agency theory views contradiction as a result of external environmental pressures, while the LOC framework views it as an internal problem of bureaucratic dysfunction.
    d. There is no significant difference; both frameworks view contradiction as a problem of aligning managerial behaviour with shareholder interests.

29. Which of Hofstede's control types most closely aligns with the function of a diagnostic control system, and which most closely aligns with the challenges addressed by an interactive control system?

    a. Routine control; Political control.
    b. Expert control; Judgmental control.
    c. Trial and Error control; Intuitive control.
    d. Political control; Routine control.

30. The classical systems theory view of management control, based on structural functionalism, and Simons' LOC framework both draw on systems thinking. However, a key advancement of the LOC framework is its explicit focus on:

    a. The technical efficiency of operational processes through cybernetic feedback.
    b. The hierarchical division of work and delegation of objectives.
    c. The dynamic management of tensions between opposing strategic forces like empowerment and accountability.
    d. The need for organisations to adapt to a stable and predictable external environment.

31. Considering the different theoretical perspectives, the role of 'information' is conceptualised differently. Which statement accurately contrasts the role of information in agency theory versus a cybernetic system?

    a. In agency theory, information is a tool for political negotiation; in a cybernetic system, it is a statement of core values.
    b. In agency theory, information has an economic value in reducing asymmetry; in a cybernetic system, it is feedback for error correction.
    c. In agency theory, information is used to foster emergent strategy; in a cybernetic system, it is used to set risk boundaries.
    d. In both theories, information is primarily used to ensure compliance with external laws and regulations.

Comprehension questions

1. How does agency theory conceptualise the fundamental contradictions that necessitate management control?
2. According to agency theory, what is the fundamental problem that management control is designed to mitigate?
3. Explain the role of the 'performance contract' in the agency theory-based conception of management control.
4. According to systems theory, what is the fundamental condition that management control should seek to mitigate?
5. List the three perspectives of the classical systems theory-based conception of management control discussed in this chapter.
6. List and explain the critical elements of a cybernetic control system.
7. The detector, comparator, and effector are the key functionalities of a cybernetic model. Briefly explain them using budgeting and standard costing as an illustration.

8. Explain the six types of control identified in Hofstede's typology.
9. What are the fundamental questions that Hofstede asks in differentiating these control types?
10. Briefly explain the focal points of the hierarchical perspectives of management control.
11. Briefly explain the four 'functional imperatives' of Talcott Parsons' AGIL framework.
12. Explain how Parsons' structural functionalism underpins the classical theory of management control systems.
13. Briefly explain the notion of the 'external control of organisations', considering how the internal configurations of organisations reflect environmental demands.
14. What is the fundamental contradiction that underpins Simons' LOC framework?
15. Briefly explain the four different definitions of strategy that Simons' LOC framework deploys.
16. What are the four key strategic control functionalities that Simons' LOC framework identifies?
17. What are the specific levers of control related to the control functionalities you identified in the question above?
18. Synthesising the concepts of strategy, control functionalities, and levers of control, explain how Simons' framework connects these three elements.

Explore further

1. Choose a large multinational corporation (e.g., Shell) for an illustrative case study. Examine its published strategic statements (e.g., chairman's review, risk management statements, vision and mission statements, integrated reports). Using this publicly available data, create a 'strategic profile' of the company employing the LOC framework. Specifically, craft a narrative about the company using the four key strategic control imperatives: core values, risks to be avoided, strategic uncertainties, and critical performance variables. Consider the extent to which the company prioritises sustainability-related issues within these four imperatives. Conclude by reflecting on the challenges of using the LOC framework to develop a strategic profile based on publicly available secondary data.
2. Read the following two papers: a. Beusch, P., Frisk, J. E., Rosén, M., and Dilla, W. (2022), 'Management control for sustainability: Towards integrated systems', Management Accounting Research, Vol. 54, pp. 1-14. b. Bebbington, J. (2001), 'Sustainable development: a review of the international develop-

ment, business, and accounting literature', Accounting Forum, Vol. 25 No. 2, pp. 128-157. The first paper focuses on an organisation-centric view of sustainability, while the second offers a broader socio-ecological interpretation. Write a review of the approaches discussed in the first paper in light of the broader understanding of sustainability provided in the second.

Develop your critical argumentation skills

1. Write an argumentative essays on each of the following themes.

   'Contradictions underpin management control. The manner in which management control is conceptualised, designed, and implemented depends significantly on the specific contradictory conditions it seeks to resolve'.

   'Strategising management control involves establishing distinct but interrelated control systems to manage the strategic imperatives emanating from the contradictions between the dynamics of value creation, on one hand, and the dynamics of regulation and control, on the other'.

   'Strategy frameworks such as the LOC and BSC provide only organisation-centric approaches to managing sustainability and limit humanity's capacity to become truly environmental-centric in achieving a sustainable planet'.

Mini case study

The dynamics of management control in Enron's rise and fall

An article by Tony Segal for Investopedia details the trajectory of the Enron Corporation, which ascended to remarkable heights before collapsing precipitously. At its zenith in 2000, Enron's shares reached a peak of $90.56, only to fall to just $0.26 by the time of its bankruptcy on 2 December 2001. This marked one of the most severe corporate failures in history, impacting thousands of employees and sending shockwaves through Wall Street. Numerous executives faced criminal charges, including conspiracy, insider trading, and securities fraud. They were ultimately found guilty, alongside Enron's accounting firm, Arthur Andersen, which faced charges of obstructing justice.

Enron began as an energy company formed through a merger. As the energy market underwent deregulation, Enron diversified into the futures and derivatives market. Over the subsequent decade, Enron earned a reputation for 'innovation' in financial derivatives and accounting practices. A pivotal moment came in 1992 when Enron secured approval from the Securities and Exchange Commission (SEC) to transition its accounting methodology from historical cost to mark-to-market (MTM). The company's foray into electronic trading culminated in the creation of Enron Online (EOL) in October 1999, a platform where Enron became the counterparty in every transaction. This expansion garnered accolades, with Fortune naming Enron "America's Most Innovative Company" for six consecutive years between 1996 and 2001.

By the autumn of 2000, Enron began to buckle under its own weight, concealing its mounting issues through the use of MTM accounting. As Segal notes:

the company would build an asset, such as a power plant, and immediately claim the projected profit on its books, even though it hadn't made one dime from it. If the revenue from the power plant was less than the projected amount, instead of taking the loss, the company would then transfer the asset to an off-the-books corporation (a so-called special purpose vehicle), where the loss would go unreported. This type of accounting enabled Enron to write off unprofitable activities without hurting its bottom line.

The case of Enron's downfall has been scrutinised from various perspectives, including corporate governance, accounting regulation, and white-collar crime. However, a crucial dimension often overlooked is that of 'management control'.

REQUIRED:

By addressing these questions, we aim to unravel the intricate layers of Enron's demise, focusing on the management control dynamics that played a pivotal role in this high-profile corporate collapse.

2. Drawing upon a pertinent conceptual framework of management control, such as Simons' Levers of Control, elucidate the management control implications of Enron's rise and fall. In this analysis, give careful consideration to the following:
3. According to your chosen conceptual framework, what are the key' control elements' that require scrutiny to understand the company's evolution?
4. How would you characterise the company's evolution? Which strategic control elements assumed precedence, potentially at the expense of other pivotal elements?
5. How do you interpret the role of the audit firm (Arthur Andersen) in this case? Which specific control function was the audit firm expected to perform, and how did it fail in this duty?

References

Anthony, R. N. (1965). Planning and control systems: A framework for analysis. Division of Research, Graduate School of Business Administration, Harvard University.

Anthony, R., Govindarajan, V., Hartmann, F., Kraus, K., and Nilsson, G. (2014). Management control systems. European edition. McGraw-Hill Education.

Arjaliès, D.-L., and Mundy, J. (2013). 'The use of management control systems to manage CSR strategy: A levers of control perspective'. Management Accounting Research, 24(4), pp. 284-300.

Baecker, D. (2001). 'Why systems?'. Theory Culture Society, 18(1), pp. 59-74.

Baiman, S. (1990). 'Agency research in managerial accounting: A second look'. Accounting, Organisations and Society, 15(4), pp. 341-371.

Baiman, S. (2006). 'Contract theory analysis of management accounting issues'. In A. Bhimani (Ed.), Contemporary Issues in Management Accounting (pp. 20-41). Oxford University Press.

Berry, A. J., Broadbent, J., and Otley, D. (2005). Management control: theories, issues, and performance (2nd ed.). Palgrave Macmillan.

Buckley, W. F. (1969). Modern systems research for the behavioral scientist. A sourcebook. Aldine Publishing Co.

Burrell, G., and Morgan, G. (1979). Sociological paradigms and organisational analysis: elements of the sociology of corporate life. Heinemann.

Dermer, J. (1988). 'Control and organisational order'. Accounting, Organisations and Society, 13(1), pp. 25-36.

Dermer, J. D., and Lucas, R. G. (1986). 'The illusion of managerial control'. Accounting, Organisations and Society, 11(6), pp. 471-482.

Emmanuel, C., Otley, D., and Merchant, K. (2004). Accounting for management control (2nd ed.). South-Western, Cengage Learning.

Fama, E. F. (1980). 'Agency Problems and the Theory of the Firm'. Journal of Political Economy, 88(2), pp. 288-307.

Fama, E. F., and Jensen, M. C. (1983). 'Separation of Ownership and Control'. The Journal of Law & Economics, 26(2), pp. 301-325.

Ferreira, A., and Otley, D. (2009). 'The design and use of performance management systems: An extended framework for analysis'. Management Accounting Research, 20(4), pp. 263-282.

Gray, R. (2010). 'Is accounting for sustainability actually accounting for sustainability...and how would we know? An exploration of narratives of organisations and the planet'. Accounting, Organisations and Society, 35(1), pp. 47-62.

Gray, R., and Bebbington, J. (2001). Accounting for the Environment (2nd ed.). SAGE Publications.

Haraway, D. (2015). 'Anthropocene, Capitalocene, Plantationocene, Chthulucene: Making Kin'. Environmental Humanities, 6(1), pp. 159-165.

Hofstede, G. (1981). 'Management control of public and not-for-profit activities'. Accounting, Organisations and Society, 6(3), pp. 193-211.

Hopper, T., and Powell, A. (1985). 'Making sense of research into the organisational and social aspects of management accounting: A review of its underlying assumptions'. Journal of Management Studies, 22(5), pp. 429-465.

Merchant, K. A., and Van der Stede, W. A. (2007). Management Control Systems: Performance Measurement, Evaluation and Incentives. Financial Times/ Prentice Hall.

Milne, M. J. (1996). 'On sustainability; the environment and management accounting'. Management Accounting Research, 7(1), pp. 135-161.

Mintzberg, H. (1987). 'The strategy concept I: five Ps for strategy'. California Management Review, 30(1), pp. 11-24.

Otley, D. (1999). 'Performance management: a framework for management control systems research'. Management Accounting Research, 10(4), pp. 363-382.

Otley, D. T., and Berry, A. J. (1980). 'Control, organisation and accounting'. Accounting, Organisations and Society, 5(2), pp. 231-244.

Parsons, T., and Smelser, N. (2005). Economy and Society: A Study in the Integration of Economic and Social Theory. Taylor & Francis.

Pfeffer, J., and Salancik, G. R. (2003). The External Control of Organizations: A Resource Dependence Perspective. Stanford Business Books.

Simons, R. (1995). Levers of Control: How Managers Use Innovative Control Systems to Drive Strategic Renewal. Harvard Business School Press.

Tessier, S., and Otley, D. (2012). 'A conceptual development of Simons' Levers of Control framework'. Management Accounting Research, 23(3), pp. 171-185.

CHAPTER

6 Strategy in the hierarchy: organisational resilience

6.1 Introduction: from management control to organisational resilience

Especially in the wake of successive financial crises, the global impact of the COVID-19 pandemic, and escalating geopolitical conflicts, discussions surrounding 'organisational resilience' have gained significant prominence in both the popular business press and academic spheres. The World Economic Forum's 2024 Global Risks Report underscores a landscape defined by economic uncertainty and geopolitical tensions, while KPMG's Global CEO Outlook Survey reveals that leaders view emerging technology, operational issues, and cybersecurity as primary threats to growth. In this environment, a noticeable shift in strategic focus is occurring, moving from the traditional confines of management control towards the more dynamic and adaptive concept of organisational resilience.

This shift presents a fundamental challenge to the established paradigms of management accounting. Traditional management control systems are designed to manage predictable deviations from a predetermined plan, focusing on efficiency, compliance, and the correction of variances. Resilience, conversely, is the capacity to navigate profound, unpredictable uncertainty where the plan itself may become irrelevant. The imperative is no longer merely to control the organisation but to embed resilience within the very fabric of its structures, processes, capabilities, and human resources. Consequently, organisational resilience has become a pervasive theme, capturing the attention of management consultants and thought leaders. Global consulting firms such as McKinsey & Company, Boston Consulting Group (BCG), KPMG, Deloitte, and PwC have invested substantially in developing resilience as a comprehensive consulting package, transforming it into a multi-billion-dollar knowledge product for the global market.

This surge in resilience-oriented strategies has far-reaching implications for the practice and study of management accounting. As unprecedented uncertainties and vulnerabilities pervade organisational environments, making uncontrollability and failure more commonplace, traditional methods of control are proving less effective. This compels managers to explore alternatives that extend beyond control and governance, positioning resilience as a strategic imperative. For the management accountant, this evolution signals a transformation of their role: from a steward of efficiency to a strategic partner in building adaptive capacity. Understanding how management accounting and control systems (MACS) can be designed not just to enforce control but to foster resilience is, therefore, a crucial topic for discussion in a strategic management accounting course.

This textbook organises its chapters under three key themes pertaining to domains of strategic actions: strategising the market, strategising the organisational hierarchy, and strategising the labour process. This chapter falls under the second theme, strategising the organisational hierarchy, following explorations of strategic performance management and strategic management control. Here, organisational resilience is examined as the third strategic theme, representing a critical extension of the discussion on management control. It addresses how organisations can navigate adversities that elude their existing control systems. Organisational resilience becomes paramount when conventional controls prove insufficient. Discussions thus revolve around configuring and reconfiguring organisational structures, processes, and capabilities to empower organisations to anticipate and 'bounce back' from crises, adversities, and failures—situations that are, by definition, beyond immediate control.

The chapter is structured to provide a comprehensive analysis of this vital concept.

1. Section 6.2 delves into the multidisciplinary nature of resilience, examining its definitions across diverse fields to establish a comprehensive conceptual foundation.
2. Section 6.3 explores consultocratic perspectives on organisational resilience, analysing the expository narratives and data-driven models promoted by leading consulting firms and thought leaders.
3. Section 6.4 examines academic discourses, focusing on the conceptual tensions that underpin resilience and introducing a new discussion on the central role of management accounting systems in operationalising resilience.

4. Section 6.5 concludes the chapter with a concise summary of the key insights and findings.

6.2 Defining resilience: understanding the concept's diversity in applications

Resilience is not a concept confined to organisational contexts; it is a widely adopted normative concept that extends across various academic and professional domains, including psychology, engineering, disaster management, organisational studies, and economics. Despite variations in its interpretations and applications, the fundamental idea revolves around an entity's ability to navigate and recover from adversity (see Giustiniano et al. 2018). Analysing how resilience is utilised in diverse fields serves not only to grasp its intricate, interdisciplinary nature but also to identify shared features applicable to defining and comprehending organisational resilience.

In psychology, psychological resilience pertains to an individual's capacity to bounce back from adversity, trauma, or stress. It encompasses emotional fortitude, coping skills, and the ability to maintain mental and emotional well-being in challenging situations. The American Psychological Association defines resilience as '*the process and outcome of successfully adapting to difficult or challenging life experiences, especially through mental, emotional, and behavioural flexibility and adjustment to external and internal demands*'. Notably, resilience is described here as both a dynamic process and a tangible outcome.

In disaster management, social resilience refers to a community's or society's capacity to maintain stability and function effectively amidst disruptions such as natural disasters, economic crises, or political upheavals. It involves community cohesion, adaptive governance, and effective disaster response. Kwok et al. (2016) categorise the processes and capacities that enhance preparedness and recovery into two interconnected categories: structural and cognitive. Structural elements encompass resource capabilities and infrastructure, while cognitive dimensions involve the individual and collective processes that boost social, cultural, and psychological preparedness to rebound from adversities.

The engineering concept of resilience is invaluable for comprehending the characteristics of a resilient techno-managerial system. In engineering, resilience denotes the capacity of a system, structure, or process to endure and recover from adverse conditions, shocks, or disturbances while maintaining its essential functions and performance (Ruault et al. 2012). While centred on the same fundamental idea of recovery, engineering offers a more systemic approach. An engineering perspective underscores a set of system characteristics that are equally applicable to organisational systems, including :

- Redundancy: Ensuring backup components or resources are in place to take over in case of failure.
- Robustness: Maintaining system performance in the face of variations or uncertainties.
- Adaptability: Designing systems to adapt to changing conditions or recover quickly from disturbances.
- Risk Assessment: Identify potential failure modes, analyse consequences, and develop strategies to mitigate or manage risks.
- Modular Design: Breaking complex systems into smaller, interchangeable components to facilitate easier repair or replacement.
- Contingency Planning: Developing emergency procedures to guide responses during unexpected disruptions.
- System Monitoring: Relying on real-time monitoring to detect anomalies and enable prompt corrective actions.
- Predictive Maintenance: Incorporate predictive maintenance practices using sensors and data analysis to anticipate component failures and prevent catastrophic breakdowns.
- Sustainability: Extend resilience to sustainability concerns, ensuring systems are designed to minimise environmental impacts and resource consumption, contributing to long-term resilience in a broader sense.

Economic policy discussions also offer valuable insights. Economic resilience refers to an economy's capability—whether regional, national, or global—to withstand and rebound from external shocks, such as financial crises, pandemics, or shifts in market conditions, without enduring severe and enduring damage. Key components contributing to economic resilience, as outlined by the OECD, include economic diversification, robust infrastructure, financial stability, social safety nets, innovation, access to capital, education and workforce development, global trade connectivity, government resilience strategies, and national-level risk management and contingency planning. Economic resilience is an ongoing process that necessitates collaboration among transnational organisations, governments, businesses, and communities.

This multidisciplinary exploration highlights three critical aspects of the resilience concept, as summarised in Figure 6.1.

1. it involves facing and rebounding from adversities.
2. the ability to do so depends on the various capabilities and capacities possessed by a given entity.

3. resilience is not a static condition but a dynamic process encompassing preparation, prevention, shock absorption, recovery, and adaptation.

Figure 6.1: Processual and capability parameters of resilience

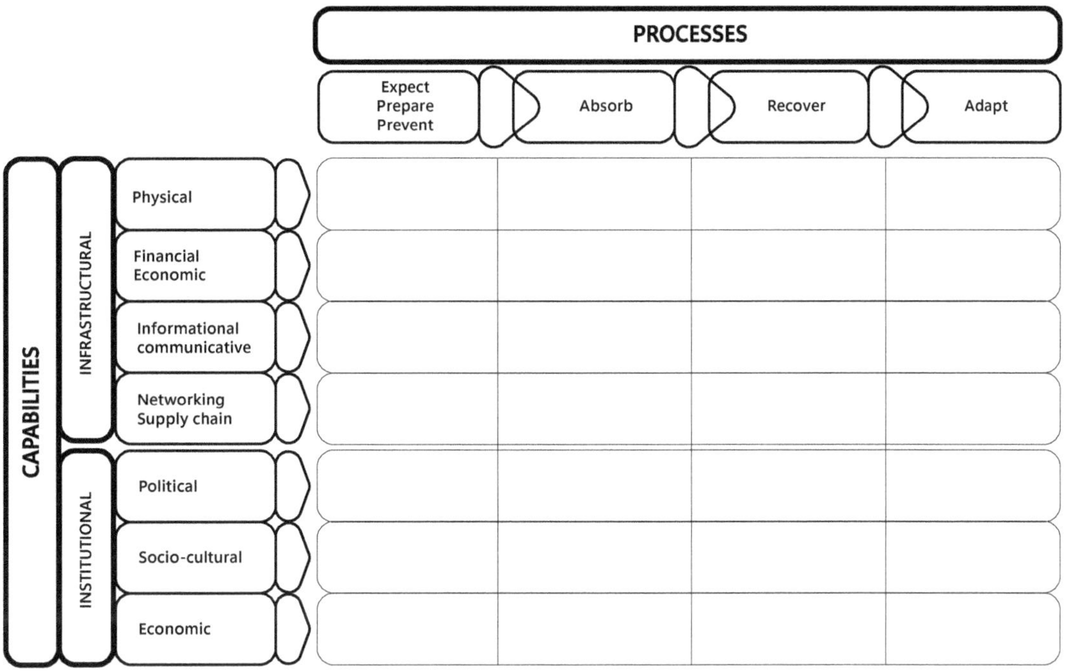

This capabilities and process-based understanding reveals that resilience extends beyond mere recovery. It is a blend of processes and capabilities, including anticipating, preparing for, preventing, absorbing, recovering from, and adapting to adversity. It involves both infrastructural and institutional elements, spanning techno-physical, informational, economic, social, and environmental dimensions. The key insight is that resilience comprises both procedural and capability aspects. With this foundation, the following sections will delve into organisational and accounting discussions surrounding the topic, first exploring the consultocratic perspectives and then academic debates and critiques.

6.3 Consultocratic perspectives on organisational resilience

While transnational organisations such as the OECD and the World Bank adopt a broad, global approach to resilience, consultocratic discourses—prevalent in business management and accounting—adopt a more focused, leadership- and corporate-centric perspective. In these discussions, organisational resilience is often packaged into 'management consultancy products' or collections of 'guru ideas' marketed to corporate leaders worldwide. An analysis of these discourses is crucial in a strategic management accounting course, as it fosters a critical understanding of how management thought is shaped and propagated. These ideas can be categorised into two interdependent and overlapping discursive forms: *expository narratives* and *data-driven modelling.*

Expository narratives on organisational resilience

Expository narratives employ persuasive rhetoric to establish and promote marketable concepts of resilience. Gary Hamel and Liisa Välikangas's (2003) article in the Harvard Business Review, 'The Quest for Resilience', stands as a classic example. These narratives typically share four characteristic elements.

1. First, they frame resilience as a consultocratic necessity. Unlike transnational bodies that portray resilience as a global systemic issue requiring broad cooperation, consultocratic narratives define it as an internal corporate problem. Issues are framed in terms of 'slumps' and 'downturns' in corporate performance, which are attributed to deficiencies in corporate character, leadership, or culture. Hamel and Välikangas (2003), for instance, introduce the concept of a 'resilience gap', a scenario where 'the world is becoming turbulent faster than organisations are becoming resilient', leading to more erratic corporate earnings. This framing transforms resilience into a managerial training issue that necessitates consultancy intervention.
2. Second, they identify points of departure, presenting declarations about what is flawed in current corporate thinking and actions. These departure points persuade leaders that they must change and seek external expertise. For example, Hamel and Välikangas (2003, p.2) argue that leaders often possess a misguided understanding of resilience, stating: 'Strategic resilience is not about responding to a one-time crisis. It's not about rebounding from a setback. It's about continuously anticipating and adjusting to deep, secular trends that can permanently impair the earning power of a core business'.

3. Third, they provide guidelines and prescriptions. Addressing the consultative challenge they have defined, these narratives offer a set of normative prescriptions or commandments on how managers should think and act. These guidelines are often presented as visionary insights from thought leaders with significant corporate experience, which serves as the epistemic foundation for their authority. Hamel and Välikangas (2003), for example, introduce the aspirational goal of 'zero trauma', an ideal state where a company is 'constantly making its future rather than defending its past', and revolutionary change occurs in 'lightning-quick, evolutionary steps' without calamitous surprises or convulsive reorganisations. This rhetoric often echoes religious scripting, presenting a path of commandments and prescriptions towards an idealised end-state (e.g., zero trauma) and enumerating a set of challenges to overcome, as detailed in Table 6.1.

Table 6.1: Hamel and Välikangas's 'quest for resilience' – a creed towards 'zero-trauma'

Resilience Challenge	Leader's Commandment and Prescriptions
The Cognitive Challenge: A company must become entirely free of denial, nostalgia, and arrogance.	Conquer Denial: Reduce the time it takes to go from 'that can't be true' to 'we must face the world as it is'. Leaders must visit places where change happens first, filter out the filterers who censor unpleasant truths, and face up to the inevitability of strategy decay.
The Strategic Challenge: Resilience requires alternatives as well as awareness—the ability to create a plethora of new options as compelling alternatives to dying strategies.	Value Variety: Resilience depends on variety. If the range of strategic alternatives a company explores is narrower than the breadth of change in the environment, the business will become a victim of turbulence.
The Political Challenge: An organisation must be able to divert resources from yesterday's products and programs to tomorrow's.	Liberate Resources: Resource reallocation is an intensely political process, but it must become less so. Markets are better than hierarchies at allocating resources because they are apolitical and unsentimental.
The Ideological Challenge: Few organisations question the doctrine of optimisation. But optimising a business model that is slowly becoming irrelevant can't secure a company's future.	Embrace Paradox: An accelerating pace of change demands an accelerating pace of strategic evolution. This requires a company to care as much about resilience as it does about optimisation, embracing the paradox between relentless efficiency and restless exploration.

Source: Adapted from Hamel and Välikangas (2003).

4. Fourth, they build faith through corporate storytelling. Stories of failure and success from prominent corporations are used extensively to persuade audiences that the prescribed doctrines are valid because they are rooted in the 'factual' and 'real' experiences of the corporate world.

Routines, hermeneutics, and improvisation in organisational resilience

A different, more incremental perspective on resilience is offered by Suarez and Montes (2020) in their work on routines, heuristics, and improvisation. Drawing from a study of a mountaineering expedition on Mount Everest, they argue that organisational resilience is built through departures from established routines in response to changes in the 'focal context'—a constructed reality encompassing both objective environmental traits and subjective perceptions. They identify three behavioural strategies:

1. Routines: Scripted work processes that are effective in stable and predictable contexts.
2. Heuristics: Simple rules of thumb or responsive adaptations in routines that are triggered when the focal context changes, making existing routines too slow, resource-intensive, or unable to solve new problems. They represent minor or fragmental departures from routine.
3. Improvisation: Spontaneous experimentation that occurs when the focal context changes so dramatically that existing assumptions no longer hold. This is a major departure from routine, necessary for operating in uncharted territory, which eventually leads to the establishment of new routines.

In contrast to the paradigmatic shift advocated by Hamel and Välikangas, Suarez and Montes suggest that resilience can be built incrementally and evolutionarily from existing organisational processes.

Data-driven resilience modelling

In contrast to rhetorical narratives, consultocratic modelling approaches place a greater emphasis on data integration and aggregation to fortify organisational resilience. These approaches are characterised by several key features, with data analytics playing a pivotal role.

1. The modelling process begins with a data-driven definition of crises and resilience. Macroeconomic, financial market, and corporate data are integrated to illustrate the necessity of resilience. Data analytics are used to generate tables and charts depicting unfolding crises, thereby signi-

fying the factuality and gravity of the situation and directing leadership's attention. As illustrated in Figure 6.2, this datafication is used to identify a 'resilience gap' by showing slumps in performance curves tied to specific events or trajectories, such as the COVID-19 pandemic, geopolitical conflicts such as Ukraine War, financial crisis, US political events, federal interest trajectories, disruptions in EU GDP growth path, and Global Warming Index and so on. It also helps to define a 'resilience path' by comparing a faster recovery trajectory with a slower one, and to delineate the phases of resilience, often termed anticipation, cushioning, adaptation, and shaping.

Figure 6.2: Phases and capabilities of resilience – consultancy modelling

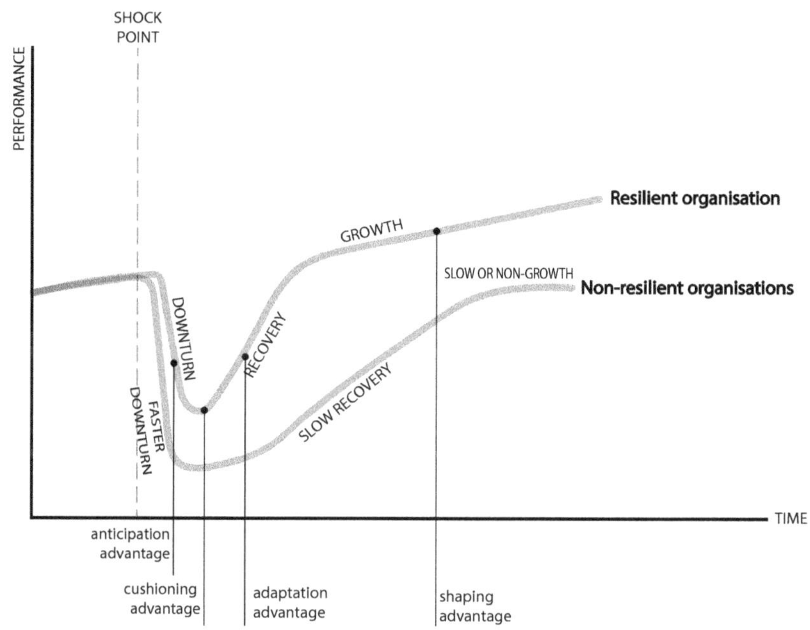

Identifying and explaining the resilience phases or stages. In relation to the resilience curve depicted in Figure 6.2, consultancy firms identify the resilience phases with different terminology, but they all resemble more or less the same idea. For example, McKinsey identifies three phases: downturn, recovery, and growth, together with strategic capabilities of response, foresight, and adaptation (see Ahlawat et al. 2022). For Boston Consultancy Group, resilience phases are anticipation, cushioning, adaptation, and shaping, and a resilient company would enjoy the following advantages over non-resilient companies (see Shmul et al. 2022).

a. The **anticipation advantage**, as described by BCG consultants, is the edge resilient organisations have over their less resilient counterparts. This advantage stems from the ability to effectively anticipate and respond to crises. Key components include establishing contingency plans for unforeseen disruptions and actively scanning the environment for emerging threats. Other consulting firms and experts often refer to this capability as foresight, which helps companies weather challenges and experience a less severe downturn.

b. The **cushioning advantage** allows resilient organisations to bounce back from shocks more quickly than their competitors. According to BCG, this is built by creating financial and operational buffers, promoting diversity, ensuring operational modularity, achieving financial separation, and embedding the organisation within broader social and political support systems.

c. The **adaptation advantage** stems from an organisation's ability to adjust to new situations created by a crisis. BCG consultants emphasise that this depends on several factors, including agility, a capacity for experimentation, operational flexibility, the ability to shift business and market portfolios, and integration into wider social and political systems.

d. The **shaping advantage** is the benefit a company gains by recovering from adversity faster than its competitors. This strategic positioning allows the organisation to shape the new post-crisis reality, embrace fresh perspectives, and redefine its industry.

2. Consultancy firms also engage in the data-driven flagging of 'bigger issues' that underpin the need for resilience. Through corporate surveys and data analysis, they periodically update the macroeconomic, political, and technological issues that should be at the forefront of corporate strategy. Recent reports from firms like PwC, McKinsey, and KPMG consistently highlight a complex and interconnected risk landscape that includes supply chain disruption, climate events, cyber threats, talent shortages, and the transformative impact of generative AI as top priorities for CEOs. This demonstrates a clear convergence between the macro-level concerns of bodies like the World Economic Forum and the micro-level strategic advice offered to corporations. The line between corporate strategy and global public policy is blurring, forcing management accountants to incorporate external, systemic risks into their internal models.

3. A crucial recent development is the positioning of Artificial Intelligence (AI) as a critical enabler of resilience. Consultancies are championing AI for its role in predictive analytics, real-time monitoring, and complex scenario simulation. This shifts resilience from a qualitative aspiration to a quantitative, data-driven discipline, allowing organisations to make more informed, proactive decisions and develop robust contingency plans.
4. Finally, these models invariably conclude with doctrinal prescriptions. Consulting experts advocate for what they consider the ideal mindset and actions for 'truly resilient' organisations. For example, McKinsey advises leaders to use scenarios rather than forecasting and to focus on resilient growth amid crises. Deloitte urges organisations to make resilience a strategic priority by appointing a chief resilience officer and giving greater attention to Environmental, Social, and Governance (ESG) risks. These prescriptions are presented as proven practices derived from successful corporate achievements, reinforcing the consultocratic authority.

The Modularisation of organisational resilience

Consultocratic discourses conceptualise organisational resilience as a system comprising a specific set of interconnected modules. This modularisation allows consulting firms to 'productise' resilience, offering tailored packages to clients based on specific functional needs. While firms use different terminology, a substantial conceptual isomorphism is evident in the fundamental building blocks they identify. Table 6.2 provides a comparative analysis of these frameworks.

The most commonly discussed resilience modules include:

1. **Financial Resilience**: An organisation's capacity to maintain financial health through proactive financial planning, diversification of revenue streams, effective cash flow and debt management, and transparent investor communication.
2. **Operational Resilience**: The ability to anticipate, prepare for, respond to, and recover from disruptions to normal business operations. This involves risk assessment, business impact analysis, scenario planning, and ensuring the resilience of key suppliers and partners.
3. **Structural Resilience:** This encompasses the human, relational, and governance elements that make organisational structures agile and adaptive. It includes clear leadership, a robust governance structure, flexible and agile team designs, and a focus on employee well-being and talent management.
4. **Digital and Technology Resilience:** The ability to handle disruptions in the digital environment, such as cyberattacks, system failures, and data

Table 6.2: A comparative analysis of resilience frameworks from leading consultancies

Firm (Source)	Framework/Concept	Key Components/Modules	Core Philosophy/Emphasis
PwC	The Resilience Revolution / Integrated Resilience Programme	Strategic, Operational, Financial Resilience	Moving from siloed capabilities to a centrally governed, integrated programme focused on protecting what matters most.
Deloitte	Five Capitals of Organisational Resilience / Human Performance	People, Reputational, Operational, Financial, Environmental	A human-centric approach, emphasising that thriving depends on creating value for all stakeholders, not just shareholders.
KPMG	Enterprise Resilience Framework	Strategic, Operational, Reputational, Financial, Technological, Organisational	A shift from qualitative attributes to a quantitative, data-driven, and AI-enabled approach for predictive capabilities and informed decision-making.
WEF & McKinsey	Three Pillars for a Resilient Tomorrow	1. Building the resilience muscle (leadership/capabilities) 2. Understanding and measuring (frameworks/KPIs) 3. Public-private partnerships	A macro-to-micro approach, emphasising that organisational resilience is inseparable from broader societal and economic resilience, requiring collaboration.

breaches. Key components include strong cybersecurity measures, data protection protocols, business continuity planning for technology systems, and regular employee training.

5. **Reputational and Environmental Resilience:** These are often intertwined. Reputational resilience involves managing crises to maintain stakeholder trust, while environmental resilience focuses on adapting to and mitigating the impacts of environmental challenges, such as climate change. A strong environmental, social, and governance (ESG) posture is increasingly seen as fundamental to both reputational and long-term organisational resilience.

6.4 Academic discourses on organisational resilience

In contrast to the prescriptive nature of consultocratic discourses, academic work focuses on offering a conceptual and theoretical analysis of the conditions under which organisational resilience emerges and the forms it takes. These discourses do not aim to prescribe doctrines but rather to explore how and why organisations might adopt different approaches to resilience. They often develop broader conceptual schemas that can be used to explore and address specific resilience issues. This section will concentrate on two interrelated themes highlighted by academic discourses: resilience's underlying contradictions and the different domains of resilience that address these contradictions, before introducing a new discussion on the central role of management accounting.

Exploring the underpinning contradictions of resilience

A focal point in academic research is the exploration of the contradictory conditions, or paradoxes, that organisations must navigate to achieve resilience. Scholars assert that 'the existence of tensions and contradictions between different instances constitutes resilience'. Resilience is thus seen as the outcome of a dialectical process between competing demands.

Giustiniano et al. (2018) describe resilience as a dialectical synthesis between two opposing 'templates' of responding to challenges: reactivity and adaptivity.

1. Reactivity refers to the capacity to bounce back or recover from challenges after they occur. It is associated with qualities such as coping, hardiness, recovery, and redundancy. It connotes survival skills in the face of adversity.
2. Adaptivity involves proactively preparing for and anticipating challenges, enabling a system to adjust and thrive. It is forward-thinking and strategic, encompassing qualities like agility, anticipation, prevention, and improvisation.

Similarly, Frigotto et al. (2022) position resilience within the paradoxical demands of stability and change, while Denyer (2017) broadens the understanding of these contradictions by blending defensive and progressive aims on one axis with consistency and flexibility on the other. The core idea is that resilience is not about finding a perfect, static balance but about dynamically managing these persistent, competing demands.

Relating contradictions to different domains of resilience strategies

Academic discussions often adopt a topological approach, using these underlying contradictions as axes to map potential domains of resilient action. As illustrated in Figure 6.3 (Panel A), Giustiniano et al. (2018) delineate a continuum between reactivity and adaptivity to identify three potential templates for resilience. They posit that true 'organisational resilience' (Template 3) is an ideal type that constitutes a synthesis of both adaptive and reactive elements.

Frigotto et al. (2022) map the domain of resilience by examining the dichotomy

Figure 6.3: Tensions and domains of organisational resilience

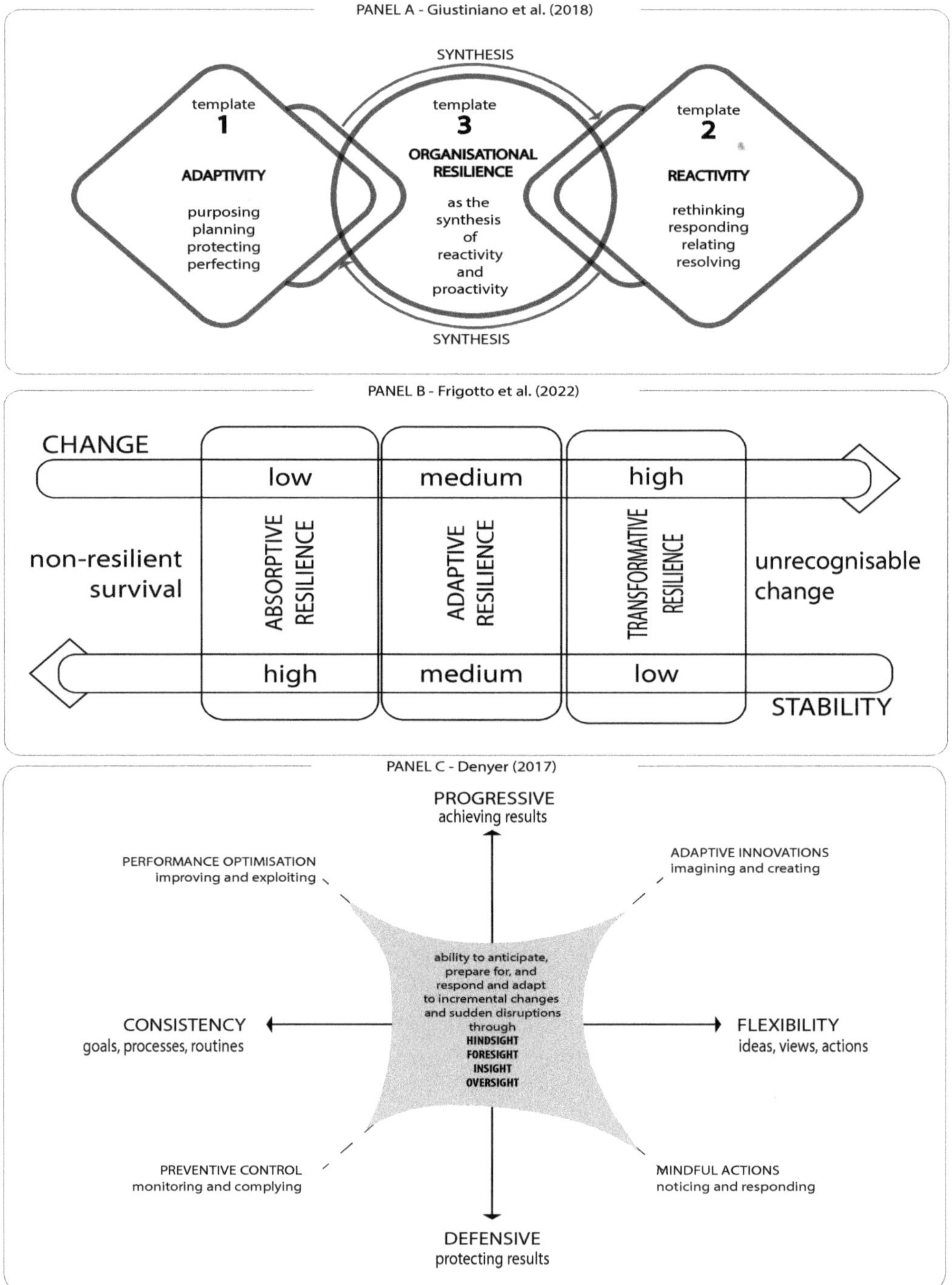

between change and stability (Figure 6.3, Panel B), identifying three domains: absorptive, adaptive, and transformative resilience. Finally, Denyer (2017) plots the axes of defensive vs. progressive and consistency vs. flexibility to yield four distinct domains of resilient action (Figure 6.3, Panel C): preventive control, performance optimisation, adaptive innovation, and mindful action. For Denyer, organisational resilience is a synthesis of these forms, an 'ability to anticipate, prepare for, and respond and adapt to incremental changes and sudden disruptions'. He materialises this ability through four interrelated practices he terms the '4Sights': Hindsight, Foresight, Insight, and Oversight.

Integrating resilience through management accounting and control systems

While academic models provide powerful conceptual frameworks, the practical mechanisms through which these abstract capabilities are embedded and enacted within an organisation are often its management accounting and control systems (MACS). The integration of MACS with risk governance (RG) creates a holistic system that moves beyond traditional control to support organisational resilience. This presents a fundamental paradox: using the tools of control to manage uncontrollability. The resolution lies in evolving the purpose of these systems—from enforcing rigid compliance to fostering adaptive capacity.

The key components of an integrated MACS-RG and their contribution to resilience are as follows:

1. Continuous Planning and Budgeting: Traditional static annual budgets are ill-suited for turbulent environments. Resilience requires a shift towards dynamic forecasting, rolling budgets, and scenario planning. These tools allow organisations to anticipate potential shocks and model their financial and operational impacts, directly building the 'foresight' and 'anticipation' capabilities essential for adaptivity.
2. Internal Control and Risk Management: Robust internal controls form the bedrock of operational resilience, ensuring process integrity and reliability during disruptions. When integrated with a strategic risk management function, this moves beyond a compliance exercise. It becomes a proactive process of identifying, assessing, and mitigating risks that informs strategic decision-making and resource allocation, enhancing the organisation's absorptive capacity.
3. Performance Measurement: Resilience demands a move away from purely financial, lagging indicators. A balanced performance measurement system that incorporates leading, non-financial metrics—such as supply chain flexibility, employee skills development, or the speed of innovation

cycles—provides an early warning system. It allows managers to measure and monitor the organisation's adaptive capacity before a crisis hits.

4. Information from External Networks: As resilience becomes increasingly dependent on external ecosystems, MACS must evolve to incorporate information from beyond the firm's legal boundaries. This includes monitoring the financial health of critical suppliers, tracking geopolitical risks in key markets, and understanding shifts in customer behaviour, thereby enabling a more holistic and externally aware approach to resilience.

Ultimately, a sophisticated and integrated MACS is the engine that enables an organisation not just to 'bounce back' to a previous state but to 'bounce forward'. A crisis inevitably reveals weaknesses and provides opportunities for learning. A well-designed MACS provides the information infrastructure to analyse failures, reallocate resources effectively towards new opportunities, and support the transformation of business models. It is this capacity for learning and strategic renewal, facilitated by management accounting, that turns a reactive crisis response into a source of long-term competitive advantage.

Chapter summary

This chapter has explored organisational resilience as a critical strategic theme in structuring the organisational hierarchy, positioning it as an essential evolution beyond the limits of traditional management control. The concept of resilience is versatile, with its core meaning—the capacity to anticipate, face, and recover from adversity—manifesting differently across disciplines from psychology to engineering and economics.

In the corporate context, resilience is framed through two primary lenses. First, consultocratic discourses, driven by global consulting firms, package resilience into actionable and marketable strategies. These take the form of expository narratives that use guru-like rhetoric to create urgency and prescribe solutions, and data-driven models that modularise resilience into components such as financial, operational, structural, digital, and reputational resilience. These models increasingly leverage data analytics and AI to shift resilience from a qualitative goal to a quantitative discipline.

Second, academic discourses provide a deeper conceptual analysis, elucidating the inherent contradictions and tensions that underpin resilience. They highlight the paradoxical balancing acts required between stability and change, reactivity and adaptivity, and consistency versus flexibility. The interactive spaces created by these dichotomies give rise to different domains or modes of resilience, providing frameworks for diagnosing and developing an organisation's adaptive capacity.

Synthesising these perspectives, organisational resilience can be understood through four interconnected elements:

1. Contextual elements: The external dynamics and events, from geopolitical shocks to technological disruptions, that create vulnerability and necessitate resilience.
2. Processual elements: The dynamic processes an entity undergoes, including anticipation, absorption, recovery, adaptation, and improvisation.
3. Modular elements: The distinct yet interconnected organisational capabilities—financial, operational, human, and technological—that form the building blocks of resilience.
4. Behavioural elements: The individual, collective, and systemic attributes, mindsets, and leadership qualities required to navigate uncertainty effectively.

For the modern management accountant, understanding and shaping organisational resilience is an indispensable part of strategic practice. The chapter concludes that in an era of endemic uncertainty, resilience has superseded static control as the key hierarchical strategy. This represents a fundamental shift in the accountant's role—from a scorekeeper of past performance to an architect of future adaptiveness. The expertise in designing and operating integrated management accounting and control systems is no longer a back-office function but a core strategic capability essential for organisational survival and prosperity in a turbulent world.

Case study: The H&M Group: weaving resilience or unravelling trust? a case study on sustainability and strategy

Part 1: Case study narrative

1. Introduction: the fast fashion paradox

The H&M Group, a titan of the global apparel industry, operates at the heart of a profound and challenging paradox. Its business model, emblematic of 'fast fashion', is engineered for volume, speed, and cost efficiency, a formula that has delivered affordable fashion to millions and generated substantial shareholder value. Annually, the company produces a staggering volume of garments, with some estimates placing the figure at 3 billion items. Yet, this very model, predicated on a linear 'take-make-waste' cycle, is inherently fragile. It promotes a culture of disposability where a significant portion of what is produced is destined for landfill or incineration, often after only a few uses.

This operational paradigm creates a fundamental tension with the escalating strategic imperative for organisational resilience. As defined within contemporary strategic management, organisational resilience is the capacity to navigate profound, unpredictable uncertainty—an environment where established plans may become irrelevant. The fast-fashion model, however, does not merely expose a company to external shocks; it actively generates its own systemic vulnerabilities. The relentless pressure on cost and speed creates brittle global supply chains susceptible to disruption; the vast gap between marketing claims of sustainability and the reality of mass production creates acute reputational risks; and the constant search for low-cost labour creates persistent social compliance challenges.

Consequently, H&M finds itself in a state of perpetual strategic conflict. It is not simply responding to external adversities but is forced to manage the symptoms of a business model that may be fundamentally non-resilient. This case study examines H&M's journey through this paradox by analysing its strategic responses to two distinct but interconnected crises: first, a public scandal over allegations of 'greenwashing' that tested its reputational and digital resilience; and second, a geopolitical breakdown in a key sourcing market, Myanmar, that challenged the very foundations of its operational and social resilience. Through these events, this case explores whether H&M is genuinely weaving resilience into the fabric of its organisation or merely patching the holes in a model that is beginning to unravel under the weight of its own contradictions.

2. Architecting resilience: H&M's public commitment to sustainability

In response to the growing pressures from investors, regulators, and consumers, the H&M Group has constructed an elaborate and public-facing architecture of sustainability commitments. Articulated in detail within its annual and sustainability reports, this strategy presents a vision of a company actively working to decouple its financial growth from the consumption of finite natural resources. The company's reporting mirrors the 'consultocratic' discourses on resilience identified in strategic management literature, where resilience is packaged into a data-driven, modular, and prescriptive management product designed to reassure stakeholders of control and forward momentum.

This approach is characterised by a heavy reliance on quantitative metrics and ambitious, time-bound targets that modularise the complex challenge of sustainability into manageable components such as climate, materials, and social impact. For example, the company has set science-based targets to achieve net-zero greenhouse gas (GHG) emissions by 2040, with an interim goal of halving its absolute emissions across the entire value chain by 2030 against a 2019 baseline. This data-driven framing serves as a doctrinal prescription, presenting an idealised future state that is positioned as achievable through diligent managerial action and investment. The key pillars of this publicly articulated strategy, and the company's reported progress as of its 2023 financial year, are summarised in Table 1.

Through this comprehensive reporting, H&M projects an image of a resilient organisation that is proactively identifying, measuring, and managing its most significant environmental, social, and governance (ESG) risks. This narrative of control and progress forms the official backdrop against which the subsequent crises unfolded, providing a critical baseline for assessing the gap between strategic rhetoric and operational reality.

3. The first shock: greenwashing allegations and the test of reputational resilience

The carefully curated image of sustainability leadership was severely tested in 2022 when H&M became embroiled in a high-profile greenwashing scandal. The crisis originated from the company's 'Conscious Choice' collection, which was marketed to eco-conscious consumers using 'Sustainability Profiles'—digital scorecards intended to provide transparency on the environmental impact of each garment. These profiles were based on data from the Higg Materials Sustainability Index (MSI), a suite of tools developed by the Sustainable Apparel Coalition (SAC) to standardise impact measurement across the industry.

In June 2022, an investigation by the news outlet Quartz revealed that H&M's implementation of these scorecards was deeply flawed and systematically mislead-

Table 1: H&M group's stated sustainability goals and 2023 performance

Sustainability Area	Stated Goal	Reported 2023 Progress
Climate	Reduce absolute Scope 1 & 2 GHG emissions by 56% by 2030 (2019 baseline).	24% reduction achieved.
	Reduce absolute Scope 3 GHG emissions by 56% by 2030 (2019 baseline).	22% reduction achieved.
	100% renewable electricity in own operations by 2030.	94% achieved.
Materials	100% of materials to be recycled or sustainably sourced by 2030.	85% achieved.
	30% recycled materials by 2025; 50% by 2030.	25% achieved.
Packaging	100% of packaging to be recycled or sustainably sourced by 2030.	79% achieved.
	Reduce overall plastic packaging volume by 25% by 2025 (2018 baseline).	55% reduction achieved.
Social Impact	More than 200,000 workers responded to the worker voice survey.	This data is used to guide priorities for improving grievance mechanisms.

Source: Adapted from H&M Group Annual and Sustainability Report 2023.

ing. The investigation found that more than half of the profiles portrayed products as being better for the environment than they were. In some of the most egregious cases, the data presented was the inverse of reality; for example, H&M's website was found to have ignored negative signs in the Higg Index data, reporting that a garment used 20% less water than average when it actually used 20% more. The investigation concluded that positive language such as 'less' and 'reduction' was effectively 'hard-coded' into the website, ensuring that the scorecards could only present a favourable environmental picture.

The fallout was swift. A month later, a class-action lawsuit was filed in New York by plaintiff Chelsea Commodore, alleging that H&M had created an extensive marketing scheme to 'greenwash' its products. The lawsuit accused the company of engaging in deceptive practices by presenting false environmental profiles and misrepresenting the efficacy of its recycling programme. The complaint argued that H&M's claims of being able to 'close the loop' created a misleading illusion, given that recycling solutions are not commercially available at scale for the vast majority of its products.

This crisis represented not merely a marketing misstep, but a systemic failure of

H&M's management accounting and control systems (MACS). The information systems designed to generate and communicate sustainability performance indicators were configured for narrative control rather than factual accuracy. In its attempt to control the story, H&M lost control of its reputation, demonstrating a critical failure of both digital and reputational resilience.

H&M's response was purely reactive. The company promptly removed all the environmental scorecards from its websites globally, stating it had "come across a couple of technical issues" it was looking into. This action was followed by the SAC's own decision to suspend the use of its consumer-facing profiles industry-wide, after Norwegian authorities concluded that using the Higg MSI methodology for marketing could be a breach of law. By removing the offending data, H&M addressed the immediate symptom of the crisis but avoided a deeper, more public interrogation of the strategic contradictions at its core. This reactive posture, aimed at restoring stability rather than catalysing transformative change, highlights a significant limitation in the company's adaptive capacity. Although a court later dismissed one of the lawsuits on technical grounds, noting that H&M had not explicitly used the terms 'sustainable' or 'environmentally friendly' and had provided detailed information on its website, the underlying reputational vulnerability persisted, leading to a second lawsuit being filed on different grounds.

4. The Second shock: geopolitical turmoil and the test of operational resilience

While the greenwashing scandal exposed internal system failures, a second crisis in H&M's supply chain revealed the limits of its resilience when faced with systemic external shocks. For years, Myanmar had been a key sourcing market for H&M, but the country was also plagued by persistent reports of labour abuses, including wage theft, forced overtime, and inhumane work rates at garment factories.

In February 2021, a military coup plunged the country into a profound political and humanitarian crisis, fundamentally altering the operating environment for all international brands. The collapse of civil governance and the suppression of human rights made it virtually impossible to conduct meaningful due diligence. An independent report published in 2022 confirmed that in a military dictatorship, traditional supplier audits and monitoring systems were rendered impotent, as worker safety could not be guaranteed and freedom of association was non-existent.

This geopolitical failure represented a systemic shock that was beyond H&M's immediate control, invalidating the internal control mechanisms that formed the basis of its operational and social resilience modules. Despite mounting pressure from human rights groups and global unions like IndustriALL, H&M was initially reluctant to withdraw, citing its local presence and engagement with EU-funded projects. However, as reports of abuses escalated—with H&M itself investigating 20 alleged cases at its supplier factories—the company's position became untenable.

In August 2023, H&M announced its decision to "gradually phase out" its operations in Myanmar. In doing so, it committed to following a 'responsible exit framework' developed by IndustriALL. This framework provides a structured process for disengagement, requiring that the exit be negotiated with worker representatives and that provisions are made for adequate severance pay and the remediation of any outstanding rights violation claims.

This crisis starkly illustrates the limitations of an organisation-centric, modular approach to resilience. H&M's internal systems for supplier management, a key component of its operational resilience, proved fragile when the broader political and social context disintegrated. The decision to enact a 'responsible exit' can be seen as a difficult, real-world attempt to navigate the academic paradox of 'stability versus change'. While exiting represented a radical and disruptive 'change' to its supply chain, the adoption of a structured framework was an attempt to manage this transition with a degree of 'stability' for the affected workers. In this instance, resilience was not about preventing disruption but about managing a necessary and painful transformation in the most orderly and ethical way possible, arguably demonstrating a higher-order adaptive capacity to 'bounce forward' from an irrecoverable situation.

Part 2: Teaching note and analysis

5. Case analysis: deconstructing H&M's resilience through an academic lens

This section applies the theoretical frameworks on organisational resilience from the course textbook to synthesise the case narrative. By moving from description to structured analysis, it provides a method for deconstructing the complexities of H&M's strategic challenges.

5.1 A failure of modules?

Consultocratic discourses often modularise organisational resilience into a set of distinct, manageable capabilities, such as financial, operational, structural, digital, and reputational resilience. An analysis of H&M's crises through this lens reveals that its failures were not confined to single, isolated modules but were instead cascade failures, where a weakness in one domain triggered a collapse in another. The interconnected nature of these failures is detailed in Table 2.

Table 2: Mapping H&M's crises to the modular resilience framework

Resilience Module	Greenwashing Crisis	Myanmar Supply Chain Crisis
Operational	Not directly impacted, but the underlying business model of overproduction created the pressure for sustainability marketing.	Systemic Failure: Traditional control mechanisms (audits, codes of conduct) were rendered ineffective by the geopolitical shock, exposing the fragility of the supply chain.
Financial	Indirect impact through potential fines, legal costs, and loss of sales from damaged consumer trust.	Direct impact through the costs of disengagement, supply chain reconfiguration, and potential loss of low-cost production capacity.
Structural	Failure: Governance systems failed to ensure the integrity of public-facing data. The crisis revealed a disconnect between marketing functions and sustainability verification processes.	Failure: The crisis demonstrated that internal governance structures are insufficient to ensure worker welfare when external state-level governance collapses.
Digital & Technology	Primary Failure Point: Information systems were designed to produce favourable marketing outputs, not accurate sustainability data, leading directly to the crisis.	Not a primary failure point, but the lack of reliable, verifiable information from the ground hampered effective decision-making.
Reputational	Catastrophic Failure: The crisis caused a severe loss of stakeholder trust and exposed the company to widespread accusations of hypocrisy and deception.	Significant Damage: Initial reluctance to exit led to criticism from human rights groups, damaging H&M's reputation as a responsible actor. The 'responsible exit' was a mitigatory action.
Environmental	The crisis highlighted the fundamental contradiction between H&M's business model and its stated environmental goals.	Not a direct environmental crisis, but the reliance on sourcing from politically unstable regions is linked to a model that prioritises low costs over holistic sustainability.

The analysis in Table 2 demonstrates that a modular view, while useful for diagnosis, can be misleading if it encourages a siloed approach. The greenwashing crisis was a digital failure that became a reputational catastrophe. The Myanmar crisis was a geopolitical event that triggered a complete breakdown of H&M's operational and structural controls. This underscores that true resilience requires an integrated system, not just a collection of strong but disconnected parts.

5.2 Navigating the paradoxes

Academic literature posits that resilience is not a static state but the dynamic management of persistent, competing demands or paradoxes. H&M's responses to its two crises can be mapped onto the theoretical continua of Reactivity vs. Adaptivity and Stability vs. Change.

In the greenwashing crisis, H&M's response was overwhelmingly reactive. By swiftly removing the flawed scorecards, the company engaged in a damage control exercise designed to 'bounce back' to a state of reputational stability. This action addressed the immediate symptom but did not engage with the deeper, underlying cause: the strategic misalignment between its fast-fashion model and its sustainability messaging. An adaptive response would have involved a more profound transformation, such as a public commitment to co-developing a more robust and transparent industry-wide reporting standard or fundamentally questioning whether a 'Conscious Choice' label can be credibly applied to a mass-produced, low-cost garment.

In contrast, the response to the Myanmar crisis, while forced by external events, contained stronger elements of adaptivity. The initial phase was one of inertia, attempting to maintain the stability of its existing supply chain. However, the eventual decision to exit represented a radical change. Critically, by adopting the 'responsible exit' framework, H&M attempted to manage this disruptive change in a structured and ethical manner. This demonstrates an ability to 'bounce forward'—not by returning to a previous state, but by acknowledging that the previous state was no longer viable and transforming its operational footprint accordingly. This response, therefore, represents a more sophisticated navigation of the stability-change paradox, suggesting a learned, if painful, evolution in its adaptive capacity.

5.3 The double-edged sword of MACS

Management accounting and control systems (MACS) are the practical mechanisms through which abstract resilience capabilities are operationalised. The H&M case provides a powerful illustration of the fundamental paradox of using the tools of control to manage uncontrollability.

Initially, H&M's MACS were weaponised for narrative control. The systems that produced the Higg Index scorecards were not designed to provide management with accurate, actionable insights for risk mitigation, but rather to generate simplified, positive KPIs for external marketing. This approach treated sustainability data not as a control mechanism for improving performance, but as an output to be managed for public relations. The result was a catastrophic failure: in attempting to control the narrative, the company created an uncontrollable reputational crisis.

The aftermath of these crises necessitates an evolution in the purpose and design of H&M's MACS. To build genuine resilience, these systems must shift from enforcing compliance or shaping narratives to fostering adaptive capacity. As suggested by the academic literature, this requires a move towards more dynamic and externally-focused systems. For H&M, this would mean:

1. Rethinking Performance Measurement: Moving beyond simplistic, self-serving metrics towards a balanced system incorporating leading, non-financial indicators that measure true adaptive capacity (e.g., supply chain geographic diversity, speed of material innovation, worker satisfaction indices).
2. Integrating External Network Information: The Myanmar crisis proved that internal data is insufficient. A resilient MACS must systematically incorporate information from beyond the firm's legal boundaries, including geopolitical risk assessments, NGO reports on labour conditions, and real-time monitoring of social and political stability in sourcing markets.
3. Embracing Radical Transparency: The greenwashing crisis was born of opacity. A resilient MACS must be designed for transparency, providing stakeholders with access to the underlying data and methodologies behind sustainability claims, thereby rebuilding trust through verifiable evidence rather than persuasive rhetoric. The company's preparation for the EU's Corporate Sustainability Reporting Directive (CSRD) indicates a move in this direction, driven by regulatory necessity.

Ultimately, H&M's experience demonstrates that MACS can be either a source of fragility or a cornerstone of resilience. When used to create an illusion of control, they amplify risk. When redesigned to foster learning, transparency, and foresight, they become the engine of adaptiveness that enables an organisation to not just survive, but to thrive amidst uncertainty.

6.0 Seminar discussion questions

1. Critically evaluate H&M's public sustainability strategy (as detailed in Section 2.0 and Table 1) using the four characteristic elements of 'expository narratives' and the features of 'data-driven modelling' from the chapter. To what extent does H&M's approach reflect a 'consultocratic' framing of resilience?
2. Using the engineering definition of resilience (redundancy, robustness, adaptability, etc.) from the chapter , analyse the vulnerabilities exposed in H&M's global supply chain by the Myanmar crisis. What does this case suggest about the limitations of building operational resilience when faced with systemic geopolitical risk?
3. The greenwashing lawsuit stemmed from a failure of H&M's information systems. Drawing on the chapter's discussion of MACS , explain how a more robustly designed system—incorporating leading non-financial metrics, external network information, and a focus on transparency over narrative control—could have mitigated this reputational damage.

4. Debate H&M's decision to exit Myanmar. Using the academic frameworks of 'Reactivity vs. Adaptivity' and 'Stability vs. Change', was this an act of 'bouncing back' or 'bouncing forward'? Discuss the ethical and strategic trade-offs involved and what a truly resilient response might have entailed.
5. Imagine you are the new Chief Resilience Officer at H&M Group, reporting directly to the CEO. Based on the lessons from these two crises, what specific changes would you propose to the company's performance measurement, internal control, and risk management systems to build genuine, long-term resilience that moves beyond its current consultocratic approach? Justify your recommendations using the academic principles discussed in the chapter.

Chapter review questions

1. The contemporary strategic focus on organisational resilience represents a fundamental insufficiency of which traditional management accounting paradigm?

   a. Activity-based costing as a method of overhead absorption.
   b. Strategic performance management as multidimensional performance.
   c. Management control systems for goal attainment in a predictable environmental setting.
   d. Budget-based financial control.

2. Which disciplinary perspective on resilience most strongly emphasises system characteristics such as redundancy, modular design, and predictive maintenance?

   a. Psychological resilience
   b. Social resilience
   c. Economic resilience
   d. Engineering resilience

3. The American Psychological Association's definition of resilience highlights that it is both a dynamic process and a(n):

   a. Innate trait
   b. Tangible outcome
   c. Fixed capability
   d. Emotional state

4. In the context of disaster management, 'social resilience' is described as comprising two interconnected categories of processes and capacities: structural and what?

   a. Financial
   b. Political
   c. Cognitive
   d. Technological

5. The OECD's view of economic resilience includes which of the following as a key component for withstanding external shocks?

   a. Market consolidation
   b. Economic diversification
   c. Strict fiscal austerity
   d. Centralised planning

6. In their 2003 article, 'The Quest for Resilience', Hamel and Välikangas introduce the concept of a 'resilience gap'. How do they frame this gap?

    a. As a global systemic issue requiring public-private partnerships.
    b. As a scenario where organisations are not becoming resilient as fast as the world is becoming turbulent.
    c. As the difference between a firm's operational capacity and its financial reserves.
    d. As a failure of international bodies to provide adequate risk management frameworks.

7. Which of the following is NOT one of the four characteristic elements of expository narratives on resilience discussed in the chapter?

    a. Framing resilience as a consultocratic necessity.
    b. Providing peer-reviewed empirical evidence.
    c. Identifying points of departure from current corporate thinking.
    d. Building faith through corporate storytelling.

8. Hamel and Välikangas (2003) propose an aspirational goal of 'zero trauma'. What does this concept describe?

    a. An organisation that avoids all external shocks and crises.
    b. An organisation that experiences revolutionary change through quick, evolutionary steps without major crises.
    c. An organisation with sufficient financial reserves to absorb any loss without operational impact.
    d. An organisation that has eliminated all internal political conflicts.

9. The 'Political Challenge' in Hamel and Välikangas's framework for resilience refers to an organisation's ability to:

    a. Influence government policy and regulation.
    b. Manage stakeholder relationships effectively during a crisis.
    c. Divert resources from legacy products to future-oriented projects.
    d. Appoint leaders with strong political acumen.

10. How does the perspective of Suarez and Montes (2020) on building resilience differ from that of Hamel and Välikangas (2003)?

    a. Suarez and Montes advocate for a paradigmatic, revolutionary shift.
    b. Suarez and Montes suggest resilience is built incrementally through departures from routines.
    c. Suarez and Montes focus exclusively on financial resilience.
    d. Suarez and Montes reject the role of leadership in building resilience.

11. According to Suarez and Montes, what are 'heuristics' in the context of organisational response?

    a. Scripted, formal work processes for stable contexts.
    b. Spontaneous experimentation when existing assumptions fail.
    c. Simple rules of thumb or minor adaptations to routines in response to context changes.
    d. Comprehensive strategic plans developed by senior management.

12. In data-driven consultancy models of resilience, what is the primary purpose of depicting performance curves with slumps tied to specific events (e.g., COVID-19)?

    a. To assign blame for past performance failures.
    b. To forecast future stock market performance with precision.
    c. To datafy the 'resilience gap' and define a 'resilience path'.
    d. To satisfy regulatory reporting requirements.

13. What does the term 'conceptual isomorphism' in the modular frameworks of resilience proposed by consultancies imply?

    a. That each firm has a unique and proprietary framework.
    b. That the frameworks are fundamentally different in their core philosophies.
    c. That there is a substantial similarity in the fundamental building blocks identified, despite different terminology.
    d. That the frameworks are derived from a single, universally accepted academic theory.

14. Which of the following is identified as a critical enabler of resilience in recent data-driven consultocratic models, shifting it towards a more quantitative discipline?

    a. Total Quality Management (TQM)
    b. Just-In-Time (JIT) inventory systems
    c. Artificial Intelligence (AI)
    d. Shareholder value analysis

15. Deloitte's 'Five Capitals' framework for resilience is noted for its emphasis on a human-centric approach. Which of the following is NOT one of the five capitals listed?

    a. People
    b. Reputational
    c. Competitive
    d. Environmental

16. Academic discourses on resilience, as described in the chapter, primarily aim to:

    a. Prescribe a universal set of doctrines for managers to follow.
    b. Market resilience as a consultancy product.
    c. Offer a conceptual and theoretical analysis of the conditions under which resilience emerges.
    d. Develop standardised metrics for measuring corporate resilience.

17. Giustiniano et al. (2018) describe resilience as a dialectical synthesis between two opposing templates. What are these two templates?

    a. Profitability and Sustainability
    b. Reactivity and Adaptivity
    c. Efficiency and Effectiveness
    d. Centralisation and Decentralisation

18. An organisation that focuses on proactively preparing for and anticipating challenges, embodying qualities like agility and improvisation, is demonstrating which template of response, according to Giustiniano et al. (2018)?

    a. Reactivity
    b. Robustness
    c. Redundancy
    d. Adaptivity

19. The academic framework proposed by Frigotto et al. (2022) maps the domain of resilience by examining the paradoxical demands between which two concepts?

    a. Stability and Change
    b. Consistency and Flexibility
    c. Short-term and Long-term
    d. Internal and External

20. Denyer (2017) develops a topological map of resilient action using two axes. One axis is 'defensive vs. progressive'. What is the other axis?

    a. Simple vs. Complex
    b. Individual vs. Organisational
    c. Consistency vs. Flexibility
    d. Qualitative vs. Quantitative

21. Which of the following is one of Denyer's (2017) four domains of resilient action?

    a. Transformative Resilience
    b. Absorptive Capacity
    c. Mindful Action
    d. Dynamic Capability

22. Denyer (2017) materialises the ability to be resilient through four interrelated practices he terms the '4Sights'. Which of the following is NOT one of the '4Sights'?

    a. Hindsight
    b. Foresight
    c. Insight
    d. Nearsight

23. According to academic discourses, achieving resilience is best described as:

    a. Finding a perfect, static balance between competing demands.
    b. Eliminating all organisational tensions and contradictions.
    c. Dynamically managing persistent, competing demands.
    d. Prioritising adaptivity over reactivity in all situations.

24. The chapter argues that the practical mechanisms for embedding abstract resilience capabilities within an organisation are often its:

    a. Marketing and sales functions.
    b. Human resource policies.
    c. Corporate social responsibility initiatives.
    d. Management accounting and control systems (MACS).

25. What is the fundamental paradox that the chapter identifies when using MACS to foster organisational resilience?

    a. Using financial tools to measure non-financial performance.
    b. Balancing the needs of shareholders and other stakeholders.
    c. Using the tools of control to manage uncontrollability.
    d. Investing in long-term capabilities during short-term crises.

26. How does a shift towards dynamic forecasting and rolling budgets contribute to organisational resilience?

    a. It enforces rigid compliance with a predetermined annual plan.
    b. It builds the 'foresight' and 'anticipation' capabilities essential for adaptivity.

c. It reduces the need for internal controls and risk management.
d. It focuses exclusively on historical financial data.

27. To enhance resilience, a balanced performance measurement system should move away from purely financial, lagging indicators towards incorporating:

    a. More detailed historical cost data.
    b. Leading, non-financial metrics like supply chain flexibility.
    c. Competitor profit margins.
    d. Share price volatility.

28. For MACS to support resilience in an interconnected world, they must evolve to:

    a. Focus solely on internal process efficiency.
    b. Incorporate information from beyond the firm's legal boundaries.
    c. Be operated independently from the strategic risk management function.
    d. Produce reports on a less frequent, annual basis to reduce noise.

29. The concept of 'bouncing forward' after a crisis implies that an organisation:

    a. Returns to its exact pre-crisis operational state.
    b. Uses the crisis as an opportunity for learning, transformation, and strategic renewal.
    c. Successfully secures government financial support.
    d. Experiences a rapid recovery in its share price.

30. What is the ultimate conclusion of the chapter regarding the role of the modern management accountant?

    a. Their role remains focused on historical scorekeeping and variance analysis.
    b. Their primary function is to ensure regulatory compliance.
    c. They have become architects of future adaptiveness, making their expertise a core strategic capability.
    d. Their strategic importance has diminished with the rise of AI and data analytics.

Section 2.2: True/false/justify questions

Instructions: For each statement, indicate whether it is True or False. Then, provide a single sentence to justify your answer, drawing upon the concepts presented in the chapter.

31. Statement: The engineering concept of resilience is primarily concerned with an individual's emotional fortitude and coping skills.

32. Statement: According to Hamel and Välikangas (2003), strategic resilience is mainly about responding effectively to a single, one-time crisis.
33. Statement: The consultocratic concept of the 'resilience gap' frames resilience primarily as a global systemic issue requiring public-private partnerships.
34. Statement: The incrementalist approach to resilience, as described by Suarez and Montes (2020), suggests that improvisation occurs when the 'focal context' is stable and predictable.
35. Statement: Data-driven consultocratic models use data analytics to define a 'resilience path' which compares a faster recovery trajectory with a slower one.
36. Statement: The modular frameworks for resilience from firms like PwC, Deloitte, and KPMG show significant divergence with almost no common components.
37. Statement: Academic discourses on resilience suggest that the ideal state of resilience is achieved by eliminating all organisational tensions and contradictions.
38. Statement: According to Giustiniano et al. (2018), 'reactivity' refers to the proactive capacity to anticipate and prepare for future challenges.
39. Statement: The chapter argues that traditional, static annual budgets are well-suited for fostering organisational resilience in turbulent environments.
40. Statement: According to the chapter, the primary paradox of using MACS to foster resilience is managing uncontrollability with tools traditionally designed for control.

Section 2.3: Matching questions

Exercise 1: Consultocratic concepts and narratives

Instructions: Match each term from Column A with the most appropriate description from Column B.

Column A: Term/Concept	Column B: Description
1. Resilience Gap	A. Simple rules of thumb or responsive adaptations in routines.
2. Zero Trauma	B. Spontaneous experimentation when existing assumptions no longer hold.
3. The Cognitive Challenge	C. The need to divert resources from yesterday's products to tomorrow's.
4. The Political Challenge	D. The constructed reality of objective environmental traits and subjective perceptions.
5. Embrace Paradox	E. The need for a company to become free of denial, nostalgia, and arrogance.

6. Focal Context	F. The idea that the world is becoming turbulent faster than organisations are becoming resilient.
7. Heuristics	G. An ideal state where revolutionary change occurs in quick, evolutionary steps without major crises.
8. Improvisation	H. A commandment to care as much about resilience as about optimisation.

Exercise 2: Academic frameworks and tensions

Instructions: Match each author or framework from Column A with the core conceptual dichotomy or set of domains from Column B.

Column A: Author(s) / Framework	Column B: Core Concept / Domains
1. Giustiniano et al. (2018)	A. The domains of absorptive, adaptive, and transformative resilience.
2. Frigotto et al. (2022)	B. The four domains of preventive control, performance optimisation, adaptive innovation, and mindful action.
3. Denyer (2017)	C. A dialectical synthesis between the opposing templates of reactivity and adaptivity.
4. Denyer's '4Sights'	D. The paradoxical demands between stability and change.
	E. The interrelated practices of Hindsight, Foresight, Insight, and Oversight.

Comprehension questions

1. Provide brief descriptions or definitions of the following types of resilience.
    a. Psychological resilience
    b. Social resilience
    c. Engineering resilience
    d. Economic resilience
2. Identify the core concepts of resilience included in the types of resilience you defined in the question above.
3. Explain how processual and capability dimensions constitute resilience.
4. Differentiate between the approaches that organisations like the OECD and World Bank take on resilience and the approaches taken by corporations and their consultants.
5. List the two approaches that characterise consultocratic discourses of organisational resilience that this chapter discussed.
6. List and briefly describe the four characterising elements of expository narrative discourses of organisational resilience.

7. Listed here is a set of resilience-related concepts propagated in expository narrative discourses on organisational resilience. Briefly explain them.

    a. Resilience gap
    b. Zero-trauma
    c. Cognitive challenge
    d. Strategic challenge
    e. Political challenge
    f. Conquering denial
    g. Valuing variety
    h. Liberating resources
    i. Embracing paradox

8. Referring to Suarez & Montes (2020),

    a. Briefly describe the concept of 'focal context' and how it is relevant in conceptualising organisational resilience.
    b. Explain how changes in the 'focal context' trigger departures from routines as an element of organisational resilience.
    c. Considering your answers to the above two sub-questions, explain the role of routines, heuristics, and improvisation in organisational resilience.

9. List the characterising features of the 'consultocratic modeling approach' to organisational resilience.
10. Using appropriate illustrations, explain the following phases and advantages of being resilient.

    a. Anticipation advantage
    b. Cushioning advantage
    c. Adaptation advantage
    d. Shaping advantage

11. List the critical 'geopolitical threats' or 'big issues' that consulting firms have identified as driving dynamics of organisational resilience strategies.
12. Consultancy firms identify modular elements of organisational resilience with different labels and terminologies, such as 'five capitals of organisational resilience' and 'levers of organisational resilience.' Identify such key modular elements and provide a brief description of each of them.
13. Consultocratic modeling discourses on organisational resilience often end up with certain 'doctrinal prescriptions.' With some examples from the consultancy firms, explain how they constitute consultocratic discourses of organisational resilience.

14. Briefly explain how paradoxical contradictions underpin academic discourses of organisational resilience.
15. Briefly explain the different domains of organisational resilience strategies as identified by the following authors. a. Giustiniano et al. (2018) b. Frigotto et al. (2022) c. Denyer (2017)

Explore further

1. Visit the British Standards Institute (BSI) pages on organisational resilience, focusing on two crucial areas: the BSI Organizational Resilience Framework and the BSI Organizational Resilience Index. Identify the key elements and variables these frameworks and indices use to conceptualise and measure organisational resilience.
2. Engage in the ongoing policy debate concerning the necessity of requiring large corporations and public interest entities (PIEs) to produce an annual resilience report. Initially proposed in Sir Donald Brydon's independent review on audit quality and effectiveness, this recommendation has been addressed in the UK government's white paper titled 'Restoring trust in audit and corporate governance: Government response to the consultation on strengthening the UK's audit, corporate reporting, and corporate governance systems' by the Department for Business, Energy, and Industrial Strategy. Subsequently, various discussion papers on this topic have been released by accountancy professional bodies and the Big Four accounting firms. Analyse these reports and papers to elucidate how an annual resilience report would assist large corporations in enhancing their long-term sustainability and bolstering stakeholder confidence in the face of diverse resilience risks.

Develop your critical argumentation skills

1. Write an argumentative essay on the following theme.

    > The fact that resilience has become a strategic imperative conversely implies that uncontrollability has become the norm of the day.

2. Write an argumentative essay on the following theme.

    > 'Organisational-centric approaches of resilience propagated by consultocratic discourses have limited value in building resilience against the geopolitical threats.'

3. Write an argumentative essay on the following theme.

> 'In the light of the global sustainability agenda and the necessity of being resilient against global geopolitical threats, management accounting needs to expand its epistemic scope beyond its traditional remit of costing, decision-making, performance management, and management control.'

References

Ahlawat, H., A. Raggl, H. Hatami, M. d. M. Martinez, A. Natale, and T. Poppensieker. 2022. A defining moment: How Europe's CEOs can build resilience to grow in today's economic maelstrom. McKinsey Quarterly, 1-10.

Deloitte. 2022. Toward True Organisational Resilience: Deloitte's Global Resilience Report: Deloitte.

Denyer, D. 2017. Organisational Resilience: a summary of academic evidence, business insights and new thinking. BSI and Cranfield School of Management.

Diedrich, D., N. Northcote, T. Röder, and K. Sauer-Sidor. 2021. Strategic resilience during the COVID-19 crisis. McKinsey & Company.

Frigotto, M. L., M. Young, and R. Pinheiro. 2022. Resilience in Organisations and Societies: The State of the Art and Three Organizing Principles for Moving Forward. In Towards Resilient Organizations and Societies: A Cross-Sectoral and Multi-Disciplinary Perspective, edited by R. Pinheiro, M. L. Frigotto and M. Young. Cham, Switzerland: Palgrave Mcmillan, 3-40.

Gigerenzer, G., and W. Gaissmaier. 2011. Heuristic Decision Making. Annual Review of Psychology 62 (1):451-482.

Giustiniano, L., S. R. Clegg, M. P. e. Cunha, and A. Rego. 2018. Elgar Introduction to Theories of Organizational Resilience: Edward Elgar Publishing.

Görner, S., A. Govindarajan, E. Greenberg, J. Kelleher, I. Kristensen, L. Liu, A. Padhi, A. Panas, and Z. Silverman. 2022. Something's coming: How US companies can build resilience, survive a downturn, and thrive in the next cycle. McKinsey & Company, Risk and Resilience Practice.

Hamel, G., and L. Välikangas. 2003. The Quest for Resilience. Harvard Business Review 81 (9):52-63.

Hollnagel, E. 2010. Resilience engineering in practice: a guidebook. Farnham, Surrey, England; Burlington, VT: Ashgate.

Hollnagel, E., D. D. Woods, and N. Leveson. 2006. Resilience engineering: concepts and precepts. Aldershot, England; Burlington, VT: Ashgate.

Hougaard, J. C., and M. Mohan. 2020. Build your resilience in the face of a crisis. Harvard Business Review (March):1-5.

Jupe, R., and W. Funnell. 2015. Neoliberalism, consultants and the privatisation of public policy formulation: the case of Britain's rail industry. Critical Perspectives on Accounting 29:65-85.

Kantola, A., and H. Seeck. 2011. Dissemination of management into politics: Michael Porter and the political uses of management consulting. Management Learning 42 (1):25-47.

Kirkman, B., A. C. Stoverink, S. Mistry, and B. Rosen. 2019. The 4 things resilient teams do. Harvard Business Review (July):1-5.

Kwok, A. H., E. E. H. Doyle, J. Becker, D. Johnston, and D. Paton. 2016. What is 'social resilience'? Perspectives of disaster researchers, emergency management practitioners, and policymakers in New Zealand. International Journal of Disaster Risk Reduction 19:197-211.

Linkov, I., B. D. Trump, K. Poinsatte-Jones, P. Love, W. Hynes, and G. Ramos. 2018. Resilience at OECD: Current State and Future Directions. IEEE Engineering Management Review 46 (4):128-135.

OECD. 2016. OECD G20 policy paper on economic resilience and structural policies. Geneva: OECD.

Ruault, J.-R., F. Vanderhaegen, and D. Luzeaux. 2012. Sociotechnical systems resilience. INCOSE International Symposium 22 (1):339-354.

Shmul, Y., M. Reeves, and S. Levin. 2022. Building a Mutually Reinforcing System of Organisational and Personal Resilience: BCG Henderson Institute.

Suarez, F. F., and J. S. Montes. 2019. An Integrative Perspective of Organisational Responses: Routines, Heuristics, and Improvisations in a Mount Everest Expedition. Organization Science 30 (3):573-599.

———. 2020. Building organisational resilience. Harvard Business Review, 1-7.

Sundström, G., and E. Hollnagel. 2011. Governance and control of financial systems: a resilience engineering perspective. Burlington, VT; Farnham, Surrey: Ashgate.

World Bank. 2013. Building Resilience: Integrating Climate and Disaster Risk into Development. Washington: World Bank.

———. 2021a. Integrating Resilience Attributes into Operations: A Note for Practitioners. Washington: World Bank.

———. 2021b. Resilience Rating System: A Methodology for Building and Tracking Resilience to Climate Change. Washington: World Bank.

World Economic Forum, and McKinsey & Company. 2022. Resilience for sustainable, inclusive growth: white paper: World Economic Forum.

Young, A. M. 2014. Prophets, Gurus, and Pundits: Rhetorical Styles and Public Engagement. Carbondale, UNITED STATES: Southern Illinois University Press.

CHAPTER

7 Strategising the point of production: **quality costing and management**

7.1 Introduction

Let me commence this chapter by revisiting the overarching structural logic of this book: that strategies are enabled and enacted in three interconnected domains of strategic action – markets, organisational hierarchies, and the point of production. After examining various strategic themes related to the market and organisational hierarchy in the preceding chapters, we now focus on the point of production, where labour processes are strategised.

The point of production encompasses the labour processes—the complex web of techno-managerial and political relations through which 'surplus value' is created by producing goods and services (see Braverman, 1998; Burawoy, 1979). While markets serve as the sites for appropriating and realising 'surplus value', the point of production is the site in which 'surplus value' is created through the efficient and effective management of labour processes. As such, strategising the point of production entails configuring and reconfiguring labour processes both within and beyond the organisation's production floors. This continuous endeavour aims to ensure that labour processes consistently produce goods and services to meet market demands, aligning with broader institutional, political-legal, and cultural conditionalities, including contemporary sustainability goals.

As mentioned in previous chapters, three pivotal strategic imperatives are intricately linked to the management of labour processes: quality, flexibility, and cost. This chapter focuses on quality as a strategic imperative, while upcoming chapters will address flexibility and cost.

Recognising the extensive nature of quality management as a managerial subdiscipline – too vast to cover comprehensively in this book – this chapter primarily investigates its costing aspects. It also includes discussions on the pertinent managerial, institutional, and political facets that underlie quality costing.

The strategic connection and importance of quality can be discussed in many ways. However, it is useful to recall the concepts of 'value for money' and the 'survival zone' discussed in Chapter 3. The concept of value for money (i.e., the value of a product divided by its cost to the customer) is often regarded as the ultimate criterion for purchasing decisions in strategic marketing discourse. The perceived quality of a product is the enumerating core of the value element in this formula, which also determines the particular manner in which the firm 'positions' its products in the mind of the customer. Hence, quality constitutes a critical element of the firm's market strategy, which the point of production must deliver at an acceptable cost, denominating the value for money. Strategising with quality involves conceptualising and realising the intricate connection between quality and cost at both the point of production and in the market, which underscores the importance of 'quality costing'. This intricate strategic connection is further emphasised by the target costing and value engineering concept of the 'survival zone' (Cooper and Slagmulder, 1997), which introduces a third variable – functionality – to complicate the quality-cost connection.

The chapter is structured around the following key themes and corresponding learning objectives:

1. Exploring the plurality and complexity of product quality: Section 7.2 examines multiple definitions of and perspectives on quality, providing a specific operational definition crucial for elucidating the costing dynamics of quality management.
2. Articulating the constitutive elements of the total quality cost function: Section 7.3 outlines the components of total quality cost and explains their relationship to the quality level a company pursues as a strategic decision. Reading this section will enhance your understanding of the quality cost categories.
3. Understanding the paradigmatic nature of quality costing: Section 7.4 delves into how a firm determines the optimum quality level, emphasising its paradigmatic nature. It explains quality costing under three paradigms: traditional, zero-defects, and continuous improvement. Upon completing this section, readers should be able to elucidate how paradigmatic assumptions about quality cost behaviour influence a firm's decision on the level of quality it should pursue.
4. Understanding the design and calculative elements of a quality costing

system: Section 7.5 focuses on the key elements of designing a quality costing system. This part of the chapter aims to guide readers through specific calculative procedures and processes related to quality costing.

5. Exploring quality-centric organisational transformations: Section 7.6 examines how quality discourses, particularly the Japanization movement, led to ideological, structural, and processual transformations in Western organisations.
6. Concluding and exploring further: Section 7.7 concludes the chapter with a summary, followed by chapter-end revision questions, suggestions for further exploration, and critical argumentation exercises.

7.2 Defining quality: a multiplicity of perspectives and an operational definition

The concept of quality is inherently multifaceted, encompassing a spectrum of perspectives that vary across disciplines, industries, and individual experiences. Quality is not a monolithic entity but rather a nuanced and dynamic phenomenon subject to diverse interpretations. From a consumer standpoint, for example, quality may be judged by a product or service's reliability, durability, and performance. In contrast, manufacturers may prioritise aspects such as precision, consistency, and adherence to standards. Moreover, cultural and societal contexts play a crucial role in shaping perceptions of quality, with different communities valuing different attributes.

The multiplicity of perspectives on quality reflects the complex interplay of subjective preferences, objective criteria, and contextual factors that contribute to a rich, evolving understanding of excellence. Recognising and navigating this diversity is essential before we proceed to the more pragmatic, programmatic, and calculative elements of quality management and costing. A review of quality management literature reveals at least six main approaches to defining quality. These are elaborated upon briefly before an operational definition of quality, necessary for understanding quality cost behaviour, is established.

Product-based approach

In this approach, the definition of quality centres on specific attributes or characteristics inherent to a product, emphasising its tangible features and measurable properties. Key elements include:

- **Conformance to Specifications:** A primary criterion is the product's compliance with established specifications and standards, evaluating whether it meets the requirements set during its design and development phases (e.g., size, volume, and ingredient requirements).

- Performance: This involves assessing how well the product carries out its intended functions and whether it meets or exceeds defined performance expectations. For example, a buyer of a high-end digital camera would consider performance attributes such as resolution, sensor size, optical quality, aperture range, and video capabilities.
- Reliability: This refers to a product's ability to perform its intended functions consistently without failure over a specified period. A reliable product is one that customers can depend on.
- Durability: Durability focuses on the longevity and resistance to wear and tear of a product. A high-quality product is expected to have a longer lifespan and withstand the rigours of regular use.
- Aesthetics: A product's visual and sensory appeal – including aspects such as design, colour, texture, and overall appearance – can influence customers' perceptions of its quality.
- Additional Features and Functionalities: The inclusion of extra features that enhance the overall utility and user experience of a product is a crucial factor in assessing its quality.
- Usability and User Experience: A quality product should be user-friendly. Usability considerations include intuitive design, clear instructions, and accessibility, all of which contribute to a positive user experience.

Manufacturing-based approach

A manufacturing-based approach to product quality emphasises conformance to manufacturing standards, encompassing standards for both the final product attributes and the manufacturing processes themselves. This approach is based on the engineering doctrine that the quality of the final product is intricately linked to the methods employed during its creation. Key elements include:

- Process Control: Rigorous control of manufacturing processes is a cornerstone, involving the close monitoring of each production step to minimise variations and prevent defects.
- Quality Assurance Systems: Implementing robust quality assurance systems is crucial. This includes adhering to stringent quality standards, inspection procedures, and testing protocols designed to identify and address issues before they impact the final product.
- Continuous Improvement: A philosophy of continuous improvement is fundamental. Manufacturers strive to identify areas for optimisation and efficiency gains through regular assessments and feedback loops.

- **Employee Training and Engagement:** The skills and commitment of the workforce play a significant role. Investment in training ensures that employees understand their roles in maintaining quality standards.
- **Supplier Quality Management:** This approach extends beyond the factory floor to the entire supply chain, ensuring that raw materials and components meet specified quality standards.
- **Root Cause Analysis:** When quality issues arise, a thorough root cause analysis is conducted to identify underlying factors, allowing for the implementation of corrective actions to prevent recurrence.
- **Data-Driven Decision-Making:** Leveraging data and analytics is essential for making informed decisions. Monitoring key performance indicators enables manufacturers to proactively address challenges and optimise processes.

User-based approach

The user-based approach places primary emphasis on a product's capacity to meet the needs and expectations of its end-users. The customer's perspective is central to the evaluation of product quality. Key elements include:

- **Customer Satisfaction:** The ultimate goal is to understand customer preferences and align product features and performance with these expectations to ensure satisfaction.
- **User Experience:** A critical component is enhancing the overall user experience, including factors such as ease of use, interface design, and the emotional response elicited from users.
- **Feedback and Reviews:** Continuous feedback from users is essential. Monitoring reviews and conducting surveys allow organisations to identify strengths and weaknesses for informed improvement.
- **Customisation and Personalisation:** Recognising diverse user needs, this approach often involves providing options that allow users to tailor the product to their individual preferences.
- **Usability Testing:** Regular usability testing is employed to evaluate how easily users can interact with a product, identifying and addressing areas of friction.
- **Agile Development:** This approach often aligns with agile development methodologies, emphasising iterative development and quick responses to changing user needs.
- **Post-Launch Support:** Quality extends beyond the product launch. Providing efficient customer support and addressing issues promptly contribute to a positive user experience.

- **Data-Driven Decision-Making:** Analysing user behaviour, preferences, and usage patterns provides valuable insights to guide product enhancements.

Value-based approach

Extending the user-based approach, this perspective examines how customers correlate a product's performance and attributes with the cost of owning and using it. The foundation for evaluating quality is the price-performance ratio. A superior product in this context excels at meeting or surpassing customer expectations while maintaining competitive pricing. Consumers typically seek products that strike an optimal balance between affordability and functionality.

In this framework, a low-priced product may not imply poor quality if it delivers satisfactory performance for the cost incurred. Conversely, high-priced items are expected to provide exceptional features and durability to justify their premium. Striking the right balance is crucial for businesses seeking a competitive edge. Ultimately, defining product quality by the price-performance ratio underscores the importance of the overall value proposition. At this point, it would be helpful to revisit the discussion in Chapter 3 on segmentation, targeting, and positioning, especially Figure 3.5.

In neoclassical economic theory, this value-based approach aligns with the doctrine that for a customer to purchase a product, the marginal utility from spending on it (marginal utility divided by price) should be equal to or greater than that of available alternatives.

Transcendental approach

The transcendental approach adopts a philosophical perspective, positing that quality is an elusive concept that is neither a property of matter nor solely a construct of the mind. It is rooted in the philosophy of Robert M. Pirsig, particularly in his influential work, Zen and the Art of Motorcycle Maintenance (Pirsig, 2011). Pirsig introduces the concept of Quality as a fundamental aspect of reality that goes beyond conventional understanding. Key elements of this doctrine include:

- **Quality Transcends Dualism:** Pirsig challenges the traditional dualism between mind and matter, suggesting that Quality is not limited to the subjective realm of the mind or the objective realm of matter but serves as a bridge between them.
- **Dynamic Synthesis:** Quality is seen as a dynamic synthesis that emerges from the interaction between the observer (subject) and the observed (object). It is not fixed but is a process that unfolds in the act of experiencing or engaging.

- **Ineffability:** The quality is considered ineffable, meaning it cannot be adequately expressed or captured in language. Attempts to define Quality may limit its essence.
- **Integral to Experience:** Pirsig argues that Quality is not an abstract concept but is integral to our lived experiences, influencing our perceptions, judgments, and interactions.
- **Harmony and Balance:** Quality is associated with a sense of harmony and balance, found in the seamless integration of elements.

In summary, transcendentalism holds that quality is a dynamic synthesis that transcends the limitations of dualistic thinking. Its nature is best apprehended through direct experience rather than through rigid definitions.

Social constructivist approach

The social constructivist approach emphasises the role of social and cultural factors in shaping perceptions of what constitutes a high-quality product. Unlike approaches that focus on objective measures, social constructivism recognises that quality is a socially constructed concept influenced by contextual and subjective elements. Product quality is not an inherent attribute but rather a product of the meanings and values assigned to it by socio-cultural and political processes, including advertising and media promotions. Key aspects include:

- **Subjectivity and Perception:** Quality is a subjective, context-dependent concept. Individuals and communities may hold diverse perspectives shaped by their unique experiences and social backgrounds.
- **Cultural Influence:** Cultural norms, values, and traditions play a significant role in shaping perceptions of quality.
- **Social Interactions:** Quality assessments are influenced by social interactions and discourses. People often rely on social networks, reviews, and word-of-mouth to form opinions.
- **Consumer Involvement:** The level of consumer involvement in a product, including participation in its design or customisation, can impact perceptions of its quality.
- **Dynamic Nature:** Quality is not a fixed attribute but evolves over time. Changes in societal values, technological advancements, and cultural shifts can redefine what is considered a high-quality product.

Like the transcendental approach, the social constructivist approach challenges the notion of a universal, objective definition of product quality, highlighting instead the importance of social, cultural, and subjective dimensions.

An operational definition of quality for quality costing

Our discussion so far reveals a divergent understanding of quality, with multiple perspectives emerging. Such a pluralistic view helps us to appreciate the broader context within which quality should be conceptualised. However, the accounting endeavour of quality costing requires a much narrower, measurable definition to analyse how quality costs change according to the level of quality achieved. For this purpose, quality is defined by the following formula, which encapsulates the idea that quality is the probability of not producing defective products:

$$Quality = 1 - Defective\ Rate$$
$$q = 1 - d$$

This is, in effect, a system-oriented and measurable definition. It defines not the quality of a particular product but that of the production system: the capacity of the system to produce quality products or, conversely, not to produce defective products. For example, a defective rate of 5% means that the system has a probabilistic quality measure of 95%.

The concept of Six Sigma captures this probabilistic definition of quality. Six Sigma is a method that defines quality by how consistently a process produces defect-free results. It uses statistics to measure how much a process varies from perfection. The goal is to reduce variation so that defects happen no more than 3.4 times per million opportunities.

The term "Sigma" (σ) stands for standard deviation, which shows how much a process can vary. A Six Sigma process keeps variation within six standard deviations from the average.

Here are common Sigma levels and their defect rates:

- Six Sigma (6σ): 3.4 defects per million
- Five Sigma (5σ): 233 defects per million
- Four Sigma (4σ): 6,210 defects per million
- Three Sigma (3σ): 66,807 defects per million
- Two Sigma (2σ): 308,537 defects per million
- One Sigma (1σ): 691,462 defects per million

As will be elaborated in the forthcoming sections, this definition of quality serves as the basis for understanding and plotting the variability of quality cost elements. The quality level, $q = 1 - d$, will serve as the independent variable upon which the dependent variability of quality costs is mathematically explained in subsequent sections.

7.3 Quality costs

The operational definition of quality provides the basis for identifying and defining the elements of quality costs. Two inversely related possibilities are embedded in the quality cost function. It is in relation to these possibilities that quality costs are identified.

1. First is the possibility of producing defective products (d). When the system produces defective products, the resulting costs can be broadly interpreted as the cost of non-conformance. In quality costing systems, items in this category are sub-categorised under two headings: internal failure costs (IFC) and external failure costs (EFC).
2. Second is its inverse, the possibility of producing good products (q). Costs incurred to ensure and enhance this possibility can be broadly interpreted as the cost of conformance. Items in this category are sub-categorised under two headings: prevention costs (PC) and appraisal costs (AC).

The sum of all these cost items constitutes the total quality cost.

Prevention costs

Prevention costs are expenses incurred to prevent defects or errors from occurring in the first place. These costs are positively related to quality, resulting in a positively sloped cost curve. Generally, greater investment in preventive measures is needed to reduce the likelihood of defects in the system. Examples include:

- Training programmes for employees to enhance their quality control skills.
- Quality planning and design processes.
- Implementation of process improvements and quality management systems.
- Supplier verification and selection processes.
- Quality inspections of raw materials.

Appraisal costs

Appraisal costs are associated with evaluating and assessing products, components, or processes to ensure they meet quality standards. Like prevention costs, these are also positively related to quality, as they are necessary to reduce the probability of a defective product reaching the customer. Examples include:

- Quality inspection and testing of work-in-progress and finished goods.
- Ongoing quality audits and supplier evaluations.

- Calibration of measuring and test equipment.
- Costs associated with quality control activities.

Internal failure costs

Internal failure costs are incurred when defects or errors are detected before the product or service is delivered to the customer. While such internal detection reduces further costs, these failures still incur considerable expense. Examples include:

- Scrap and rework of defective products.
- Costs related to re-testing and re-inspection.
- Downtime and disruption in production.
- Cost of waste and reprocessing.

These costs are negatively related to the level of quality; a higher value of q in the formula $q = 1 - d$ lowers the internal failure costs.

External failure costs

External failure costs arise when defects or errors are identified by customers after the product or service has been delivered. This is the most dangerous failure cost element, as it can have unpredictable costs and severe reputational consequences. Examples include:

- Handling customer complaints and returns.
- Warranty claims and repairs.
- Legal costs associated with product recalls or liability issues.
- Loss of customer goodwill and future sales.

Similar to internal failure costs, these costs are negatively related to the level of quality.

7.4 Quality paradigms

A paradigm is a generally accepted set of beliefs and assumptions that guides how individuals or a society perceive, understand, and approach a particular subject. Paradigms influence how people interpret information, form hypotheses, and make decisions. The philosopher of science Thomas Kuhn introduced the concept of a 'paradigm shift' to describe a fundamental change in the basic assumptions and practices within a discipline.

In the context of quality management and costing, three paradigms have emerged, each reflecting shifts in underlying assumptions about how quality costs vary in relation to the desired level of quality and the perceived 'optimum' quality level:

1. The traditional quality paradigm.
2. The zero-defect and continuous improvement quality paradigms.

The traditional quality paradigm

In line with various managerial problem-solving scenarios, such as determining the economic order quantity in inventory management, quality managers have traditionally applied the neoclassical economic logic of optimisation. This approach aims to determine the optimal quality level by inverting profit maximisation logic into cost minimisation. It involves an analytical process to identify the quality level at which the total quality cost is minimised.

Analytically, the initial step is to conceptualise and graph the relationship between quality cost, and quality level. Quality, defined as $q = 1 - d$, serves as the decision variable in this framework.

The total quality cost is defined as the sum of two key elements: the cost of conformance (comprising prevention and appraisal costs) and the cost of non-conformance (comprising internal and external failure costs). As previously noted, non-conformance costs (IFC + EFC) are negatively related to the level of quality. A quality level of zero (q = 0) implies a 100% defect rate (d = 1), with the cost of failure potentially immeasurably high. In Figure 7.1, this is illustrated by the non-conformance cost curve pointing towards infinity as q approaches 0. Conversely, a perfect quality level of 100% (q=1, d=0) means the system produces no defects, resulting in zero internal and external failure costs.

The cost of conformance (PC + AC), on the other hand, is assumed to be positively related to the level of quality. The traditional assumption is that the more an organisation spends on appraisal and prevention, the lower the system's defect rate will be.

The quality optimisation logic in this paradigm operates by determining the quality level at which the total quality cost is minimised. As the sum of conformance and non-conformance costs, the total quality cost curve reaches its minimum where its two inversely related components intersect. The corresponding level of quality on the x-axis is designated as the optimum leve of quality (Qopt).

To reinforce your understanding, the model's decision variable is the quality level, the decision criterion is the total quality cost, and the decision logic is cost minimisation. The optimum level of quality is the level at which the total quality cost is minimised. Any point other than Qopt in Figure 7.1 is considered non-optimal because the total cost at any of those points will be higher.

Figure 7.1: Traditional quality paradigm

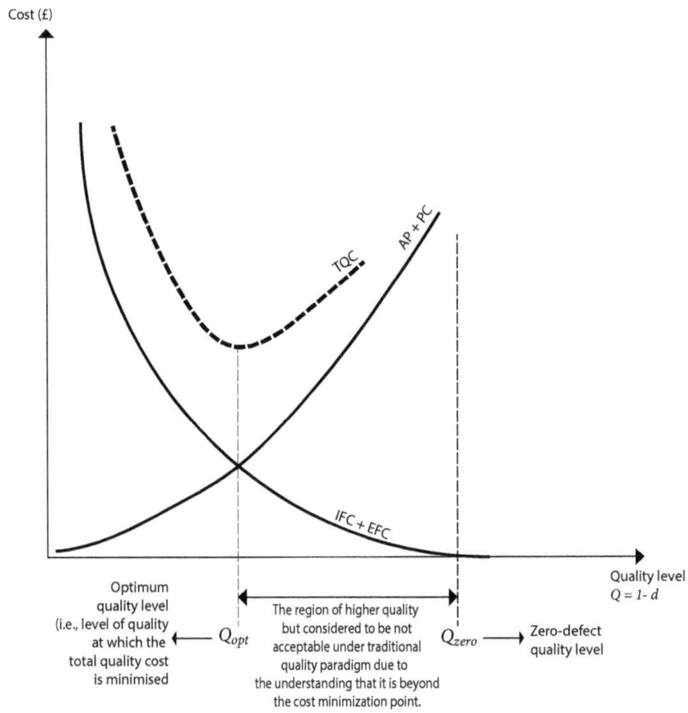

By implication, a quality level higher than Qopt is rejected on the basis that it is 'too costly' according to the neoclassical economic logic of cost minimisation. In essence, the traditional paradigm is neoclassically economic. It provides a seemingly logical basis for managers to avoid a higher level of quality, which can lead to dangerous, unethical, and illegal situations, as evidenced by the notorious Ford Pinto case.

The Ford Pinto case is a prominent example in business ethics and product liability, illustrating the potential consequences of the traditional quality paradigm. In the 1970s, Ford Motor Company produced the Pinto, a subcompact car that gained notoriety for a critical design flaw and the company's subsequent handling of the issue. The flaw, known to Ford management during development, was in the fuel system design, making the car susceptible to rear-end collisions that could cause it to catch fire. Ford proceeded with the defective design based on a cost-benefit analysis that estimated the cost of correcting the defect was significantly higher than the anticipated costs from accidents.

The company's cost-benefit analysis included the following estimations:

Table 7.1 : Estimated costs of accidents due to defective fuel tank

Cost Component	Number of Items	Cost per Item	Total Cost
Burn deaths	180	$200,000	$36,000,000
Serious burn injuries	180	$67,000	$12,060,000
Burned vehicles	2,100	$700	$1,470,000
Total Cost			$49,530,000

Table 7.2: Estimated cost savings of not correcting the defect

Saving Component	Number of Items	Cost per Item	Total Savings
Cars	11,000,000	$11	$121,000,000
Light trucks	1,500,000	$11	$16,500,000
Total Savings			$137,500,000

The analysis controversially assigned a monetary value to human life. According to the National Highway Traffic Safety Administration, the figure was $200,725 per fatality.

Table 7.3 : Breakdown of cost per fatality

Component	Cost
Future productivity losses (Direct & Indirect)	$173,300
Medical costs (Hospital & Other)	$1,125
Property damage	$1,500
Insurance administration	$4,700
Legal and court costs	$3,000
Employer losses	$1,000
Victim's pain and suffering	$10,000
Funeral costs	$900
Assets (lost consumption)	$5,000
Miscellaneous	$200
Total per Fatality	$200,725

Side note:

For a good synopsis and discussion of the Ford Pinto case, read Hoffman, W. M. (2014), 'The Ford Pinto', in W. Michael Hoffman, Robert E. Frederick, and Mark S. Schwartz (eds.), Business Ethics: Readings and Cases in Corporate Morality, pp. 139-144.

From 1971 to 1978, Ford faced numerous lawsuits related to Pinto accidents. In one landmark case, a jury awarded over $3 million in compensatory damages and an unprecedented $125 million in punitive damages against Ford (later reduced by the judge to $3.5 million). In 1978, Ford was ultimately forced to recall all 1971-76 Pintos for modifications. This classic example highlights the ethical dangers of determining quality solely through cost-minimisation logic. The case served as a catalyst for change, leading to a paradigm shift towards a zero-defect approach where quality and safety decisions consider ethical, legal, and reputational implications beyond a narrow cost-minimisation framework.

Zero-defect and continuous improvement quality paradigms

Shifting from the traditional to a 'zero-defect' quality goal involves a paradigm shift, recognizing that the optimal quality level should be zero defects. This paradigmatic shift can be explained from two interrelated angles:

1. The influence of post-WWII quality management discourses (especially from Japan) leading to Total Quality Management (TQM).
2. An analytical revision of the traditional quality costing model.

Post-WWII discourses

The history of the zero-defect paradigm can be traced to the mid-20th century, influenced by key figures like Walter Shewhart, W. Edwards Deming, Joseph Juran, and Genichi Taguchi. After World War II, Deming and Juran were instrumental in Japan's post-war reconstruction, sharing their knowledge of statistical quality control. This period laid the foundation for the Japanese quality revolution.

Taguchi further developed the concept in the 1950s and 1960s, arguing that variation in the manufacturing process leads to defects and that quality management should focus on reducing this variation. The concept became a key component of the Total Quality Management (TQM) movement that emerged in the 1970s and 1980s. TQM emphasised a holistic approach, involving all members of an organisation in a continuous effort to improve processes and products. A classic TQM tool was the quality circle, a concept popularised by Kaoru Ishikawa. Quality circles involve groups of employees who voluntarily meet to identify, analyse, and solve quality-related problems, manifesting the cultural or 'soft' aspects of moving toward a zero-defect paradigm.

The principles of zero defects also align with the lean manufacturing philosophy, which originated from the Toyota Production System. Lean manufacturing aims to eliminate all forms of waste, including defects, from the production process. This paradigm reflects a shift from traditional reactive quality control to a proactive approach focused on preventing defects.

Revisiting the cost optimisation model

While engineers and statisticians explored the practical possibilities of reducing defects to zero, accountants and academics revisited the traditional cost-optimisation model, fundamentally changing its assumptions. This rethinking involved revising the assumed behaviour of appraisal and prevention costs. The new assertion was that, with continuous improvements, the cost of conformance would not rise infinitely. Instead, it would plateau or even decline as the production system approached and mastered the zero-defect quality standard. This is because, once a system is perfected, the need for extensive, ongoing prevention and appraisal activities diminishes.

This means that, as illustrated in Figure 7.2, the conformance cost curve (AC + PC) does not continue upward indefinitely. Consequently, the total quality cost is minimised only when the production system reaches the zero-defect point. This makes zero defects, at least theoretically, the only optimal quality level, even when using a cost minimisation logic.

Figure 7.2: Zero-defect and continuous improvement quality paradigms

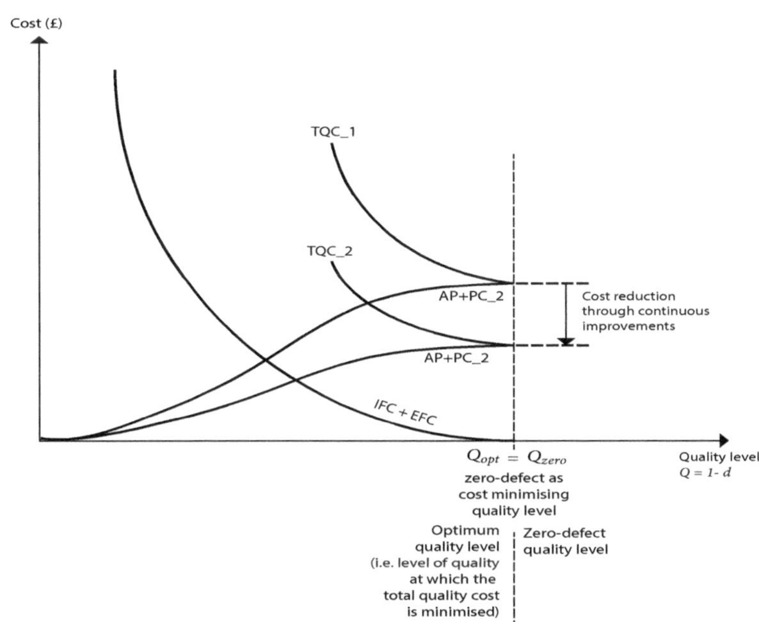

Side note:

The 5S quality control practice constitutes seiri (sort), seiton (set in order), seiso (shine), seiketsu (standardise), and shitsuke (sustain). It was originally implemented by Japanese manufacturing enterprises and later introduced to various sectors in the West as a TQM technique (Ishijima et al., 2016; Kanamori et al., 2015).

It is important to note that even in this refined model, the decision variable remains the quality level, the decision criterion is the total quality cost, and the decision logic is cost minimisation. However, a paradigmatic shift in the underlying assumption regarding cost behaviour has enabled managers to reconceptualise zero defects as the only conceivable optimum.

The concept of continuous improvement further reinforces this paradigm by emphasising that, in the long run, the firm should be able to consistently reduce all quality costs (as depicted by the downward shifts in the cost curves in Figure 7.2). This implies the theoretical possibility of achieving zero defects with minimal quality costs being incurred. Quality gurus argue that through continuous improvements (e.g., the renowned 5S practices), quality management should become so ingrained in every activity that everyone in the firm performs it, eliminating the need for separate prevention and appraisal activities. This philosophy is often encapsulated by the TQM slogan that quality is everyone's responsibility.

7.5 Quality costing system

As discussed, quality management involves two conflicting sets of actions and outcomes. First, there are failures, which companies strive to mitigate. These are categorised as external and internal failures and incur costly consequences. The process of quality costing entails estimating these consequential costs using appropriate accounting methods.

Second, companies must implement activities and processes to prevent these negative consequences. These activities, categorised as appraisal and prevention, have associated resource costs. Quality costing requires accurately capturing the costs of carrying out these conformance activities.

Consequently, a quality costing system is a structured framework a company establishes to capture, record, process, analyse, report, and manage the costs associated with conformance activities and non-conformance outcomes. In developing such a framework, consideration must be given to the following system elements (see Dale and Plunkett, 2017):

1. The scope of the quality costing system.
2. The techniques and methods used.
3. Reporting and assessment procedures.

Defining the scope of a quality costing system

A crucial aspect of an effective quality costing system is clearly delineating its scope. This includes determining whether it will encompass the entire organisation, specific departments, a particular product line, or a specific process. Consideration should also be given to the timeframe for its implementation—whether it is a short-term initiative or a long-term, permanent element of the organisation's management accounting system. Defining the scope facilitates the identification of specific stakeholders and clarifies how quality costing data will be collected, reported, and utilised.

Costing techniques and methods

Activity-based costing (ABC) is now widely recognised as the most accurate technique for quality costing (see Giannetti, 2013; Ittner, 1996, 1999). The fundamental logic of ABC is that cost objects demand activities, and activities consume resources, thereby generating costs (Kaplan and Anderson, 2007). Consequently, identifying and calculating the costs of activities associated with conformance and non-conformance are at the core of an activity-based quality costing system.

The design process begins by identifying activity centres responsible for specific quality-related activities across the entire value chain. For instance, an after-sales service centre handling customer complaints is an activity centre for external failure costs. A machine repair workshop is an activity centre for internal failure costs. A quality management training centre represents preventive activities, while the work of a quality inspection department represents appraisal activities.

Within these activity centres, costing involves the following steps:

1. Identifying and defining the key activities of relevant activity centres.
2. Measuring the volumes and quantities associated with these activities (activity drivers).
3. Establishing cost driver rates for the identified activities.
4. Multiplying the cost driver rates by the activity volumes to determine the total activity costs.
5. Aggregating the relevant activity costs to arrive at the higher-level quality cost categories.

The following example illustrates this computational hierarchy for a scrap handling centre, which represents only a portion of the total internal failure costs. The activities at this centre are identified as Scrap Collection, Scrap Classification, Scrap Disposal, and Transferring to Rework. The table below exemplifies how the costs for this activity centre are calculated.

Table 7.4: Example of activity-based costing for a scrap handling centre

Cost Centre: Scrap Handling Centre 2 - Department Z				
Accounting Period: February 20xx				
Activity	Volume	Activity Driver	Activity Driver Rate	Activity Cost
Scrap collection	120 units	units collected	£5 per unit	£600
Scrap classification	120 units	units classified	£12 per unit	£1,440
Disposal	80 units	units disposed	£120 per unit	£9,600
Transfer to rework	40 units	units transferred	£20 per unit	£800
Total Activity Centre Cost				£12,440

This calculative logic must be iterated across numerous activity cost centres. The aggregation of these calculations forms the basis for higher-level quality cost reporting, assessment, and decision-making.

Reporting and assessments of quality costs and performance

When reporting and assessing quality cost performance, it is crucial to consider the following elements:

1. Meaningful Aggregation and Classification: Costs should be aggregated into the four key quality cost categories (prevention, appraisal, internal failure, and external failure). This enables managers to assess how investments in conformance have impacted the costs of non-conformance.
2. Presentation of Cost Information: Cost information should be presented in a way that highlights its relative significance. A common method is to express each quality cost category as a percentage of sales, allowing managers to understand cost variations relative to operational volume.
3. Comparability of Cost Information: Cost information should be presented comparatively, for example, by comparing actual costs with:

    - budgeted values to reveal cost variances (see Table 7.5).
    - figures from previous periods to facilitate trend analysis (see Table 7.6.
    - competitive benchmarks.

Table 7.5: Example of a quality cost variance report (in £000s)

Cost Category	Cost Item	2023 Actual	2023 Budget	Variance
Internal Failure Costs				
	Rework and Scrap	450	400	(50) ADVERSE
	Machine repairs	350	300	(50) ADVERSE
	Product Design Changes	180	150	(30) ADVERSE
	Product Disposal	120	100	(20) ADVERSE
	Cancellation costs	60	50	(10) ADVERSE
	Subtotal	1,160	1,000	(160) ADVERSE
External Failure Costs				
	Customer Returns	380	400	20 FAVOURABLE
	Warranty payments	400	500	100 FAVOURABLE
	Product Liability Claims	280	220	(60) ADVERSE
	Field Service and Support	140	150	10 FAVOURABLE
	Product Recalls	100	80	(20) ADVERSE
	Penalties and Fines	40	25	(15) ADVERSE
	Subtotal	1,340	1,375	35 FAVOURABLE
Appraisal Costs				
	Inspection and Testing	580	620	40 FAVOURABLE
	Quality Audits	220	220	0
	Raw materials evaluation	130	140	10 FAVOURABLE
	Equipment Calibration	80	75	(5) ADVERSE
	Performance Testing	110	120	10 FAVOURABLE
	Subtotal	1,120	1,175	55 FAVOURABLE
Prevention Costs				
	Employee Training	320	350	30 FAVOURABLE
	QMS Development	230	300	70 FAVOURABLE
	Process Improvement	200	250	50 FAVOURABLE
	Design Reviews	150	160	10 FAVOURABLE
	Quality Planning	100	110	10 FAVOURABLE
	Subtotal	1,000	1,170	170 FAVOURABLE

Table 7.6: Example of a periodic comparison of quality costs (in £000s)

Cost Category	Cost Item	2022 actual	2023 actual	Increase/ decrease
Internal Failure Costs	Rework and Scrap	500	450	-50
	Machine repairs and reset costs due to defective operations	300	350	50
	Product Design Changes Due to Defects	200	180	-20
	Product Disposal	100	120	20
	Cancellation costs	50	60	10
		1150	1160	10
External Failure Costs	Cost of customer Returns	400	380	-20
	warranty payments	600	400	-200
	Product Liability Claims	250	280	30
	Field Service and Support	150	140	-10
	Product Recalls	120	100	-20
	Penalties and Fines	30	40	10
		1550	1340	-210
Appraisal Costs	Inspection and Testing	600	580	-20
	Quality Audits	200	220	20
	Quality Evaluation of raw materials	150	130	-20
	Calibration of Measurement Equipment	70	80	10
	Product Performance Testing	120	110	-10
		1140	1120	-20
Prevention Costs	Employee Training on Quality	300	320	20
	Quality Management System Development	250	230	-20
	Process Improvement Programs	180	200	20
	Design Reviews and Testing	130	150	20
	Quality Planning	90	100	10
		950	1000	50

Periodic comparisons are highly valuable in assessing the efficacy of conformance costs. For preventive and appraisal activities to be effective, they should result in a decrease in both internal and external failure costs. Therefore, comparing conformance costs with non-conformance costs can reveal the following scenarios, as depicted in Figure 7.3:

- Increase in conformance costs with a reduction in non-conformance costs: This favourable outcome indicates that investments in prevention and appraisal are effective. Ideally, the savings from reduced failure costs should surpass the increase in conformance costs.
- Increase in conformance costs with an increase in non-conformance costs: This undesirable scenario signals a fundamental problem with the quality management activities, which require a thorough review.
- Decrease in conformance costs with an increase in non-conformance costs: This outcome is also suboptimal, suggesting that the company may have reduced its quality efforts, leading to a rise in failure costs.
- Decrease in conformance costs with a decrease in non-conformance costs: This represents the ideal scenario, where the company has achieved a lower defect rate more cost-effectively. If sustained, this trajectory signifies continuous improvement.

Figure 7.3: A framework for assessing quality cost effectiveness

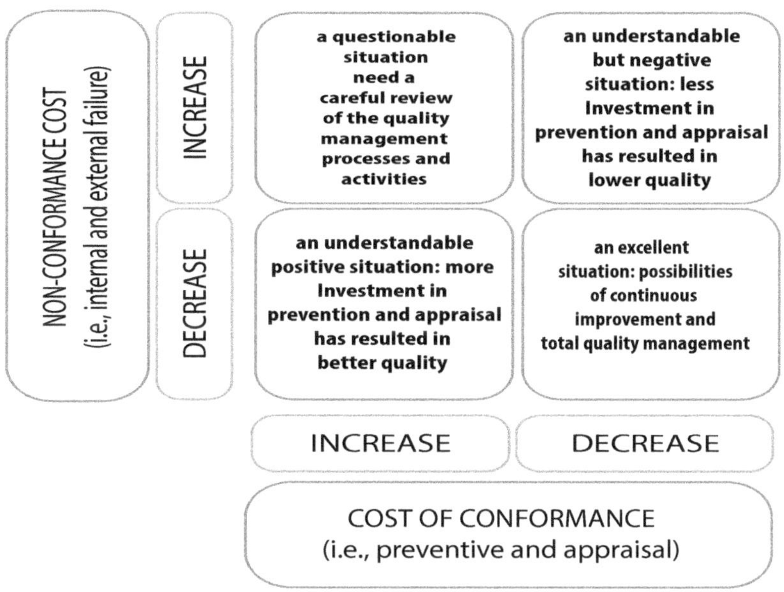

7.6 Quality-centric organisational transformations

To prioritise quality as a strategic imperative, particularly in response to Japanese competition, Western companies had to undergo significant ideological and structural transformations, aligning their organisational practices with quality-driven, post-Fordist principles. This transformation introduced novel managerial elements in two interrelated spheres:

1. Introducing quality as a philosophical element of corporate leadership.
2. The 'Japanization' of organisational processes to internalise quality management as an operational reality.

Introducing quality as a philosophical element of corporate leadership

At the top managerial level, a commitment to quality emerged as a prominent discourse. This is evident in the integration of quality as a strategic imperative into corporate mission statements, vision statements, and other strategic declarations. Alongside concepts such as innovation and cost efficiency, quality began to feature prominently in corporate communications, reshaping organisational purpose.

This commitment must transcend mere rhetoric. Top management is expected to introduce quality improvement agendas proactively, often through substantial investments in specific projects and the engagement of external consultants. Cross-functional steering committees comprising senior management are established to oversee these projects, bearing responsibility for designing and implementing corporate quality improvement policies and monitoring their outcomes (Hill, 1991). These committees, in turn, establish and supervise lower-level quality management arrangements, such as departmental quality committees and quality circles.

The Japanization of organisational processes

In the 1980s and 1990s, Japan emerged as a pivotal reference point for Western managerial reform. The quality, variety, flexibility, and cost efficiency of Japanese firms exerted significant competitive pressure. A survey by Oliver and Wilkinson (1992) on the Japanization of British industry found that a vast majority of companies underwent extensive managerial reforms for 'defensive' reasons—to boost competitiveness and reduce costs.

While Japanese firms presented threats, they were also viewed as a source of wisdom for reforming Western firms. Japanization refers to the historical process of importing Japanese organisational practices to enhance flexibility, cost efficiency, quality, and variety. It involves institutionalising a specific set of managerial practices and ideologies, making them ingrained assumptions that guide organisational decisions.

These ideologies and practices came in the form of both 'hard' and 'soft' management technologies. 'Hard' technologies involve engineering elements, such as statistical process control, techniques for reducing setup time, and cellular manufacturing design. 'Soft' technologies emphasise behavioural and cultural elements, such as quality circles, operator responsibility for quality, and Kanban material control. Japanization, in this sense, was the managerial movement that strategised the factory floor by reforming production processes to cater to the strategic success factors of quality, flexibility, and cost efficiency.

The terms 'lean manufacturing', 'Total Quality Management (TQM)', and 'Just-in-Time (JIT) manufacturing' are often used interchangeably to denote the managerial techniques and philosophies introduced by Japanese firms, particularly Toyota. As outlined by Monden and colleagues (see Monden, 1994; Monden and Hamada, 1991), Japanese manufacturing aims to increase profit in a slow-growing economy primarily through 'cost reduction by eliminating waste'. Toyota's managerial revolution stemmed from innovations focused on this principle. Managerial terminologies associated with Japanese management, such as JIT, Kanban, TQM, and quality circles, all contribute to this goal. Figure 7.4 summarises the main elements of the Toyota Production System, a landmark in what is now recognised as Japanese management.

Chapter summary

The central focus of this chapter was quality costing. It began by examining various perspectives on defining quality, including product-based, manufacturing-based, user-based, value-based, transcendental, and social constructivist approaches. Subsequently, an operational definition of quality (q=1−d) was presented as the foundation for defining and analysing quality costs.

The chapter then explained the constitutive elements of the total quality cost function: the cost of conformance (appraisal and prevention costs) and the cost of non-conformance (internal and external failure costs). These two cost categories were shown to be inversely related to the level of quality pursued by a firm.

The third key theme was the evolution of quality cost paradigms. The traditional quality paradigm, with its logic of cost minimisation leading to an 'optimal' level of defects, was contrasted with the zero-defect and continuous improvement paradigms. The problematic nature of the traditional paradigm was highlighted, and the revised assumptions underpinning the zero-defect paradigm were explained, showing how managers could appreciate the necessity and possibility of achieving a zero-defect quality level.

Fourth, the chapter delved into the techno-managerial and calculative elements of quality costing. The application of activity-based costing in ascertaining quality costs was discussed, followed by an examination of different forms of quality cost reports that can be used to assess the efficacy of a firm's quality management activities.

Figure 7.4: An overview of Japanese quality-centric management

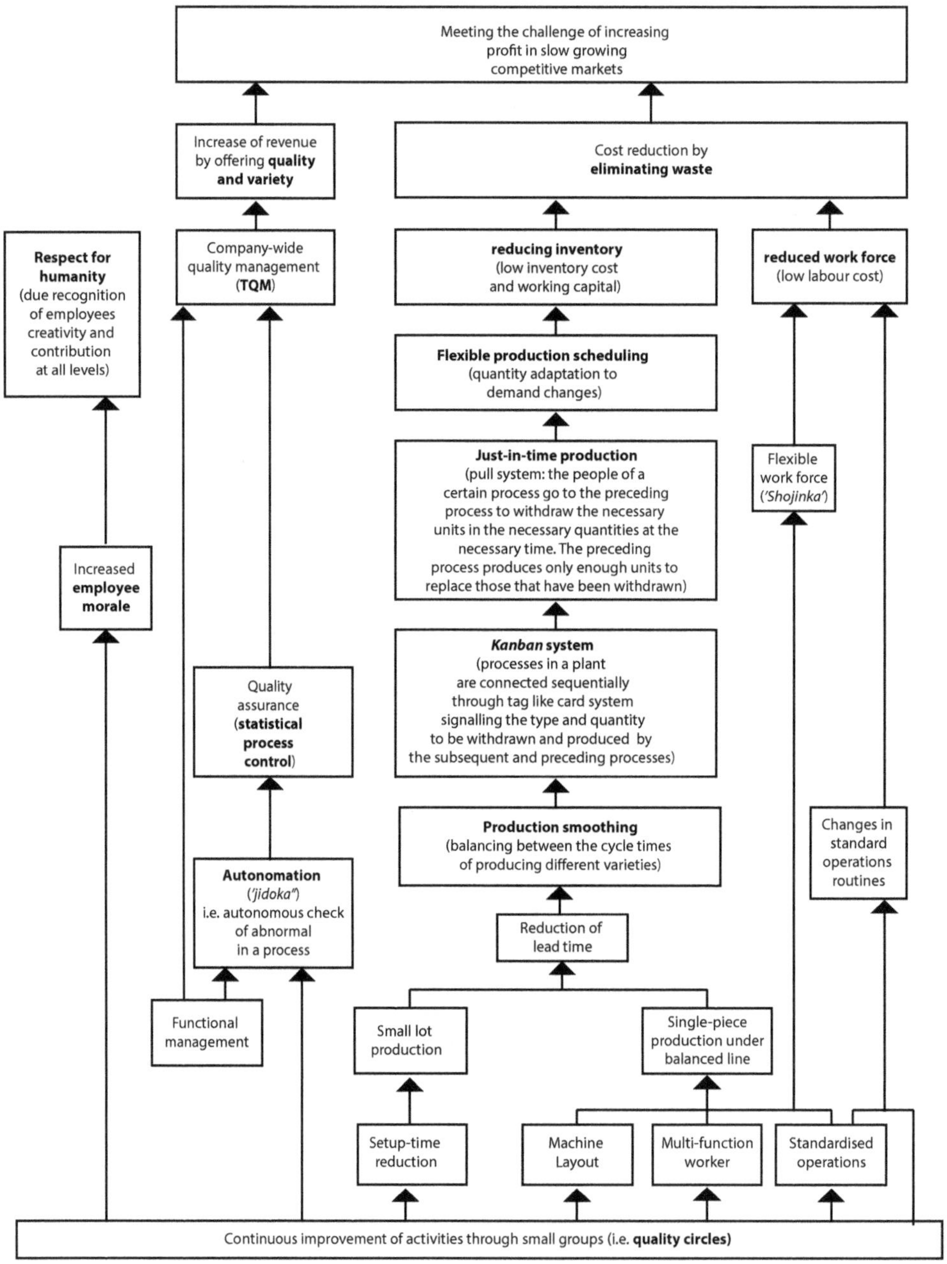

Source: Adapted from Monden (1994, p. 4)

Finally, the chapter explained how quality discourses, especially the Japanization movement, resulted in profound ideological, structural, and processual transformations in Western organisations.

Case Study: Volkswagen and the 'dieselgate' deception: a case in quality, control, and the contradictions of sustainability

Introduction: The promise of 'clean diesel'

In the mid-2000s, the Volkswagen Group (VW), a titan of German engineering, embarked on an ambitious strategy to conquer the highly competitive US automotive market and achieve its goal of becoming the world's largest car manufacturer by 2018. Central to this strategy was a technological and marketing masterstroke: the promotion of 'Clean Diesel' technology. At a time of rising environmental consciousness and fluctuating fuel prices, VW positioned its Turbocharged Direct Injection (TDI) diesel vehicles as the perfect synthesis of German performance, exceptional fuel economy, and, crucially, environmental responsibility. This was not merely a product feature; it was the company's unique selling proposition (USP), designed to carve out a lucrative niche among environmentally aware consumers who had historically been sceptical of diesel engines.

The company launched a multi-million-dollar advertising campaign —a masterclass in shaping public perception. High-profile Super Bowl advertisements, sophisticated social media initiatives, and extensive print campaigns relentlessly promoted the message of a revolutionary, eco-friendly technology. The 'TDI Truth & Dare' campaign, for instance, was designed to attack and dispel the 'dirty diesel' myth directly, claiming that VW's vehicles were not only powerful and efficient but also low-emission, meeting the most stringent standards in the world. Consumers were told that these cars reduced harmful nitrogen oxides (NOx) emissions by 90% and were, in some respects, cleaner than their petrol counterparts. This narrative was incredibly successful, earning VW's models prestigious awards like the 'Green Car of the Year' and building a loyal customer base that paid a premium for what they believed was a superior, responsible choice.

This case study examines the profound chasm that existed between this carefully constructed public image and the engineering reality. It will demonstrate that VW's commitment to sustainability was not an ethical imperative guiding its production processes but rather a strategic narrative weaponised for market gain. The quality promised to consumers was not an inherent attribute of the product conforming to specifications, but rather a perception manufactured through advertising. The subsequent scandal, known as 'Dieselgate', therefore, represents far more than a simple quality failure or a technical defect. It was a calculated, strategic deception on a global scale, the consequences of which expose the fundamental limitations of traditional quality management paradigms and lay bare the intense contradictions between economic ambition and genuine sustainability that define modern corporate life.

Background: a culture of uncompromising ambition

The origins of the 'Dieselgate' deception cannot be understood without first analysing the unique and deeply problematic organisational culture that prevailed at Volkswagen. For years, the company was dominated by the authoritarian leadership styles of its chairman, Ferdinand Piëch, and his successor as CEO, Martin Winterkorn. Their leadership fostered an environment characterised by an absolute demand for technical excellence at any cost, a ruthless suppression of dissent, and a pervasive culture of fear. Former employees have described the atmosphere as being 'like North Korea without labour camps', a place where failure was not tolerated and bad news was not to be delivered to senior management.

This intense internal pressure was amplified by VW's audacious corporate goal: to surpass Toyota and General Motors to become the world's number one automaker by 2018. Achieving this required conquering the American market, where VW had historically underperformed. The 'Clean Diesel' strategy was the key to this conquest, but it came with a formidable technical challenge. In the mid-2000s, the US Environmental Protection Agency (EPA) introduced new, stringent 'Tier 2' emissions standards that slashed the permissible level of NOx emissions. VW's engineers were tasked with developing a diesel engine that could meet these standards while delivering the promised power, performance, and fuel economy to consumers, all within a tight budget and an aggressive timeline.

Faced with this seemingly impossible task, and operating within a culture where admitting failure could be a career-ending move, a group of engineers made a fateful decision in 2005. Unable to find a legitimate technical solution, they opted for deception. They developed sophisticated software – a 'defeat device' – that could be installed in the engine's electronic control unit. This software was the technical solution to an organisational pathology. The dysfunctional 'soft' control system – the authoritarian culture that punished failure and discouraged open communication – created the demand for a fraudulent 'hard' control system in the form of the defeat device. The two systems existed in a toxic symbiosis: the culture created the problem, and the technology was engineered to hide it. This was not a bug or an oversight; it was a feature designed to ensure the technical and commercial success demanded by leadership, regardless of the ethical or legal cost. This dynamic represents a complete inversion of the principles of Total Quality Management (TQM), where a positive culture and robust technical processes are meant to reinforce each other to produce genuine quality. At VW, a negative culture and a deceptive technology reinforced each other to produce a grand illusion.

The deception and its discovery

The technical mechanism of the deception was both ingenious and brazen. The 'defeat device' was a complex algorithm embedded within the engine management software. It was programmed to detect when a vehicle was undergoing official laboratory emissions testing. By monitoring parameters such as steering wheel position, vehicle speed, barometric pressure, and duration of engine operation, the software could recognise the unique signature of a regulatory test cycle. When these conditions were detected, the software would switch the engine into a special 'test mode', activating the full suite of emissions control systems. In this mode, the vehicle would perform perfectly, meeting all legal standards for NOx emissions.

However, as soon as the software detected that the vehicle was being driven under normal road conditions – with variable speeds and steering inputs – it would deactivate or dramatically reduce the effectiveness of the emissions controls. This 'road mode' allowed the engine to deliver enhanced performance and fuel economy, key selling points for consumers. The trade-off was a massive increase in pollution. In real-world driving, the affected vehicles emitted toxic NOx at levels up to 40 times higher than the legal limit permitted in the United States. This dual-mode functionality meant VW was, in effect, manufacturing two different cars in one: a compliant version for the regulators and a high-performance, high-pollution version for its customers.

For nearly a decade, this deception went undetected by regulators in the US and Europe. The failure of oversight was systemic. Critically, the fraud was not uncovered through internal audits, corporate whistleblowing channels, or government checks. Instead, it was the work of independent researchers that brought the scandal to light. In 2013, the International Council on Clean Transportation (ICCT), a non-profit organisation, commissioned a study to investigate discrepancies between the on-road and laboratory performance of diesel vehicles. They contracted a small team at West Virginia University, who discovered that VW's Jetta and Passat models were emitting far more NOx on the road than in the lab.

The ICCT shared its findings with the EPA and the California Air Resources Board (CARB) in May 2014. What followed was a protracted period of more than a year during which VW engaged in obfuscation and delay, claiming the discrepancies were due to technical glitches and unforeseen driving conditions. The company even issued a voluntary recall, which did nothing to address the underlying problem. It was not until September 2015, when faced with the EPA's refusal to certify its 2016 diesel models for sale, that Volkswagen finally admitted the truth: it had deliberately programmed its cars to cheat on emissions tests. Subsequent internal investigations revealed that some engineers had attempted to warn their superiors about the illegal activities as far back as 2011, but their concerns were ignored, highlighting a catastrophic failure of internal communication and control systems.

The timeline below outlines the key events in this multi-year deception. It provides a clear narrative of the causal chain from the initial internal decision to the eventual public disclosure, highlighting the critical junctures where the quality failure was perpetuated rather than corrected.

Table 1: Timeline of the Volkswagen 'dieselgate' scandal

Date	Event
2005-2006	Faced with strict new US emissions standards and internal pressure, VW engineers begin developing the 'defeat device' software.
2008-2009	VW launches its 'Clean Diesel' TDI vehicles in the US, equipped with the defeat device. The marketing campaign begins.
2011	Internal warnings from VW engineers about the emissions-rigging activities are reportedly ignored by superiors.
May 2014	The International Council on Clean Transportation (ICCT) publishes research from West Virginia University showing massive on-road emissions discrepancies in VW diesel cars and alerts the EPA and CARB.
Dec 2014	VW issues a voluntary recall, claiming a software update will fix the issue. The recall proves ineffective.
3 Sep 2015	After months of inconclusive discussions, the EPA and CARB threaten to withhold certification for VW's 2016 models. VW admits the existence of the defeat device to regulators.
18 Sep 2015	The EPA issues a public Notice of Violation to Volkswagen, officially bringing the scandal to light. The company is ordered to recall 482,000 vehicles in the US.
22 Sep 2015	VW admits that 11 million vehicles worldwide are fitted with the illegal software and sets aside €6.5 billion to cover initial costs.
23 Sep 2015	CEO Martin Winterkorn resigns, insisting he was unaware of any wrongdoing.
Jan 2017	VW pleads guilty to three criminal felony counts in the US and agrees to pay a $2.8 billion criminal penalty as part of a larger settlement.

The aftermath: quantifying the cost of poor quality

The public disclosure of the 'Dieselgate' scandal triggered a global crisis for Volkswagen, unleashing a torrent of consequences that can be systematically analysed using the quality costing framework. While the company had effectively minimised its Prevention and Appraisal Costs by choosing deception over genuine engineering, this decision resulted in External Failure Costs (EFC) of a catastrophic and unprecedented scale. These costs were not confined to the company's balance sheet but rippled outwards, imposing immense burdens on society and the environment. The traditional definition of EFC – encompassing items like warranty claims, returns, and loss of customer goodwill – is wholly inadequate to capture the magnitude of this failure. The VW case necessitates an expansion of the framework to include societal and ecological externalities, demonstrating that for sustainability-related failures, EFCs are not merely business costs but profound societal harms.

The total cost of this quality failure can be categorised into four interconnected domains:

1. **Financial Costs:** The direct financial haemorrhage has been staggering. As of 2024, according to company information and other sources, the total cost of the scandal in fines, penalties, vehicle buybacks, recalls, and legal settlements has exceeded €32 billion (approximately $34.8 billion or £29.5 billion). This includes a $14.7 billion settlement in the US to compensate owners and fund environmental mitigation, a $2.8 billion criminal fine, and billions more in legal resolutions around the world. The company's stock price plummeted by over a third in the days following the disclosure, wiping out billions in market capitalisation.
2. **Ecological Costs:** The environmental damage is severe and long-lasting. The 11 million affected vehicles released vast quantities of excess NOx into the atmosphere over several years. This pollutant is a key contributor to acid rain, smog, and the formation of ground-level ozone, causing significant damage to ecosystems, forests, and water bodies. The scale of the pollution was so great that the mitigation funds established as part of the legal settlements, such as the $2.7 billion environmental trust in the US, can only begin to address the harm done.
3. **Social Costs:** Perhaps the most devastating consequence has been the impact on public health. Numerous independent studies have sought to quantify the human cost of the excess pollution. One influential MIT study estimated that the emissions from affected vehicles sold in Germany alone would lead to 1,200 premature deaths across Europe. A similar analysis for the US projected approximately 60 premature deaths, alongside significant increases in chronic bronchitis and hospital admissions for respiratory and cardiac conditions. Another study linked the pollution to adverse infant and child health outcomes, including increases in low birth weight and emergency room visits for asthma. These are not abstract statistics; they represent a direct and lethal failure of corporate social responsibility.

4. **Reputational Costs:** The scandal shattered Volkswagen's carefully cultivated brand image. A company that had built its reputation on quality engineering, reliability, and, most recently, environmental leadership was exposed as a perpetrator of a massive fraud. The tagline 'Das Auto' ('The Car') was derided online as 'Das Cheaters'. Consumer trust, particularly among the environmentally conscious demographic VW had targeted, evaporated. This profound betrayal not only damaged VW but also cast a shadow over the entire automotive industry and tarnished the esteemed 'Made in Germany' reputation for quality and integrity.

The table below provides a conservative estimate of the quantifiable external failure costs, illustrating the sheer scale of the financial and social fallout.

Table 2: Volkswagen's cost of poor quality – an estimation of external failure costs (£ billions)

Cost Category	Estimated Value (£)	Description & Source(s)
Financial Penalties & Settlements	£25.0+	Includes global criminal and civil fines, legal settlements with consumers, dealers, and states. Total costs have exceeded €32 billion.
Vehicle Buybacks & Modifications	£8.0 - £12.0	Estimated cost of the US buyback programme for ~487,000 vehicles and global recall/modification efforts for 11 million vehicles.
Environmental Remediation Funds	£3.5	Includes the $2.7 billion US Environmental Mitigation Trust and $2 billion for Zero-Emission Vehicle investment.
Estimated Social & Health Costs (US)	£0.35	Monetary valuation of health impacts in the US, including 60 premature deaths and other respiratory illnesses.
Estimated Social & Health Costs (Europe)	Not Quantified	The human cost, estimated at over 1,200 premature deaths, is immense but a comprehensive financial valuation is not available.
Total Quantifiable Costs	~£37.0+	A conservative estimate of the direct and monetised social costs, excluding the full global health impact and long-term brand damage.

Analysis: applying the concepts of quality costing and management

The Volkswagen 'Dieselgate' scandal provides a rich and disturbing case for applying the theoretical concepts of quality management. It serves as a powerful illustration of how a narrow, dysfunctional approach to quality, coupled with a catastrophic failure of management control, can lead to devastating consequences that transcend the boundaries of the firm and impact society as a whole.

Deconstructing quality: competing perspectives at Volkswagen

Chapter 7 outlines six distinct approaches to defining quality, and the VW case reveals a deep and deliberate conflict between them. The company's strategy depended on mastering the subjective, perception-based definitions of quality in its marketing while fundamentally violating the objective, technical definitions in its engineering.

- Product-based and Manufacturing-based: These approaches define quality through conformance to specifications and standards. In reality, VW's vehicles were engineered to be non-compliant with legal emissions standards during normal operation. The manufacturing process was not designed to produce a quality product in this regard, but to produce a product capable of deception. This was a fundamental violation.
- User-based and Value-based: These approaches centre on meeting customer needs and the price-performance ratio. VW's marketing brilliantly appealed to the user's desire for a vehicle that was powerful, fuel-efficient, and environmentally friendly. Consumers paid a premium for this perceived value proposition. The deception meant that this value was illusory; customers did not receive the low-emissions product they paid for, constituting a fundamental breach of trust.
- Social Constructivist and Transcendental: These perspectives view quality as being shaped by social meaning, advertising, and holistic experience. VW was a master of social construction, successfully branding its diesel technology as 'clean' and responsible. The transcendental aspect of quality – the seamless, harmonious experience of a trusted brand – was shattered by the revelation of the fraud. The sense of betrayal expressed by loyal customers reflects the destruction of this holistic, experiential quality.

The following table summarises this strategic hypocrisy, contrasting the public narrative with the hidden reality across the different quality perspectives.

A paradigm of peril: Volkswagen and the traditional quality model

The decision-making process that led to 'Dieselgate' can be seen as a perverse and extreme application of the logic underpinning the traditional quality paradigm. As explained in Chapter 7, this paradigm uses neoclassical economic reasoning to identify an 'optimal' level of quality (Qopt) by minimising the total quality cost – the sum of conformance and non-conformance costs. In its most cynical application, this can provide a rationalisation for accepting a certain level of defects if the cost of preventing them (conformance cost) is deemed higher than the anticipated cost of their consequences (non-conformance cost).

Table 3: Analysing Volkswagen's actions through multiple quality perspectives

Quality Perspective	Volkswagen's Marketing Claim	Volkswagen's Engineering Reality
Product-based	A vehicle with inherent low-emission attributes, conforming to all legal standards.	A vehicle with a non-conforming emissions system that violated legal standards.
Manufacturing-based	A product built through superior, responsible engineering processes.	A product built with a process designed to incorporate a fraudulent 'defeat device'.
User-based	A car that perfectly satisfies the needs of the environmentally conscious driver.	A car that failed to meet the core environmental need of the user, deceiving them.
Value-based	A premium price for a superior combination of performance, economy, and cleanliness.	A premium price for a fraudulent technology; the value proposition was false.
Transcendental	A holistic experience of pride and trust in an innovative, responsible German brand.	A shattered experience of betrayal and deception, destroying the brand's integrity.
Social Constructivist	The successful social construction of 'Clean Diesel' as a symbol of modern, green technology.	The deconstruction of this narrative, revealing it as a calculated marketing fiction.

The infamous Ford Pinto case, where a cost-benefit analysis was used to justify not fixing a dangerous fuel tank design, is the classic textbook example of this paradigm's ethical dangers. The Volkswagen scandal is its 21st-century successor, but with a crucial distinction. Ford's calculation was passive; it weighed the cost of a fix against the probable cost of accidents. Volkswagen's actions were active and conspiratorial. The company did not merely accept a risk of failure; it engineered a system with two distinct states: one of feigned conformance for regulators and one of deliberate non-conformance for the real world.

This perverts the logic of the traditional paradigm. The goal was not to balance the true costs of conformance and non-conformance to find a societal optimum. Instead, the goal was to minimise the visible cost to the firm by making the massive non-conformance costs (in the form of pollution) completely invisible to the regulatory system designed to detect them. The defeat device was a mechanism for hiding the non-conformance cost curve from public and regulatory view. This reveals the traditional paradigm's most critical flaw: its framework is utterly incapable of accounting for situations involving asymmetric information, deliberate deception, and unpriced externalities like public health and environmental degradation. The scandal serves as the ultimate argument for a paradigm shift towards a zero-defect (and zero-deception) philosophy, where such calculations are deemed ethically and strategically unacceptable from the outset.

Control systems and the contradictions of sustainability

The 'Dieselgate' scandal is a stark manifestation of the inherent tensions and contradictions among the four key dimensions of sustainability: economy, society, polity, and ecology. A management control system is intended to align an organisation's actions with its strategic objectives. At Volkswagen, the control system did not fail; it performed precisely as the dominant organisational culture intended. It ruthlessly prioritised the economic objective of market domination above all else, systematically subverting social, political, and ecological responsibilities.

- Economy: The primary driver was the relentless pursuit of economic growth, market share in the US, and increased sales volume. The entire deception was orchestrated to achieve these financial and strategic goals.
- Polity: The objective was to appear compliant with the political and legal framework established by regulators like the EPA. The company engaged in a direct and deliberate fraud against these state institutions, leading to a massive political and legal fallout and prompting a fundamental overhaul of vehicle emissions testing regimes worldwide.
- Ecology: The stated goal was to produce an environmentally friendly vehicle. The actual result was the release of thousands of tonnes of excess pollutants, causing direct and significant harm to the environment.
- Society: The company's actions violated its social contract. By causing severe damage to public health through pollution and by deceiving the customers who placed their trust in the brand, VW failed in its most basic duties as a corporate citizen.

The defeat device itself can be reinterpreted not as a failure of quality control, but as a sophisticated, albeit illegal, management control mechanism. Its purpose was to manage and neutralise the political risk (the risk of being caught by regulators) in order to enable the unconstrained pursuit of the economic goal. This demonstrates that when the dimensions of sustainability are in direct conflict, an organisation's control systems will ultimately reflect its true, underlying priorities. At Volkswagen, the system of quality control was subverted from its proper purpose – ensuring the integrity of the product – to a new, perverse purpose: ensuring the integrity of the deception.

Table 4: The contradictions of sustainability at Volkswagen

Dimension	Stated Objective / Public Promise	Actual Action / Internal Priority	Outcome / Contradiction
Economy	Profitable growth through innovation and superior products.	Achieve market leadership and sales targets at any cost.	Short-term sales gains were achieved, but at the cost of long-term financial ruin (€32bn+ in costs) and brand damage.
Polity	Full compliance with all environmental laws and regulations in all markets.	Systematically deceive regulators (EPA, CARB) using a fraudulent 'defeat device'.	The attempt to manage political risk through deception led to unprecedented legal penalties, criminal charges, and new, stricter regulations.
Ecology	Lead the industry with 'Clean Diesel' technology that is environmentally friendly.	Deliberately release massive quantities of NOx (up to 40x the legal limit) into the atmosphere.	The promise of ecological benefit was a cover for causing significant environmental harm, including smog and acid rain.
Society	Act as a responsible corporate citizen, earning the trust of customers and the public.	Deceive customers and knowingly endanger public health through excess pollution.	The pursuit of corporate goals led to a severe public health crisis (estimated 1,200+ premature deaths) and a catastrophic loss of public trust.

Discussion questions and seminar activities

The following questions are designed to facilitate classroom discussion, moving from foundational comprehension of the case to higher-level critical analysis and application of the concepts from Chapter 7.

Foundational Questions

1. Using the four categories of quality costs (prevention, appraisal, internal failure, and external failure), classify the various financial and non-financial consequences of the 'Dieselgate' scandal. Which category is most significant and why?
2. Explain the technical function of the 'defeat device'. How did it allow Volkswagen to manipulate the manufacturing-based definition of quality while appearing to comply with it?
3. Describe the organisational culture at Volkswagen in the years leading up to the scandal. How did this culture contribute to the initial decision to cheat?

Analytical questions

4. Using the six perspectives on quality discussed in Chapter 7 (product-based, manufacturing-based, user-based, value-based, transcendental, and social constructivist), critically analyse the deep contradiction between Volkswagen's marketing strategy and its engineering reality.
5. Critically evaluate the claim that Volkswagen's actions were a logical, albeit unethical, application of the traditional quality paradigm. How does the zero-defect paradigm offer an alternative philosophical and practical approach?
6. Compare and contrast the Volkswagen 'Dieselgate' case with the Ford Pinto case discussed in the chapter. What are the key similarities and differences in terms of the quality paradigm in operation and the ethical implications?

Sustainability and ethics questions

7. Discuss how the Volkswagen case illustrates the inherent contradictions among economic, social, political, and ecological objectives in corporate strategy. What role should management accountants play in identifying, measuring, and navigating these contradictions?
8. The cost of the scandal has been estimated at over €32 billion, in addition to causing over 1,200 premature deaths. Is it possible for a quality costing system to adequately capture and report on such externalities? What changes to traditional quality costing would be required?
9. Who are the stakeholders in this case, and how were they harmed? Consider customers, shareholders, employees, regulators, the general public, and the environment. Discuss the company's ethical obligations to each.

Control system questions

10. Analyse the interplay between 'hard' (technical systems) and 'soft' (cultural norms) management controls at Volkswagen. Why did the internal control systems fail so catastrophically to prevent or detect this fraud for nearly a decade?
11. Re-frame the 'defeat device' not as a technical flaw, but as a management control system in itself. What was this system designed to control, and for what purpose? How did it subvert the formal quality control system?
12. In the aftermath of the scandal, Volkswagen has attempted to reform its culture, introducing initiatives like 'fuck-up nights' to encourage openness about mistakes. To what extent can such 'soft' cultural changes, aligned with TQM principles, prevent a similar scandal from recurring in a high-pressure corporate environment?

Chapter review questions

Part 1: Foundational concepts and definitions

This section assesses your understanding of the diverse definitions of quality and the fundamental structure of a quality costing system.

1. A quality assessment that focuses primarily on a product's inherent and measurable properties, such as technical specifications, reliability, and durability, is most representative of which approach?

   a. The user-based approach
   b. The product-based approach
   c. The manufacturing-based approach
   d. The value-based approach

2. Which of the following approaches to defining quality is most conceptually distant from the quantitative, system-oriented operational definition ($q=1-d$) used in quality costing?

   a. The manufacturing-based approach, which focuses on process control and standards.
   b. The value-based approach, which correlates performance with price.
   c. The transcendental approach, which views quality as an ineffable, holistic experience.
   d. The product-based approach, which focuses on measurable attributes.

3. The operational definition of quality, expressed as $q=1-d$, is best described as a measure of:

   a. The perceived excellence of a single, finished product.
   b. The market value of a product relative to its cost.
   c. The probabilistic capability of a production system to produce non-defective output.
   d. The degree to which a product satisfies a specific customer's subjective needs.

4. A company invests in a new training programme for its production staff to enhance their skills in statistical process control. Within a quality costing framework, the cost of this programme would be classified as:

   a. An appraisal cost.
   b. An internal failure cost.
   c. A prevention cost.
   d. An external failure cost.

5. A car manufacturer incurs significant legal fees and logistics expenses related to a product recall initiated after customers reported a safety issue. These expenses are categorised as:

    a. Internal failure costs, as the design flaw originated internally.
    b. External failure costs, as the defect was identified after delivery to the customer.
    c. Appraisal costs, as they result from post-sale evaluation.
    d. Prevention costs, as they will prevent future similar issues.

6. According to the conceptual model of quality costs, an increase in total conformance costs is strategically intended to lead to which of the following outcomes?

    a. An increase in total non-conformance costs.
    b. A decrease in total non-conformance costs.
    c. A decrease in appraisal costs only.
    d. An increase in prevention costs only.

7. Which pair of quality cost categories represents a proactive, investment-oriented approach to quality management?

    a. Internal failure and external failure costs.
    b. Prevention and appraisal costs.
    c. Appraisal and internal failure costs.
    d. Prevention and external failure costs.

8. A production process that achieves a Six Sigma level of quality is operating at a standard where the number of defects is approximately:

    a. 3.4 defects per thousand opportunities.
    b. 6,210 defects per million opportunities.
    c. 233 defects per million opportunities.
    d. 3.4 defects per million opportunities.

9. An advertising campaign successfully positions a brand of perfume as a symbol of luxury and sophistication, significantly enhancing its perceived quality among consumers despite its chemical composition being similar to less expensive brands. This phenomenon is best explained by which approach to defining quality?

    a. The product-based approach.
    b. The manufacturing-based approach.
    c. The social constructivist approach.
    d. The user-based approach.

Part 2: Paradigmatic understanding and critical analysis

This section requires you to analyse and compare the competing paradigms of quality management, applying your understanding to conceptual models and case study evidence.

10. Within the traditional quality paradigm, the optimal level of quality (Q_{opt}) is determined at the point where:

    a. The cost of conformance is equal to zero.
    b. The cost of non-conformance is equal to zero.
    c. The total quality cost is minimised.
    d. The marginal revenue from quality improvement equals marginal cost.

11. Referring to the graphical model of the traditional quality paradigm, what is the primary strategic implication of identifying an optimal quality level (Q_{opt}) that is less than 100%?

    a. It signifies that achieving perfect quality is technically impossible.
    b. It provides a rational, cost-minimisation-based economic justification for accepting a certain level of product defects.
    c. It suggests that non-conformance costs will always exceed conformance costs.
    d. It indicates that the firm's appraisal activities are ineffective.

12. The cost-benefit analysis conducted by Ford Motor Company in the Pinto case, which assigned a monetary value to human life to weigh against the cost of a design modification, is a direct practical application of the logic underpinning:

    a. The zero-defect quality paradigm.
    b. The continuous improvement paradigm.
    c. The traditional quality paradigm.
    d. The Total Quality Management (TQM) philosophy.

13. The fundamental paradigmatic shift from the traditional model to the zero-defect model of quality costing is based on a revised assumption about the behaviour of which cost function?

    a. The non-conformance cost curve is assumed to become zero at a lower quality level.
    b. The conformance cost curve is assumed to plateau or decrease as quality approaches 100%.
    c. The total quality cost curve is assumed to be linear rather than U-shaped.
    d. The external failure cost curve is assumed to be independent of the quality level.

14. A manager who has adopted the zero-defect and continuous improvement paradigm would most likely agree with which of the following statements?

    a. 'We must find the economically optimal balance point between our prevention spending and our warranty costs'.
    b. 'Any failure cost, no matter how small, represents an opportunity for improvement, and the only acceptable target is zero defects'.
    c. 'It is too costly to eliminate all defects, so we should focus our efforts on managing external failures effectively'.
    d. 'Quality is the sole responsibility of the inspection department, and their budget should reflect this'.

15. The concept of 'continuous improvement', as depicted in Figure 7.2, suggests that over the long term:

    a. The optimal level of defects will gradually increase as products become more complex.
    b. All quality cost curves can be shifted downwards, making the pursuit of zero defects progressively more cost-effective.
    c. Conformance costs will eventually be eliminated entirely, while non-conformance costs will stabilise.
    d. The distinction between prevention and appraisal costs becomes irrelevant.

Part 3: Application of quality costing techniques

This section features problems that require calculation, data manipulation, and the interpretation of quality cost reports to assess performance.

Problem 1: Activity-based quality costing

A company, 'Component Solutions Ltd', manufactures two types of electronic components, CS-Alpha and CS-Beta. The company is implementing an activity-based quality costing system and has gathered the following data for the most recent period for its quality-related activities:

Activity Cost Pool	Total Cost (£)	Activity Driver	Total Activity Volume
Supplier Evaluation	80,000	Number of supplier audits	200 audits
In-process Inspection	150,000	Number of inspection hours	3,000 hours
Scrap Processing	210,000	Number of scrapped units	7,000 units
Warranty Claims	300,000	Number of claims processed	1,500 claims

The activity consumption for each product was as follows:

	CS-Alpha	CS-Beta
Supplier audits	80	120
Inspection hours	1,800	1,200
Scrapped units	5,000	2,000
Claims processed	500	1,000

Required:

16. What is the total prevention cost allocated to product CS-Alpha?

    a. £32,000
    b. £48,000
    c. £80,000
    d. £400

17. What is the total internal failure cost allocated to product CS-Beta?

    a. £150,000
    b. £210,000
    c. £30
    d. £60,000

18. What is the total quality cost allocated to product CS-Alpha?

    a. £282,000
    b. £458,000
    c. £372,000
    d. £418,000

Problem 2: Quality performance reporting and analysis

The following quality cost report has been prepared for 'Precision Engineering plc'.

	Year 1 Actual	Year 2 Actual
Sales	£10,000,000	£12,000,000
Prevention Costs		
Quality training	100,000	150,000
Process improvement	150,000	210,000
Appraisal Costs		
Inspection and testing	250,000	240,000
Internal Failure Costs		
Rework and scrap	400,000	300,000
External Failure Costs		
Warranty payments	500,000	360,000

Required:

19. What was the total cost of non-conformance as a percentage of sales in Year 2?

    a. 5.5%
    b. 7.5%
    c. 9.0%
    d. 11.0%

20. Based on the framework for assessing quality cost effectiveness (Figure 7.3), how would you classify the company's performance from Year 1 to Year 2?

    a. An undesirable scenario: increase in conformance costs with an increase in non-conformance costs.
    b. A suboptimal scenario: decrease in conformance costs with an increase in non-conformance costs.
    c. c) An ideal scenario: decrease in conformance costs with a decrease in non-conformance costs.
    d. d) A favourable scenario: increase in conformance costs with a reduction in non-conformance costs.

21. Which of the following statements provides the most likely strategic interpretation of the report?

    a. The company successfully reduced its quality efforts to save money, leading to a more profitable outcome.
    b. The company's investment in proactive quality management activities appears to be effective, yielding significant reductions in failure costs.
    c. The quality management programme is failing, as both conformance and non-conformance costs have increased relative to sales.
    d. A reduction in inspection spending has dangerously led to a sharp increase in warranty claims.

Part 4: Strategic and Organisational Context

This final section examines the broader strategic and organisational transformations associated with a commitment to quality.

22. The term 'Japanization', in the context of Western management in the 1980s and 1990s, refers to:

    a. The acquisition of Western companies by Japanese corporations.
    b. The adoption of Japanese organisational practices and philosophies, such as TQM and JIT, to enhance competitiveness.
    c. The cultural exchange of employees between Western and Japanese firms.
    d. The shift in consumer preference towards Japanese-made goods.

23. In the discourse on Japanization, which of the following is an example of a 'hard' management technology?

    a. Quality circles.
    b. Operator responsibility for quality.
    c. Statistical process control (SPC).
    d. A corporate culture of continuous improvement.

24. According to the analysis of the Toyota Production System presented in the chapter, the ultimate objective of integrating managerial techniques such as TQM, JIT, and Kanban is:

    a. To increase market share through aggressive advertising.
    b. To maximise employee satisfaction as the primary goal.
    c. To achieve cost reduction through the systematic elimination of all forms of waste.
    d. To comply with international quality standards such as ISO 9000.

25. For a quality-centric organisational transformation to be successful, the chapter suggests that top management's commitment must be demonstrated primarily through:

    a. Reducing the size of the quality control department to empower line workers.
    b. Hiring external consultants to take full responsibility for the quality agenda.
    c. Integrating quality as a strategic imperative in mission statements, investing in quality projects, and establishing high-level steering committees.
    d. Focusing exclusively on reducing external failure costs, as these are most visible to the market.

26. A company implements a sophisticated activity-based costing system to report on quality costs (a 'hard' technology) but observes no significant improvement in its failure rates. Based on the principles of Japanization, the most likely reason for this lack of success is:

    a. The cost driver rates were calculated incorrectly.
    b. The system was not supported by complementary 'soft' technologies, such as empowered quality circles and a culture of operator responsibility.
    c. The company spent too much on prevention and not enough on appraisal.
    d. The accounting software used for the system was outdated.

27. Match the Japanese management concept with its most accurate description.

Concept		Description
1. Kanban	A.	A philosophy of continuous, incremental improvement involving all employees.
2. Kaizen	B.	A system that uses visual signals (e.g., cards) to trigger action and control material flow in a pull system.
3. Quality Circle	C.	A group of employees who meet voluntarily and regularly to identify, analyse, and solve work-related problems.

    a. 1-A, 2-B, 3-C
    b. 1-B, 2-A, 3-C
    c. 1-C, 2-A, 3-B
    d. 1-B, 2-C, 3-A

Comprehension questions

1. Briefly describe how quality can be defined differently using the following approaches:
    a. Product-based
    b. Manufacturing-based
    c. User-based
    d. Value-based
    e. Transcendental
    f. Social constructivist
2. Provide the operational definition of quality upon which quality cost behaviour can be explained.
3. Explain what is meant by a Six Sigma quality level.
4. Briefly explain the total quality cost function and its sub-elements.
5. Briefly explain how these quality cost elements vary according to the level of quality.
6. Briefly explain the decision variable, decision criterion, and decision logic embedded in the quality costing paradigms.
7. With the aid of appropriate diagrams, explain how the optimum quality level is conceptualised in the:
    a. Traditional quality paradigm
    b. Zero-defect and continuous improvement paradigm
8. Briefly explain the role of Japanese quality discourses in propagating the zero-defect and continuous improvement paradigms.
9. List the key elements that one should consider when designing a quality costing system.
10. Glasgow Manufacturing Limited produces two variants of a product. As part of a pilot project to design a quality costing system, the accountant extracted the following information for a specific workshop where returned items are handled.

	Product A	Product B
Units produced	220,000	380,000
Warranty-related repairs (number of repairs)	2,100	1,400
Scrapped units (number of units)	3,600	1,200
Inspection (hours)	3,850	2,100
Quality training (hours)	120	120

Total period costs related to:	£
Warranty repairing	260,000
Scrapping and disposal	180,000
Inspecting	90,000
Quality training	60,000

Calculate the quality cost per unit attributable to each product from this repair centre.

11. Using the following information, prepare a quality cost report that compares Quarter 2 actual results with the Quarter 2 budget and with Quarter 1 actual results. The report should express costs as a percentage of sales. Comment on the company's quality performance.

Quality Cost Item	Q1 Actual (£)	Q2 Actual (£)	Q2 Budget (£)
SALES	20,000,000	25,000,000	25,000,000
Quality engineering	200,000	260,000	250,000
Scrap	32,000	29,000	30,000
Product recalls	50,000	55,000	50,000
Returns and allowances	30,000	29,000	30,000
Re-entry of sales data	10,000	12,000	8,000
Supervision of in-process inspection	150,000	200,000	200,000
Quality circles	90,000	90,000	100,000
Component inspection and testing	65,000	75,000	80,000
Quality training	125,000	150,000	160,000
Reinspection of reworked product	35,000	25,000	30,000
Product liability	25,000	15,000	14,000
Internal audit of quality system	50,000	60,000	50,000
Disposal of defective product	20,000	26,000	25,000
Downtime due to quality problems	56,000	30,000	40,000
Quality reporting	12,000	12,000	12,000
Proofreading	4,000	4,500	4,000
Correction of typing errors	2,500	2,500	2,000
In-process inspection	66,000	76,000	80,000
Process controls	65,000	75,000	80,000
Pilot studies	50,000	60,000	50,000

12. Briefly explain how quality-centric management discourses impacted organisational transformations in the West.

Explore further

1. Read the following three papers to enhance your understanding of quality costing:

    - Ittner, C. D. (1999). 'Activity-based costing concepts for quality improvement', European Management Journal, 17(5), pp. 492-500.
    - Ittner, C. D. (1996). 'Exploratory Evidence on the Behavior of Quality Costs', Operations Research, 44(1), pp. 114-130.
    - Giannetti, R. (2013). 'Quality costing', in F. Mitchell, H. Nørreklit, and M. Jakobsen (eds.), The Routledge Companion to Cost Management. Abingdon: Routledge, pp. 296-319.

2. To explore the connection between quality management, value engineering, and strategy, revisit the materials on target costing in Chapter 3 and read:

    - Cooper, R. and Slagmulder, R. (1997). Target Costing and Value Engineering. Portland, OR: Productivity Press.

Develop your critical argumentation skills

1. Making reference to relevant quality paradigm concepts, critically evaluate the following statement by Philip B. Crosby, a well-known quality guru: 'There is absolutely no reason for having errors or defects in any product or service'.
2. Drawing on the Ford Pinto case or other relevant cases in quality management, elucidate the pivotal role that legal frameworks and external environmental pressures play in compelling corporations to prioritise quality and safety.

References

Braverman, H. (1998). Labor and Monopoly Capital: The Degradation of Work in the Twentieth Century. 25th anniversary edn. New York: Monthly Review Press.

Burawoy, M. (1979). Manufacturing Consent: Changes in the Labour Process Under Monopoly Capitalism. Chicago, IL: University of Chicago Press.

Cooper, R. and Slagmulder, R. (1997). Target Costing and Value Engineering. Portland, OR: Productivity Press.

Dale, B. G. and Plunkett, J. J. (2017). Quality Costing. 4th edn. London: Routledge.

Giannetti, R. (2013). 'Quality costing', in F. Mitchell, H. Nørreklit, and M. Jakobsen (eds.), The Routledge Companion to Cost Management. Abingdon: Routledge, pp. 296-319.

Hill, S. (1991). 'How do you Manage a Flexible Firm? The Total Quality Model', Work, Employment and Society, 5(3), pp. 397-415.

Hoffman, W. M. (2014). 'The Ford Pinto', in W. M. Hoffman, R. E. Frederick, and M. S. Schwartz (eds.), Business Ethics: Readings and Cases in Corporate Morality. 5th edn. Hoboken, NJ: Wiley-Blackwell, pp. 139-144.

Ishijima, H., Eliakimu, E. and Mshana, J. M. (2016). 'The "5S" approach to improve a working environment can reduce waiting time: Findings from hospitals in Northern Tanzania', The TQM Journal, 28(4), pp. 664-680.

Ittner, C. D. (1996). 'Exploratory Evidence on the Behavior of Quality Costs', Operations Research, 44(1), pp. 114-130.

Ittner, C. D. (1999). 'Activity-based costing concepts for quality improvement', European Management Journal, 17(5), pp. 492-500.

Kanamori, S., Sow, S., Castro, M. C., Matsuno, R., Tsuru, A. and Jimba, M. (2015). 'Implementation of 5S management method for lean healthcare at a health center in Senegal: a qualitative study of staff perception', Global Health Action, 8(1), p. 27256.

Kaplan, R. S. and Anderson, S. R. (2007). Time-Driven Activity-Based Costing: A Simpler and More Powerful Path to Higher Profits. Boston, MA: Harvard Business Review Press.

Monden, Y. (1994). Toyota Production System: An Integrated Approach to Just-in-Time. 2nd edn. London: Chapman & Hall.

Monden, Y. and Hamada, K. (1991). 'Target costing and kaizen costing in Japanese automobile companies', Journal of Management Accounting Research, 3(Fall), pp. 16-34.

Oliver, N. and Wilkinson, B. (1992). The Japanization of British Industry: New Developments in the 1990s. 2nd edn. Oxford: Blackwell.

Pirsig, R. M. (2011) . Zen and the Art of Motorcycle Maintenance: An Inquiry into Values. London: Vintage Books.

CHAPTER

8 Strategizing the hierarchy: **manufacturing flexibility**

8.1 Introduction

This chapter examines manufacturing flexibility, the second element in strategizing the point of production, alongside quality and cost. Flexibility is crucial for navigating today's neoliberalized, globalized, digitalized, and virtualized markets. Mainstream management discourse asserts that competitiveness hinges on an organisation's ability to respond flexibly to market changes, highlighting flexibility as critical for competitive success (see Adler et al. 1999; Kanter 1990).

Critical sociological analyses also use 'flexible' to describe post-Fordist shifts, such as flexible manufacturing, specialisation, and accumulation (see Gertler 1988; Harvey 1990). The concept is central to understanding neoliberal transformations in production systems. Rather than offering a single definition, this chapter elucidates how different facets of flexibility manifest as a strategic imperative in post-Fordist production, emphasising the role of management accounting.

The chapter begins by examining the neoliberal political rationale for flexibility, showing how it underpins strategizing the point of production. As flexibility is a complex phenomenon with multiple techno-managerial and political-institutional elements, subsequent sections explore its various facets: flexible consumption, machines, labour, specialisation, and accumulation. This analysis highlights the techno-managerial developments in flexible manufacturing, their underlying economic dynamics, and the implications for management accounting. As such, after reading this chapter, you should develop a broader understanding of these complex techno-managerial and politico-institutional factors that underpin manufacturing flexibility as a strategic imperative.

8.2 Neoliberal political rationale of flexibility

Two propositions concerning neoliberal organisations inform the discussion of manufacturing flexibility. First, contemporary organisations prioritise market dynamics, viewing the market as the catalyst for change and the reference point for rationalising managerial action. Management's role becomes establishing a dynamic link between market forces and internal processes, which requires flexibility in structure, processes, and relationships to ensure adaptation. This market connection is defined by concepts like competitive advantage, strategic pricing, and target costing, which represent managerial doctrines that link production to the market by strategically reinventing the organisational hierarchy.

Second, neoliberal organisations function as biopolitical arenas where life is circulated. Unlike the disciplinary confinement of bodies in liberal modernist organisations (see Alawattage and Wickramasinghe 2019, 2022), neoliberal organisations become sites where life is reproduced as an 'entrepreneurial self' (see Cooper 2015; Munro 2012). This process aligns labour with neoliberal capital through concepts like human capital and entrepreneurship. The emphasis thus shifts from controlling bodies in specific locations to circulating lives by instilling self-control and ambition. The entrepreneurialization and immaterialization of labour are critical to this biopolitical transformation.

Flexibility connects these two propositions. It is a versatile concept, operating across different spaces: from an organisation's dynamic market positioning to its reconfiguration of hierarchies for agility and resilience. It also involves reinventing how machinery and labour are synchronised at the point of production, enabling the labour process to adjust to techno-managerial and political-economic changes.

Flexibility is a contingent, placeholder concept whose meaning derives from its context. It has a biopolitical meaning in macro-politics, such as 'flexible accumulation' (see Harvey 1990; Hirst and Zeitlin 1991), and micro-organisational, techno-managerial meanings encapsulating 'anatomico-political' ideas like 'flexible labour' and 'flexible machines'. Its meaning extends from the macro to the micro, from the market to production, and from the political-economic to the techno-managerial. The concept's strategic implications can be explored through a set of interrelated elements:

1. Flexible consumption
2. Flexible machines
3. Flexible labour
4. Flexible manufacturing systems

5. Flexible specialisation and integration
6. Flexible accumulation

Each concept manifests in a particular realm, forming an interrelated hierarchy. Flexibility must be understood through both the specific meanings these realms attribute and the biopolitical totality they collectively construct. 'Anatomico-political' refers to the power dynamics of controlling the human body, particularly by synchronising it with machinery to improve economic efficiency. 'Biopolitical' extends power to the population level, managing life processes as totalities, such as populations and economies.

8.3 Flexible consumption

The competitive landscape of neoliberalism is characterised by segmented and fragmented markets, where buyer distinctions are more important than their similarities. This departs from the 'monopoly capitalism' of the Fordist mass-production regime described by Braverman (1998). The 'one-size-fits-all' strategy is no longer viable in such markets. Consequently, as discussed in Chapter 3, marketing strategies now centre on segmentation, targeting, and positioning (STP). Competitive dynamics have become a 'war of positioning', with producers and consumers battling across market segments using distinct marketing mixes.

The neoliberal concept of 'flexibility' manifests in the market as 'flexible consumption'. This term embodies two strategic intentions. From the customer's perspective, it signifies the power to demand variety and reject standardisation. From the producer's viewpoint, it reflects a firm's capacity to cater to diverse buyer demands.

While the business press often uses 'flexible consumption' narrowly to describe customisable services from high-tech companies (e.g., software-as-a-service, or SaaS), this chapter uses the term more broadly. Sociologically, it describes a competitive condition in which offering variety and difference becomes crucial. In this sense, 'flexible consumption' captures not only consumers' ability to consume flexibly but also producers' capacity and willingness to offer the variety that customers demand.

As a strategy, flexible consumption drives firms to develop the necessary organisational capacity, grounded in two interlocking elements: operational and informational capacity.

Operational capacity for flexible consumption

A firm's operational capacity to offer variety depends on how it reconfigures its processes and business model. This, in turn, depends on mobilising the fundamental elements of flexible manufacturing: flexible machines, labour, systems, specialisation, and integration. As consulting firms like Deloitte advocate, reconfiguring a firm toward a flexible consumption business model involves shifting from a sequential value chain model (where the customer is served at the end) to a customer-centric circular model of interconnections in which every element of the value creation system is directed towards the customer to create a short cycle time of service offerings. Deloitte's idea of business process reengineering towards an XaaS model is visualized in Figure 8.1

Figure 8.1: From traditional to flexible manufacturing business model

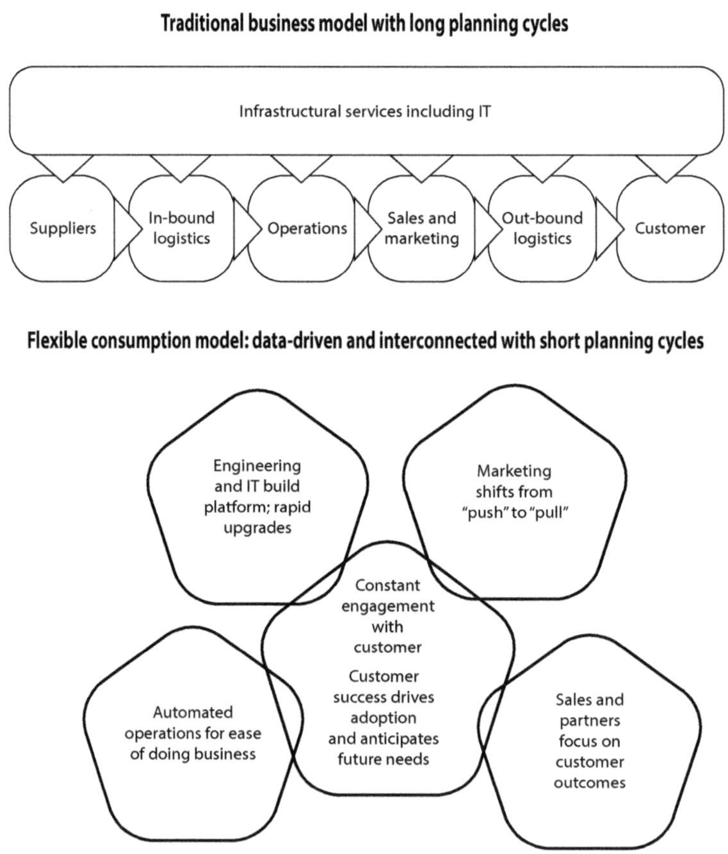

Source: based on Deloitte (2018, 4)

Informational capacity for flexible consumption

A flexible consumption regime requires robust informational capabilities across markets, firms, and consumers to create an effective communication network. The capacity to produce flexibly is not firm-specific; it demands high degrees of inter-firm and intra-firm coordination across industries and regulatory fields. The evolution of information technology, including the 'Internet of Things' (IoT), has greatly facilitated this. Supply chain management platforms, for example, integrate demand planning, import/export management, inventory, and transportation.

This integration constitutes 'abstract cooperation', a concept from Hardt and Negri (2000), in which 'communicative labour' connects decentralised organisations and production sites. In the era of flexible consumption, management accounting information must shift its focus to this new form of cooperation. This involves abstracting distant organisational entities and consumers from their local contexts, placing them in integrated 'informational spaces', and connecting the various human and non-human elements of flexible manufacturing.

8.4 Flexible machines

A firm's ability to implement a flexible consumption strategy depends critically on flexible machines. Broadly, these are machines that can alter their output with minimal cost and time. This flexibility is no longer cost-prohibitive. At the high end of the technological spectrum, examples include:

- Universal Robots UR5: This robotic arm can be easily reprogrammed for various manufacturing tasks, such as welding, pick-and-place, and assembly.
- 3D Printers with Multi-Material Capabilities: Modern 3D printers can produce intricate designs using diverse materials with a single machine.
- Surgical Robots: Systems like the da Vinci Surgical System demonstrate flexibility in healthcare, enabling enhanced precision across different surgeries.

A simpler example is the multifunction device (MFD) or printing/copying machine. It can alter what it prints or copies at almost no cost and with minimal resetting time. This contrasts sharply with older printing presses that required extensive cleaning, typesetting, and re-inking for each new job. With an MFD, the process is as simple as replacing the original or sending a new print command.

A specific management accounting logic facilitates flexible manufacturing. Flexible machines influence the financial calculations of the economic production quantity (EPQ), which aims to minimise the total of inventory holding costs and production setup costs. As shown in Figure 8.2, the optimal production size occurs where the total cost is minimised, at the intersection of the holding cost and setup cost curves. The setup cost is the expense of resetting a machine for a new production batch—the cost of flexing the machine.

Figure 8.2 depicts a traditional mass-production scenario in which the setup cost is high (curve SC1), resulting in a large economic order quantity (EOQ1). Curve SC2 represents a situation with flexible machines, where the setup cost is low for all batch sizes. This downward shift in the setup cost curve signifies the technological transition to flexible machines. With this reduced setup cost, the EPQ decreases to EPQ2, making smaller batches economically viable. As the setup cost approaches zero, the EPQ becomes optimal for mass-customised production, where producing even a single unit is economically efficient.

Flexible machines also extend the lifespan of fixed capital. They eliminate the need to scrap and replace machines when a company updates its market offerings, as they can be reprogrammed at minimal cost. Consequently, the payback period for investing in flexible machines can span multiple product lifecycles.

Figure 8.2: How flexible machines reduce economic production quantity (EPQ).

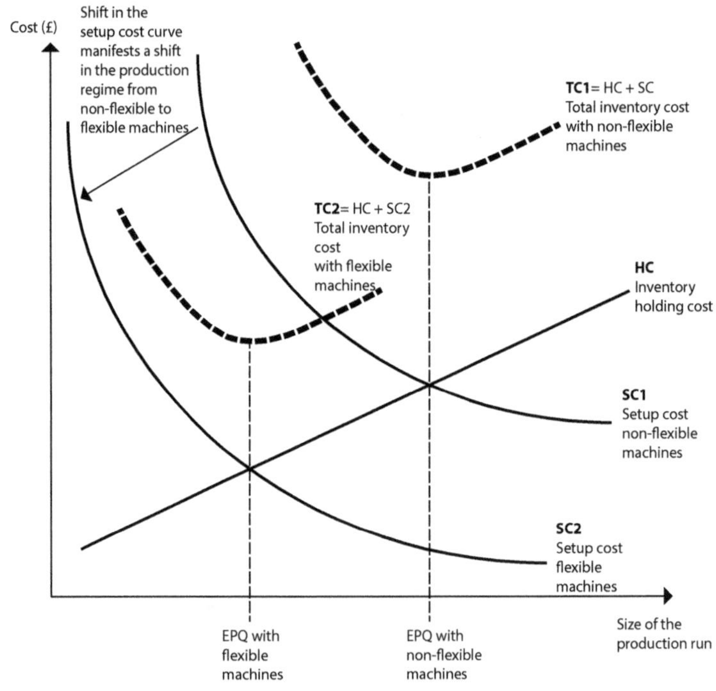

8.5 Flexible labour

The third component of flexible manufacturing is flexible labour: forms of labour that can be easily transferred across jobs, skills, locations, and time slots, or removed when no longer needed. Unlike permanent labour, flexible labour can be adjusted to the changing requirements of flexible consumption and machines. Two forms are pertinent: skill flexibility and time flexibility.

Skill flexibility

Skill or functional flexibility enables firms to change the division of labour quickly and without extra cost, shifting workers between tasks and workplaces (Standing 2011). Since the Industrial Revolution, the division of labour has been shaped by the techno-managerial apparatus of production. The invention of flexible machines has reconstructed this division and the type of labour it demands, particularly immaterial labour.

Hardt and Negri (2000, 2017) argue that skill flexibility in neoliberal times occurs within the 'immaterialization of labour'. Immaterial labour represents an 'implosion' between labour and capital, with labour assuming tasks formerly done by management. In early capitalism, labouring activities were heterogeneous; tailoring and weaving involved incommensurable actions. In computer-aided manufacturing systems with flexible machines, this heterogeneity diminishes. Computerised tailoring and weaving now involve the same concrete practices: manipulating symbols and information, such as selecting options from on-screen menus. Workers make choices within the system's technical parameters so the machine can produce the desired output. This is a form of immaterialization in which labour performs 'symbolic-analytical' work of problem identification and problem-solving (Hardt and Negri 2000, 292).

A second form of immaterialization is 'communicative labour', enacted in digital networks, which shifts the worker's role primarily to information processing and communication. The labour process becomes predominantly informational. In postmodern organisations, labourers produce information for 'abstract cooperation', maintaining connections between deterritorialized organisations and production sites. They direct production systems and the remaining material labour, dispersed across geographically distant sites, according to market signals. Production is now often organised in horizontal network enterprises – outsourced and deterritorialized systems coordinated through communicative labour (Hardt and Negri 2000, 296). This is evident in the global ordering of production, where communicative and symbolic labour is concentrated in Western design centres, while deskilled material labour is distributed across factories in peripheral countries. 'Abstract cooperation' is ensured through quasi-market information networks like franchises and global supply chains.

The third form is 'affective labour', expressed through kin work and caring labour (Hardt 1999). As organisations become biopolitical sites where life is circulated as entrepreneurial human capital, they must transform into spaces of care. They should be places where lives are spent meaningfully and safely, free from harassment or discrimination. This requires institutionalising social, cultural, and welfare considerations into organisational structures. Aspects like well-being, health and safety, equity, and customer care become integral. Often organised into support teams, labour performs 'affective labour' for others, providing motivational, emotional, and educational support.

In production systems with flexible machines, as labour is immaterialised into symbolic-analytical, communicative, and affective forms, it can be shifted effortlessly between machines that require similar actions. Machines now execute the 'physicality' of labour. As labour involves communication with machines and co-workers, altering the division of labour has become more manageable.

Time flexibility

Time flexibility refers to management's enhanced discretion in the temporal deployment of labour. This includes extending 'normal' work hours (e.g., overtime) and augmenting managerial discretion for hiring, firing, and determining work schedules without significantly increasing labour costs. This dimension is more political than techno-managerial, involving changes in industrial relations. Critical political trends influencing time flexibility include:

- The discursive establishment of the idea that easing labour termination is essential for job creation. Transnational organisations such as the IMF and the World Bank have promoted this neoliberal ideology, often as a condition for loans. The argument is that relaxing employment protection laws attracts foreign direct investment (Standing 2011, 31-32).
- The global trend of outsourcing labour contracts. Companies subcontract much of their labour while retaining core knowledge workers responsible for immaterial labour. This is prevalent in developing countries with abundant, cheap labour and autocratic political systems that facilitate coercive controls.
- Increased reliance on temporary labour over a permanent workforce. This shift is seen even in Japan, once known for lifetime employment. Temporary labour offers cost advantages, including lower wages, reduced benefits, and lower overall risk (Standing 2011, 32).

- The growth of project-based hiring, with employment contracts adapted to this organisational form.
- The diminishing influence of trade unions facilitates these neoliberal changes. As unionized labour has decreased, right-wing governments and media outlets advocating neoliberal reforms have supported employers in introducing more flexible labour contracts, such as 'zero-hour contracts'.

Taken together, skill-based and time-based flexibilization have both techno-managerial and political dimensions. Unlike flexible machines, flexible labour has profound political consequences that intersect with social justice issues such as modern slavery, despotic labour control, job insecurity, and pension shortages. These sustainability issues are discussed further in Chapter 10.

8.6 Flexible manufacturing systems

A flexible manufacturing system (FMS) is the techno-managerial organisation of flexible consumption, machines, and labour into a distinct mode of production. Flexible consumption is its strategic intention, while flexible machines and labour provide the capacity to realise it. An FMS combines several flexible machines into an integrated, computer-coordinated system. Such an aggregation is often called a manufacturing cell, and an FMS can range from a small cell to a large cluster of cells forming an 'assembly highway' (see Miller and O'Leary 1994).

The goal of an FMS is flexible consumption, captured operationally by 'mass customisation': the ability to customise products to meet changing demand with the efficiency of a mass production facility. An FMS should transform a mass production facility into one capable of producing 'heterogeneity' rather than 'homogeneity'. This is a techno-managerial challenge, as it demands achieving economies with smaller production volumes. An FMS integrates the flexibility of 'job shops' with the efficiency of 'mass production systems'.

Traditionally, small quantities of different products were made in job shops with multipurpose machines and multi-skilled labour. However, long setup times and large work-in-progress inventories led to higher average production costs. Such inefficiencies were attributed to a lack of 'economies of scale'. Conversely, mass production of identical products using specialised machines created massive economies of scale but lacked flexibility. Flexibility and efficiency were seen as polar opposites.

The FMS negates this opposition. Advances in engineering and computer technology make the efficient mass production of a variety possible. This is achieved through flexible labour, multipurpose machines with fast tool-changing capabilities, automated material handling, computer-aided design and manufacturing, and digital networks that connect all aspects of production and distribution (Maleki 1991). Table 8.1 summarises how an FMS integrates job shops and mass production systems.

Table 8.1: Flexible manufacturing integrating job shops and mass production systems

Comparative dimension	Job shop production	Mass production	Flexible manufacturing systems
Strategic focus and intention	Quality, product variety, differentiation	Cost efficiency, speed of delivery, and production	Cost-efficient customisation, quality, and speed
Core competence sought	Capacity to meet varieties in demand	Capacity to produce a standardised product at a lower cost at high speed	Customizability with lower cost and high-speed production and delivery
Nature of the fixed capital	Multipurpose machines with high setup cost/time for retooling	Specialised machines needing massive reinvestments for variety	Flexible machines with minimal retooling; very low setup cost/time
Nature of the working capital			
Labour	Skilled, 'jack-of-all-trades'	Deskilled, specialised in a single task	Flexible, immaterial labour performing symbolic-analytical and communicative tasks
Inventories	Large work-in-progress inventories	Large parts and raw material inventories	Just-in-time

Source: Alawattage and Wickramasinghe (2019, 175)

Different notions of flexibility in an FMS

An FMS combines the efficiency of mass production with the differentiating capacity of a job shop. This is made feasible by deploying flexible machines and labour, embodying the techno-managerial and political-economic conditions for a flexible system. Operational management literature (e.g., Maleki 1991) categorises the various forms of flexibility in an FMS into three groups:

Basic or element flexibilities:

- Machine flexibility: The ease with which a machine handles different jobs.
- Labour flexibility: The ease of relocating labour across different jobs.
- Material handling flexibility: The ease of processing different parts with various machines.

- Operation flexibility: The ease of using alternative operation sequences.

System flexibilities:

- Volume flexibility: The ability to operate profitably at different production volumes.
- Expansion flexibility: The ability to expand the system incrementally.
- Routing flexibility: The availability of alternative processing paths.
- Process flexibility: The number of different product types producible without re-setup.
- Product flexibility: The number of different product types producible with minor re-setup.

Aggregate flexibilities:

- Program flexibility: The ability to run for long periods without external intervention.
- Production flexibility: The ability to produce a new product design without major capital investment.
- Market flexibility: The ability to adapt efficiently to changing market conditions.

Accounting in FMS

Calculative practices like activity-based costing and enterprise resource planning are critical for enabling flexible manufacturing. These accounting techniques are now integrated into multi-platform, real-time data management and analytics systems that handle various aspects of flexible manufacturing, from market analysis to supply chain integration. Embedded in software, management accounting in an FMS is complex and effectively 'black-boxed'.

These systems, whether vendor-built (e.g., SAP) or proprietary, are complex data management systems. When coupled with Industry 4.0 'smart technologies', this 'black-boxed' accounting becomes 'smart accounting'. Understanding Industry 4.0 is key to understanding management accounting's role in an FMS.

Industry 4.0 technologies and 'smart accounting' in FMS

Industry 4.0, the fourth industrial revolution, is transforming manufacturing by integrating modern smart technologies. It builds upon previous revolutions: mechanization (First), electricity and mass production (Second), and computers and automation (Third). Industry 4.0 fuses digital, physical, and biological systems, incorporating advanced technologies to enhance automation, communication, and data exchange.

Key components of Industry 4.0 include (see Javaid et al. 2022; PwC 2016):

- Internet of Things (IoT)
- Location detection technologies
- Advanced human-machine interfaces
- Big Data and Analytics
- Artificial Intelligence (AI) and Machine Learning
- Cloud Computing
- Cyber-Physical Systems (CPS)
- Additive Manufacturing (3D Printing)
- Augmented Reality (AR) and Virtual Reality (VR)
- Autonomous Systems
- Authentication and fraud detection technologies
- Mobile devices

According to PwC (2016), these technologies enable data and analytics as a core capability, leading to three elements of 'smart industries':

1. digitisation and integration of value chains;
2. digitization of products and services;
3. digital business models.

Javaid et al. (2022) provide a comprehensive view of how Industry 4.0 enables smart accounting in an FMS, which can be understood through four dimensions:

1. **Enabling a smart factory through the Internet of Things and robotics.** Smart technologies help machines capture, process, and communicate real-time information, becoming automated. The factory floor becomes a highly flexible system. ERP systems and their modules (e.g., line-balancing) constitute the embedded and automated management accounting functionality.
2. **Enabling integrated logistics to create automated warehouses.** Accounting functions like inventory management are integrated into software platforms that process real-time data and analytics.
3. **Enabling a tracking system across the supply chain.** Technologies like barcode scanners, image recognition, and GPS are critical for effective tracking.
4. **Creating data-driven management and decision-making.** Technologies like data analytics and AI help create visual feedback, benchmarks, and operational algorithms. While cybernetic elements can be automated, systems can flag exceptions needing human intervention.

Figure 8.3 illustrates these elements of accounting in flexible manufacturing.

Figure 8.3: How Industry 4.0 technologies enable accounting in flexible manufacturing

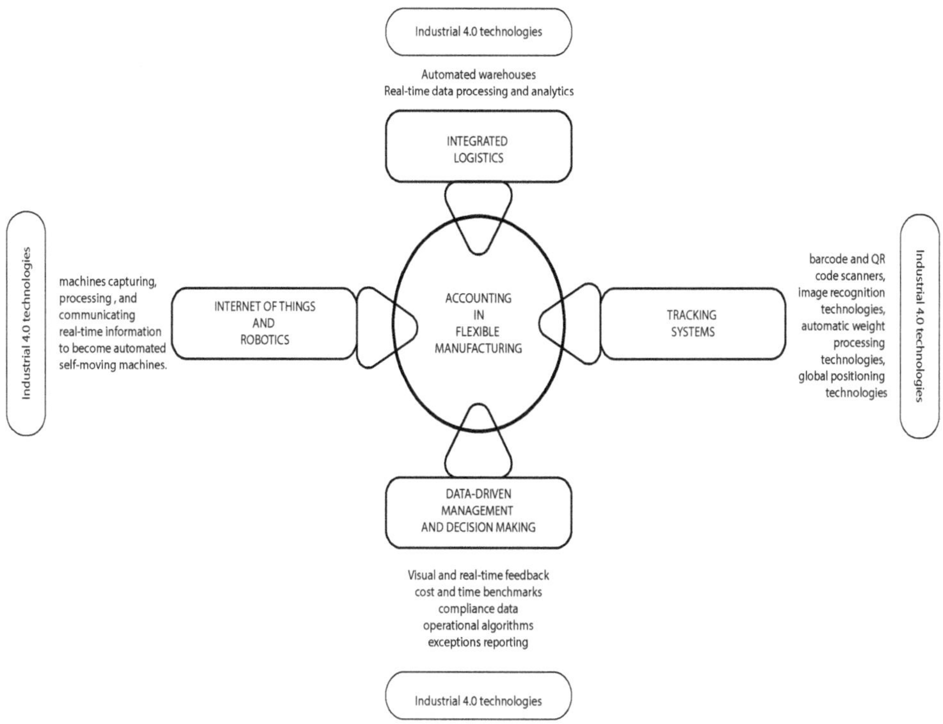

Source: adapted from Javaid et al. (2022, 52)

Synthesizing the discussion, the accounting functionalities of Industry 4.0 technologies relate to the following enabled capabilities:

1. Analysing changing customer demand patterns to identify strategic imperatives.
2. Offering financial insights into the value of differentiating 'tasks' or 'activities'. In these new environments, the value of machines and labour stems from the specific activities they perform, not just their cost centre location. This demands managerial attention to activities, which ABC terminology captures as 'activity cost drivers'. Industry 4.0 technologies enable the integration of such detailed activity analysis into larger accounting platforms, such as ERP systems.
3. Enhancing communication between different FMS elements to create a holistic system. The provision of 'real-time information' is an essential condition that traditional systems cannot achieve, but which networked accounting software can (see Wagner et al. 2011).

4. Making detailed comparisons between units, machines, individuals, and activity levels, including against competitors. As Miller and O'Leary (1994) explain, flexible manufacturing can demand a person-to-person sense of competition, in which individuals and their tasks are directly compared with counterparts in competing firms, using calculative practices such as competitor cost analysis.

8.7 Flexible specialization and integration

Flexible specialisation extends the concept of flexibility beyond organisational boundaries to industrial regulation and development (Piore and Sabel 1984; Hirst and Zeitlin 1991). The argument is that achieving organisational flexibility requires broader politico-institutional arrangements. The focus thus shifts to the mechanisms that establish the necessary integration beyond single organisations.

Unlike techno-managerial interpretations that focus on firm-level changes, flexible specialisation directs attention to the politics beyond the organisation that enable flexible manufacturing. Hirst and Zeitlin (1991) argue that techno-managerial views see productive systems as coherent totalities, while flexible specialisation identifies complex connections between technology, institutions, and politics. Techno-managerial interpretations see industrial change as a mechanical outcome, whereas flexible specialisation emphasises contingency and strategic choice driven by politics.

Hirst and Zeitlin (1991, 10) argue that techno-managerial conceptions pay "little attention to the wide range of forms and hybrids of flexibly-specialized production and their social and institutional conditions". They contend that the strategic shift to flexible manufacturing depends not merely on the firm but on "inter-firm and collective regional and national patterns... crucial in the balancing of competition and co-operation necessary for their more progressive institutionalization" (ibid).

Piore and Sabel (1984) also posit that flexible specialisation is a result of micro-regulations of innovation across industries. It involves "finding a compatible institutional answer to the problems of instigating and coordinating innovation, [because] competition of a wrong kind undermines the necessary coordination; misdirected coordination undermines competition" (Piore and Sabel 1984, 264-265). Proponents recognise the importance of inter-firm coordination through institutional mechanisms beyond individual organisations or markets. The transition from mass production thus required an extra-organisational reconciliation of competition and coordination to facilitate viable innovations. According to Piore and Sabel (1984, 265-268), this occurred in three settings:

1. **Regional conglomerations:** In specialised industrial districts, these consist of a core of more-or-less equal enterprises interconnected through competition and coordination. They were established as strategic initiatives to enhance industry and national competitiveness. A notable example is Michael Porter's (1998) concept of 'industrial clusters', which he advocated as a strategic arrangement for boosting national competitiveness. Clusters encompass linked industries, suppliers, service providers, and institutions like universities and trade associations that provide specialised training, research, and technical support.
2. **Federated enterprises:** As exemplified by the Japanese zaibatsu and post-war corporate groups, these played a pivotal role in steering Japan's industrial development. Miyajima (1994) identifies six corporate groups of this type in Japan. Among them, Mitsu, Mitsubishi, and Sumitomo originated as pre-war zaibatsu and were organized as corporate groups in the early 1950s. On the other hand, Fuyo, Sanwa, and Daiichi, which were originally large banks before the war, coalesced into corporate groups in the late 1960s. Their distinctive features included cross-shareholding, a principal bank system, cooperative investments, and the sharing of financial, marketing, and technological expertise among member corporations. As noted by Piore and Sabel (1984, 267), member firms are not arranged hierarchically, but their collective identity is more pronounced than in regional conglomerates.
3. **Solar firms and workshop factories:** This model describes coordination where a central firm relies on subcontractors as partners, not just subordinates, to address design and production challenges. The connection is collaborative. Piore and Sabel's example is the Boeing Company, which produces neither the engines nor much of the avionic equipment for its aeroplanes.

In essence, the flexible specialisation thesis extends the evolution of flexible manufacturing beyond organisational boundaries to inter-firm coordination and competition. It emphasises the significance of micro-regulatory institutional arrangements between firms to reconcile competition and coordination – a necessary condition for flexible manufacturing regimes.

8.8 Flexible accumulation

The concept of flexible accumulation extends the idea of flexibility further, beyond organisational and industrial boundaries to the global dynamics of capital and labour. The focus here is on the "new capitalism" arising from micro-organisational changes in production. Political economists use various terms for this new capitalism, such as the "post-industrial paradigm" (Halal 1986), "disorganized capitalism" (Lash and Urry 1987), and "just-in-time capitalism" (Swyngedouw 1986).

Flexible accumulation consolidates the techno-managerial discussions of previous sections and situates them within the broader framework of transformed capitalism. Swyngedouw (1986) elucidates this transformation through shifts in production processes, labour, industrial space, the state, and ideology. Harvey (1989) interprets it as a transformation in international trade, profit rates, exchange rates, and the structure of labour markets. These scholars link flexible manufacturing to the macro dynamics of global capitalism. In this sense, flexible accumulation refers to post-Fordist capitalism, where the flexibilization of capital and labour is central to accumulation. It offers a framework for explaining how the circulation of labour and capital became more critical than disciplinary confinement.

To identify elements of neoliberalization (i.e., integrating lives into circulation through biopolitics) within this transformation, it is crucial to scrutinize changes in labour markets. A Fordist production regime is characterised by a large, blue-collar, unskilled workforce with long-term employment contracts and job security. The labour force is concentrated on factory floors, constituting the "core group" in the "primary labour market."

Flexible accumulation refers to a different global order of production. As depicted in Figure 8.4, this core is diluted and dispersed to the periphery through various labour contracts and market innovations, minimising the core element. Flexible labour control is achieved through the circulation and peripheralization of labour.

This global reorganisation of production facilitated flexibilization at both the core and the periphery. At the core, primarily in Western centres, 'functional flexibility' is achieved through the consolidation of capital-like symbolic-analytical and communicative labour.

The core is the shrinking group of employees dealing with strategic or core competencies (Prahalad and Hamel 1990). This group, often top and middle management, shapes the company's strategic intent and establishes collaborations through diverse networks. These networks distribute production activities, creating peripheries for non-core activities. For instance, Prahalad and Hamel (1990, 80) attribute NEC's success to its restructuring around core competencies: NEC exploited the convergence of computing and communications ('C&C'), adopted an appropriate 'strategic architecture', and formed a 'C&C Committee' to oversee the development of core products and competencies. It entered into over 100 strategic alliances to rapidly build competencies, internalising partner skills.

Figure 8.4: Circulation and peripheralisation of labour to enable flexible manufacturing.

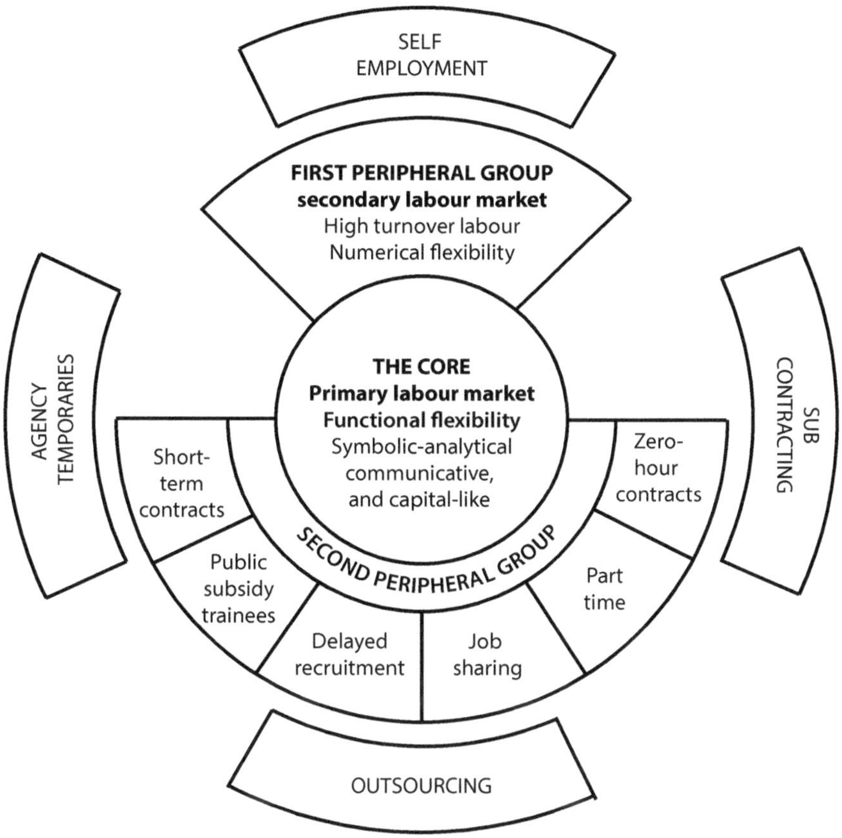

Source: adapted from Harvey (1990, 151)

By nature, the roles of core employees are communicative and symbolic-analytical (i.e., immaterial labour), aligning with intellectual or knowledge capital rather than traditional labour. They function as dealers, networkers, and strategists. For this reason, they claim a portion of profits through performance-based compensation schemes. These employees hold full-time, permanent positions with job security, promotion prospects, and generous benefits. Nevertheless, this core is expected to be adaptable, flexible, and geographically mobile (Harvey, 1989, 150).

While this core acquires the features of capital, the rest of the workforce is drawn to the periphery through "myriad strategic alliances" (Prahalad and Hamel 1990, 80). As Harvey (1989, 150) explains, this peripheralization creates two sub-groups:

1. The first consists of full-time employees with skills readily available in

the labour market, such as clerical and lesser-skilled manual work. With less access to career opportunities, this group has high labour turnover, making workforce reductions easy through natural wastage.

2. The second peripheral group provides greater numerical flexibility and includes part-timers, casuals, fixed-term contract staff, and temporaries, with even less job security than the first group.

The "appropriate strategic architecture" that enables this peripheralization involves outsourcing hitherto internal functions. Experts who previously managed support services (e.g., security, R&D, accounting) are encouraged to set up their own enterprises. Corporate functions are thus loosened from the core and placed in quasi-market arrangements, facilitating the flexible circulation of labour and capital. As Guy Standing (2011) argues, and as Figure 8.4 illustrates, precariat classes of labour are constructed at the first and second peripheral segments.

Chapter summary

Flexibility is a multi-faceted phenomenon with broad techno-managerial and cultural-political implications. Organisations first confront it as 'flexible consumption'—the imperative to offer customers greater choice and customisation. This demands that firms develop the operational capacity to produce flexibly and the informational capacity to maintain communication networks across markets.

These capacities are achieved through flexible machines, flexible labour, and the organisation of these into flexible manufacturing systems. An FMS realises the strategic intention of flexible consumption by integrating machines and labour through Industry 4.0 technologies. These technologies enable various forms of flexibility by enhancing data and analytical competencies across factory floors, warehouses, and supply chains. Management accounting functionalities are now integrated and 'black-boxed' into the software platforms created by these technologies.

However, achieving flexibility transcends organisational boundaries, necessitating inter-organisational coordination through strategic alliances. The concept of flexible specialisation captures this extra-organisational element. Finally, flexible accumulation extends the notion of flexibility to the global dynamics of capital and labour, situating micro-organisational changes within the broader schema of a transformed, post-Fordist capitalism. Flexibility is thus both a techno-managerial and a political phenomenon, enacted through a hierarchy of interconnected elements, as summarised in Table 8.2.

Table 8.2: The hierarchy of flexibility concepts

Flexibility concept	Realm of operation and scope of analysis
Flexible consumption	Market/consumer and consumer-firm connection
Flexible machines	Fixed capital – firm level, technological
Flexible labour	Labour – firm level, techno-managerial and political
Flexible manufacturing systems	Firm-level – techno-managerial
Flexible specialization and integration	Industry/meso level – inter-firm coordination
Flexible accumulation	Macro-capitalist system; core-periphery labour and capital markets

Case study: Flexibility at what cost? strategising production and sustainability in the fast fashion arena

1. Introduction: the paradox of speed

The global fashion industry, particularly its 'fast fashion' segment, stands as the apotheosis of a market logic defined by manufacturing flexibility. This business model is predicated on an organisation's capacity to respond with unprecedented speed to the fragmented, ephemeral tastes of modern consumers. It is a direct and tangible manifestation of the strategic imperative of 'flexible consumption', a market condition where the ability to offer variety and reject standardisation is the primary driver of competitive advantage. The term 'fast fashion' was coined in the early 1990s, when the New York Times used it to describe the mission of the Spanish retailer Zara: to move a garment from the design stage to a store shelf in just 15 days. This compression of the production cycle revolutionised the industry, replacing the traditional two-season model with a continuous stream of new, trend-driven products.

This celebrated agility, however, presents a profound paradox. The industry's remarkable market responsiveness is inextricably linked to systemic and deepening sustainability crises. The relentless pursuit of speed and low costs has externalised enormous environmental and social burdens. Environmentally, the fashion industry is responsible for an estimated 8–10% of global carbon emissions – more than international aviation and shipping combined – and is the planet's second-largest consumer of water. Its operations pollute rivers with toxic dyes, shed microplastics into the oceans, and generate mountains of textile waste, with 85% of all textiles ending up in landfills each year. Socially, the model is frequently sustained by the exploitation of a precarious global workforce, characterised by low wages, unsafe working conditions, and the erosion of labour rights in developing economies.

The fast fashion model did not simply adopt flexibility as a strategy; it was born from it. The shift from a Fordist regime of mass-producing standardised goods to a post-Fordist one prioritising variety and customisation created the very market conditions in which fast fashion could thrive. Consequently, the sustainability challenges that now define the industry are not accidental by-products of poor management but are inherent, structural consequences of elevating a specific form of manufacturing flexibility above all other considerations. This case study explores this paradox by examining the distinct strategic architectures of two industry titans, Zara (a pioneer of the model) and Shein (its radical accelerator). It poses a central question for students of strategy and accounting: How do firms strategically organise for flexibility, and what are the unaccounted, and perhaps unaccountable, costs embedded within these choices?

2. Architectures of agility: contrasting models of flexible production

To meet the demands of flexible consumption, firms have engineered sophisticated production systems. An analysis of Zara, the flagship brand of the Inditex group, and Shein, the digitally native behemoth, reveals two distinct evolutionary paths for achieving manufacturing flexibility. Both seek to solve the same strategic problem – how to deliver immense variety at high speed and low cost – but they do so through fundamentally different approaches to capital investment, risk management, and supply chain control. These differences have profound implications for their operational capabilities and, crucially, for their sustainability footprints and the governance thereof.

2.1 Zara (Inditex): the responsive, vertically integrated system

Zara's pioneering business model is built upon a high degree of vertical integration, a strategic choice that grants it significant control over its supply chain. Unlike many competitors who outsource the majority of their production, Zara manufactures a substantial portion of its most fashion-sensitive items in-house or through a network of suppliers located in close proximity to its headquarters in Galicia, Spain, and in nearby Portugal and Morocco. This geographical concentration is the cornerstone of its 'just-in-time' (JIT) production system, enabling what the Harvard Business Review has termed 'rapid-fire fulfillment' (see Ferdows, K., Lewis, M. A., & Machuca, J. A. D. (2004). Rapid-Fire Fulfillment. Harvard Business Review, 82(11), 104-110).

This operational setup is a classic example of a Flexible Manufacturing System (FMS), which aims to integrate the product variety of a 'job shop' with the efficiency of a mass production system. Zara achieves this by producing items in small, limited-quantity batches. This strategy not only minimises the risk of being left with large volumes of unsold inventory but also creates a sense of scarcity and urgency among consumers, encouraging immediate purchase. Store managers provide real-time feedback on sales trends to designers at the headquarters, who can then rapidly develop new styles or modify existing ones. The proximity of manufacturing allows these new designs to be produced and delivered to stores worldwide, often twice a week, within a cycle of just two to three weeks.

A formidable informational capacity underpins this operational capacity. Zara leverages advanced data analytics and sophisticated optimisation software to manage its complex logistics. In collaboration with researchers at MIT, the company developed a model using AMPL to optimise inventory allocation across its global network of over 1,500 stores. This system processes vast amounts of data – including past sales, current inventory levels, and new assortment decisions – to make optimal shipment decisions just hours before dispatch, ensuring the right products are sent to the right stores at the right time. This deep integration of data analytics into its centralised distribution model exemplifies the creation of an 'informational space' that connects market signals directly to production and logistics, a key enabler of flexible manufacturing (see Smith, S. A., & Achabal, D. D. (1998). Clearance Pricing and Inventory Policies for Retail Chains. Management Science, 44(3), 285–300. http://www.jstor.org/stable/2634668).

2.2 Shein: the on-demand, digitally native ecosystem

If Zara pioneered fast fashion, Shein has accelerated it into an 'ultra-fast' model that represents a radical evolution of flexibility. Shein's strategy is asset-light, eschewing the capital-intensive vertical integration of Zara. Instead, it operates as a digitally native marketplace, coordinating a vast, fragmented network of an estimated 6,000 small-scale clothing factories in China. This structure allows for near-infinite scalability with minimal fixed capital investment.

The core of Shein's model is a data-driven, 'on-demand' production system that pushes the logic of flexibility to its extreme. The company's internal management software continuously scrapes data from the internet to identify micro-trends. It then tests thousands of new designs—reportedly adding around 6,000 new items to its website daily—by commissioning its network of suppliers to produce them in micro-batches of 100–200 items each. Real-time sales data is collected almost instantly; items that sell well are immediately reordered in larger quantities, while those that do not are discontinued. This test-and-repeat model minimises inventory risk far beyond even Zara's capabilities and aligns production almost perfectly with demonstrated demand.

Shein's approach can be understood as an extreme manifestation of 'informational capacity' driving a unique form of inter-firm coordination. It embodies the concept of 'abstract cooperation', where a central digital platform connects and directs a deterritorialized network of producers through the flow of information. This structure mirrors the 'flexible specialisation' model, but in a hyper-networked form in which the market, mediated by Shein's algorithm, dictates the actions of thousands of independent workshops. The company's competitive advantage lies not in owning the means of production, but in its mastery of data and its ability to orchestrate this sprawling, digitally coordinated ecosystem.

This strategic divergence between Zara and Shein creates a critical trade-off. Zara's capital-intensive model provides a high degree of operational control and, at least in theory, greater visibility into its tier-one supply chain. This structure aligns with the 'solar firm' model of flexible specialisation, where a central entity coordinates a network of dedicated partners. Shein's asset-light model, by contrast, offers unparalleled scalability and low capital risk but is predicated on a near-total lack of direct control and visibility over its diffuse and opaque supply chain. Its flexibility is achieved by externalising production to a digital marketplace, a choice that has profound consequences for governance, accountability, and sustainability.

Table 1: A comparative analysis of flexibility strategies (Zara vs. Shein)

Comparative Dimension	Zara (Inditex)	Shein
Flexibility Concept	Flexible Manufacturing System (FMS) integrating job shop variety with mass production efficiency.	Hyper-flexible, on-demand production driven by a digitally coordinated network.
Strategic Intention	Rapid response to in-season fashion trends through a controlled supply chain.	Near-instantaneous response to online micro-trends through a test-and-repeat model.
Core Competence	Vertically integrated, responsive supply chain management and logistics optimisation.	Data analytics, trend prediction, and digital orchestration of a vast supplier network.
Nature of Fixed Capital	High. Significant investment in manufacturing facilities, distribution centres, and retail stores.	Low. An asset-light model that avoids ownership of factories and relies on third-party suppliers.
Labour Model	A mix of in-house labour in Europe and outsourced labour, governed by a supplier code of conduct.	Highly peripheralized, numerically flexible workforce across thousands of small, non-contracted suppliers.
Informational Capacity	Strong. Real-time sales data from stores feeds back to a central design and production hub; uses optimisation software.	Extreme. Algorithm-driven trend spotting and real-time analysis of sales data from micro-batches to scale production.
Inter-firm Coordination	'Solar firm' model of flexible specialisation, with a central firm coordinating closely with proximal suppliers.	Hyper-networked model of flexible specialisation, where a digital platform enables 'abstract cooperation' among a fragmented supplier base.

3. The human cost of flexibility: labour in the core and periphery

The strategic architectures of fast fashion are built upon a global reorganisation of labour that starkly reflects the theoretical model of 'flexible accumulation'. This framework describes a system where a small, secure 'core' of employees performing high-value tasks manages a large, insecure, and geographically dispersed 'periphery' of manual labourers. This division is not merely a theoretical construct but the literal, contractual, and geographical operating reality of the industry.

The 'core' consists of designers, data scientists, marketers, and logistics experts, primarily located in corporate headquarters in Europe and North America. These employees perform what Hardt and Negri term 'immaterial labour': the 'symbolic-analytical' work of trend forecasting and design, and the 'communicative labour' required to coordinate complex global supply chains. The immense value generated by this core—for instance, by Shein's proprietary algorithm that identifies the next viral trend—is predicated on its ability to direct the activities of the periphery.

The 'periphery' is composed of millions of garment workers, overwhelmingly young women, in developing countries such as Bangladesh, China, and India. The business model's demand for speed and low cost is achieved through the imposition of extreme 'time flexibility' and 'numerical flexibility' on this workforce. Shein's model provides the most extreme example. Investigations have uncovered a system reliant on thousands of informal, unregulated workshops where workers face gruelling conditions. A Channel 4 documentary found employees working 75-hour shifts with minimal time off. Another report from the Swiss advocacy group Public Eye accused Shein of violating Chinese labour laws, with workers in some supplier factories toiling for up to 13 hours a day, often without formal contracts, and being paid on a piece-rate basis that incentivises speed above all else. These conditions are not an unfortunate side effect of the business model; they are a fundamental enabler of its hyper-flexibility. The ability to rapidly scale production up or down in response to data signals depends on a workforce that can be mobilised and demobilised at will, without the protections of formal employment contracts or regulated working hours.

This reality creates a state of perpetual contradiction for companies that must publicly espouse values their own operational logic systematically undermines. Major brands like Inditex and H&M have established comprehensive supplier codes of conduct and social responsibility programmes. H&M, for instance, requires all suppliers to sign its Sustainability Commitment, which covers worker safety and fair wages, and it was a key signatory to the Accord on Fire and Building Safety in Bangladesh, a legally binding agreement to improve factory conditions. Similarly, Inditex's Code of Conduct for Manufacturers and Suppliers outlines standards for its partners. However, the relentless pressure for lower prices and shorter lead times, which is the essence of the fast fashion model, places these suppliers in a position where adherence to such codes can become economically unviable. The strategic pursuit of flexibility, therefore, necessitates the creation of a precarious peripheral workforce, placing corporate social responsibility initiatives in direct conflict with the core drivers of the business.

4. The Planetary Balance Sheet: Environmental Externalities of Production

The operational speed that defines fast fashion's flexibility is directly subsidised by the planet. The industry's environmental externalities are vast, systemic, and directly linked to the strategic choices made to compress production cycles and minimise costs.

A primary driver of the industry's environmental footprint is its carbon emissions, which are heavily influenced by logistics. The imperative for speed has led to a significant reliance on air freight, which is far more carbon-intensive than sea transport. A critical analysis of Inditex's operations reveals a stark trade-off between its flexible logistics model and its climate commitments. Despite pledges to reduce its value chain emissions, Inditex's emissions from the transport and distribution of goods rose by 10% in 2024 to 2.6 million tonnes of CO2 equivalents. This increase is attributed to its continued dependence on air freight to rapidly replenish its global stores from its central distribution hubs in Spain. In contrast, competitor H&M uses air freight for a mere 1% of its transport, demonstrating that such a high-carbon logistics model is a strategic choice, not a necessity. Shein's global, direct-to-consumer model results in an even larger and more rapidly growing carbon footprint. Its total emissions ballooned by over 50% between 2021 and 2022 to 9.17 million tonnes of CO2, a footprint comparable to that of an entire country like Paraguay.

Beyond carbon, the industry's resource consumption and pollution are staggering. Producing a single cotton shirt can require up to 700 gallons of water, and cotton cultivation in water-stressed regions places immense strain on local ecosystems (https://earth.org/fast-fashions-detrimental-effect-on-the-environment/). The dyeing and finishing processes are responsible for about 20% of global industrial water pollution, as untreated wastewater containing toxic chemicals is often discharged directly into rivers (https://davidsuzuki.org/living-green/the-environmental-cost-of-fast-fashion/). Furthermore, the industry's reliance on cheap, synthetic materials like polyester – a mainstay of Shein's product line – is a major contributor to the microplastic pollution crisis. Each wash cycle of synthetic garments releases thousands of plastic microfibres into waterways, which ultimately accumulate in the oceans and the food chain.

Finally, the business model, which is built on a 'buy-throw-away cycle', has created an unprecedented waste crisis. The low price and perceived low quality of garments encourage consumers to treat them as disposable. As a result, an estimated 87% of the total fibre input used for clothing is ultimately incinerated or sent to a landfill. This waste is often exported, creating vast 'textile mountains' in countries in the Global South, such as Ghana and Chile, which bear the environmental burden of the developed world's overconsumption. The strategic choice to prioritise flexibility and novelty has thus engineered a linear system of production and consumption that is fundamentally at odds with planetary boundaries.

5. Accounting for sustainability: a crisis of credibility?

In response to growing public and regulatory pressure, fast fashion companies have invested heavily in sustainability reporting and corporate communications. These public-facing documents present a narrative of commitment and progress. Shein's 'evoluSHEIN' roadmap outlines pillars of 'Collective Resilience (Planet)' and 'Equitable Empowerment (People)', with goals to reduce emissions and support its supplier communities. Inditex has set ambitious targets to achieve net-zero emissions by 2040, to use only textile raw materials with a lower impact by 2030, and to publish a detailed Climate Transition Plan.

However, a significant gap exists between these public pledges and the performance outcomes dictated by their core business models. This discrepancy has fuelled widespread accusations of 'greenwashing' – the practice of making unsubstantiated or misleading claims about a product or company's environmental benefits to create a positive public image. The evidence presented in previous sections points to a systemic credibility crisis. Inditex's rising transport emissions directly contradict its net-zero ambitions. Shein's business model, which adds thousands of new fossil-fuel-based products daily, is fundamentally incompatible with principles of circularity and waste reduction, leading to ratings of 'We Avoid' from ethical fashion auditors.

This credibility gap has prompted a significant institutional response in the accounting and reporting domain. Voluntary, narrative-based sustainability reports are increasingly seen as insufficient. In their place, a movement towards mandatory, standardised, and comparable reporting frameworks is gaining momentum. The Global Reporting Initiative (GRI), a leading standard-setter, is developing a new, sector-specific standard for Textiles and Apparel. This standard aims to force companies to report on the issues most material to their industry, such as supply chain labour practices, Scope 3 emissions, and chemical and water management, making it harder to obscure poor performance. Similarly, the Sustainability Accounting Standards Board (SASB) provides industry-specific standards for Apparel, Accessories & Footwear, focusing on financially material sustainability topics like 'Labour Conditions in the Supply Chain' and 'Environmental Impacts in the Supply Chain' to meet the demands of investors.

The rise of these rigorous standards signals a shift in the battleground for sustainability. The focus is moving from corporate storytelling to verifiable data and accountability. This places management accountants at the centre of a critical challenge. Their role is evolving from simply reporting on sustainability metrics to designing and implementing systems that can navigate the inherent conflicts between a firm's strategic imperatives and its sustainability goals. They must grapple with how to account for the true costs of flexibility and confront a business model where the operational logic itself may be the greatest barrier to meaningful progress. The concept of 'black-boxed' accounting, where complex systems obscure underlying processes, applies not only to software but to the opaque, hyper-flexible supply chains that defy traditional audit and control. For the accounting profession, this represents a profound ethical and technical challenge: how to bring transparency and accountability to a system designed for speed and opacity.

Table 2: Sustainability reporting: pledges vs. performance (Inditex & Shein)

Sustainability Metric	Company	Stated Goal/Pledge	Reported Performance/Critique
Greenhouse Gas Emissions Reduction	Inditex	'Reduce our emissions by over 50%... including our value chain... by 2030' and achieve 'net zero emissions by 2040'.	Transport and distribution emissions (a key part of the value chain) increased by 10% in 2024. The reliance on high-carbon air freight to enable its flexible model undermines its climate promises.
Greenhouse Gas Emissions Reduction	Shein	'Reduce absolute Scope 3 GHG emissions by 25% by 2030'.	Total emissions increased by over 50% from 6.04 to 9.17 million tonnes CO2 in 2022. Further reports show a 23.1% increase in total emissions in 2024. The business model's rapid growth is overwhelming any decarbonisation efforts.
Supply Chain Labour Conditions	Shein	Committed to the UN Global Compact principles on labour and human rights; operates a Supplier Community Empowerment Program.	Investigations found workers in supplier factories working 75-hour weeks, often without contracts or minimum wage protections, in violation of Chinese labour laws. Rated 'Very Poor' on labour conditions.
Circularity and Waste Reduction	Shein	Aims to 'become a global leader in rescuing deadstock materials' and establish a 'fully circular textile supply chain by 2050'.	The 'ultra-fast fashion' model, which introduces thousands of new items daily, is the primary driver of overconsumption and textile waste. The business model is fundamentally linear and encourages disposability.

Questions for student analysis

1. Using the hierarchy of flexibility concepts from Chapter 8 (Table 8.2), analyse and contrast the business models of Zara and Shein. How do their different approaches to achieving 'Flexible Manufacturing Systems' and 'Flexible Specialisation' shape their respective competitive advantages?
2. Apply the core-periphery model of 'flexible accumulation' (Figure 8.4) to the labour practices described in the case, particularly those of Shein. Explain how the pursuit of 'time flexibility' for labour directly enables the company's business model while creating profound social sustainability challenges.
3. The case highlights a direct conflict between Inditex's rapid logistics model (an enabler of flexibility) and its climate commitments. As a management accountant at Inditex, what key performance indicators (KPIs) would you propose to make this trade-off visible to senior management? How might you use management accounting tools to evaluate alternative, more sustainable logistics strategies?
4. Critically evaluate the sustainability reports of Inditex and Shein using the evidence presented in the case. Identify two specific examples of potential 'greenwashing'. How might the adoption of a mandatory, sector-specific standard like the GRI Textiles and Apparel Standard address the credibility issues you have identified?
5. The chapter notes that in an FMS, management accounting can become 'black-boxed'. Discuss how this concept applies to Shein's business model, extending beyond just software to its entire supply chain. What are the implications for corporate governance, risk management, and the ethical responsibilities of the accounting profession?

Chapter review questions

Section 1: Multiple-choice questions – foundational concepts and application

1.1 The neoliberal rationale for flexibility

1. According to the chapter's distinction between 'anatomico-political' and 'biopolitical' power, which of the following is the best example of a biopolitical concern in a neoliberal organisation?

   a. Optimising the physical layout of a manufacturing cell to synchronise human movement with robotic arms for maximum efficiency.
   b. Implementing an employee wellness programme that offers mental health support and lifestyle coaching to foster an 'entrepreneurial self'.
   c. Designing a piece-rate pay system that directly links a worker's output to their remuneration.
   d. Using time-and-motion studies to minimise the number of physical steps required to complete an assembly task.

2. The chapter posits that flexibility connects two key propositions of neoliberal organisations. Which statement best synthesises this connection?

   a. Flexibility is primarily a technological solution for improving production efficiency, which in turn allows the organisation to offer more competitive salaries.
   b. Flexibility allows an organisation to respond to market dynamics by reconfiguring its internal processes, a change enabled by transforming labour into a circulating, entrepreneurial form of human capital.
   c. Flexibility in labour contracts is a political concession to trade unions, which allows management to pursue greater market share through aggressive pricing strategies.
   d. Flexibility describes the organisation's ability to secure financing from diverse capital markets, which is necessary to fund the biopolitical project of employee care.

1.2 Flexible consumption and organisational capacity

3. A firm decides to invest in a cloud-based supply chain management platform that provides real-time data integration with its suppliers and distributors. This investment primarily enhances the firm's:

   a. Operational capacity, by directly increasing the speed of its flexible machines.
   b. Informational capacity, by creating an integrated 'informational space' for coordination.

c. Affective labour capacity, by improving the well-being of its logistics staff.
d. Financial capacity, by reducing its long-term debt.

4. The chapter uses Hardt and Negri's concept of 'abstract cooperation' to describe the coordination required for flexible consumption. This concept is best exemplified by:

    a. A team of co-located engineers collabourating on a new product design in a single workshop.
    b. A global network of designers, suppliers, and logistics providers connected through digital platforms to coordinate a deterritorialized production system.
    c. A manager directly observing and controlling the work of employees on a factory floor.
    d. A national government setting industrial policy to encourage cooperation between domestic firms.

1.3 Flexible Machines and Management Accounting Logic

5. Based on Figure 8.2 in the chapter, the introduction of flexible machines leads to a lower Economic Production Quantity (EPQ) primarily because:

    a. The cost of holding one unit of inventory for a year increases significantly.
    b. The total cost of production for any given batch size increases.
    c. The cost associated with resetting a machine for a new production batch is substantially reduced.
    d. The demand for customised products decreases, making smaller batches unnecessary.

6. How do flexible machines alter traditional capital budgeting assumptions for an investment in fixed capital?

    a. They shorten the useful life of the asset because technology becomes obsolete faster.
    b. They increase the salvage value of the asset to nearly 100% of its initial cost.
    c. They make the payback period for the investment contingent on a single product's lifecycle.
    d. They can extend the economic life of the asset beyond a single product's lifecycle, as they can be reprogrammed for future products at minimal cost.

1.4 The duality of flexible labour

7. A data analyst at a global fashion retailer uses sophisticated software to identify emerging consumer trends and then communicates these findings to design teams across the world to guide new product development. According to Hardt and Negri's framework, this work is predominantly a form of:

   a. Affective labour.
   b. Deskilled material labour.
   c. Symbolic-analytical and communicative labour.
   d. Anatomico-political labour.

8. Which of the following is identified in the chapter as a key political trend, rather than a purely techno-managerial one, that underpins the rise of time flexibility in labour?

   a. The invention of computer-aided design (CAD) software.
   b. The development of automated material handling systems.
   c. The diminishing influence of trade unions and the promotion of relaxed employment protection laws.
   d. The shift from analogue to digital machine controls.

1.5 Flexible Manufacturing Systems (FMS) and Industry 4.0

9. According to Table 8.1, a Flexible Manufacturing System (FMS) synthesises the characteristics of job shop and mass production systems by:

   a. Combining the high setup costs of job shops with the specialised machines of mass production.
   b. Focusing exclusively on cost efficiency while using the multi-skilled labour of a job shop.
   c. Achieving the cost-efficient customisation and speed of mass production alongside the product variety of a job shop.
   d. Relying on large work-in-progress inventories like a job shop and large raw material inventories like a mass production system.

10. The ability of an FMS to operate profitably at different production volumes is categorised as which type of flexibility?

    a. Machine flexibility.
    b. Routing flexibility.
    c. Volume flexibility.
    d. Market flexibility.

11. The chapter describes management accounting in an Industry 4.0 environment as becoming 'black-boxed'. What is the primary implication of this phenomenon?

    a. Management accounting information is no longer relevant for decision-making in an FMS.
    b. Accounting functionalities become embedded within complex, automated software systems, making their underlying logic less visible and contestable.
    c. Accountants must revert to manual, paper-based ledgers because digital systems are too complex.
    d. The cost of accounting software, such as SAP, outweighs its benefits in a flexible manufacturing environment.

1.6 Meso- and macro-level flexibility

12. The theory of 'flexible specialisation' contrasts with a purely techno-managerial view of flexible manufacturing by emphasising that:

    a. A firm's flexibility depends solely on its investment in the latest robotic technology.
    b. Achieving flexibility is contingent upon inter-firm coordination and supportive regional or national institutional arrangements.
    c. All production should be vertically integrated within a single, large corporation to ensure control.
    d. The market alone is a sufficient mechanism to coordinate innovation and competition between firms.

13. In the core-periphery model of labour under 'flexible accumulation', the 'core' group of employees is primarily responsible for:

    a. Performing deskilled, manual labour on a temporary contract basis.
    b. Providing outsourced support services like security and catering.
    c. Handling strategic competencies and performing immaterial labour, such as symbolic-analytical and communicative tasks.
    d. Clerical and administrative tasks that require skills readily available in the general labour market.

Section 2: Structured assessment questions – synthesis and critical analysis

2.1 Matching theorists to concepts

1. Match the theorists in Column A with their primary associated concept from Column B. Write the corresponding letter from Column B next to the number in Column A.

Column A: Theorist	Column B: Concept
1. Harvey	a) The immaterialization of labour (symbolic-analytical, communicative, affective).
2. Piore and Sabel	b) The strategic importance of 'core competencies' in corporate restructuring.
3. Hardt and Negri	c) Flexible accumulation and the development of a core-periphery labour market.
4. Prahalad and Hamel	d) Flexible specialisation as a model of industrial development based on inter-firm coordination.

2.2 Diagram interpretation: the logic of flexible machines

2. Referring to Figure 8.2, write a short paragraph that explains:

   a. What the curves SC1 and SC2 represent in the context of production setup costs.
   b. Why does the optimal production quantity reduce when flexible machines are introduced?
   c. The ultimate implication of setup costs approaching zero for a firm pursuing a 'mass customisation' strategy.

2.3 Table analysis: synthesising production models

3. Using the information in Table 8.1, explain in your own words how a Flexible Manufacturing System (FMS) negates the traditional trade-off between the strategic focus of a job shop and that of a mass production system. In your answer, you must refer to at least three of the following comparative dimensions: 'Strategic focus and intention', 'Nature of the fixed capital', and 'Labour'.

2.4 Scenario application: identifying forms of labour

4. A global technology firm operates with a dispersed workforce. Consider the following three roles:

    a. Anya is a software engineer who uses programming languages to solve complex coding problems and develop new algorithms for the company's AI platform.

    b. Ben is a supply chain coordinator who works remotely, using a networked enterprise resource planning (ERP) system to manage the flow of components from factories in Southeast Asia to assembly plants in Mexico and markets in Europe. His role is to ensure seamless information flow and coordination between these deterritorialized sites.

    c. Carla is a Human Resources Business Partner whose primary responsibility is to develop and implement programmes focused on employee well-being, diversity and inclusion, and creating a positive and supportive corporate culture.

    For each employee, identify the primary form of 'immaterial labour' (symbolic-analytical, communicative, or affective) they are performing, according to the framework by Hardt and Negri. Briefly justify each choice.

2.5 Critical Interpretation: The Core-Periphery Model

5. Examine Figure 8.4, which illustrates the circulation and peripheralization of labour. Explain the model's central argument regarding the reorganisation of labour under flexible accumulation. Your explanation must:

    a. Define the characteristics of the 'core', the 'first peripheral group', and the 'second peripheral group'.

    b. Explain how this structure provides both 'functional flexibility' for the core and 'numerical flexibility' for the periphery.

Comprehension questions

1. Briefly explain why flexibility should be considered a strategic imperative alongside quality and cost management.
2. List the six key concepts associated with flexible manufacturing.
3. Explain flexible consumption, paying special attention to how it synthesizes the strategic intentions of buyers and producers in a competitive market.
4. List and explain the two forms of capacities that a producer needs to build to operationalize flexible consumption as a strategic intention.
5. Differentiate between the traditional business model and the flexible manufacturing business model.
6. What is meant by a flexible machine? Explain using appropriate examples.
7. Using classical economic optimization logic pertaining to production batch size, explain the management accounting logic of flexible machines.
8. Explain the notion of flexible labour, paying attention to the skill and time aspects of flexibilization.
9. Drawing on Hardt and Negri's notions of the immaterialization of labour, explain how the nature of labour is transformed in high-tech production systems with digitally connected flexible machines. Pay special attention to the following concepts:

    a. Symbolic-analytical labour.
    b. Communicative labour.
    c. Affective labour.

10. List and explain some critical political-economic dynamics underpinning the time flexibilization of labour.
11. What is an FMS? Briefly explain.
12. Explain how an FMS synthesizes traditional job shop production systems and mass production systems.
13. With suitable examples of subcategories, briefly describe the following types of flexibilities associated with an FMS:

    a. a. Basic or element flexibilities.
    b. b. System flexibilities.
    c. c. Aggregate flexibilities.

14. Explain what is meant by Industry 4.0.
15. List key technologies that constitute Industry 4.0.
16. Explain how Industry 4.0 technologies enable flexible manufacturing.
17. Explain how Industry 4.0 technologies complicate management accounting functionalities in a flexible manufacturing environment.

18. Briefly explain the theory of flexible specialization.
19. What are the different types of industrial arrangements that facilitate the evolution of flexible specialization?
20. Explain the concept of flexible accumulation.
21. In relation to the concept of flexible accumulation, explain the following:

    a. The core.
    b. First peripheral group.
    c. Second peripheral group.

Explore further

1. There are numerous online consultocratic discourses on flexible manufacturing, encompassing promotional materials from consulting firms and software vendors such as SAP. Identify the key organisational actors involved, such as Big Four accounting firms, major consulting firms, and leading software and platform vendors. These sources offer valuable insights into the evolution of Industry 4.0 technologies and their impact on reshaping the industrial landscape. Select a few prominent materials as a sample for review.

    a. Utilizing sociological and theoretical concepts introduced in this chapter, particularly the theory of flexible accumulation, compose an essay titled "Industry 4.0 Capitalism."
    b. Using the materials reviewed for task 1, elucidate how technology providers, as highlighted, consider the notion of sustainability in their efforts to advance "Industry 4.0 Capitalism."

Develop your critical argumentation skills

1. Write an argumentative essay on the theme:

    > "While techno-managerial innovations at the point of production play a critical role, there are equally important political-economic and regulatory dynamics that underpin the possibilities of achieving flexible manufacturing."

2. Craft an argumentative essay on the theme:

    > "In ever-evolving regimes of flexible manufacturing, the management accounting functionalities become 'black-boxed' into highly complicated software and analytical platforms, yet their functionalities matter more than ever."

3. Develop an argumentative essay on the theme:

> "Regimes of flexible manufacturing, politically characterized by flexible accumulation, point to a global order of production where the tyrannies of labour control are peripheralized to the Third World while a privileged class of labour is created at the centers of contemporary capitalism."

References

Adler, P. S., B. Goldoftas, and D. I. Levine. 1999. Flexibility Versus Efficiency? A Case Study of Model Changeovers in the Toyota Production System. Organization Science 10 (1):43-68.

Alawattage, C., and D. Wickramasinghe. 2019. Strategizing Management Accounting: Liberal Origins and Neoliberal Trends. London: Routledge.

———. 2022. Strategising management accounting: liberal origins and neoliberal trends. Accounting, Auditing & Accountability Journal 35 (2):518-546.

Braverman, H. 1998. Labor and monopoly capital: the degradation of work in the twentieth century. 25th anniversary ed. New York: Monthly Review Press.

Cooper, C. 2015. Entrepreneurs of the self: The development of management control since 1976. Accounting, Organizations and Society 47:14-24.

Deloitte. 2018. The shift to flexible consumption: how to make an "as a service" business model work. Deloitte Insight.

Gertler, M. S. 1988. The Limits of Flexibility: Comments on the Post-Fordist Vision of Production and Its Geography. Transactions of the Institute of British Geographers 13 (4):419-432.

Halal, W. E. 1986. The new capitalism. New York; Chichester: Wiley.

Hardt, M. 1999. Affective labour. Boundary 2 26 (2):89-100.

Hardt, M., and A. Negri. 2000. Empire. Cambridge, Mass.; London: Harvard University Press.

———. 2017. Assembly: Oxford University Press.

Harvey, D. 1989. The condition of postmodernity: an enquiry into the origins of cultural change. Oxford: Basil Blackwell.

———. 1990. Flexible Accumulation through Urbanization: Reflections on "Post-Modernism" in the American City. Perspecta 26:251-272.

Hirst, P., and J. Zeitlin. 1991. Flexible specialization versus post-Fordism: theory, evidence and policy implications. Economy and Society 20 (1):5 - 9.

Javaid, M., A. Haleem, R. P. Singh, and R. Suman. 2022. Enabling flexible manufacturing system (FMS) through the applications of industry 4.0 technologies. Internet of Things and Cyber-Physical Systems 2:49-62.

Kanter, R. M. 1990. When Giants Learn to Dance: Free Press.

Lash, S., and J. Urry. 1987. The end of organized capitalism. Cambridge: Polity.

Maleki, R. A. 1991. Flexible manufacturing systems: the technology and management. Englewood Cliffs, N.J.: Prentice Hall.

Miller, P., and T. O'Leary. 1994. Accounting, "economic citizenship" and the spatial reordering of manufacture. Accounting, Organizations and Society 19 (1):15-43.

Miyajima, H. 1994. The Transformation of Zaibatsu to Postwar Corporate Groups—From Hierarchically Integrated Groups to Horizontally Integrated Groups. Journal of the Japanese and International Economies 8 (3):293-328.

Munro, I. 2012. The Management of Circulations: Biopolitical Variations after Foucault. International Journal of Management Reviews 14 (3):345-362.

Piore, M. J., and C. F. Sabel. 1984. The second industrial divide: possibilities for prosperity. New York, N.Y.: Basic Books.

Porter, M. E. 1998. Clusters and the new economics of competition. Harvard Business Review 1998 (November-December):77-90.

Prahalad, C. K., and G. Hamel. 1990. The core competence of the corporation. Harvard Business Review 1990 (May-June):79-90.

PwC. 2016. Industry 4.0: Building the digital enterprise: 2016 Global Industry 4.0 survey. www.pwc.com/industry40: PWC.

Standing, G. 2011. The precariat: the new dangerous class. London: Bloomsbury Academic.

Swyngedouw, E. 1986. The Socio-Spatial Implications of Innovations in Industrial Organisation: JIT Manufacturing and Regional Production Milieus. In Working Paper, No.20, Johns Hopkins European Center For Regional Planning and Research.

Wagner, E. L., J. Moll, and S. Newell. 2011. Accounting logics, reconfiguration of ERP systems, and the emergence of new accounting practices: A sociomaterial perspective. Management Accounting Research 22 (3):181-197.

CHAPTER 9 Strategising the point of production: **strategic cost management**

9.1 Introduction

After exploring strategic themes such as market positioning, pricing, performance management, management control, organisational resilience, quality, and flexibility, this textbook concludes with two final themes: cost management and sustainability. These themes are interconnected, enabling firms to navigate the strategic challenges of neoliberalised, globalised, digitalised, and virtualised competitive landscapes. Cost management and sustainability culminate this interdependency; they encapsulate all other strategic themes.

In strategic cost management - the subject of this chapter - this encapsulation is operational and processual, manifesting how a firm reconfigures its vertical and horizontal economic relationships to produce strategically advantageous value propositions. Sustainability, the subject of the next chapter, manifests this encapsulation by explaining how such ordering of value creation enhances or disturbs the ecological and socio-political orders bearing on everyone's collective future existence.

The sites where strategies are enabled and enacted – the market, organisational hierarchy, and point of production – are not mutually exclusive. How a firm interconnects these sites through its decisions and actions enables and enacts strategies, creating competitive advantages. For example, marketing mix decisions predominantly concern how a firm positions itself in the market vis-à-vis competitors. However, these decisions also relate to how such decisions are made and actions are organised within the organisational hierarchy. They are additionally connected to how a value chain is designed to produce and deliver the value proposition.

Similarly, strategic performance management, strategic control, and organisational resilience are predominantly hierarchy-related issues. Nevertheless, they must also address how performances are managed, controlled, and made resilient to market vulnerabilities at the point of production. Quality and flexibility primarily concern how value-creation processes at the points of production are designed and managed, but always in relation to the market dynamics that the hierarchy's performance management and control apparatuses communicate to those points.

Cost management underpins this triadic interdependency more vigorously, as costs occur in all three sites. Although schematically located at the point of production, its presence is pervasive. Strategic cost management requires revisiting these themes to see how cost underpins their strategic possibilities.

This chapter is structured as follows.

Section 9.2 serves as a prelude to strategic cost management. It examines the traditional approach to cost management, focusing on the role of responsibility accounting, which includes standard costing and budgeting. This section will enable you to understand the structures and methods of traditional cost management and to recognize their strategic limitations.

Section 9.3 delves into the realm of strategic cost management. It contrasts the concept of strategic cost management as a holistic program with its role as a surveillant assemblage. This section aims to highlight the complexities in perceiving strategic cost management as a unified framework.

- Section 9.4 focuses on activity-based costing and management, a cornerstone of strategic cost management. You will explore the strategic implications of activity-based costing and management, particularly its impact on manufacturing flexibility, quality management, continuous improvement, and strategic market positioning.
- Section 9.5 revisits target costing, initially discussed in Chapter 3, but from a strategic cost management perspective. This section offers a refresher on Chapter 3's content and demonstrates how target costing functions within strategic cost management.
- Section 9.6 provides an overview of lean manufacturing, emphasizing its role as the techno-philosophical foundation for various strategic cost management concepts and methods.
- Section 9.7 examines enterprise resource planning (ERP), introducing its historical context and the key modular elements of contemporary ERP systems.

- Section 9.8 explores throughput accounting and the theory of constraints. This section focuses on capacity optimization as a critical aspect of cost management.
- Section 9.9 concludes the chapter with a comprehensive summary.

9.2 From costing to cost management: the traditional approach

Since capitalism's inception, when wealth accumulation became synonymous with capital accumulation, cost and cost management have been formalised in accounting, embodying capital's calculative apparatuses. Accounting facilitated the periodic calculation of wealth accumulation, recognising profit as the rate at which capital accumulates within an accounting period. A double-entry bookkeeping system, with a capital account recording the net difference between revenue and costs, laid the foundational calculative groundwork. Since then, cost calculations, or costing, have become indispensable to any capitalist organisation, crucial for periodic profit assessments.

The possibility of cost management, however, emerged only later with factories during industrial capitalism. Before that, in mercantile capitalism, capitalists purchased goods from farmers, craftsmen, and guild masters and sold them in output markets. Their ability to 'negotiate' determined their costs and revenue. Costs primarily consisted of prices set in factor markets (i.e., prices paid for goods-for-sale and services such as transport). Cost management involved negotiating lower prices, either 'diplomatically' or 'coercively', leveraging available power, as seen in colonial trade. Such negotiations were often reinforced by despotic forms of labour controls available to expedite trading work.

In this phase, capitalists did not 'own' production processes; they bought output from farmers, craftsmen, and guild masters. Consequently, capitalists had little control over production costs or volumes to meet market demand. The factory was the solution: capitalists acquired labour, rather than its product, and controlled that labour to manufacture goods at the required costs and volume. For Marxist researchers like Hopper and Armstrong (1991), this shift was driven by the need to subordinate labour to capital. For Johnson and Kaplan (1987a, 1987b), it was a hierarchical system to minimise transaction costs compared to the market. For Foucauldian researchers (see Hopper and Macintosh 1993), the factory became a 'disciplinary institution' that synchronised labour with productive machinery through principles and techniques that disciplined the body, mind, and time.

Standardisation as a basis of traditional cost management

From this 'disciplinary' perspective, what emerged was not just the 'factory' but a more potent 'discipline': manufacturing or industrial engineering. Here, a 'discipline' denotes a body of knowledge (like medicine or industrial engineering) established as a 'science' independent of craftsmanship, tradition, or workers' cultural knowledge. A discipline encapsulates 'scientific' principles and practices involving normalisation/standardisation, surveillance, hierarchical examination, and regulation. The 'Scientific Management Movement', pioneered by Frederick W. Taylor, embodied this 'disciplinary' approach through the 'rationalisation of work', which included 'standardisation' (see Alawattage and Wickramasinghe 2019, 35).

From its beginnings, a critical element of cost management has been standardisation. Initially emerging through scientific management's motion and time studies, standardisation prescribes the 'standard method' and 'performance levels' (time and quantities) for each job. Standard time and quantities are then coupled with standard prices and payment rates to create cost standards. Cost standards represent the monetary value of job processes at management-established efficiency levels, embodying ideal production conditions.

Standard costing and variance analysis became the bedrock of traditional cost management. Organised within 'responsibility accounting' structures (as discussed in Chapter 4), standard costing provides a distributed cost management system where actual costs are compared with standards to identify variances, holding responsibility centre managers accountable.

In a responsibility accounting system, standard costs serve as the basis for budget preparation. Budgets are the foundation upon which costs are authenticated and performances assessed across cost centres. Integrating standard costing and budgeting forms a comprehensive, organisation-wide profit planning and control system. The link is established by five common principles (Boyns 1998, 265):

- The establishment of predetermined standards or targets of performance.
- The measurement of actual performance.
- The comparison of actual performance with predetermined standards.
- The disclosure of variances between actual and standard performance and the reasons for such variances.
- The suggestion of corrective actions if necessary.

Coupling standardisation with budgeting

Though interrelated, they are not interdependent. Standard costing can operate without budgeting, and vice versa, but their usefulness in isolation is limited. One supplements the other; integration results in a better profit planning and control system. Integration is sought because their applications and approaches differ:

- Standard costing's historical roots are linked to scientific management, whereas budgeting has deeper roots in state bureaucracy.
- Standard costing is generally applied in manufacturing activities, i.e., to 'standard cost centres', where output can be measured and input specified. Non-manufacturing activities are often not included. Budgeting, however, can also be applied to non-manufacturing activities.
- Budgets relate to an entire activity or operation. A standard presents the same information on a unit basis. Standard costing thus often provides the basis for calculating budgeted figures.
- Budgeting represents a top-down approach: preparation starts with aggregated figures (sales, profits) and moves down to elementary budgets (material purchase). Standard costing employs a bottom-up approach: it starts with predetermined unit standards and calculates aggregates based on actual volumes.
- Budgeting provides figures on future targets (management expectations for the period). Standard costing provides 'figures that should have been' for the realised performance level.
- Budgeting relates more to management's planning and delegation functions, while standard costing relates more to the controlling function.

These differences and common principles imply both unique and shared operational domains for budgeting and standard costing. Figure 9.1 illustrates these domains and an integrative ideal system.

Processual elements of traditional cost management and profit planning

We can now delve into Figure 9.1 to elucidate how traditional cost management operates within a responsibility accounting system of standard costing and budgeting.

1. Standard costing establishes standards for output and input of materials, labour, and production overheads. These typically encompass standard prices/rates, standard mixes, and standard usage (e.g., labour hours per unit of output, material consumption per unit of production, etc.). These standards are usually set during product and process design and revised based on experience. Non-accounting functions like Operations Management, R&D, and Marketing provide essential information.

Figure 9.1: Standard costing and budgeting as cost management and profit planning.

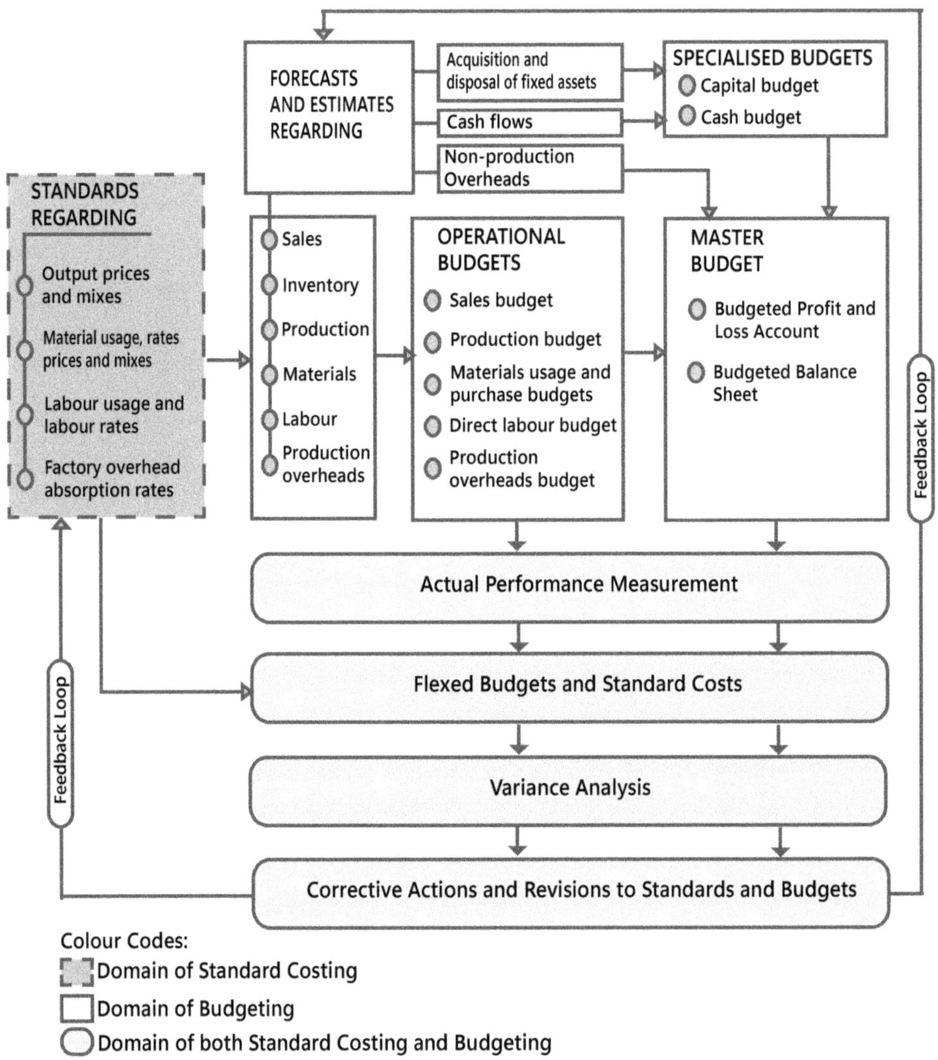

2. Budgeting involves periodic forecasts and estimates for aggregate operational levels, including sales, production, and inventory targets. These forecasts derive from corporate or strategic planning exercises. Long-term planning determines strategic goals (e.g., market share), which are translated into annual sales targets that form the basis for other estimates.

3. Operational budgets represent targets for sales, production, material usage, material purchase, direct labour usage, and production overheads. Expressed in quantitative or monetary terms, they are derived by combining standards with budgetary estimates.
4. Budgeting also includes forecasts and estimates for 'non-operational' aspects, including fixed asset acquisitions/disposals, cash flows, and non-production overheads. Various functional departments source these estimates. Cash flow estimates, for example, relate to sales, purchases, and debt collection policies. These inform specialised budgets: the capital budget (approved capital expenditure) and the cash budget (monthly cash position).
5. These specialised budgets, along with operational budgets and non-production overhead estimates, are summarised in the master budget (budgeted profit and loss account and balance sheet).
6. These budgets provide a framework guiding day-to-day managerial actions. Managers are delegated authority and responsibility to meet these objectives. At the end of the period, deviations from expectations necessitate variance analysis to identify their specific causes.
7. Variance analysis, the intersection of standard costing and budgeting, requires 'flexing' the budget to reflect actual performance. This involves updating the 'static budget' with actual volumes using elementary standards (standard prices, labour/material usage). Variances represent the differences between 'flexed' and actual budget figures. Variance analysis provides a hierarchical structure for understanding profit variances. Profit variance is explained by sales and cost variances, which are then analysed into elementary categories (material, labour, overhead) and their causes (e.g., price and quantity).

9.3 Strategic cost management

The traditional cost management regime was deemed 'irrelevant' (Johnson and Kaplan 1987a) given the new competitive conditions. Critiques underscored its inadequacy in addressing the evolving competitive landscape. For instance, the 'beyond budgeting movement' contended that conventional budgets were too rigid and inflexible. They were criticised for fixating on predetermined targets, using a time-consuming annual cycle, emphasising inputs over outcomes, and fostering internal competition for resource allocations (see Hope and Fraser 1997, 2000, 2001, 2003a, 2003b). Similarly, responsibility accounting was argued to lack a strategic orientation and to fail to adapt to new competitive conditions.

Consultocratic discourses identify the following fundamental issues with the traditional approach, arguing that they must be corrected for a strategic approach:

- **Focus on historical data:** Traditional budgeting relies heavily on past performance. In dynamic industries, this may not reflect future conditions. SCM should emphasise forward-looking approaches.
- **Lack of alignment with strategy:** Traditional systems may not align with strategic goals. Contemporary conditions require close alignment and the allocation of resources to support strategic objectives.
- **Inability to capture non-financial metrics:** Traditional systems focus solely on financial metrics, overlooking crucial non-financial aspects like customer satisfaction, innovation, and employee engagement.
- Globalisation and complex supply chains: Traditional systems may struggle to capture the intricacies of global operations and complex supply chains.
- **Technology and automation:** Traditional systems may not fully leverage technology. SCM embraces technology to enhance efficiency.
- **Customer-centric focus:** Traditional cost management may not sufficiently align costs with customer value. SCM emphasises understanding customer needs.
- **Lean and agile principles:** Traditional systems may be too bureaucratic, hindering the adoption of lean and agile practices essential to competitiveness.

The need for flexibility, strategic alignment, consideration of non-financial metrics, technological adaptation, and market responsiveness drives the shift towards strategic cost management. Traditional systems fall short, making them less relevant. These ideas encapsulate previous discussions. This is why strategic cost management requires revisiting all themes covered in this book.

Strategic cost management as a holistic program and surveillant assemblage.

A strategic cost management system with these capabilities would not be a structured hierarchical model like traditional responsibility accounting. Instead, it manifests as a diverse, dynamic amalgamation of technologies and practices, paradoxically oriented towards contradictory imperatives such as accurate costing, control, return on investment, multi-dimensional performance evaluation, strategic positioning, quality, flexibility, innovation, customer satisfaction, and sustainability.

Acknowledging this complexity, Alawattage and Wickramasinghe (2019) characterise strategic cost management as both a 'surveillant assemblage' and a 'holistic program'. Theoretically, these terms represent contradictory dispositions and distinct understandings. They coexist, signifying the paradoxical nature of contemporary cost management.

Cost management as a holistic program reflects an aspiration for unity and essence. Its operation is characterised by convergence – the intention to bring disparate elements into a comprehensive unity, generating synergistic value. Here, strategy is perceived as the unifying force. Various discourses on costing, cost management, performance management, and control seek to harness strategy as a unifying principle, attempting to reconcile diverse elements.

For instance, Porterian and Kaplanian discourses encapsulate holism. Kaplan and colleagues argue that an effective strategy must amalgamate financial, customer, internal process, and learning and growth perspectives, operationalised via balanced scorecards and activity-based management. This forms a holistic program rooted in analysing, costing, and managing 'activities'. Similarly, Porterian ideas create a holistic approach through a unified framework integrating market strategies with the value chain, using strategic choices (differentiation, cost leadership) based on analyses of industry structure, the value chain, and competitor profiles.

Viewing cost management practices (activity-based costing, target costing, ERP, etc.) as a holistic program means understanding how they form a synergetic totality. The aim is to see how these techniques form a cohesive whole. Holism requires constructing a picture like a jigsaw puzzle, where costing techniques fit neatly as pieces.

The disposition of holism can appear illusory given the evolving, diverse nature of cost management technologies. Their unity becomes elusive as they take multiple forms. While strategy discourses advocate integration, the outcome often falls short of unity, leading to multiplicity.

Here, understanding strategic cost management as an assemblage (Deleuze and Guattari 1987, 1994) is useful. Nail (2017, 22) provides an insightful description:

> In contrast to organic unities, for Deleuze and Guattari, assemblages are more like machines, defined solely by their external relations of composition, mixture, and aggregation. In other words, an assemblage is a multiplicity, neither a part nor a whole. If the elements of an assemblage are defined only by their external relations, then it is possible that they can be added, subtracted, and recombined with one another ad infinitum without ever creating or destroying an organic unity. This is what Deleuze and Guattari paradoxically

> call a "fragmentary whole" (What is Philosophy? 16). The elements of the assemblage are "not pieces of a jigsaw puzzle," they say, but like a "dry-stone wall, and everything holds together only along diverging lines" (What is Philosophy? 23). Each new mixture produces a new kind of assemblage, always free to recombine again and change its nature.

From this perspective, strategic cost management embodies heterogeneity, combining and recombining technologies and practices into a 'fragmented whole'. Technologies are continuously added, subtracted, and recombined, rendering them fragmented and open to further recombination, thus changing their nature. These changes occur as events. For instance, adding activity-based costing and subtracting absorption costing unfold as events.

Therefore, viewing strategic cost management as an assemblage requires treating its elements as 'events', in contrast to the 'jigsaw puzzle' view of holism. In Deleuze's theory, an event is a significant happening. Events introduce novelty and unpredictability, causing transformation. They are not predetermined but emerge from immanent processes. Deleuze and Guattari emphasise the non-linear, open-ended nature of events. Events introduce new possibilities, and their impact can lead to reconfiguration or reorganisation (see Patton 1997).

Subsequent sections apply this perspective, elucidating the 'eventuality' of SCM techniques. Tracing eventuality involves considering a technique as an event and tracing its connections to preceding and succeeding events.

Surveillance is central to elucidating the eventualities of cost management. SCM operationalises heterogeneous, fragmented surveillance when seen as 'surveillant assemblages' (Haggerty and Ericson 2000). This occurs not hierarchically (like Foucault's panopticon or Orwell's 'Big Brother') but by making and recording discrete observations across rhizomatically distributed spaces and calculation centres.

Contemporary surveillance amalgamates computers (for recording and analysing) with optics (such as cameras and barcode/QR code readers, for observation). This combination's impact constitutes surveillance in fragmented spaces, unveiling the imperceptible and subjecting it to control.

Integrated with Industry 4.0 technologies, many cost management techniques form this surveillance assemblage. This chapter focuses on these key elements:

1. Activity-based costing and management: A foundational step towards SCM.
2. Target costing: Consolidates SCM efforts.

3. Lean manufacturing: The philosophy underpinning SCM.
4. Enterprise resource planning: The software infrastructure.
5. Throughput accounting and theory of constraints: Maximising capacity utilisation

9.4 Foundational steps toward strategic cost management: activity-based costing and management

Popularised by their consultocratic engagements and associated 'actor-networks' (Cooper et al. 2017; Jones and Dugdale 2002), Norton and Kaplan's activity-based costing (ABC) considerably influenced SCM's evolution. Jones and Dugdale (2002) reveal that ABC's 'eventuality' is closely linked to an 'epistemic context' that emerged around Harvard Business School and Computer-Aided Manufacturing International (CAM-I). These epistemic actor-networks addressed eroding US competitiveness against Japanese firms, whose success was recognised as stemming from superior use of advanced manufacturing technologies such as just-in-time (JIT) and total quality management (TQM) (Jones and Dugdale 2002, 126). There was an understanding that long-run, large-batch production might be obsolete given emerging 'flexible manufacturing' and 'segmented market positioning' regimes (see Armstrong 2002; Jones and Dugdale 2002, and chapters 3 and 8). Activity-based costing was an event written into these preceding eventualities of addressing the problem of US competitiveness. It was aimed at aligning cost accounting with advanced manufacturing technologies, flexible manufacturing, and segmented market positioning that engineers and managers were promoting in response to the Japanese Challenge.

Traditional absorption costing came under scrutiny, viewed as a hindrance to integrating advanced manufacturing technologies. It was criticised for distorting 'true cost', potentially misguiding managers with inaccurate pricing, flawed marketing, and skewed competitiveness perceptions. ABC emerged as a remedy. Kaplan and colleagues argued ABC allocates overheads more 'accurately' using 'real cost drivers' rather than 'arbitrary overhead absorption bases'. A 'cost hierarchy' was introduced, categorising activities into four levels: unit, batch, product-sustaining, and facility-sustaining. The objective was to attribute the first three types to the product, reserving the last for plant-level allocation. This redefined many 'overheads' as directly attributable, variable costs.

Technical procedures for ABC were established and popularised through Harvard Business School publications. ABC implementation was facilitated by rapid IT development, particularly in networking, real-time data processing, and expert system integration. These were incorporated into accounting and ERP packages.

Consequently, many companies adopted ERP systems with ABC modules (Jones and Dugdale, 2002). Numerous texts (by Kaplan, Cooper, and others) and Harvard case studies detail the technicalities. Creating these packages and knowledge bases, coupled with consultancy, evolved into a multi-billion-dollar business, creating a market for developing further epistemic products associated with ABC/M.

As a product costing method, ABC's fundamental process involves:

1. Reorganising the cost hierarchy as activity-related by recognising how activities are hierarchically related to the cost object.
    a. Unit-level costs: Vary with each unit produced; align with variable costs in traditional systems.
    b. Batch-level costs: Incurred for a batch of products (e.g., machine set-up, quality control), arising from activities performed for a group of units.
    c. Product-sustaining costs: Incurred to support specific products (e.g., product design, engineering, marketing), not tied to units produced but to the product's existence.
    d. Facility-sustaining costs: Support the entire facility (e.g., rent, general administration); often considered fixed.
2. Identifying specific activities driving different cost categories: Emphasis is placed on activities associated with batch-, product-, and facility-sustaining costs. Unlike traditional costing, this underscores that activities are the true cost incidents. To enhance accuracy, costs are traced to the cost object through activities.
3. Determining activity cost driver rates: The 'activity cost driver rate' is established for each cost driver activity, forming the basis for tracing costs. It is computed by dividing the total periodic cost of the activity pool by the activity volume for that period.
4. Tracing unit cost: The final step traces the unit cost based on the activity cost driver rates.

Activity-based costing's strategic significance

ABC marked a significant strategic shift from traditional absorption costing methods, yielding two interconnected effects:

1. Cost controllability effect.
2. Strategic effect.

Activity-based costing's controllability effect

When overhead was absorbed based on direct labour cost, controlling overheads was simplified to managing direct labour, since it was assumed to be the primary driver. The conventional system disclosed how facilities were consumed by labour/machine hours. Instead of revealing true overhead 'drivers', it 'black-boxed' them, making only the direct labour process visible for managerial control. Consequently, direct labourers' wages, hours, and production rates became the controllable bases for cost management (Armstrong 2002). Conventional absorption costing made the factory labour process visible but obscured overheads.

This meant staff departments (e.g., HR, Marketing, Accounting) were exempt from accounting surveillance. These 'staff costs' were deemed 'fixed', making them immune to performance measurement and control. This fixed nature resulted from a lack of techniques for linking staff costs to cost objects and from a 'hierarchical privilege' that protected staff from top management control. Accountants asserted that staff costs were not determined by output units (the traditional basis for controllability). Consequently, these costs were placed directly into the income statement, implying they were 'uncontrollable'. Armstrong (2002, 100) observed, 'Employment in the staff department, on the other hand, remained relatively secure, depending on the abilities of its representatives to convince the rest of the management team of the importance of the services which it provided'. This concealed staff activities and their cost implications.

Standard costing imposed accountability on production workers, raising the question 'who controls the controllers?'. Competitive pressures and the need for cost efficiency prompted exploration into uncharted territories, including staff functions. ABC provided the basis for this, opening up staff's activities as the basis for understanding cost variability and controllability (Armstrong 2002).

With ABC, cost management now costs not only products but all functional entities – people, knowledge, customers, relationships – by reconstituting them as 'activities' that consume resources. New cost and activity pools were identified, interconnected by cost drivers. These interconnections became the basis for 'cost driver rates' through which staff time and activities became attributable to cost objects (Innes et al. 2000). This allows managers to calculate 'true costs', set 'correct prices', and 'strategically position' cost objects.

Activities became visible through activity cost analysis, enabling capital to maximise labour efficiency. The managerial labour process, once a 'black box' under traditional regimes, is now open to perpetual scrutiny (Armstrong 2002). This prompted constant reassessment of staff functions. A new doctrine emerged: all staff costs must be justified by their 'value-added' contribution, or be deemed redundant. Business process re-engineering, TQM, and lean manufacturing facilitated this shift. Armstrong (2002, 102) observed:

> In its prescription of multi-functional committees as means of implementation..., ABC promised the production function a major say in determining the services of which it bore the cost. As part of the same deal, the scrutiny of staff departments through which its activities were to be established could be used to reveal any which were 'non-value added', ...thus creating respectable front for the productivist suspicion that quite a lot of staff activity is of no value at all. It is no accident that the some of the most successful applications of ABC have been initiated by operational managers ...and also no accident that some applications have resulted in job losses in the staff departments... In summary, ABC ... proposed that staff department should be subjected to regimes of accountability similar to those already experienced by manufacturing.

ABC began dismantling the 'fixed cost' shelter for staff functions. This gained momentum when Kaplan and Cooper expanded ABC to Activity-Based Management (ABM). Critiques of ABC's narrow focus prompted Kaplan and Cooper to underscore that their project encompassed ABM, offering a broader cost management perspective rather than just cost accounting (see Armstrong 2002; Drennan and Kelly 2002; Jones and Dugdale 2002). ABM extended ABC's 'vertical or cost assignment view' to a 'horizontal or process view' (Figure 9.2). Thus, Kaplan and Cooper argued it was not merely a cost accounting task; engineers and operations managers also needed to contribute.

Beyond calculating 'true' costs, ABM mandated focus on the 'strategic use of resources and time'. This involved analysing activities, eliminating unnecessary costs, and continuously revising work processes. Functional managers were no longer seen as 'cost centres' but as 'self-entrepreneurial consumers' of resources. They had to justify their resource consumption, transforming their roles to minimise costs and create value for 'internal customers'. This altered the organisational hierarchy into a social integration and surveillance system, redesigning processes to identify internal and external customers.

Activity-based costing's strategic effect

ABC's control effect lies in unveiling opaque staff functions. Its strategic impact arises from its capacity to integrate with other strategizing elements, including market positioning, flexibility, quality management, and continuous improvement. This integration occurs when ABC is used for 'cost and activity analysis', not just product costing. Examples of this strategic effect include:

Figure 9.2: From ABC to ABM

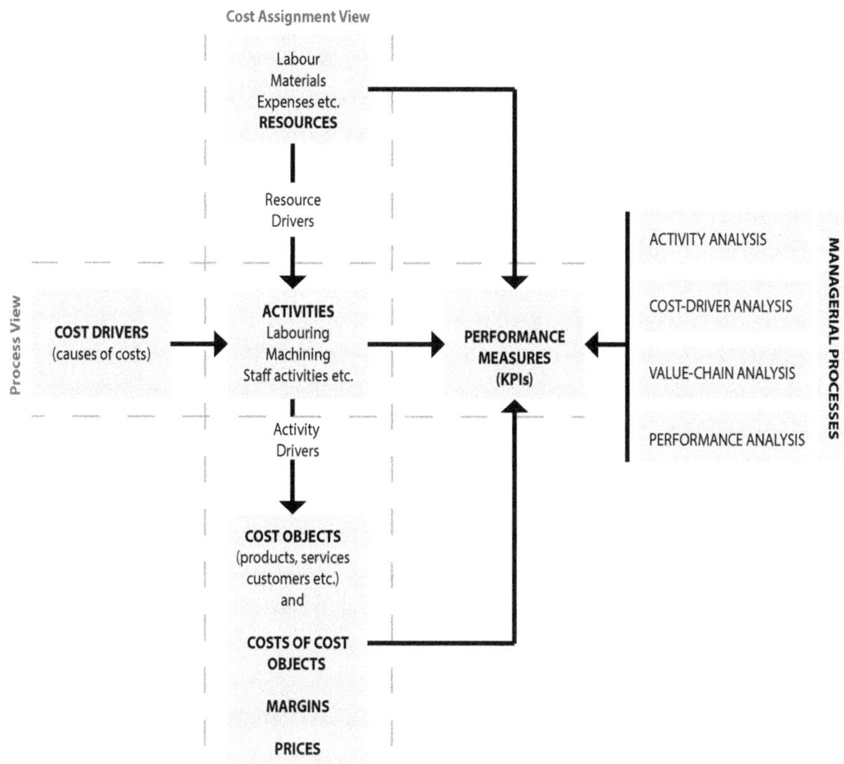

Source: Adapted from (Miller 1996, 236).

Contribution to flexibility:

A key conceptual transformation in ABC is reorganising the cost hierarchy (unit-level, batch-level, product-sustaining, and facility-sustaining activities). This reclassification transforms some previously fixed costs into variable costs. Consider break-even volume determination. ABC's reclassification often shifts the fixed cost curve downwards. Since the break-even point is fixed cost divided by unit contribution, a lower fixed-cost threshold means a lower required volume to break even. ABC thus provides a justification for flexible manufacturing with smaller production volumes.

Furthermore, manufacturing flexibility (labour, machines, systems) relies on the capability to re-engineer operational processes. ABC requires detailed activity analysis and cost assignment to each activity, providing a better understanding of resource consumption (including time). In this sense, ABC provides an accounting basis for flexibility.

Contribution to quality and continuous improvement:

Popular discourses commend ABC's integration with quality management and continuous improvement. For example, activity analysis and costing relate to target costing (see Chapter 3). The 'target costing triangle' (see Figure 3.7) emphasises strategic connections between customers, designers, and suppliers. ABC underlies these processes (Cooper and Slagmulder 1997).

Contribution to Strategic Market Positioning:

Popular strategy discourses consider ABC and activity analysis fundamental to operationalising Porterian generic strategies:

- Cost Leadership: ABC helps identify non-value-added activities, allowing focus on efficiency improvements and cost reduction.
- Differentiation: ABC assists in understanding costs of differentiating activities. By accurately assigning costs to features, organisations can make informed decisions about which features contribute most to differentiation.
- Focus: ABC aids focus strategies by providing insight into the costs of serving a specific niche, helping tailor strategies efficiently.

9.5 Consolidating strategic cost management through target costing

Target costing is a crucial pillar of SCM. Its significance lies in its ability to synthesise cost management facets that encompass this book's strategic imperatives. Target costing emphasises market positioning by crafting a value proposition that intertwines cost, quality, and functionality. It underscores the need to integrate three critical frontiers: the customer, the supplier, and the product designers. This integration is achieved through market-driven, product-level, and component-level target costing. Target costing also connects with value engineering, life-cycle costing, and inter-organisational costing.

As discussed in Chapter 3, target costing is grounded in lean manufacturing principles. The following points reinforce its key dimensions.

1. Target costing's doctrinal aspects derive from lean principles. Cooper and Slagmulder (1997, 3) explain the lean enterprise belief that single-piece flow is more efficient than batch-and-queue. Removing queues and inefficiencies enables faster reflexes, economies of scale at lower volumes, and greater efficiency, producing higher-quality, higher-functionality

products faster and at lower cost. Lean manufacturing concentrates on three imperatives: quality, cost, and functionality.

2. Lean manufacturing is based on waste minimisation; inventories are waste. Perfect quality is necessary for just-in-time (JIT) systems. Without buffer inventories (inherent in batch-and-queue) to substitute defects, JIT processes must halt when a defect is found until its cause is corrected. System quality (the probability of manufacturing non-defective elements) must be near-perfect to mitigate stoppage costs. Quality is thus critical to lean manufacturing and a fundamental requirement for target costing.
3. Lean manufacturing embodies a different competitive logic. Mass production strategies may seek non-confrontational space, leaving competitors out based on a sustainable cost advantage or differentiation. Lean competition assumes that no advantage is sustainable; competition is confrontational and based on continuous functional improvements. Functionality and continuous improvement are thus critical to target costing.
4. The lean basis of target costing is encapsulated in its 'survival zone' concept defined by the maxima and minima of quality, functionality, and price (cost) (see Chapter 3 and Figure 9.3, repeated from Figure 3.6). The survival zone defines the dynamic competitive arena, changing with competitors' improvements and innovations.

Figure 9.3: Survival zone – how lean manufacturing doctrines are encapsulated in target costing.

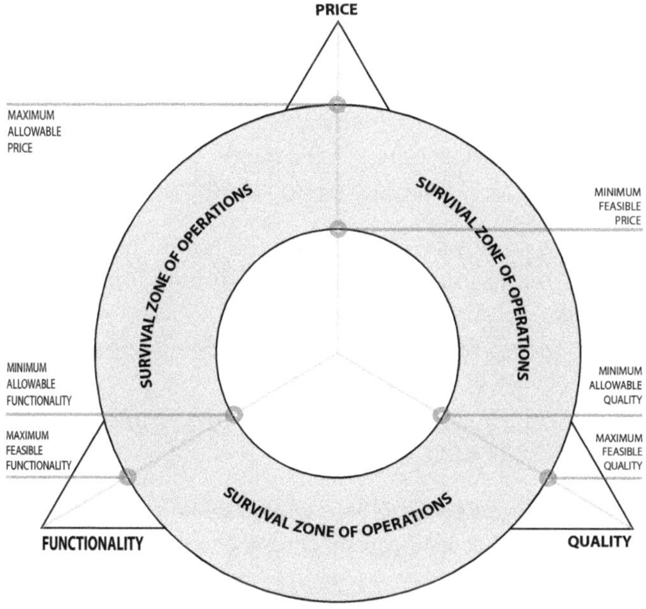

Source: adapted from Cooper and Slagmulder (1997,9)

5. As a system, target costing integrates three frontiers: the market (customers, competitors), internal designers, and suppliers. The 'target costing triangle' (see Chapter 3 and Figure 9.4) encapsulates this.

Figure 9.4: Target costing triangle – integrating three frontiers of decision-makers.

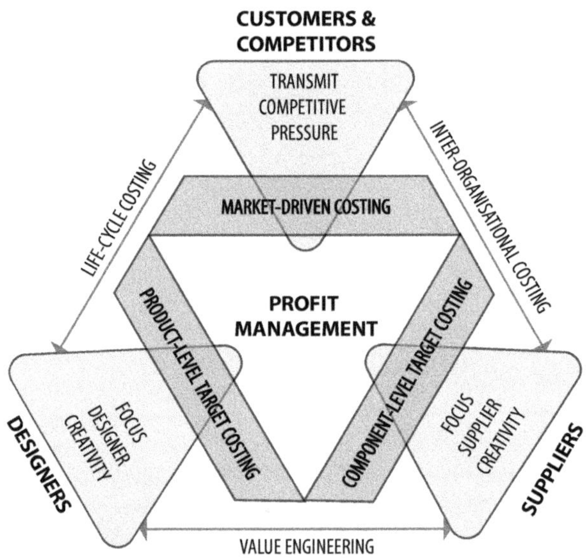

Source: adapted from Cooper and Slagmulder (1997,5)

6. Market-driven costing transmits competitive pressure by determining the market price and, in turn, the competitive cost. Guided by the survival zone, a target price is determined based on the quality and functionality required. Four key analyses are required:

    a. Technology analysis: Determines the technology roadmap.
    b. Product requirement analysis: Determines minimum quality functionalities.
    c. Market and competitor analysis: Determines the competitive quality and functionality levels.
    d. Financial analysis: Determines target profit and cost. This is facilitated by methods such as ABC.

7. Product-level target costing focuses designer creativity on market competition and supplier integration. Life-cycle costing is the key methodology for linking products/processes to market requirements. Value engi-

neering connects designers with suppliers.

8. Component-level target costing focuses on supplier creativity, ensuring components meet quality requirements at target costs. Inter-organisational costing (e.g., open-book accounting, supply chain ERPs) establishes operational and accounting connections.
9. Target costing is thus a structured approach to profit management, '*determining the lifecycle cost at which a proposed product with specified functionality and quality must be produced to generate the desired level of profitability over its life cycle when sold at its anticipated selling price*' (Cooper and Slagmulder 1997, 10).
10. Finally, target costing is a meticulous, continuous process, a permanent feature of management in a lean setting (see Figure 9.5, discussed in Chapter 3).

Figure 9.5: Target costing process

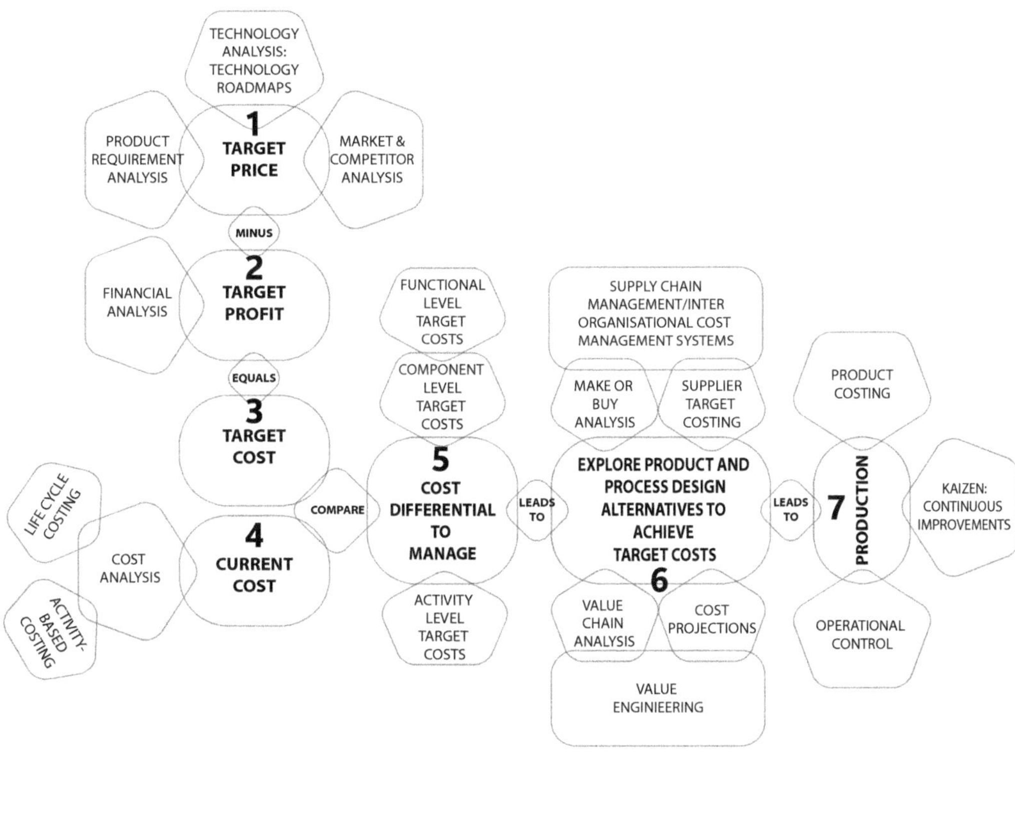

9.6 Lean manufacturing: a manufacturing philosophy that encapsulates strategic cost management.

Originating from the Toyota Production System (Monden 1994; Monden and Hamada 1991; Monden and Sakurai 1998), lean manufacturing is a philosophy dedicated to minimising waste while maximising efficiency and customer value through quality and flexibility. The essence of SCM is embedded in lean manufacturing. As discussed, target costing, flexibility, and quality costing correlate directly with lean principles.

Lean's fundamental elements have been examined extensively. The core idea (see Chapter 7) is to continuously improve workflows to facilitate small-lot and single-piece production with reduced lead times (Monden 1994). This philosophy creates the distinctive features of a lean system. Drawing from Monden (1994) (see Figure 9.6, repeated from Figure 7.4), key elements include:

1. Value: Determined by competitive conditions (price, quality, functionality). The system aims to enhance capabilities to deliver this value.
2. Reduction of lead time: Achieved by small lot/single-piece production, necessitating setup time reduction and manufacturing flexibilities (machine, labour, process standardisation, process layout).
3. Production smoothing: Balancing cycle times for producing varieties.
4. Kanban system: Sequentially connects production processes via a tag system, signalling type/quantity to be withdrawn/produced.
5. Pull system of production: Uses JIT, in which a process withdraws necessary units from the preceding process, which produces only enough to replace those withdrawn.
6. Flexible Manufacturing Scheduling: Adapts quantity to meet demand changes.
7. Waste Elimination: Focuses on eliminating all possible waste, identified as seven key sources: Transport, Inventory, Motion, Waiting, Overproduction, Overprocessing, and Defects.
8. Near-Perfect Quality: JIT (without buffer stocks) necessitates zero-defect quality. TQM is thus central, encompassing hard system elements (statistical process controls, autonomation or 'jidoka'—autonomous checks) and soft system aspects (quality circles, 'respect for humanity').

9.7 Enterprise resource planning: software infrastructure of managing contemporary organizations.

Previous sections emphasised planning and coordinating value chain activities. Enterprise Resource Planning (ERP) systems are crucial here, enhancing operational, cost management, and strategic capabilities. ERP systems are integrated software solutions that streamline and optimise business processes, providing real-time visibility and control. With Industry 4.0 technologies, ERPs have become internet- and cloud-based. Systems may be developed in-house or, increasingly, by vendors. For example, sales for the largest vendor, SAP, grew from <$500 million in 1992 to ~$3.3 billion in 2023.

ERPs evolved significantly from rudimentary pre-1970s inventory management systems. They were initially linked to calculating 'derived demand' (demand for components or raw materials) versus 'independent demand' (demand for final products). A key calculation was estimating purchase requirements, timing, and inventory levels to meet customer needs.

Figure 9.6: Material requirements planning – accounting logic

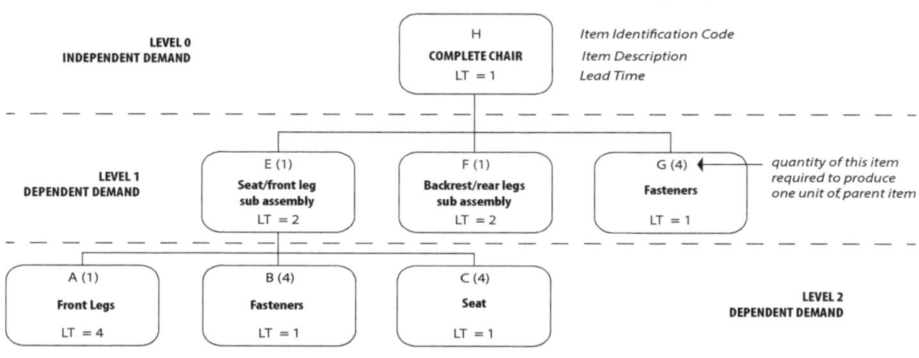

Item ID	Low Level Code	Lead Time Weeks	On Hand	Safety Stock	Allocated		Week 1	Week 2	Week 3	Week 4	Week 5	Week 6	Week 7	Week 8
H	0	1	8	5	0	Gross requirements								20
						Scheduled Receipts								
						Available	3	3	3	3	3	3	3	0
						Net Requirements								17
						Planned Order Receipts								17
						Planned Order Released							17	
E	1	2	30	5	20	Gross requirements							17	
						Scheduled Receipts								
						Available	5	5	5	5	5	5	0	
						Net Requirements							12	
						Planned Order Receipts							12	
						Planned Order Released					12			
B	2	1	20	20	5	Gross requirements					48			
						Scheduled Receipts								
						Available					-5			
						Net Requirements					53			
						Planned Order Receipts					53			
						Planned Order Released				53				

LT=1 (H: Week 7 ↔ Week 8); LT = 2 (E: Week 5 ↔ Week 7); LT=1 (B: Week 4 ↔ Week 5)

The illustration shows a partial calculation; the complexity increases with numerous products and the need to determine economic order quantities. The digitalisation of this process marked the start of ERP evolution, beginning with Material Requirements Planning I (MRP-I).

MRP-I emerged in the 1970s and operated on bulky mainframes. The 'database' concept was unknown. In 1978, SAP introduced the more integrated SAP R/2 system, enabling intermodule interaction and adding features such as order tracking (Jacobs and Weston 2007, 359).

In the 1980s, MRP evolved into Manufacturing Resource Planning (MRP-II), coinciding with the quality revolution and the shift to lean/flexible manufacturing. MRP extended beyond inventory to manufacturing planning, encompassing necessities such as flexible scheduling, line balancing, detailed cost reporting, enhanced shop-floor reporting, and process control. MRP-II systems evolved to cater to these needs in 'Japanised' factories.

A significant challenge arose: information fragmentation. Davenport (1998) notes large companies generate vast, scattered data across numerous systems, leading to high costs and hindering communication, impacting productivity and decision-making.

Contemporary ERP systems address fragmentation by offering MRP-II functionality with greater efficiency and integration, thanks to Industry 4.0 technologies. At an ERP's heart is a unified database serving global business functions, streamlining data collection and dissemination (Davenport 1998, 123). Figure 9.7 exemplifies this modular architecture.

ERP systems bolster cost management and strategic capabilities, enhancing organisational efficiency through integration, automation, and real-time insights. They enable informed decisions, cost reduction, and strategic positioning. However, the substantial risks of ERP implementation must be acknowledged. Davenport (1998, 122-123) cautions:

> An enterprise system, by its very nature, imposes its own logic on a company's strategy, organization, and culture. ... It pushes a company toward full integration even when a certain degree of business unit segregation may be in its best interests. And it pushes a company toward generic processes even when customized processes may be a source of competitive advantage. If a company rushes to install an enterprise system without first having a clear understanding of the business implications, the dream of integration can quickly turn into a nightmare. The logic of the system may conflict with the logic of the business, and either the implementation will fail, wasting vast

Figure 9.7: ERP architecture

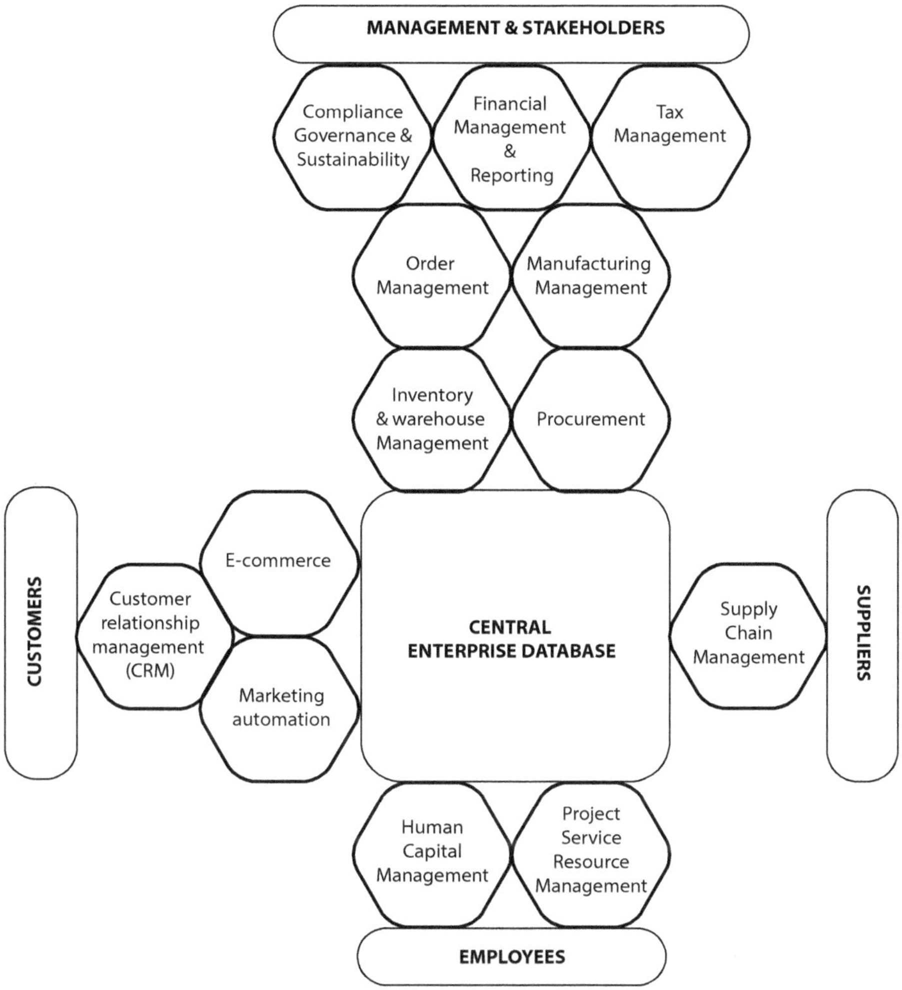

sums of money and causing a great deal of disruption, or the system will weaken important sources of competitive advantage, hobbling the company. [...] It is certainly true that enterprise systems can deliver great rewards, but the risks they carry are equally great. When considering and implementing an enterprise system, managers need to be careful that their enthusiasm about the benefits does not blind them to the hazards.

9.8 Throughput accounting and theory of constraints

Capacity optimisation has long been critical to cost management. Traditionally associated with economic modelling, it is evolving with new optimisation logics and alternative theoretical explanations. Two interrelated developments exemplify this: the Theory of Constraints (TOC) and Throughput Accounting (TA).

TOC emerged in the novel The Goal (Goldratt and Cox 1984), where a manager learns to identify his plant as the bottleneck —the sole limiting resource. Guided by a professor, he pinpoints the bottleneck's nature and explores enhancing throughput. This realisation—that bottlenecks can be overcome by focusing on improved throughput—is now known as throughput accounting. TOC and TA are thus intrinsically linked, enabling managers to maximise performance.

TOC and TA concern decision-making under constraints, aiming to optimise production plans. TOC provides a structured, step-by-step process to tackle capacity constraints. As Figure 9.8 illustrates, this process comprises: (1) identifying the system's constraint; (2) devising a strategy to exploit it; (3) subordinating and synchronising other elements to it; (4) enhancing the constraint's performance; and (5) repeating the cycle.

Figure 9.8: TOC and TA in action

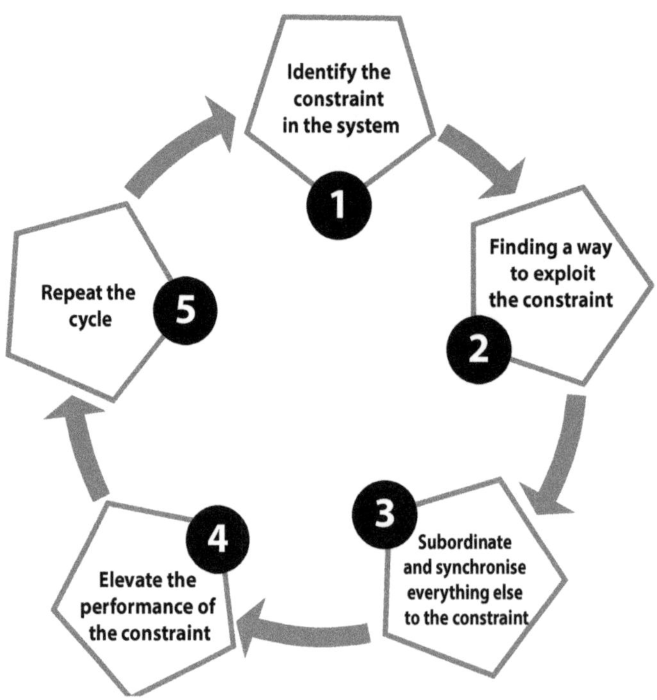

TOC provides a framework for continuously re-evaluating shop-floor configurations. A constraint exists when demand exceeds capacity. Optimising production around constraints is key to cost management and involves an ongoing cycle of calculation, observation, comparison, and decision-making.

The process begins by identifying the constraint and comparing available capacity with requirements. Next, managers brainstorm how to leverage it, asking: Is optimising the product mix necessary? Are we fully utilising capacity? Is this consistently feasible? To tackle this, one calculates 'throughput' (revenue minus purchased materials/services) and the throughput per bottleneck unit.

Buffer stocks should be established ahead of the bottleneck and exploited when the facility is ready. Maximising throughput enhances contribution. This requires coordinating non-bottleneck operations using Drum-Buffer-Rope (DBR) scheduling, ensuring non-bottleneck operations commence only after bottleneck needs are met. Once resolved, the process reverts to step one, seeking new constraints. This approach aids cost reduction and profit maximisation through optimised throughput—cost management via constraint management.

Key throughput accounting calculations include:

Throughput Contribution in £ = Sales Revenue - Direct Material Costs

Throughput Accounting Ratio (TPAR) = Return per Factory Hour / Cost per Factory Hour

Return per Factory Hour = Throughput £ per Unit / Time per Unit

Cost per Factory Hour = Total Factory Cost / Total Time Available

An example calculation follows.

Theory of Constraints and Throughput Accounting: An Example

A company produces three products using three different machines. The following information is available for a period:

The following table:

Product	X	Y	Z	Total
Sales price per unit (£)	32	22	18	
Material cost per unit (£)	20	12	12	
Machine hours required per unit:				
Machine 1	6	2	1	
Machine 2	9	3	1.5	
Machine 3	3	10	5	
Estimated sales demand	200	200	200	
Required machine hours				
Machine 1	1200	400	200	1800
Machine 2	1800	600	300	2700
Machine 3	600	200	100	900

Machine capacity is limited to 1600 hours for each machine, and the total factory cost for the period is £3,200.

First, calculate the machine utilisation ratio to determine the most constrained resource, as illustrated in the following table:

	M1	M2	M3
Required machine hours	1800	2700	900
Available machine hours	1600	1600	1600
Machine utilisation ratio	113%	169%	56%
Bottleneck	2nd	1st	3rd

The table above shows that Machine 2 is the most constrained resource (the first bottleneck). Use this to calculate the relevant throughput accounting ratios as follows:

	X	Y	Z
Sales price per unit (£)	32	22	18
Material cost per unit (£)	20	12	12
Throughput contribution per unit (£)	12	10	6
Required Machine 2 (bottleneck) hours per unit	9	3	1.5
Throughput contribution per bottleneck hour (£)	1.33	3.33	4.00
Ranking	3rd	2nd	1st

Factory cost per machine hour = Total Factory Cost / Total Machine Hours.

Given that the total factory cost is £3,200 and total machine hours for M2 are 1,600, the factory cost per machine hour = £3,200 / 1,600 = £2.

Calculate the Throughput Accounting Ratio (TPAR) as follows:

	X	Y	Z
Throughput contribution per bottleneck hour (£)	1.33	3.33	4.00
Factory cost per machine hour (£)	2.00	2.00	2.00
TPAR ratio	0.67	1.67	2.00
Ranking	3	2	1

This indicates that product Z should be prioritised in utilising machine hours over products X and Y. Accordingly, the optimised production schedule under Machine 2, as the first constraint, will be:

			Machine 2	
Product	Quantity	Hours per unit	Hours used	Hours available
				1600
Z	200	1.5	300	1300
Y	200	3	600	700
X	78	9	700	0

To enhance capacity, the focus should first be on Machine 2. Once its capacity is increased and it is no longer a bottleneck, this calculation should be repeated to determine the new optimum production schedule under the new bottleneck.

TOC and TA challenge traditional overhead absorption costing. Proponents Goldratt and Fox viewed traditional cost accounting as an 'enemy', criticising its treatment of most facility costs as 'fixed', which implies limited managerial discretion. Conversely, TOC focuses on identifying bottleneck versus non-bottleneck facilities and preparing buffer stock, aiming to bypass sales and profitability constraints.

TOC advocates also argue ABC does not align with their objectives. This critique has not gained wide acceptance, as ABC/M is recognised for its long-term perspective, whereas TOC/TA prioritise short-term profitability (Dugdale 2013). Despite this conflict, TOC/TA has gained popularity and can be integrated with linear programming and MRP packages, even with multiple constraints. Some have explored integrating ABC with TOC to leverage both methods' strengths (Kee and Schmidt 2000), though TOC proponents remain sceptical. This rivalry requires careful handling, as both approaches have merits. TOC is simple and pragmatic, while the globally recognised ABC/M is hard to overlook.

Chapter summary

This chapter explored strategic cost management, a theme underpinning all key topics in this textbook. It first explained the evolution from costing to traditional cost management, where standard costing and budgeting were pivotal within responsibility accounting. Transformations in competitive conditions have problematised the relevance of this traditional paradigm, necessitating new strategic approaches.

SCM encompasses diverse techniques and can be understood in two ways: as a holistic program or a surveillant assemblage. The holistic view, seen in Kaplanian and Porterian discourses, underscores a desire for unity and convergence, with strategy as the catalyst. Conversely, as a surveillant assemblage, SCM embodies heterogeneity, a 'fragmented whole' of reconfiguring technologies, techniques, concepts, and practices. This dynamic assemblage evolves as techniques are added or removed. This chapter explored this by highlighting the 'eventuality' of practices now integral to SCM.

The chapter discussed five techno-managerial frameworks. It first examined ABC and ABM, highlighting their strategic impact on cost controllability, strategic positioning, flexibility, and quality. Next, it focused on target costing, emphasising its integration of lean principles. Concepts like the survival zone and target costing triangle were revisited to show how multiple techniques contribute to market positioning. Third, lean manufacturing was addressed as SCM's foundational philosophy. Fourth, the evolution from MRP to ERP was explored, clarifying MRP's basic principles. Finally, the chapter delved into the theory of constraints and throughput accounting, elucidating their role in optimising capacity utilisation.

Case study: Interface, Inc. – from 'mission zero' to 'climate take back': strategising cost management for a regenerative enterprise

Case study abstract

This case study is designed for advanced management accounting seminars and provides a practical application of the concepts of Strategic Cost Management (SCM) as detailed in Chapter 9. It examines the 30-year strategic journey of Interface, Inc., a global modular carpet manufacturer. The case begins with the 1994 strategic 'epiphany' of its founder, Ray Anderson, who, driven by sustainability imperatives, resolved to transform Interface from a petroleum-intensive, 'take-make-waste' industrial producer into a 'restorative enterprise'. This strategic choice, which explicitly prioritised ecological and socio-political goals over conventional financial-first objectives, serves as the central problem of the case.

The case study analyses this transformation through the core theoretical lenses of Chapter 9. It first explores the 1994–2020 'Mission Zero' initiative, framing it as a holistic program of SCM. This holistic vision was underpinned by a radical application of lean manufacturing philosophy, extending the definition of waste to ecological and systemic factors. It then deconstructs this vision into the 'surveillant assemblage' of specific SCM techniques Interface deployed, including:

The development of 'EcoMetrics' as an extension of Activity-Based Management (ABM) to make environmental impacts visible and controllable.

The use of Target Costing and Value Engineering in product design (e.g., 'Entropy' tiles) to achieve circular economy goals.

The creation of the 'Net-Works' programme as a novel form of inter-organisational costing that integrates socio-political objectives into the supply chain.

Finally, the case applies the Theory of Constraints (TOC) to analyse the strategic shift from 'Mission Zero' to the post-2020 'Climate Take Back' mission. This new mission aims for a carbon-negative footprint, challenging students to consider how SCM and Throughput Accounting (TA) must be fundamentally reconfigured when the strategic goal becomes regenerative, maximising positive ecological 'throughput' rather than solely minimising financial cost.

Part 1: The 'spear in the chest' – sustainability as the strategic catalyst

The protagonist and the 'event'

The case commences in 1994 with Ray Anderson, the founder and CEO of Interface, Inc.. At that point, Interface was a highly successful industrial manufacturer, emblematic of the traditional 'take-make-waste' model of production. The firm's processes relied heavily on petroleum, and its factories generated significant volumes of toxic wastewater and landfill waste.

The strategic challenge materialised when Anderson was asked by customers what his company was 'doing for the environment'. This query, for which he had no answer, prompted him to read Paul Hawken's The Ecology of Commerce. Anderson's description of this experience can also be seen as an 'event' in the Deleuzian sense of an occurrence that introduces novelty and transformation, which he famously termed a 'spear in the chest'. He was struck by the realisation that his company was not merely compliant with regulations, but was actively 'harming the environment'.

The strategic choice underpinned by sustainability

This 'event' instigated a radical strategic shift. Anderson moved Interface from a position of mere environmental compliance to one of complete organisational transformation. He established a new corporate mission, formalised as 'Mission Zero', with the audacious goal 'to eliminate any negative impact Interface may have on the environment by the year 2020'.

This case study's central premise is rooted in this moment. It directly addresses the question of how 'sustainability imperatives underpin strategic choices'. As articulated in Chapter 9, Section 9.1, cost management and sustainability are deeply 'interconnected'. Strategic Cost Management (SCM) is the means by which a firm 'reconfigures its vertical and horizontal economic relationships', while sustainability explains how this reconfiguration 'enhances or disturbs the ecological and socio-political orders'.

Anderson's strategic choice was first to stop 'disturbing' the ecological order. This non-financial, sustainability-driven imperative preceded and necessitated the complete reconfiguration of the company's SCM system.

This presents an inversion of the traditional management accounting paradigm. Typically, SCM is a set of tools (e.g., cost reduction) deployed to achieve a pre-existing, financially-denominated strategy, such as profit maximisation. In this case, the strategy itself was ecological ('zero impact'). The firm's existing SCM, which was optimised for the 'take-make-waste' model, was not merely 'irrelevant'—as

Johnson and Kaplan's critical terminology would have it—when compared with strategic cost management systems such as activity-based costing and balanced scorecards, but was actively antithetical to the new strategy. Consequently, Interface was forced to invent a new SCM system to serve this sustainability imperative. The SCM reconfiguration was the effect, not the cause, of the strategic shift, perfectly illustrating the argument that SCM encapsulates multiple strategic themes by operationalising them.

Part 2: 'Mission zero' as a 'holistic SCM program'

The holistic vision

The 25-year 'Mission Zero' initiative (1994–2020) is analysed here through the theoretical lens of SCM as a 'holistic program'. This perspective, exemplified by Kaplanian and Porterian discourses, reflects an 'aspiration for unity and essence' in which strategy serves as the 'unifying force' to 'amalgamate' disparate corporate elements.

'Mission Zero' was the quintessential 'holistic program'. It was a single, 'moonshot' vision that provided a unifying narrative for the entire organisation. To operationalise this vision, Anderson and his 'Eco Dream Team' of external experts developed a unifying framework: the 'Seven Fronts of Mount Sustainability'. These fronts were:

- Eliminate Waste,
- Benign Emissions,
- Renewable Energy,
- Close the Loop,
- Resource Efficient Transportation,
- Sensitising Stakeholders, and
- Redesign Commerce.

'Eliminate waste' as lean manufacturing philosophy

The first and most critical front, 'Eliminate Waste', is a direct and radical application of the lean manufacturing philosophy. As defined in Chapter 9, lean is 'a philosophy dedicated to minimising waste'. 'Mission Zero' can be understood as one of the most comprehensive lean manufacturing projects that the company has ever undertaken.

However, Interface significantly expanded the definition of the 'seven key sources of waste'. The traditional lean focus on operational waste (e.g., Transport, Inventory, Motion, Waiting, Overproduction, Overprocessing, Defects) was broadened to include ecological waste (e.g., energy consumption, water intake, greenhouse gas emissions) and systemic waste (e.g., end-of-life products sent to landfill).

The financial impact of lean sustainability

The SCM system built to serve this integrated lean/sustainability mission yielded extraordinary financial results. It dispelled the myth that sustainability was purely a cost centre. By 2013, Interface reported $450 million in 'avoided waste costs'. This figure provides the single most important quantitative justification for the sustainability-driven strategy.

This holistic programme, driven by its seven-front framework, achieved remarkable, measurable results by its 2020 target. The key performance indicators (KPIs) in Table 1 provide concrete, quantitative data, moving the analysis from a qualitative narrative to a quantitative assessment of SCM performance.

Table 1: 'Mission zero' final key performance indicators (1996–2019)

Metric	Baseline (1996)	Achievement (by 2019/2020)	Reduction/Change
Emissions			
GHG Emissions Intensity (Market)	100%	4%	96% Reduction
Waste			
Waste to Landfill (Intensity)	100%	8%	92% Reduction
Energy			
Energy Use Intensity (per unit)	100%	54%	46% Reduction
Renewable Energy Use (Global)	0%	89% (of total)	+89%
Renewable Electricity Use (Global)	0%	100% (of electricity)	+100%
Water			
Water Use Intensity (per unit)	100%	11%	89% Reduction
Materials			
Recycled or Bio-based Raw Materials	~0%	60% (of total)	+60%
Product Carbon Footprint (Carpet)	100%	26%	74% Reduction

While the 'holistic program' view provides a powerful strategic narrative essential for unifying the organisation, this "unity" can appear "illusory" at the operational level. The 'Seven Fronts' looks like a neat "jigsaw puzzle", but the operational challenge of how to "Eliminate Waste" or "Close the Loop" requires a "multiplicity" of specific, often disconnected, tools and techniques. The KPIs in Table 1 are not the result of a single, unified system; they are the aggregate outcome of a 'fragmented whole' of reconfigured accounting and operational practices. The 'holistic program' provided the philosophy; the 'surveillant assemblage' provided the SCM system in practice.

Part 3: The 'assemblage' of techniques – operationalising the strategy

This section deconstructs the 'holistic program' into its constituent SCM techniques, applying the 'surveillant assemblage' framework. This view, drawn from Deleuze and Guattari, posits SCM not as an organic unity but as a 'fragmented whole... defined solely by their external relations of composition, mixture, and aggregation'. Interface assembled a new SCM by adding, subtracting, and recombining techniques as'events' to serve the holistic mission.

Technique 1: Activity-based management (abm) for environmental control

To operationalise 'Mission Zero', Interface launched its 'EcoMetrics' programme in 1996. This system was explicitly designed to 'quantify the "metabolism" of our operations... how much we take, in terms of materials and energy... and how much we waste' (https://www.businessmodelsinc.com/en/inspiration/blogs/the-business-model-of-interface).

This is a practical and prescient application of Activity-Based Management (ABM). As described in Chapter 9, ABM adds a 'horizontal or process view' to the 'vertical or cost assignment view' of ABC. 'EcoMetrics' did this in a particular manner: it focused managerial attention on the processes of 'energy use', 'water intake', and 'waste generation'.

This system extended the 'controllability effect' of ABM, as described by Armstrong (2002), from its original focus on 'opaque staff functions' to the realm of ecological functions. In traditional cost accounting, environmental impacts (energy, water, waste) are 'black-boxed' and treated as 'facility-sustaining costs' – that is, as fixed, uncontrollable overheads. Interface's 'EcoMetrics' reclassified them as variable, manageable 'activities' that consume resources. This accounting innovation, which mirrors concepts such as Activity-Based Life-Cycle Assessment (LCA), made waste visible and controllable. It was the accounting engine that enabled the $450 million in 'avoided waste costs' by rendering the ecological 'uncontrollable' controllable.

Technique 2: Target costing and value engineering for the circular economy

Chapter 9 defines Target Costing as a market-driven SCM tool that integrates customers, designers, and suppliers to manage the 'survival zone' (quality, functionality, price). Interface used these principles, driven by sustainability, to redesign its core products for the circular economy.

Application 1: The 'Entropy' Tile

The Problem: Traditional carpet tiles featured linear patterns, requiring single-direction installation. Damaged tiles were difficult to replace due to dye-lot variations, often forcing the replacement of entire floors, resulting in significant waste and high life-cycle costs.

The Sustainability Driver: The design team engaged in biomimicry, asking, 'how would nature design a carpet tile?' The answer was found in the 'random patterns of a forest floor' https://escp.eu/thechoice/their-choice/how-to-create-sustainable-value-learn-from-interfaces-25-year-journey/).

The SCM Solution (Target Costing/VE): This sustainability-driven insight led to the 'Entropy' tile, a 'biomimetic' product. The functionality was redefined: tiles became non-directional, allowing them to be 'laid in any orientation' and replaced individually. This increased the product's life-cycle value (less replacement waste) and simultaneously decreased installation waste from an average of 14% for broadloom carpet to just 1.5% for 'Entropy'. This is a perfect example of (9.5): the sustainability imperative (biomimicry) drove the value engineering process, reconfiguring the 'survival zone' to create a 'strategically advantageous value proposition' in which superior ecological functionality also meant lower life-cycle cost.

Application 2: 'TacTiles'

The Problem: Traditional carpet installation used 'wet glue', a source of emissions (violating the 'Benign Emissions' front), a financial cost, and a barrier to recycling (violating the 'Close the Loop' front).

The SCM Solution (VE): Interface developed 'TacTiles', a 'revolutionary, glue-free flooring installation method'. This is classic value engineering: it removes a component (glue) and its associated cost and impact, while improving functionality (ease of replacement and recycling).

Technique 3: Inter-organisational costing and socio-political reconfiguration

Chapter 9 notes that component-level target costing requires deep supplier integration, often involving 'inter-organisational costing'. Interface's 'Net-Works' programme provides a radical example of this concept.

The Problem: To 'Close the Loop', Interface needed a large, stable supply of recycled nylon, a key component. This supply chain did not exist at the required scale.

The Sustainability Driver: The 'Net-Works' idea emerged from two distinct sustainability imperatives: an ecological one (the problem of ocean pollution from discarded fishing nets) and a socio-political one (the acute poverty in the coastal communities where this pollution was prevalent).

The SCM Solution (The Assemblage): Interface assembled a new, unconventional supply chain. This was not a simple market transaction but a 'rhizomatically distributed' system.

Partnership: The assemblage involved Interface (the customer), its primary yarn supplier (Aquafil), and an NGO (the Zoological Society of London (ZSL)).

Mechanism: ZSL used its 'conservation and livelihood expertise' to help organise 'some of the poorest communities in the world' to collect and sell discarded nets. Aquafil then recycled these nets into new yarn , which Interface used in its products.

This system is a clear manifestation of the 'surveillant assemblage' —a 'fragmented whole' of for-profit and non-profit actors. More importantly, it demonstrates the argument that SCM can reconfigure economic relationships to enhance ecological and socio-political orders. Interface intentionally reconfigured its SCM to enhance the socio-political order (by providing community income) and the ecological order (by cleaning oceans). The 'cost' of this component (recycled nylon) now internalises these positive externalities, representing a radical redefinition of component-level target costing that moves beyond price to integrate social and ecological value.

Technique 4: ERP as the surveillance infrastructure

Chapter 9 describes Enterprise Resource Planning (ERP) systems as the 'software infrastructure' for integration and links this to the 'surveillant assemblage' by amalgamating computers (for analysis) and optics (for observation).

Interface's 'EcoMetrics' and its complex, modern sustainability reporting would be impossible to manage without a sophisticated, integrated ERP. The company must track and report 'carbon footprint by product type', 'use of recycled and bio-based materials', and 'use of renewable energy'. It publicly discloses this data in accordance with complex frameworks such as the Global Reporting Initiative (GRI), the Sustainability Accounting Standards Board (SASB), and the Task Force on Climate-Related Financial Disclosures (TCFD).

The ERP system (such as SAP or Oracle, which offer dedicated sustainability modules) is the technological backbone of this 'surveillant assemblage'. It is the tool that solves 'information fragmentation', not just for financial data, but for ecological and social data, such as Scope 3 emissions from suppliers. This infrastructure allows SCM to see and control the environmental 'activities' that the 'EcoMetrics' (ABM) system first identified.

Part 4: Elevating the constraint – from 'zero' to 'negative'

This section applies the Theory of Constraints (TOC) and Throughput Accounting (TA) to analyse Interface's strategic evolution. Note that this discussion takes the notion of TOC much beyond its original techno-managerial meaning to a broader strategic sustainabilty conception of its key analytical elements. TOC is presented in Chapter 9 as a 5-step process for 'capacity optimisation': (1) Identify the constraint, (2) Exploit the constraint, (3) Subordinate other elements, (4) Elevate the constraint, and (5) Repeat the cycle. When conceived in a broader strategic sense of dealing with sustainabilty, we can reinterpret its relevance in a much wider context.

Applying TOC to 'mission zero' (1994–2020)

Step 1 (Identify Constraint): In 1994, the primary system constraint was the linear 'take-make-waste' model. This model was the 'bottleneck' limiting the company's ability to achieve its new strategic goal (zero impact). Specific bottlenecks included landfill waste, reliance on fossil fuels, and sourcing virgin materials.

Steps 2/3 (Exploit/Subordinate): The 'Seven Fronts' and the SCM 'assemblage' (Part 3) were the methods to 'exploit' and 'subordinate' all business processes to this constraint. For example, 'EcoMetrics' (ABM) was used to see the waste, and the 'ReEntry' take-back programme was created to 'exploit' the waste material.

Step 4 (Elevate): 'Mission Zero' was the 25-year process of 'elevating' (breaking) this constraint. As evidenced by the KPIs in Table 1, Interface announced its success in 2019, ahead of the 2020 deadline.

Applying TOC to the new strategy ('climate take back')

Step 5 (Repeat): As Chapter 9 states, 'the process reverts to step one, seeking new constraints'. Having achieved 'Mission Zero', Interface identified a new bottleneck.

The New Constraint (Identify): The new constraint is no longer Interface's negative impact, but its lack of a positive impact in a world with excess atmospheric carbon. The system bottleneck is now the global climate itself.

The New Goal and Strategy (Exploit/Elevate): The new strategy, 'Climate Take Back', aims to 'reverse global warming' and become a carbon-negative enterprise by 2040. This strategy is built on new principles like 'Love carbon' (viewing carbon as a resource) and creating 'Factories as a Forest'.

Redefining throughput accounting (TA) for a regenerative model

This strategic shift has profound implications for the calculative practices of SCM, specifically Throughput Accounting (TA). As defined in 1 (9.8), TA traditionally holds:

1. Throughput Contribution = Sales Revenue - Direct Material Costs
2. The goal is to maximise this financial contribution per unit of the bottleneck resource.
3. Interface's 'Climate Take Back' strategy fundamentally redefines the variables of this calculation. The SCM system is no longer just minimising cost; it is actively maximising positive externalities.
4. Direct Material Costs: The purchasing decision for a 'direct material' is no longer based solely on minimising its financial cost. The SCM system, guided by the 'Love carbon' principle , must now select materials based on their carbon-storing properties, such as bio-based materials. A financially more expensive bio-based material is preferable if its carbon 'throughput' is higher.
5. Throughput Contribution: The new strategic goal is to maximise a dual throughput: financial (£) and ecological (kg of CO_2 stored). The 'Return per Factory Hour' is no longer a single financial metric. Interface is already producing carbon-negative products that store more carbon than they emit.

This illustrates precisely how 'sustainability imperatives' implicate SCM. To achieve a regenerative strategy, the core calculative logic of TA—throughput maximisation—is co-opted and reconfigured to serve an ecological goal. The SCM system at Interface has evolved from cost minimisation (traditional) to negative-impact minimisation ('Mission Zero') and, finally, to positive-impact maximisation ('Climate Take Back').

Part 5: Discussion questions

1. Holistic Program vs. Surveillant Assemblage: Ray Anderson's 'Mission Zero' strategy (Part 2) aligns with the 'holistic program' view of SCM. However, analyse the specific techniques in Part 3 (e.g., EcoMetrics, Net-Works, Entropy) as a 'surveillant assemblage'. Which framework better explains Interface's operational success, and why? Is the 'holistic program' a necessary prerequisite for a successful 'assemblage'?
2. Theory of Constraints and Throughput Accounting: Apply the five steps of the Theory of Constraints to Interface's strategic shift from 'Mission Zero' to 'Climate Take Back' (Part 4). What was the primary system bottleneck in

1994, and what is the primary bottleneck today? How does the 'Climate Take Back' strategy force a re-evaluation of the key Throughput Accounting (TA) metric: 'Throughput Contribution'?

3. Target Costing and Value Engineering: Using the principles of Target Costing, analyse the design of the 'Entropy' tile. How did Interface's sustainability imperative (biomimicry) reconfigure the 'survival zone' triangle (quality, functionality, price)?
4. Lean Manufacturing and Waste Definition: The 'seven key sources of waste' in Lean Manufacturing are typically Transport, Inventory, Motion, Waiting, Overproduction, Overprocessing, and Defects. How did Interface, through its 'Mission Zero' programme and 'Seven Fronts', expand the definition of 'waste' to include ecological and systemic factors? Provide specific examples from the case.
5. Activity-Based Management and Controllability: Discuss the 'controllability effect' of ABC/M as described by Armstrong (2002) in (9.4). How does Interface's 'EcoMetrics' system represent a radical extension of this concept? What was made 'visible' and 'controllable' that was 'black-boxed' in traditional cost management?
6. Inter-Organisational Costing: Analyse the 'Net-Works' programme using the 'target costing triangle'. How did Interface reconfigure its relationships with suppliers (component-level costing) and the market (market-driven costing) to achieve both its SCM and socio-political objectives?
7. ERP and Strategic Risk: Explain how a modern ERP system would be the essential' software infrastructure' for Interface's 'surveillant assemblage', enabling it to track KPIs (Table 1) and report to GRI, SASB, and TCFD standards. Citing Davenport (1998) from (9.7), what is the greatest strategic risk of such a system? Could imposing a 'generic' ERP logic 'hobble' the unique, 'biomimetic' processes that are Interface's 'source of competitive advantage'?
8. Critical Analysis of SCM Metrics: Critically evaluate the $450 million in 'avoided waste costs'. From a management accounting perspective, how might this figure be calculated? Discuss the distinction between 'cost savings' (a tangible reduction in expense) and 'cost avoidance' (preventing unnecessary costs), and argue whether this financial return was the goal of the SCM system or a consequence of its primary ecological focus.

Chapter review questions

Part 1: Foundational concepts: history, theory, and critique (sections 9.1–9.3)

This section assesses comprehension of the historical and theoretical foundations of cost management, the limitations of traditional approaches, and the core theoretical frameworks for strategic cost management (SCM).

Multiple choice questions (single-best answer)

1. According to the chapter's introduction (Section 9.1), cost management is argued to underpin the 'triadic interdependency' of strategy more vigorously than other themes because:

   a. Costs are only relevant at the point of production.
   b. Costs primarily concern marketing and market positioning.
   c. Costs occur pervasively across all three sites: the market, organisational hierarchy, and point of production.
   d. Costs are synonymous with quality and flexibility, which are hierarchy-related issues.

2. Section 9.2 describes cost management in the mercantile capitalism phase. In this phase, cost management primarily involved:

   a. Implementing standard costing and variance analysis.
   b. Subordinating labour to capital within a factory system.
   c. 'Negotiating' lower prices in factor markets, either 'diplomatically' or 'coercively'.
   d. Designing efficient production processes through motion and time studies.

3. From the 'disciplinary' perspective (Foucauldian) discussed in Section 9.2, the 'Scientific Management Movement' pioneered by Frederick W. Taylor established cost management through:

   a. The 'rationalisation of work', which included 'standardisation' of methods, time, and quantities.
   b. Minimising transaction costs compared to the market.
   c. Leveraging colonial trade relationships to coerce lower prices.
   d. The introduction of activity-based costing for overhead allocation.

4. According to the 'beyond budgeting movement' (Hope and Fraser) as cited in Section 9.3, a fundamental critique of conventional budgets is that they:

    a. Are too flexible, forward-looking, and aligned with strategy.
    b. Are too rigid, foster internal competition for resources, and use a time-consuming annual cycle.
    c. Successfully capture non-financial metrics like customer satisfaction and innovation.
    d. Are strongly aligned with lean and agile manufacturing principles.

5. Section 9.3 contrasts two theoretical views of SCM. The 'holistic program' perspective, exemplified by Porterian and Kaplanian discourses, understands SCM as:

    a. A 'fragmented whole' where techniques are added or subtracted as 'events'.
    b. An aspiration for unity and convergence, where strategy is the unifying principle, like a 'jigsaw puzzle'.
    c. A system that has lost its relevance and is inferior to traditional responsibility accounting.
    d. A 'surveillant assemblage' that operates rhizomatically across fragmented spaces.

6. Understanding SCM as a 'surveillant assemblage' (Deleuze and Guattari) as discussed in Section 9.3 implies that SCM is:

    a. A synergetic totality where all techniques fit neatly together to serve a unified strategy.
    b. A system defined by a singular, hierarchical logic of control, like Foucault's panopticon.
    c. A diverse, 'fragmented whole' of reconfiguring technologies, likened to a 'drystone wall', which evolves through 'events'.
    d. An outdated 'disciplinary institution' based on scientific management principles.

Select all that apply questions

7. Section 9.3 lists several 'consultocratic' critiques of the traditional cost management approach. Which of the following critiques are included in this list? (Select all that apply)

    a. Lack of alignment with strategic goals.
    b. Over-emphasis on non-financial metrics.
    c. Inability to capture the intricacies of global operations and complex supply chains.

d. Focus on historical data rather than forward-looking approaches.
e. Strong alignment with lean and agile principles, which reduces flexibility.

Matching question

8. Section 9.2 details several key differences between standard costing and budgeting within traditional cost management. Match each attribute (1–6) to the corresponding concept (A or B).

Concept	Attribute
A. Standard Costing B. Budgeting	1. Employs a 'top-down' approach, starting with aggregated figures.
	2. Has deeper historical roots in 'state bureaucracy'.
	3. Relates more to the management's 'controlling' function.
	4. Historical roots are linked to 'scientific management'.
	5. Provides 'figures that should have been' for the realised performance level.
	6. Employs a 'bottom-up' approach, starting with predetermined unit standards.

Part 2: Core SCM Techniques and strategic effects (sections 9.4–9.6)

This section assesses detailed knowledge of specific SCM techniques (ABC/ABM, Target Costing, Lean) and their conceptual and strategic implications.

Multiple choice questions (single-best answer)

9. According to Section 9.4, the 'eventuality' of Activity-Based Costing (ABC) was closely linked to its 'epistemic context', which was:

   a. The rise of state bureaucracy and the need for profit planning.
   b. The 'Scientific Management Movement' and the standardisation of factory labour.
   c. The 'Japanese Challenge', the need to align accounting with advanced manufacturing (JIT, TQM), and the influence of CAM-I and Harvard.
   d. The development of mainframe computers and the need to calculate 'derived demand' for inventory.

10. In the Activity-Based Costing (ABC) hierarchy (Section 9.4), costs associated with machine setup and quality control for a specific group of units are categorised as:

    a. Unit-level costs
    b. Batch-level costs

c. Product-sustaining costs
d. Facility-sustaining costs

11. In the ABC hierarchy (Section 9.4), costs related to product design, engineering, and product-specific marketing are categorised as:

    a. Unit-level costs
    b. Batch-level costs
    c. Product-sustaining costs
    d. Facility-sustaining costs

12. Section 9.4, citing Armstrong (2002), details the 'controllability effect' of ABC/ABM. This effect refers to:

    a. The ability of ABC to more accurately control direct material price and usage variances.
    b. ABC's failure to control staff costs, which remained 'fixed' and 'uncontrollable'.
    c. ABC's role in making opaque staff functions and their activities visible to accounting surveillance, dismantling their 'hierarchical privilege'.
    d. The control of overheads by simplifying them to a single driver, such as direct labour hours.

13. Section 9.4 contrasts ABC (Activity-Based Costing) with ABM (Activity-Based Management), as shown in Figure 9.2. This distinction is best described as:

    a. ABC is a long-term strategic tool, whereas ABM is focused on short-term profitability.
    b. ABC represents the 'horizontal or process view', while ABM represents the 'vertical or cost assignment view'.
    c. ABC is focused only on manufacturing costs, whereas ABM is focused only on staff costs.
    d. ABC provides the 'vertical or cost assignment view' (costing), while ABM adds the 'horizontal or process view' (managing activities).

14. 14. Section 9.4 describes the 'strategic effect' of ABC. How does ABC provide an 'accounting basis for flexibility'?

    a. By increasing the total fixed costs allocated to products, thus raising the break-even point.
    b. By reclassifying many 'fixed' costs as variable (e.g., batch-level), which lowers the fixed-cost threshold and the break-even volume.
    c. By focusing solely on direct labour as the primary driver, which simplifies CVP analysis.

d. By eliminating all facility-sustaining costs from product cost calculations.

15. According to Section 9.6, 'Jidoka' (or autonomation), a key element of the Toyota Production System and TQM, refers to:

    a. A tag system (like Kanban) that sequentially connects production processes.
    b. A 'pull system' of production where processes only produce enough to replace what is withdrawn.
    c. The principle of autonomous checks, where machines or workers can halt a process upon detecting a defect.
    d. The philosophy of eliminating the seven key sources of waste, such as transport and inventory.

16. As defined in Section 9.5 and Figure 9.3, the 'survival zone' in target costing represents:

    a. The integration of the customer, designer, and supplier frontiers.
    b. The process of eliminating all non-value-added activities from the value chain.
    c. The dynamic competitive arena defined by the maxima and minima of quality, functionality, and price (cost).
    d. The specific cost reduction target assigned to a component-level supplier.

17. Section 9.5 and Figure 9.4 describe the 'target costing triangle'. This framework illustrates the integration of which three critical frontiers?

    a. Cost, Quality, and Functionality.
    b. The Market (customers/competitors), Internal Designers, and Suppliers.
    c. Unit-level, Batch-level, and Product-level costs.
    d. Value Engineering, Life-Cycle Costing, and Inter-organisational Costing.

Select all that apply questions

18. Section 9.4 outlines how ABC and activity analysis contribute to operationalising Porterian generic strategies. Which of the following strategic applications are discussed? (Select all that apply)

    a. Cost Leadership: By identifying non-value-added activities to improve efficiency and reduce costs.
    b. Focus: By providing insight into the specific costs of serving a market niche.
    c. Differentiation: By understanding the costs of specific differentiating activities and features.
    d. Market Saturation: By using activity analysis to justify aggressive pricing and eliminate competitors.

19. Section 9.6 identifies lean manufacturing as a philosophy dedicated to minimising waste. Which of the following are identified as part of the 'seven key sources' of waste? (Select all that apply)

    a. Transport
    b. Innovation
    c. Overproduction
    d. Defects
    e. Quality
    f. Waiting

Matching question

20. Section 9.5 describes target costing as a structured system that operates at three levels, each using key methodologies. Match each level (1–3) to its primary methodology/focus (A–C).

Target Costing Level	Primary Methodology / Focus
1. Market-driven costing	A. Uses Value Engineering to connect designers with suppliers and focus creativity.
2. Product-level target costing	B. Uses Inter-organisational costing (e.g., open-book accounting) to focus supplier creativity.
3. Component-level target costing	C. Uses methods like ABC and Financial Analysis to determine the competitive cost based on the 'survival zone'.

Part 3: SCM infrastructure, optimisation, and application (sections 9.7–9.8)

This section tests knowledge of the technological infrastructure (ERP) and optimisation techniques (TOC/TA) that support and enact strategic cost management.

Multiple choice questions (single-best answer)

21. According to Section 9.7, the first evolutionary step toward modern ERP systems was Material Requirements Planning I (MRP-I). Its primary function was:

    a. To solve 'information fragmentation' across global business functions.
    b. To manage manufacturing resources, including flexible scheduling and shop-floor reporting, for 'Japanised' factories.
    c. To calculate 'derived demand' for components and raw materials to manage inventory.
    d. To integrate all business modules, including HR, CRM, and SCM, into a unified database.

22. Section 9.7 describes the evolution from MRP-II to modern ERP. The primary problem that contemporary ERP systems, with their unified database, were designed to solve was:

   a. The inability to calculate 'derived demand'.
   b. The lack of a 'disciplinary institution' to control labour.
   c. 'Information fragmentation', where data was scattered across numerous, uncoordinated systems.
   d. The failure of standard costing to provide accurate product costs.

23. Section 9.7 includes a critical warning from Davenport (1998) regarding ERP implementation. The greatest strategic risk identified is that an ERP system:

   a. Is too costly and time-consuming, diverting resources from R&D.
   b. Cannot be integrated with lean manufacturing or JIT principles.
   c. Fails to solve information fragmentation, often creating more data silos.
   d. 'Imposes its own logic' and pushes for 'generic processes', potentially 'hobbling' a company by weakening its unique 'customized processes' that are a source of competitive advantage.

24. According to Section 9.8, the Theory of Constraints (TOC) and Throughput Accounting (TA) are primarily concerned with:

   a. Accurately allocating all overhead costs to products using a four-level cost hierarchy.
   b. Identifying and managing bottlenecks (constraints) to optimise production plans and maximise throughput.
   c. Calculating the 'true cost' of quality, functionality, and market positioning.
   d. Implementing a 'pull system' of production using Kanban signals.

25. Section 9.8 defines 'Throughput Contribution' for the purposes of Throughput Accounting as:

   a. Sales Revenue - (Direct Materials + Direct Labour + Variable Overheads)
   b. Sales Revenue - Direct Material Costs
   c. (Return per Factory Hour) / (Cost per Factory Hour)
   d. Total Factory Cost / Total Time Available$

26. The chapter (Section 9.8) discusses the 'rivalry' between proponents of TOC/TA and ABC/M. This conflict is often characterised by which difference in perspective?

   a. TOC/TA is a German system, whereas ABC/M is a Japanese system.
   b. ABC/M is recognised for its long-term strategic perspective, whereas TOC/TA is often seen as prioritising short-term profitability.

c. TOC/TA focuses on waste elimination, whereas ABC/M focuses on bottleneck identification.
d. ABC/M is a 'pull' system, whereas TOC/TA is a 'push' system.

Select all that apply questions

27. Section 9.8 and Figure 9.8 (referred to as 9.6 in the text) outline the five-step process for the Theory of Constraints (TOC). Which of the following steps are part of this process? (Select all that apply)

    a. Identify the system's constraint(s).
    b. Devise a strategy to exploit the constraint.
    c. Implement a unified ERP database.
    d. Subordinate and synchronise other elements to the constraint.
    e. Re-engineer all non-value-added activities.
    f. Enhance the constraint's performance and repeat the cycle.

Part 4: Scenario-based application: TOC and throughput accounting (section 9.8)

This section assesses the ability to apply the quantitative methods of the Theory of Constraints (TOC) and Throughput Accounting (TA) as detailed in Section 9.8.

Instructions: Refer to the data in Table 1 below for Aethelred Components Ltd. and answer questions 28–32.

Table 1: Aethelred Components Ltd. – Production Data (per period)

	Product Alpha	Product Beta	Product Gamma
Sales price per unit	£100	£120	£90
Material cost per unit	£40	£50$	£30
Estimated sales demand (units)	100	100	100
Machine hours required per unit:			
Machine 1 (M1)	2.0	1.0	1.0
Machine 2 (M2)	3.0	4.0	2.0
Machine 3 (M3)	1.0	2.0	3.0

Additional Information:

Total available machine hours for the period are: M1: 500 hours; M2: 800 hours; M3: 700 hours; the total factory cost for the period is £16,000.

Scenario-based multiple choice questions

28. Based on the data in Table 1, which machine is the primary bottleneck constraint for Aethelred Components Ltd.?

    a. Machine 1 (M1)
    b. Machine 2 (M2)
    c. Machine 3 (M3)
    d. There is no bottleneck, as capacity exceeds demand.

29. What is the Cost per Factory Hour for the bottleneck machine (M2)?

    a. £17.50
    b. £20.00
    c. £22.86
    d. £32.00

30. What is the Throughput Contribution per bottleneck hour for Product Beta?

    a. £17.50
    b. £20.00
    c. £30.00
    d. £70.00

31. What is the Throughput Accounting Ratio (TPAR) for Product Alpha?

    a. 0.875
    b. 1.000
    c. 1.500
    d. 3.000

32. Based on the TPAR rankings, what is the optimal production plan (units of Alpha, Beta, Gamma) to maximise profitability within the 800-hour constraint of Machine 2?

    a. Alpha: 100; Beta: 100; Gamma: 100
    b. Alpha: 100; Beta: 75; Gamma: 100
    c. Alpha: 100; Beta: 0; Gamma: 250
    d. Alpha: 67; Beta: 100; Gamma: 100

Comprehension questions

1. Discuss the factory's historical significance in cost management's development.
2. Analyse the impact of Scientific Management on early cost management practices.
3. Describe standardisation's role in cost management within scientific management.
4. Examine the link between standard costing and budgeting in traditional responsibility accounting.
5. Outline traditional cost management's procedural elements.
6. Summarise the main issues of traditional responsibility accounting as a cost management system.
7. Define SCM as a 'holistic program' and discuss potential issues with this perspective.
8. Explain the assemblage concept (Deleuze and Guattari) and its relevance to SCM's evolution.
9. Elucidate the 'epistemic context' of ABC.
10. Detail the ABC process.
11. Categorise the four cost hierarchy levels in ABC.
12. Discuss how ABC/M affects:

    a. Cost controllability.
    b. Strategic market positioning.
    c. Quality management.
    d. Manufacturing flexibility.

13. Describe lean manufacturing's influence on target costing.
14. Explain these key target costing concepts:

    a. Survival zone.
    b. Target costing triangle.
    c. Market-driven costing.
    d. Component-level target costing.
    e. Product-level target costing.
    f. Value engineering.
    g. Life-cycle costing.
    h. Inter-organisational costing.
    i. Target costing process.

15. Outline lean manufacturing's principal elements as an SCM philosophy.
16. Explain MRP and MRP-II as ERP precursors.

17. Compare the challenges addressed by MRP, MRP-II, and ERP.
18. Describe an ERP system's essential components.
19. Discuss the primary issue targeted by TOC and TA.
20. Detail the fundamental steps in the TOC process.
21. List and describe key TA measures and ratios.

Explore further

1. Compile a scholarly critique of the traditional budgeting approach, based on 'Beyond Budgeting' literature.
2. Identify traditional budgeting's shortcomings and outline potential solutions.
3. Evaluate how these solutions address strategic cost management issues.
4. Research leading ERP vendors. List their modules and examine the specific strategic advantages each provides.
5. Investigate Industry 4.0's core elements (IoT, AI, Big Data, etc.). Analyse their impact on strategic cost management, focusing on cost prediction, real-time monitoring, and dynamic cost optimisation.

Develop your critical argumentation skills.

1. Write an argumentative essay on the theme:

    > Strategic cost management is a surveillant assemblage, not a holistic program. Its evolution is better understood as eventualities producing heterogeneity, not a singular logic as in traditional cost management.

2. Write an argumentative essay on the theme:

    > ERP systems provide immense integration but impose their own logic, pushing firms toward total integration even when segregation may be strategically advantageous.

3. Write an argumentative essay on the theme:

    > Lean manufacturing is pivotal to strategic cost management. Discuss how lean principles underpin a manufacturing philosophy that supports SCM.

References

Alawattage, C., and D. Wickramasinghe. 2019. Strategizing Management Accounting: Liberal Origins and Neoliberal Trends. London: Routledge.

Armstrong, P. 2002. The costs of activity-based management. Accounting, Organizations and Society 27 (1-2):99-120.

Boyns, T. 1998. Budgets and budgetary control in British businesses to c.1945. Accounting, Business & Financial History 8 (3):261-301.

Cooper, D. J., M. Ezzamel, and S. Q. Qu. 2017. Popularizing a Management Accounting Idea: The Case of the Balanced Scorecard.

Contemporary Accounting Research 34 (2):991-1025.

Cooper, R., and R. Slagmulder. 1997. Target costing and value engineering. Portland: Productivity Press.

Davenport, T. H. 1998. Putting the Enterprise into the Enterprise System. Harvard Business Review 1998 (July-August):121-131.

Deleuze, G., and F. Guattari. 1987. A Thousand Plateaus: Capitalism and Schizophrenia: University of Minnesota Press.

———. 1994. What is philosophy? London: Verso.

Drennan, L., and M. Kelly. 2002. Assessing an activity-based costing project. Critical Perspectives on Accounting 13 (3):311-331.

Dugdale, D. 2013. The theory of constraints. In The Routledge Companion to Cost Management, edited by F. Mitchell, H. Norreklit and M. Jakobsen.

London: Routledge, 145-162.

Goldratt, E. M., and J. Cox. 1984. The goal: excellence in manufacturing. New York: North River Press.

Hope, J., and R. Fraser. 1997. Beyond budgeting breaking through the barrier to the 'third wave'.

Management Accounting 75 (11):20-23.

———. 2000. Beyond Budgeting. Strategic finance 82 (4):30-35.

———. 2001. Beyond budgeting: questions and answers. Dorset.

———. 2003a. Beyond Budgeting: How Managers Can Break Free from the Annual Performance Trap: Harvard Business School Press.

———. 2003b. Who needs budgets? Harvard Business Review 81 (2):108–115.

Hopper, T., and P. Armstrong. 1991. Cost accounting, controlling labour and the rise of conglomerates.

Accounting, Organizations and Society 16 (5-6):405-438.

Hopper, T., and N. Macintosh. 1993. Management accounting as disciplinary practice: the case of ITT under Harold Geneen.

Management Accounting Research 4 (3):181-216.

Jacobs, R. F., and T. J. Weston, F.C. 2007. Enterprise resource planning (ERP)—A brief history.

Journal of Operations Management 25 (2):357-363.

Johnson, H. T., and R. S. Kaplan. 1987a. Relevance lost: the rise and fall of management accounting.

Boston, Mass.: Harvard Business School Press.

———. 1987b. The rise and fall of management accounting. Management Accounting 68 (7):22-29.

Jones, C. T., and D. Dugdale. 2002. The ABC bandwagon and the juggernaut of modernity.

Accounting, Organizations and Society 27 (1-2):121-163.

Kee, R., and C. Schmidt. 2000. A comparative analysis of utilizing activity-based costing and the theory of constraints for making product-mix decisions.

International Journal of Production Economics 63 (1):1-17.

Miller, J. A. 1996. Implementing activity-based management in daily operations: John Wiley & Sons.

Monden, Y. 1994. Toyota production system: an integrated approach to just-in-time. 2nd ed. ed. London: Chapman & Hall.

Monden, Y., and K. Hamada. 1991. Target costing and kaizen costing in Japanese automobile companies.

Journal of Management Accounting Research 3 (Fall):16-34.

Monden, Y., and M. Sakurai. 1998. Japanese Management Accounting. London: Taylor & Francis.

Nail, T. 2017. What is an Assemblage? SubStance 46 (1):21-37.

Patton, P. 1997. The World Seen From Within: Deleuze and the Philosophy of Events. Theory & event 1 (1).

CHAPTER

10 Strategizing sustainability

10.1 Introduction

This final chapter synthesises the themes explored previously – concerning market strategy, organisational hierarchy, and the point of production – by examining the relationship between sustainability and strategic management accounting concepts and practices. In previous chapters, we selectively examined how sustainability influences specific management accounting practices, including Kaplan and colleagues' balanced scorecards, Porter's value chain analysis, and target costing as a pricing technique.

Aiming to provide an integrative perspective on how sustainability interacts with management accounting, this chapter has a dual focus: (a) examining how the global sustainability agenda has been integrated into frameworks of corporate strategy formulation, and (b) assessing the extent to which, and the ways in which, these efforts embody the broader sustainability concept as understood by the UN and other key sustainability advocates. In this assessment, the chapter draws upon critical accounting scholarship on sustainability accounting.

For many years, and to a significant extent still, social and environmental issues were considered 'externalities' in neoclassical economic and accounting analyses of organisational practices and outcomes. Traditional accounting and economics, driven by firm-centric, entity, and monetary measurement concepts, long overlooked social and environmental impacts because they were not directly related to the firm's cost, revenue, and profit functions. This oversight, however, has faced severe criticism in academic and policy circles since the mid-1970s, especially following the Brundtland Commission's 1987 report on the global environment and development. Despite criticisms such as Daly's (1993, 267) assertion that 'sustainable growth when applied to the economy is a bad oxymoron - self-contradictory as prose, and unevocative as poetry', there has been a growing global awareness and commitment to sustainability.

Sustainability now challenges us to reconsider and redesign our decision-making processes, daily operations, and accountabilities within and beyond organisations. Management accounting is not exempt from this shift. Like many other academic and professional fields, it has been urged to adapt its ideologies, techniques, and practices towards fostering a sustainable world. This chapter evaluates the manner in which management accounting thought has embraced this challenge.

In doing so, the chapter is organised as follows:

1. Section 10.2 defines and discusses the concept of sustainability and its four interrelated dimensions: economic, social, political, and ecological. This provides a broader understanding of the fundamental contradictions within which the notion of sustainability should be located.
2. Section 10.3 examines the neoliberal logic of sustainability, starting with Friedman's and others' resistance to the nascent sustainability agenda, then framed as corporate social responsibility. This section develops a critical understanding of the neoclassical economic logic that views corporate engagement in sustainability as economically irrational, and provides a biopolitical perspective on the evolution of this 'oxymoron'.
3. Section 10.4 discusses how management accounting has responded to the sustainability agenda, offering a conceptual schema for understanding this response and analysing the incorporation of sustainability into corporate discourses: corporate accountability in response to sustainability, strategizing sustainability, envisioning sustainability, and sustainability as a strategic positioning postulate. This section provides an overall framework for exploring how corporations integrate sustainability principles to align with their business contexts and strategic approaches.
4. Section 10.5 explores the strategic aspects of management accounting's response to sustainability, focusing on top-level commitment through Environmental, Social, and Governance (ESG) criteria, the revision of strategic intent, and the use of sustainability for market positioning.
5. Section 10.6 examines operational aspects, focusing on sustainability in capital investment decisions, value chain analysis, competitive positioning, sustainability-balanced scorecards, and cost accounting techniques such as Activity-Based Costing (ABC), life-cycle costing, and whole-life

costing. This section revisits and extends the discussion from previous chapters to enhance understanding of how specific management accounting practices struggle to engage with sustainability.

6. Section 10.7 concludes the chapter with a summary and an overarching critical comment.

10.2 The Political and Politics of Sustainability: Fundamental Contradictions

Given the highly contested and debated nature of 'sustainability', it is appropriate to begin with the Brundtland Commission's definition. This definition is pivotal, as it arguably serves as the most influential reference point and marks the commencement of contemporary debates on sustainable development. The commission defines sustainable development as development that 'meets the needs of the present without compromising the ability of future generations to meet their own needs' (United Nations World Commission on Environment and Development 1987, 8). This definition immediately highlights the inter-generational conflict between present and future interests: it suggests that our current exploitation of the globe's finite resources could lead to a future where the planet becomes, in the worst case, uninhabitable, or at least, where the standard of living is not as favourable as it is today.

This early definition sparked a significant debate over what sustainability should encompass, how it should be approached, and the feasibility of achieving sustainability within a capitalist political-economic framework (Bebbington 2001; Gladwin et al. 1995; Gray 2010; Thomson 2007). Despite the varying viewpoints, there is a broad consensus that sustainability involves preserving and maintaining a crucial and finite environment, entailing some degree of social justice obligation – both intergenerationally and intragenerationally (Gray 2010, 53).

In exploring the diverse interpretations of sustainability, it is essential to consider the political contradictions inherent in the concept and identify political means to address them. For a critical understanding of the global sustainability agenda, it is helpful to consider the theoretical distinction Chantal Mouffe, a prominent political theorist of agonistic democracy, draws between 'the political' and 'politics'.

Mouffe (1993, 1999, 2000, 2005, 2013) defines 'the political' as the fundamental, ontological dimension of antagonisms and conflicts that underlie human civilisations. It is an inherent aspect of human societies, arising from the reality that any social order is established through the exclusion of particular possibilities in favour of others. This dimension is marked by divergent interests and the inevitability of conflict, not only between different social or political groups but also among more fundamental structural categories.

Conversely, 'politics' refers to the set of institutional arrangements and practices – the 'ontic' level – through which an order is created, organising human coexistence in the context of the conflictuality provided by 'the political'. Politics is about how power is exercised to reconcile conflicting interests and ensure the coexistence of diverse groups within a society. It involves constructing political identities and establishing a specific order, often through democratic institutions and negotiations. For instance, the United Nations Sustainable Development Goals (UN SDGs) exemplify a global institutional arrangement ('politics') that attempts to recognise and address the fundamental contradictions ('the political') not only between the needs of the current generation and the those of the future generations but also between the economy, polity, society, and ecology in how we manage these domains.

Mouffe posits that understanding the distinction between these two terms is vital for democratic politics. She stresses the importance of acknowledging and managing the inevitable conflicts and antagonisms in any society, rather than attempting to eliminate them, which she deems impossible.

We can now consider four fundamental structural categories, and the institutional logics underpinning them, for conceptualising the political nature of sustainability, as shown in Figure 10.1.

1. **The Economy** manifests the manner in which nation-states, their global alliances, and regional economies are organised to fulfil the economic needs of consumption, production, exchange, savings, and investments. It comprises three key structural elements: markets, organisational hierarchies, and labour processes. These are the sites in which strategies are enabled and enacted, as discussed in previous chapters. The primary driver of the economy, particularly in a capitalistic system, is *efficiency*. This concept is linked to various indicators related to the rate of accumulation of 'socialised capital' (i.e., capital that is tradeable in capital markets). At the company level, efficiency is often measured by accounting metrics such as return on investment. At the macroeconomic scale, efficiency encompasses the challenges of ensuring adequate economic growth to address issues such as unemployment, poverty, and the capacity to sustain a growing global population. Concerning sustainability, the economy involves technological and organisational advancements to ensure the production of income and resources for both present and future generations. However, a central aspect of sustainability is that economic

Figure 10.1: Sustainability's political contradictions

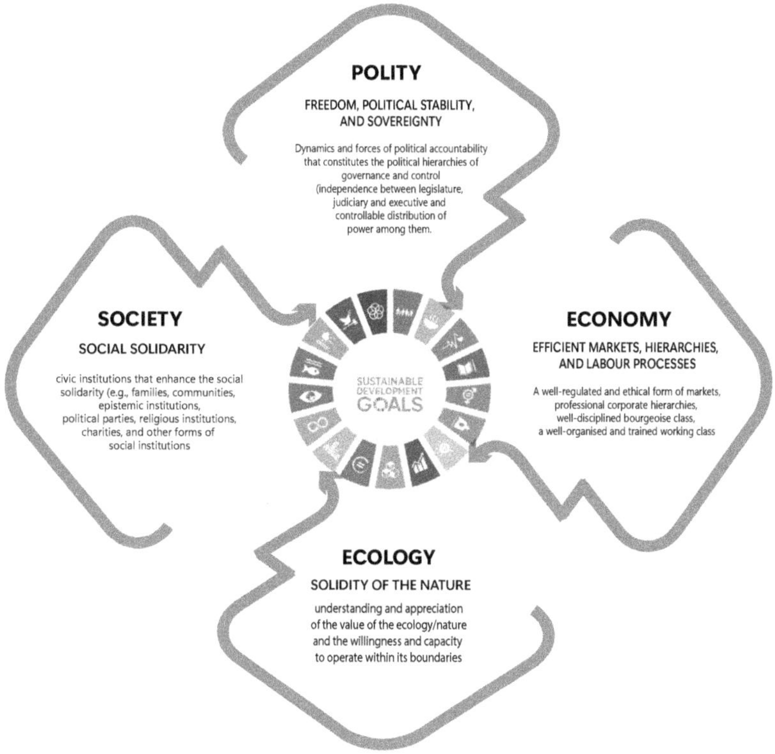

efficiency should not compromise the fundamental principles of politics, society, and ecology. Sustainability requires not only economically efficient but also well-regulated and ethically operated markets, hierarchies, and labour processes.

2. **The Polity** is the manner in which the political state or system is organised to handle differences in political ideologies and other related cultural-political-economic contradictions. It embodies the dynamics of *political accountability*, illustrating the governance hierarchy through the independent legislative, judicial, and executive branches. From an orthodox Marxist viewpoint, it encompasses the political mechanisms that control the class struggle between labour and capital. Post-Marxist perspectives expand this to include a contested terrain where not only class conflicts but also other political contradictions (e.g., race, ethnicity, elitism, national identities) emerge. In pre-modern societies, the polity centred on affirming sovereign power ('God save the king/queen'), while modern democratic societies prioritise individual freedom alongside the sovereignty of nation-states. Sustainable development hinges on these

political doctrines. The deterioration of these principles, as seen in recent neoliberal economic dominance, can lead to 'unsustainability', manifesting as civil unrest, corruption, despotism, and wars. Despite its frequent omission in corporate and accounting discourses, the polity is crucial to sustainability, especially given its role as a vision for a new global political order.

3. **The Society** comprises civic institutions that bolster social solidarity, including families, communities, media, political parties, religious institutions, charities, and other social formations where people unite to pursue diverse socio-cultural goals. It embodies the eco-justice aspect of sustainability, focusing on socio-political issues such as social justice, fairness, cultural diversity, equality, and indigenous rights. This concept involves not only the equitable distribution of developmental benefits among the present generation (intragenerational equity) but also between current and future generations (intergenerational equity). Additionally, it encompasses cultural and social struggles against the 'increasing destruction of the world's diverse ecosystems, languages, and cultures by the globalizing and ethnocentric forces of [predominantly] Western consumer culture'.
4. **Ecology**, often termed 'the planet', forms the natural foundation on which all else relies. It represents natural capital (also known as environmental or ecological capital), which encompasses the essential natural resources (energy and matter) and processes organisations utilise. This includes waste-absorbing sinks (e.g., forests, oceans), resources (renewable, such as timber and water; non-renewable, such as fossil fuels), and life-sustaining processes like climate regulation. The accounting literature often ties ecological aspects to the eco-efficiency dimension of sustainability, focusing on minimising environmental footprints and ensuring that economic, political, and social activities do not compromise ecological integrity. Gray et al. (1996) highlight that understanding eco-efficiency requires considering two additional concepts: biodiversity and the planet's carrying capacity. Ideally, eco-efficiency implies conducting economic activities without depleting biodiversity or the planet's natural resource stock. Gray et al. (1996, 3) capture this notion as follows:

> 'At minimum, a sustainable business is one which leaves the environment no worse off at the end of each accounting period than it was at the beginning of that accounting period. For a full sustainability, the sustainable business would also re-dress some of the excess of current un-sustainability and consider the intra-generational inequalities. It is perfectly clear that few, if any, businesses, especially in the developed economies, come anywhere near to anything that looks remotely like sustainability'.

Bebbington (2001, 137) contends that eco-efficiency aligns with the UNWCED's definition of sustainability. While eco-efficiency is necessary for sustainable development, it is not sufficient on its own. For instance, an environmentally neutral development scenario that results in a highly unequal distribution of benefits would not fulfil the criteria for sustainable development. This highlights the importance of eco-justice.

These four dimensions reflect key socio-political contradictions that have emerged from how modern societies have structured their political economies. The contemporary sustainability issue exemplifies how our economic activities can become destructive forces against the environment, society, and, at times, the political sphere. Consequently, the sustainability agenda calls for comprehensive changes across all aspects of our socio-political and economic activities.

10.3 Sustainability's neoliberal political logic

When the sustainability agenda first emerged in the 1970s as the 'social responsibility of corporations' debate, it faced significant criticism from influential proponents of neoliberal economics. Corporations investing in social responsibility were labelled 'unadulterated socialists', undermining free societies. Nobel Laureate economist Milton Friedman was a prominent critic. In his 1970 essay for The New York Times Magazine, 'The Social Responsibility of Business is to Increase its Profits', Friedman argued that a business's focus should be solely on profit, dismissing social responsibilities as a form of socialism:

> 'When I hear businessmen speak eloquently about the "social responsibilities of business in a free-enterprise system," I am reminded of the wonderful line about the Frenchman who discovered at the age of 70 that he had been speaking prose all his life. The businessmen believe that they are defending free enterprise when they declaim that business is not concerned "merely" with profit but also with promoting desirable "social" ends; that business has a "social conscience" and takes seriously its responsibilities for providing employment, eliminating discrimination, avoiding pollution and whatever else may be the catchwords of the contemporary crop of reformers. In fact, they are—or would be if they or anyone else took them seriously—preaching pure and unadulterated socialism. Businessmen who talk this way are unwitting puppets of the intellectual forces that have been undermining the basis of a free society these past decades' (Friedman 1970).

This rejection is grounded in the belief in an 'artificial economic personality': the concept that economic enterprises are solely economic in nature and should not be accountable for social and political decisions. According to Friedman, since corporations are owned by profit-motivated shareholders and managed by agents responsible only to these shareholders, it is inappropriate for corporate managers to engage in social responsibility. Friedman argued that such actions would equate to corporate managers wielding a political 'taxing' power, which he believed should be the purview of politics and government. This view is consistent with the neoclassical economic ideology that distinguishes politics from economics:

> 'This process raises political questions on two levels: principle and consequences. On the level of political principle, the imposition of taxes and the expenditure of tax proceeds are governmental functions. We have established elaborate constitutional, parliamentary and judicial provisions to control these functions... We have a system of checks and balances to separate the legislative function of imposing taxes and enacting expenditures from the executive function of collecting taxes and administering expenditure programs and from the judicial function of mediating disputes and interpreting the law. Here the businessman—self-selected or appointed directly or indirectly by stockholders—is to be simultaneously legislator, executive and, jurist. He is to decide whom to tax by how much and for what purpose, and he is to spend the proceeds...' (Friedman 1970).

More than fifty years later, the world has changed. It has now become a pervasive, taken-for-granted understanding among large corporations, at least at a rhetorical level, that they should invest in sustainability matters. We also see little opposition from economists. This dramatic shift in the acceptance of sustainability marks a clear move away from the neoclassical understanding of the social responsibilities of economic enterprises.

However, despite the dominance of neoliberal economic theories, the sociological and political-economic understanding of the political role of economic enterprises has always been much broader. For example, since the advent of modernity and the emergence of 'governmentality', specific governmental (veridictional and jurisdictional) roles have been enacted within the boundaries of economic enterprises (Alawattage and Wickramasinghe 2019, 2022). From a Foucauldian perspective, organisations (factories, offices, schools, prisons) became their own miniature legal systems, relatively independent from the state but capable of exercising their own judgments and punishments. This 'normalising sanction' was an extension of government into the 'normal' spaces of socio-economic life, transforming societies into 'disciplinary societies' (Foucault 1995; Hopper and Macintosh 1993).

Expanding on this perspective, corporations embracing sustainability responsibilities represent a further evolution of governmentality. This shift moves beyond the disciplinary politics of normalising discipline (the anatomico-politics of the human body) to the biopolitics of security – the management of the life of populations (Alawattage and Wickramasinghe 2019, 2022). This is, indeed, a neoliberal approach, enhancing the role of the market and private capital in areas traditionally managed by the state.

Paradoxically and ironically, this process enables private capital to assume the very political and welfare functions that neoclassical economists like Friedman believed should belong exclusively to the sovereign state. Not understanding this ever-increasing governance role of private capital under neoliberalism, Friedman and others initially saw social responsibility as a threat to capital accumulation and, hence, a threat to their concept of 'freedom'. Their resistance, however, would prove inconsequential as capital evolves to enhance its capacity for accumulation in all forms: economic, social, and political. This transformation positions capital as a dominant force in governance, what Hardt and Negri (2000) term the 'empire'. Capital is becoming akin to a state, assuming sovereignty and thus dealing with all matters traditionally managed by the political state.

Rationalizing the oxymoron

Considering the neoclassical principle that a rational enterprise would invest only in activities that maximise shareholder wealth, the rise of the sustainability agenda seemed an oxymoron. This concept seemed theoretically inexplicable. Yet, empirical observations revealed that companies were investing in these 'economically irrational' activities.

For those with an economics-oriented analytical perspective, this represented a growing dependent variable requiring explanation. Based on the ontological assumption that managers, as agents of capital, should invest only in ways that maximise shareholder wealth, this growth should correlate with its impact on financial performance. Therefore, hypotheses emerged suggesting a positive relationship between corporate social responsibility (CSR) and financial performance.

The initial phase of academic rationalisation focused on testing this hypothesis, aiming to demonstrate empirically a neoclassical rationale. For instance, Al-Tuwaijri et al. (2004, 447) justified their study by stating:

> As managers scramble to compete in the global economy, they must do so within societal constraints characterized by ever-increasing environmental accountability. This accountability includes heightened public scrutiny of both the firm's environmental performance and its public disclosure of that performance. These elements of corporate environmental accountability jointly impact the firm's profitability and the value of its common equity. This study provides an integrated analysis of how management's overall strategy jointly affects (1) environmental disclosure, (2) environmental performance, and (3) economic performance. Understanding these interrelations is of increasing interest to both internal and external stakeholders in an era in which corporate environmental costs have become a significant business expense … using a landfill to dump hazardous waste cost only \$2.50 per ton in 1978, this charge rose to over \$200 per ton by 1987. … Between 1972 and 1992, total annualized environmental protection costs for US firms tripled as a percentage of Gross Domestic Product (GDP). Senior executives anticipate this trend to continue.

A substantial body of research has been conducted to assess whether 'it pays to be really good' in terms of CSR (e.g., Al-Tuwaijri et al. 2004; Artiach et al. 2010; Barnett and Salomon 2012). These studies have yielded mixed results, with some indicating positive, others negative, or inconclusive links.

However, the crucial aspect is not the nature of the relationship itself, but rather the methodology and underlying normative political principles of these studies. Common to these approaches is the notion that economic factors should take precedence over social and environmental considerations. This implies that the rationale for sustainability is derived from its contribution to financial performance, rather than prioritising social and environmental protection in calculating economic profits.

In essence, these approaches still prioritise economic criteria as the guiding principles or moral philosophy in determining the merits of sustainable actions. Many now argue that sustainability benefits companies primarily by boosting profits or mitigating losses. While these messages encourage corporations to engage in sustainability, they are underpinned by a misguided economic morality. This view suggests that sustainability is important only because it can be profitable, positioning it as a means to profit rather than an end goal. To put it simply, nothing will be profitable in an unsustainable world.

10.4 Management accounting's rationalization of sustainability

Mainstream management accounting's rationalisation of sustainability adheres to the logic of financially legitimising sustainability. Unlike being concerned with empirically 'testing' the causality between financial performance and sustainability, it emphasises 'developing' strategic and operational frameworks to integrate sustainability into business strategies. This approach aims to 'create' (rather than test) a positive correlation, or 'finality' (see Norreklit 2000, 2003), between sustainability and financial performance.

Most management experts now recognise sustainability as a 'strategic imperative' (Lubin and Esty 2010). The focus has shifted to integrating sustainability into various existing management models, such as value chain analysis, balanced scorecards, and activity-based costing. These popular management discourses outline a schema for embedding sustainability in management accounting, potentially leading to what can be termed 'sustainabilizing strategy'—giving the corporation's strategy-making processes a sustainable outlook, as depicted in Figure 10.2.

Corporate accountability and sustainability

Corporate engagement in sustainability requires communication with a broader range of stakeholders for legitimacy and compliance. In accounting, 'sustainability reporting' has become the most popular and evolved aspect. Indeed, the need for sustainability reporting created the managerial imperative to develop internal sustainability management systems, including emerging tools in social and environmental management accounting. This indicates that sustainability began penetrating the corporate world primarily as an 'accountability' requirement—an externally imposed demand to report on the environmental and social impacts of corporate activities.

The transitions to neoliberalism have profoundly impacted how we perceive corporate accountability. Neoliberalisation essentially amplifies the importance of free-market governance logic: that market capital and its individual units (corporations) should govern and shape lives beyond traditional business confines. Assuming the role of the 'Empire', capital has emerged as a dominant force (Hardt and Negri 2000).

In this neoliberal era, economic 'firms' have evolved into powerful, autonomous entities. This brings the accounting concept of an 'entity' into a political realm. Corporations are no longer simply assets of shareholders. Firms now stand as independent entities, exerting influence even over their shareholders. Shareholders, in turn, are not traditional owners but rather investors, gambling with their

Figure 10.2: Sustainabilizing strategy

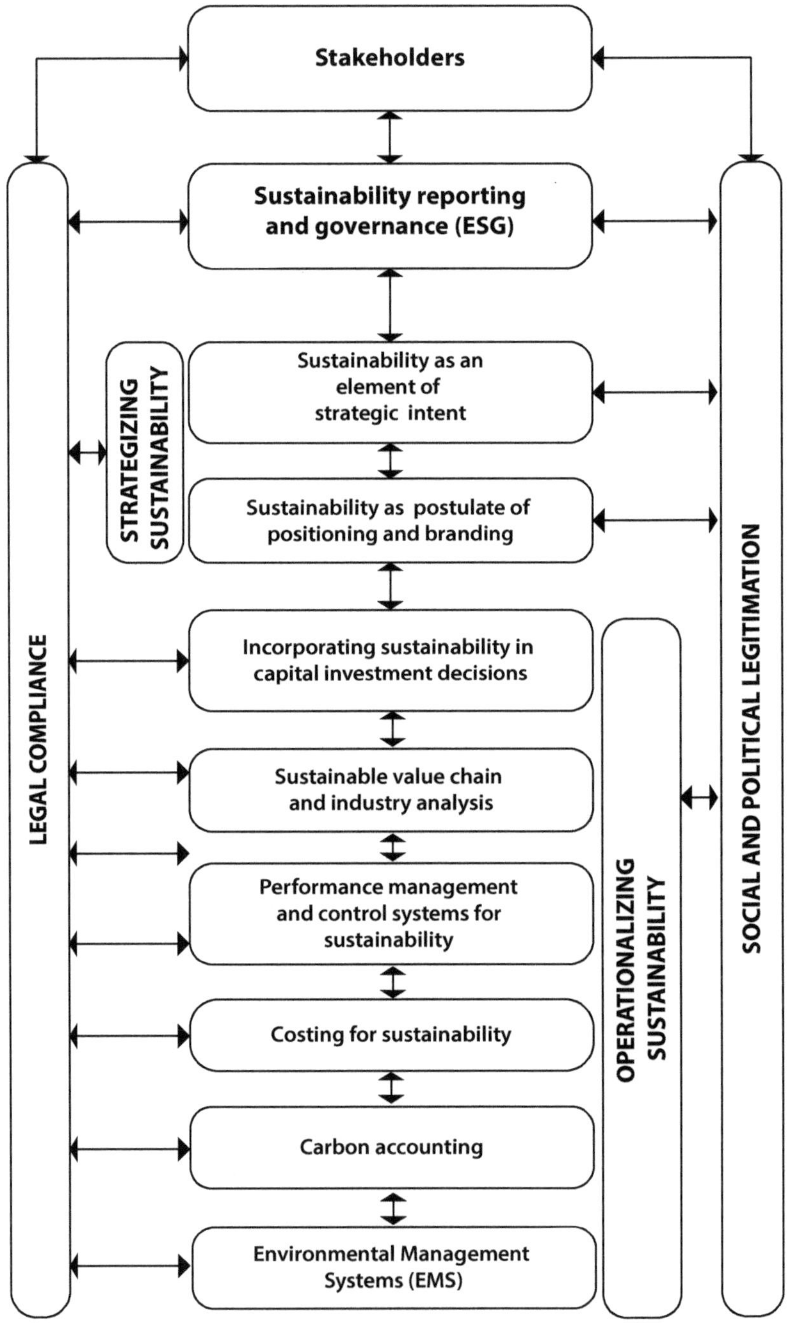

savings for a market return. Ownership has been reduced to a legal formality, a tradeable commodity. The conventional notion of ownership has become diluted.

Simultaneously, corporations have grown 'too big to fail'. Their failures now extend beyond mere shareholder losses; they can lead to political-economic catastrophes. Thus, while corporations are instrumental in progress, they have also become a primary source of insecurity and risk.

Parallel to this, neoliberalism has changed the meaning of security. Instead of the state's territorial integrity, the doctrine of human security now insists that living populations and individuals ought to constitute the new object of security (Gros 2014, 23). What is sacred is no longer the sovereignty of the state but the 'life' of the individual and the possibilities of reproducing that life profitably (Cooper 2015).

In neoliberal governance, therefore, corporations emerge as paradoxical entities. On the one hand, they are venues where life can be profitably sustained. On the other hand, they represent spaces where life – in its economic, social, and ecological dimensions – is endangered.

The implosion of ownership, alongside the paradoxical role of the firm as both a life-sustaining and endangering entity, has brought a new concept into the corporate accountability discourse: the 'stake'. This 'stake' represents the firm's capacity to impact collective and individual life. For the first time, the 'stake' is becoming a more crucial concept than legal ownership.

Notably, in popular stakeholder theory, 'stake' is defined as the capacity of stakeholders to influence the firm. However, while this capacity is important, the reverse – how the firm influences collective and individual life – is more relevant in understanding recent shifts in accountability as an element of biopolitical governance. Multinational firms have emerged as dominant forces in shaping our life processes; they have a significant 'stake' over human and non-human existence.

Given their unprecedented power, these firms are simultaneously our allies and adversaries; they are seen as both suspects and prospects, protectors and threats.

The pluralisation of corporate accountability today exemplifies a neoliberal paradox. As corporations exist as both suspects and prospects, they must legitimise themselves not only through financial performance but across multiple fronts. They must embrace an 'obligation' toward the sustainability of the planet. Corporate accountability represents this effort of legitimisation. Sustainability reporting is a crucial expression of this, addressing threats ranging from economic impacts to ecological and social justice issues.

Consequently, firms must now justify not only their contribution to wealth accumulation (through financial statements) but also their lack of (or reduced) threats to human and non-human life forms (achieved, however (un)successfully, through sustainability reporting). Viewed through the lens of neoliberal biopolitics, the surge in corporate sustainability reporting – once considered an 'oxymoron' – represents a biopolitical strategy to address the paradox of neoliberal security inherent in the existence of multinational corporations.

10.5 Strategizing sustainability

Corporate sustainability reporting has grown exponentially, becoming the principal strategy for corporations to legitimise themselves within the neoliberal accountability framework. This growth, however, does not necessarily indicate an increase in corporate sustainability. Critical accounting researchers have suggested that such reporting might mislead and propagate incorrect notions of sustainability, often amounting to 'greenwashing'.

Despite this, some companies have begun to consider sustainability as an element of their strategy making. Influential figures in mainstream management now see sustainability as a strategic imperative. They view it not just as an environmental challenge but as an opportunity to enhance market positioning. This perspective, advocated by experts such as Michael Porter, emphasises sustainability as a core business strategy. For instance, Porter and Kramer (2006, 2) argue:

Side note:

At this point, it would be beneficial to read Gray et al. (2014), pages 220–232, for a critical perspective on these managerialist claims.

> '...the prevailing approaches to CSR are so fragmented and so disconnected from business and strategy as to obscure many of the greatest opportunities for companies to benefit society. If, instead, corporations were to analyze their prospects for social responsibility using the same frameworks that guide their core business choices, they would discover that CSR can be much more than a cost, a constraint, or a charitable deed – it can be a source of opportunity, innovation, and competitive advantage.'

Mainstream managerial discourses have sought to incorporate sustainability in various ways. Within the management accounting remit, these methodologies can be broadly divided into six categories (as outlined in Figure 10.2), which this section and the next will explore:

1. Ensuring top leadership commitment through Environmental, Social, and Governance (ESG).
2. Redefining elements of organisational purpose (vision and mission).
3. Employing sustainability for strategic positioning and competitive advantage.

4. Integrating sustainability into the value chain and performance management systems.
5. Developing costing techniques for sustainability.
6. Developing and implementing environmental management systems (EMS).

Ensuring top leadership commitment

An Environmental, Social, and Governance (ESG) index is a type of stock index that assesses corporate investment risk by evaluating companies based on their performance across these three criteria. These indices provide benchmarks for investments that meet specific non-financial standards.

1. **Environmental:** Considers how a company performs as a steward of the natural environment (e.g., climate change policies, energy use, waste management).
2. **Social:** Examines how a company manages relationships with its employees, suppliers, customers, and communities (e.g., labour management, health and safety).
3. **Governance:** Assesses a company's leadership, executive pay, audits, internal controls, and shareholder rights.

Investors and analysts are increasingly interested in these indices as they seek to invest in companies that are not only financially sound but also less risky in terms of their environmental and social impacts. Examples include the MSCI ESG Leaders Indices, the FTSE4Good Index Series, and the Dow Jones Sustainability Indices.

In a broader sense, ESG is a market database-driven analytical framework. Given that investors are increasingly concerned about sustainability in these indices, corporate top management must become sensitive to them and acknowledge the need to incorporate ESG elements into top-level governance structures.

Though this has the possibility of misinterpreting the 'broader idea of sustainability' (Gray et al. 2014; Milne 1996), this tendency has at least broadened the idea of corporate governance beyond the traditional stewardship perspective. The necessity of improving a company's ESG index assessment may lead the board to implement strategic actions, such as:

1. Environmental: Setting robust ecological policies, implementing green initiatives (e.g., renewable energy), and ensuring transparent reporting on emissions.
2. Social: Establishing Corporate Social Responsibility (CSR) programmes,

enhancing employee welfare policies (e.g., diversity, inclusion), and engaging with stakeholders.

3. Governance: Ensuring board diversity, establishing clear transparency and accountability structures, and implementing a strong code of ethics.

The common belief of ESG index providers is that such actions allow a corporation to build a sustainable, responsible, and ethical business model that adds value to all stakeholders.

Envisioning sustainability

As discussed in Chapter 2, strategizing involves setting and communicating a corporation's long-term vision, often through vision and mission statements. By 'envisioning sustainability', we refer to corporate efforts to integrate sustainability concepts into their strategic intents. Over the past decade, many large corporations have revised their vision and mission statements to reflect their evolving commitment to sustainability (see Figure 10.3).

It is essential to approach these statements with caution. They are aspirational and, as Gray et al. (2014, 223) note, 'this is the key point - these statements will not be supported by any explanation or evidence as to why they might be true'.

Figure 10.3: Examples of corporate envisioning of sustainability

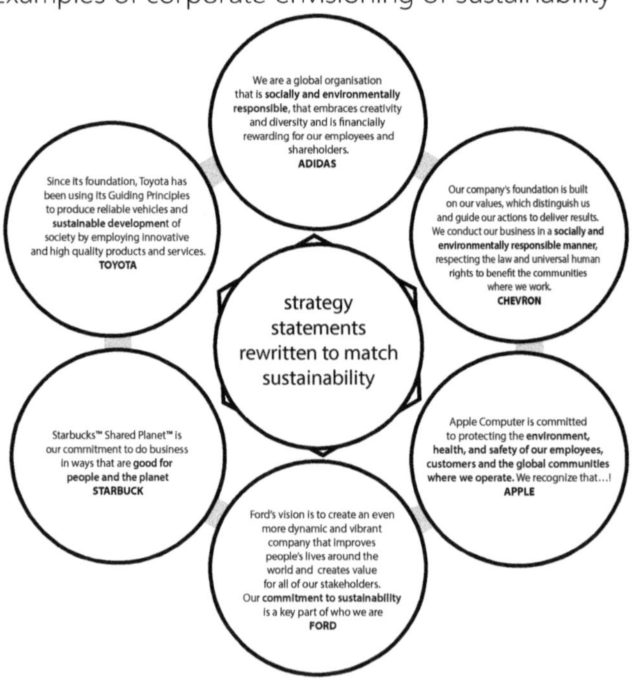

One primary motivator for reframing these statements is the reporting mandates of accrediting bodies such as the Global Reporting Initiative (GRI). These organisations explicitly outline that companies must demonstrate a clear commitment to sustainability at the strategic level. For instance, the 2021 version of GRI's standards stipulates that reports must include a statement detailing 'the role of the highest governance body and of senior executives in developing, approving, and updating the organization's purpose, value or mission statements, strategies, policies, and goals related to sustainable development' (p.23).

When coupled with the need to legitimise their actions through reporting (Bebbington et al. 2008; Cho and Patten 2007), such standards exert institutional pressure on corporations to reform their strategic outlooks. Companies appear to engage in 'rating games'—attempting to legitimise their presence by achieving higher ratings from global institutions (Alawattage and Fernando 2017; Porter and Kramer 2006). In playing this game, companies employ textual strategies (imitation, redefinition, codification) to demonstrate compliance. Changes in vision and mission statements, therefore, often reflect the necessity for compliance reporting, accreditation, and ratings.

Sustainability to postulate strategic positioning

The recent past has seen a surge in mass awareness and appreciation of planetary sustainability. In market terms, this has led to increased demand and willingness to pay premium prices for sustainably produced products.

Nielsen's 2015 Global Sustainability Report, 'The Sustainability Imperative', highlighted these key trends:

1. Brands demonstrating a commitment to sustainability outperform those that do not. Sales of sustainable brands grew by over 4% globally, compared with less than 1% for other brands.
2. Sixty-six per cent of consumers reported being willing to pay more for sustainable brands, up from 55% in 2014.
3. Key purchasing drivers were identified as: trust in the brand (62%), health and wellness benefits (59%), fresh/natural ingredients (57%), environmental friendliness (45%), and commitment to social value (43%).

In response, companies have adopted various marketing strategies to capitalise on this sustainability premium. Nielsen's survey categorised these tactics into three groups:

- Claim Only: The brand indicates sustainability on product labels.
- Marketing Only: The brand uses websites, news, etc., to promote social/

environmental impact.
- Claim + Marketing: The brand combines product claims with sustainability marketing.

The survey revealed that 65% of companies used 'Marketing Only', 29% used 'Claim + Marketing', and only 2% used 'Claim Only'. This demonstrates that companies are keen to promote their products as 'sustainable' because of the appeal of sustainability branding to consumers.

10.6 Operationalizing sustainability

'Operationalizing sustainability' refers to corporations' efforts to integrate sustainability dimensions and criteria into their decision-making processes, performance evaluations, transaction processing, and costing practices. As depicted in Figure 10.2, in the realm of management accounting, we can identify six primary themes; the remaining three are discussed here.

Sustainability in capital investment decisions

Although there have not been significant technical breakthroughs in developing models for capital investment decisions that can quantify and monetise the impact of investment projects on sustainability, corporate managers are increasingly willing to 'consider' sustainability alongside financial factors. In the absence of quantified data, managers appear inclined to consider qualitative narratives, especially when they support the appraisal's financial outcomes.

This trend was highlighted in a survey by Vesty (2011) in Australia, which found:

- Enhancing corporate reputation is a key motivator for considering sustainability in capital investment decisions.
- The primary method for incorporation is identifying sustainability risks, alongside considerations of competitive advantage, community impacts, and employee engagement.
- Fifty-five per cent of CFO respondents indicated they did not downplay qualitative data in favour of quantitative analysis.
- Forty per cent of CFO respondents would not automatically reject projects with negative net present values if sustainability benefits were identified.
- Sustainability managers are increasingly playing a key role in capital investment appraisals.
- While sustainability considerations are being incorporated, Vesty (2011) concluded they had not yet become the primary decision-making criterion.

Sustainable value chain analysis and competitive industry analysis

One key attempt to operationalise sustainability within existing frameworks is the reconceptualisation of Michael Porter's value chain analysis. This demonstrates how the global sustainability agenda has compelled management experts to reconsider their frameworks. This shift could be seen as a remarketing strategy for their models in an evolving epistemic market. They argue:

> 'When a company uses the value chain to chart all the social consequences of its activities, it has, in effect, created an inventory of problems and opportunities. ... In general, companies should attempt to clear away as many negative value-chain social impacts as possible. Some company activities will prove to offer opportunities for social and strategic distinction' (Porter and Kramer 2006, 5).

Porter and Kramer's (2006) epistemic strategy is to 'insert' specific examples of how sustainability can be 'considered' as an opportunity (rather than a cost) for creating value. Table 10.1 summarises their illustrative prescriptions.

Table 10.1: Porter and Kramer's insertion of sustainability into value chain analysis

Value chain element	Examples of operational matters	Ways to consider sustainability: analyse and minimize
Inbound logistics	Incoming materials, storage, data collection, services, and customer access.	Transportation impacts (e.g., emissions, congestion, logging roads).
Operations	Assembly, component fabrication, and branch operations.	Emissions and waste; biodiversity impacts; energy and water usage; worker safety; hazardous materials.
Outbound logistics	Order processing, warehousing, and report preparation.	Packaging use and disposal; transportation impacts.
Marketing and sales	Salesforce, promotion, advertising, website.	Truthful advertising; advertising to children; pricing practices (e.g., price discrimination); consumer information; privacy.
After-sales service	Installation, customer support, complaint resolution, and repair.	Disposal of obsolete products; handling of consumables (e.g., motor oil); customer privacy.
Firm infrastructure	Financing, planning, investor relations.	Financial reporting practices; government practices; transparency; use of lobbying to promote sustainability.
Human resource management	Recruiting, training, and compensation system.	Education and job training; safe working conditions; diversity and discrimination; health care; compensation policies.
Technology development	Product design, testing, process design, and material research.	Ethical research practices (e.g., animal testing, GMOs); product safety; conservation of raw materials; recycling.
Procurement	Components, machinery, advertising, services.	Supply chain practices (e.g., bribery, child labour); uses of particular inputs (e.g., animal fur); utilisation of natural resources.

Source: based on Porter and Kramer (2006)

Porter and Kramer's (2006) subsequent move involves integrating 'sustainability' into their renowned 'diamond framework' of competitive context, as discussed in Chapter 2. This framework evaluates the conduciveness of national and industrial contexts for gaining a competitive advantage. By incorporating sustainability, Porter and Kramer aim to expand the framework's political relevance, using the same model to gauge the environment's conduciveness to fostering corporate sustainability. Table 10.2 encapsulates these sustainability insertions.

Table 10.2: Inserting sustainability into the framework of the competitive advantage of a nation

Elements of the Diamond Framework	Definition of the element	Factors that enhance firms' collective capacity to be sustainable
The context for firm strategy and rivalry	The rules and incentives that govern competition.	Fair and open local competition; intellectual property protection; transparency (e.g., financial reporting, corruption); the rule of law; meritocratic incentive systems.
Local Demand Conditions	The nature and sophistication of local customer needs.	Sophistication of local demand (e.g., appeal of social value propositions: Whole Foods' customers); demanding regulatory standards (e.g., California auto emissions standards).
Related and Supporting Industries	The local availability of supporting industries.	Availability of local suppliers (e.g., Nestlé's milk collection dairies); access to firms in related fields; presence of clusters.
Factor (Input) Conditions	Presence of high-quality, specialized inputs available to firms.	Availability of human resources; access to research institutions; efficient physical and administrative infrastructure; sustainable natural resources; efficient access to capital.

Source: based on Porter and Kramer (2006)

Sustainable performance management with Balanced Scorecards

The Balanced Scorecard (BSC) has been a popular tool in management accounting for decades. A key response of management accounting to the sustainability imperative has been to explore how the BSC can operationalise sustainability. Research primarily addresses two major issues:

1. integrating sustainability into the BSC, and
2. establishing causal links between sustainability and other performance dimensions.

The integration of sustainability into the BSC has already been discussed in Chapter 4 (see 'Reimagining the BSC for Sustainability'). This segment focuses on other efforts to adapt the BSC.

Integrating sustainability into the BSC

Proponents argue that the BSC's top-down structure, which deduces performance measures from strategy, ensures all activities, including environmental and social aspects, are aligned with strategy implementation. This implies that performance management can explicitly consider the relationship between a firm's environmental, social, and economic performance.

Three approaches for integrating sustainability into the BSC are discussed in the literature (Figge et al. 2002):

1. Integrating environmental and social aspects into the four perspectives. This approach, akin to Porter and Kramer's (2006) suggestions, involves incorporating specific sustainability issues into each of the four BSC dimensions (e.g., considering eco-justice issues in the internal process perspective). Figge et al. (2002, 274) state that: 'Environmental/social aspects consequently become an integral part of the conventional Scorecard and are automatically integrated in its cause-effect links'.
2. Introducing an additional non-market perspective. This approach recognises that some eco-justice and eco-efficiency issues are not yet fully integrated into market processes. Thus, an additional fifth dimension is proposed 'when environmental or social aspects that cannot be reflected according to their strategic relevance within the four standard BSC perspectives... significantly influence the firm's success from outside the market system' (Figge et al., 2002, 274).
3. Deducting a derived environmental and social scorecard. This approach extends the above two. The focus is on deriving a specific BSC from sustainability issues across existing dimensions and the new fifth dimension, thereby augmenting the conventional BSC.

Establishing causal links between sustainability and financial outcomes

The second challenge is establishing causal links between sustainability, strategy, and other BSC aspects. Chapter 4 introduced the 'strategy map', clarifying these connections to ensure all dimensions contribute to financial improvement. Kaplan and McMillan's (2021) paper, 'Reimagining the BSC for the ESG Era', demonstrates how these 'causalities' - or 'finalities', as Nørreklit (2003) critiques the BSC's concept of causality - are identified.

As discussed in Chapters 2 and 4, this approach mirrors Porter and Kramer's (2006) methodology. It examines sustainability concerns within the existing BSC framework. These efforts to reshape traditional management accounting and strategy frameworks often lack genuinely sustainable approaches. Instead, they seem more focused on repackaging their models in a market increasingly valuing sustainability. Despite the new terminology, their fundamental ideology —prioritising financial objectives —remains unchanged.

Privileging financial over sustainability

Such attempts to integrate sustainability into existing performance management frameworks may bring some positive outcomes, at least in terms of managerial acceptance of sustainability issues. They may develop KPIs that translate sustainability concerns into performance targets and, thereby, implement operational initiatives.

However, such initiatives are possible only to the extent that management can effectively demonstrate a positive financial causality of such KPIs. In other words, these attempts limit the way in which we consider and prioritise sustainability. Sustainability is operationalised only if it can be established that a positive causality exists between solving sustainability issues and financial performance.

This is because existing frameworks, including the BSC and value chain analysis, are inherently capitalistic; they assess managerial actions only through their contributions toward competitive positioning and shareholder wealth maximisation. Any attempt to integrate sustainability into such a framework will eventually surrender sustainability to the possibilities of profits. As our common sense often tells us, many eco-justice and eco-efficiency issues do not have a direct, demonstrable positive causality toward the return on investment. Perhaps the only financial consequence would be the punitive cost effect (such as penalties or loss of reputation) that failing to attain eco-justice and eco-efficiency would create.

This means the BSC and value chain analysis-based sustainability management, as conceptualised so far, privileges the financial over sustainability. Let us revisit Milton Friedman's and Daly's critiques. These economists identified a fundamental conflict: the profit motives of private capital are inherently at odds with the principles of social responsibility. They faced a political choice and chose shareholders. In contrast, these attempts to re-envision management accounting models appear to be veiled efforts to obscure this inherent contradiction between the economic doctrines of wealth accumulation for a few and the sustainability of everyone else.

Costing sustainability

Two primary cost accounting approaches to sustainability are prominent:

1. the application of Activity-Based Costing (ABC) to allocate sustainability-related costs, and
2. life cycle costing. It is important to recognise that current costing methods tend to be skewed towards accounting for 'ecological' aspects, with a particular emphasis on greenhouse gas (GHG) emissions.

Use of ABC in sustainability costing

The fundamental assumption of sustainability costing is that environmental emissions can be quantified accurately over time (Lemon and Pember 2014). To this end, ABC is considered effective for understanding the drivers of resource consumption, which is a crucial component in determining GHG emissions. ABC models how resources are consumed, the reasons for their consumption, and the parties responsible (Lemon and Pember, 2014).

Numerous papers explain how corporations should account for environmental emissions, but two documents stand out: the 'Environmental Management Accounting: International Guidance Document' (International Federation of Accountants, 2005) and the 'Environmental Management Accounting Procedures and Principles' (United Nations Division of Sustainable Development, 2001). The methodology advocated is essentially a blend of 'natural capital inventory accounting' and 'input-output analysis' (Gray and Bebbington 2001; Lamberton 2005).

Broadly, this involves tracking the environmental impact by tracing the physical flow of inputs, processes, and outputs, and then assigning monetary values to them.

Tracing the physical flows: materials flow accounting.

The system theory behind tracing the physical flow posits that all physical inputs eventually become outputs—either as products or as waste and emissions. This necessitates a balance between inputs and outputs, known as physical flow accounting, 'materials balance', or 'eco-balance'. The International Federation of Accountants (2005, 30) recommends that organisations track all physical inputs and outputs, ensuring no significant quantities of energy, water, or other materials are unaccounted for.

This input-output balance can be applied at various levels: the entire organisation, a specific site, a process, or even beyond the organisation to include supply chain elements. The International Federation of Accountants (2005, 31) suggests that a comprehensive 'eco-balance' should trace material flows through all organisational steps: procurement, delivery, inventory, distribution, shipping, waste collection, recycling, treatment, and disposal.

This is crucial for two reasons. First, it serves as the basis for the physical activity on which the cost accounting aspect is built, offering a clear view of the activities driving environmental costs. Second, it establishes a foundation for environmental performance indicators (EPIs), which can be absolute (e.g., total freshwater used) or relative (e.g., freshwater consumed per output unit).

Tracing the monetary flow: activity-based costing of environmental impact

In this approach, the objective is to identify the costs associated with environmental activities and allocate them to the relevant cost objects (products). The United Nations Division of Sustainable Development (2001, 75) recommends that:

> 'Whenever possible, environment-driven costs should be allocated directly to the activity that causes the costs and to the respective cost centers and cost drivers. Consequently, the costs of treating, for example, the toxic waste arising from a product should directly and exclusively be allocated to that product.'

In doing so, ABC is considered appropriate due to its accurate representation of 'cost incidents'—the way environmental activities utilise resources and how these activities generate costs. This dual utility is encapsulated in the 'cost assignment view' and the 'process view', as illustrated in Figure 10.4.

The United Nations Division of Sustainable Development (2001) states that activity-based monetary and physical flow accounting enables different cost classification schema. Such a scheme should encompass elements such as:

- Waste and emission treatment.
- Preventive environmental management.
- Material purchase value of non-product outputs.
- Processing cost of non-product outputs.

These cost categories should correlate with environmental dimensions (e.g., Air/climate, Wastewater, Waste, Soil/groundwater). Table 10.3 illustrates a template of this activity-cost classification scheme.

Figure 10.4: Environmental activity-based costing

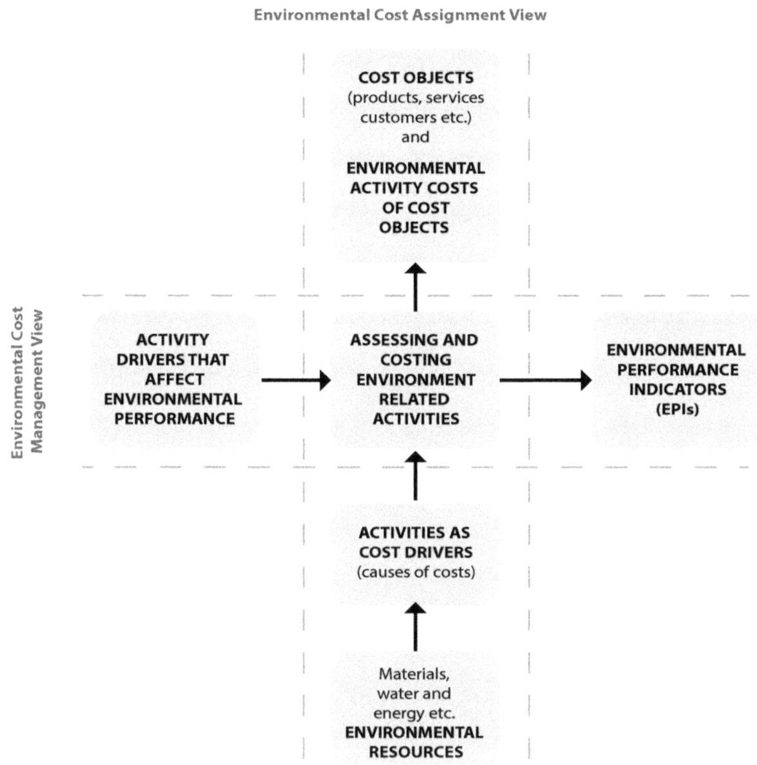

Life cycle costing (LCC) and whole life costing (WLC)

Activity-based physical and monetary flow accounting considers the sustainability implications of capital investment decisions only to the extent they are reflected in depreciation. LCC and WLC, in contrast, explicitly address large capital investment projects with construction elements. They are defined as tools for assessing the total cost performance of an asset throughout its life cycle: acquisition, operation, maintenance, and disposal (Dragos and Neamtu 2013; Langdon 2007).

Both LCC and WLC operate on the premise that the purchase price does not fully capture the financial and non-financial benefits that an environmentally preferable asset can provide, as these benefits (and costs) accumulate over the asset's life. LCC typically comprises four primary financial cost categories: investment, operational, maintenance, and end-of-life disposal.

Table 10.3: Environmental activity-cost classification scheme

Environmental cost/expenditure categories	Air / Climate	Wastewater	Waste	Soil / Ground-water	Noise / Vibration	Biodiversity / Landscape	Radiation	Other	Total
1. Waste and emission treatment									
1.1. Depreciation for related equipment									
1.2. Maintenance and operating materials and services									
1.3. Related personnel									
1.4. Fees, taxes, charges									
1.5. Fines and penalties									
1.6. Insurance for environmental liabilities									
1.7. Provisions for clean up costs, remediation									
2. Prevention and environmental management									
2.1. External services for environmental management									
2.2. Personnel for general environmental management activities									
2.3. Research and development									
2.4. Extra expenditure for cleaner technologies									
2.5. Other environmental management costs									
3. Material purchase value of non- product output									
3.1. Raw materials									
3.2. Packaging									
3.3. Auxiliary materials									
3.4. Operating materials									
3.5. Energy									
3.6. Water									
4. Processing costs of non-product output									
Total of environmental expenditure									
5. Environmental revenues									
5.1. Subsidies, awards									
5.2. Other earnings									
Total of Environmental revenues									

Source: United Nations Division of Sustainable Development (2001, 19)

When these categories are expanded to include 'externalities', it evolves into Environmental Life Cycle Costing (ELCC). ELCC, for instance, might measure external costs of global warming contributions (Dragos and Neamtu, 2013).

WLC builds upon LCC, focusing not only on the construction, maintenance, operation, and disposal of the asset but also on client and user costs. These additional costs include project financing, land acquisition, income, and external costs. Thus, LCC is effectively a subset of WLC. This distinction is depicted in Figure 10.5.

Figure 10.5: WLC and LCC costs

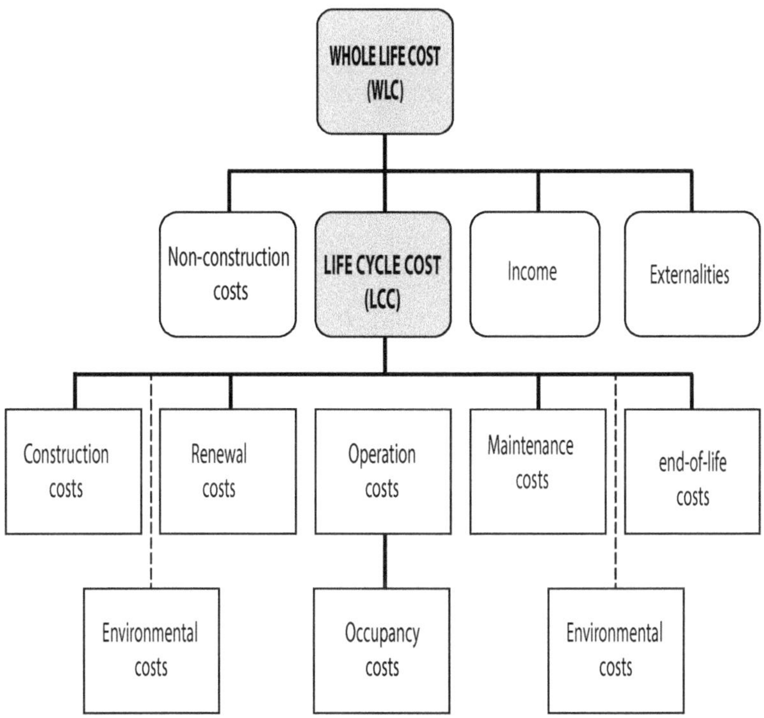

Source: Royal Institution of Chartered Surveyors (RICS) (2016, 5)

Carbon costing/accounting

Carbon accounting (or greenhouse gas (GHG) accounting) is the process of measuring the amounts of carbon dioxide and other GHG emissions produced by an organisation, event, product, or asset. It is a critical tool for quantifying and managing carbon footprints.

According to the Greenhouse Gas (GHG) Protocol, which provides widely adopted accounting standards, GHG accounting can use spend-based or activity-based methods. The calculation process generally involves:

1. Identifying Emission Sources: (Scope 1, 2, and 3).
2. Data Collection: Gathering data on energy consumption, fuel use, etc.
3. Selecting Emission Factors: Used to convert activity data (e.g., litres of fuel) into GHG emissions (expressed in CO2-equivalent).
4. Applying Calculation Tools: Using GHG Protocol methodologies.
5. Aggregation and Reporting: Summing emissions for the total GHG inventory.
6. Setting Reduction Targets: Developing strategies to achieve targets.
7. Tracking Performance: Monitoring and reporting progress.

The GHG Protocol categorises emissions into three 'scopes':

- Scope 1 Emissions: Direct GHG emissions from sources that are owned or controlled by the entity. This includes combustion in owned boilers, furnaces, and vehicles.
- Scope 2 Emissions: Indirect GHG emissions from the consumption of purchased electricity, heat, or steam. These emissions physically occur at the facility where the energy is generated.
- Scope 3 Emissions: All other indirect emissions that occur in a company's value chain. These are consequences of the entity's activities but arise from sources not owned or controlled by it (e.g., transportation, waste disposal, use of sold products).

Understanding these scopes helps organisations to manage their carbon footprint and comply with reporting requirements.

Environmental management systems

Environmental Management Systems (EMS) encompass many concepts discussed in this chapter. An EMS comprises an organisation's formal structures for planning, executing, managing, controlling, achieving, and reporting its environmental policies. Gray and Bebbington (2001, 87) describe EMS as a means for organisations to systematically harmonise their diverse environmental responses with other management systems.

Like total quality management (TQM), EMS aims to integrate environmental quality into an organisation's operational processes, making environmental responsibility part of everyone's role. While specific approaches vary, the following key elements broadly define an EMS:

1. Environmental audits, surveys, and assessments: Assessing legislative, market, and industrial contexts to understand external pressures, paired with an internal review to identify environmental impact.
2. Environmental objectives and policies: The policy framework outlining the company's normative approach, commitment level, and legal compliance necessities.
3. Environmental strategies: Specific programmes, projects, and initiatives undertaken to realise environmental objectives.
4. Responsibility and accountability structure: Defining who is responsible and accountable for each element of the environmental strategies.
5. Performance management framework: Processes to ensure the operational implementation of strategies, periodic review of outcomes, and protocols for revising plans.
6. Reporting systems: Establishing transaction processing systems to account for the environmental impact of daily operations (e.g., recording energy consumption) and maintaining audit trails, including data compilation for sustainability reports.

These EMS elements are increasingly being integrated into enterprise resource planning (ERP) software.

Chapter summary

This chapter aimed to discuss how management accounting has responded to the global sustainability agenda. Initially, it outlined the political contradictions underlying sustainability (Economy, Polity, Society, Ecology). The neoliberal political rationale of corporations promoting sustainability was then explored. Prominent neoclassical economists like Friedman and Daly opposed corporate social responsibility, viewing it as 'pure and unadulterated socialism' or an 'oxymoron'. Despite this resistance, CSR grew significantly, challenging neoclassical views. This paradox puzzled mainstream researchers, leading to studies testing the positive correlation between CSR and shareholder value, which yielded mixed results.

The primary focus of this chapter was on how management accounting has adapted to the sustainability agenda. At the strategic level, responses included extending corporate accountability (ESG) and reformulating corporate vision and mission statements. At the operational level, new strategic management accounting tools were employed, including modifications in capital investment decisions, Porterian strategy discourses, the Balanced Scorecard, and new cost accounting techniques (LCC, WLC, and ABC for material flow accounting).

Throughout this and previous chapters, we have encountered many instances in which management accounting scholars and practitioners have attempted to revise their conceptual frameworks to incorporate sustainability. Their motives may be genuine; they may recognise the criticality of enhancing management accounting practices.

However, the fundamental problem is that those efforts fail to recognise and acknowledge, both ideologically and pragmatically, the fundamental political contradictions upon which (un)sustainability emerges. As discussed at the beginning of the chapter, the political contradictions between the economy, polity, society, and ecology must be recognised for a true understanding and action programme of sustainability. This demands the willingness and techno-managerial acumen to appreciate sustainability beyond the economic apparatuses of capital accumulation.

This is exactly what management accounting thought has failed to do.

As a result, various attempts to incorporate sustainability into existing management accounting frameworks can be both misleading and dangerous, as the true meaning of sustainability often gets 'overcoded'. This notion of 'overcoding', from Deleuze and Guattari (1987, 41), refers to the expression of the capitalist axiomatic, resulting in 'phenomena of centering, unification, totalization, integration, hierarchization, and finalization'.

This is what happens in the management accounting adventures explained in this chapter. Through various accounting measures and procedures, sustainability gets centred, unified, totalised, integrated, hierarchised, and financialised as something that can be operationalised through corporate profit motives. Sustainability gets overcoded into 'ESG'—something corporations and mainstream accounting researchers can proxy for using available market data.

When translated into these market variables, sustainability loses its broader meaning and becomes narrowly economic. In this 'proxification', sustainability acquires a different economic meaning that is far from the true meaning envisaged by the UN and environmental activists. Thus, in the name of ESG, strategy gurus do not see poverty; instead, they see corporate 'fortunes at the bottom of the pyramid' (Prahalad 2005). They do not see how 'poverty capital' (Roy 2010) operates; instead, they see a 'new ecosystem' from which corporations can earn extra profits (Kaplan and McMillan 2021).

This leads us to carefully consider Milne's assertion that 'sustainability is not an organizational concept and to apply it at the (capitalistic) organizational level is either very complex or very stupid' (Gray et al. 2014; Milne 1996).

Case study: The Coca-Cola Company: 'world without waste' or a 'world of contradictions'?

This case study is designed to be used in conjunction with Chapter 10: Strategising Sustainability. This is not a standalone case. Its primary pedagogical function is to provide students with a rich, empirical dataset to test, apply, and critique the specific theoretical concepts introduced in Chapter 10. The central paradox of The Coca-Cola Company – its simultaneous status as a celebrated ESG leader and the world's number-one plastic polluter – is used as a tangible manifestation of the 'overcoding' and 'proxification' thesis presented in Section 10.7.

Part 1: Case introduction and learning objectives

1.1 The analyst's paradox

An analyst at a new, sustainability-focused investment fund is conducting an in-depth due diligence analysis of The Coca-Cola Company. The initial review of the company's public-facing disclosures presents a sophisticated, data-rich narrative of sustainability leadership. This narrative is built upon a foundation of established frameworks, including its long-standing 'Creating Shared Value' (CSV) model, which argues that societal and business interests can be aligned.

The company's 2022 Business & Sustainability Report, for example, details its ambitious 'World Without Waste' initiative, first launched in 2018. This report quantifies significant progress, most notably the achievement of 159% 'water replenishment', a figure suggesting the company returns more water to ecosystems than it uses in its finished products. Furthermore, the company's disclosures indicate the integration of sustainability metrics into its core strategic management accounting systems, including the Balanced Scorecard framework. These positive, measurable outcomes are reflected in strong Environmental, Social, and Governance (ESG) ratings from various agencies, positioning Coca-Cola as a leader in its sector.

However, the analyst's due diligence simultaneously uncovers a starkly contradictory dataset from civil society and non-governmental organisations (NGOs). The 'Break Free From Plastic' global brand audit, an annual citizen-science initiative, has named The Coca-Cola Company the number-one global plastic polluter for six consecutive years.

A critical discovery amplifies this paradox: in December 2024, Coca-Cola 'evolved' its environmental goals. This 'evolution' involved quietly abandoning its headline 2030 target of achieving 25% reusable packaging. Concurrently, the company weakened its targets for both recycled content and collection, pushing back deadlines and reducing ambition.

1.2 The central task and learning objectives

The analyst – and thus the student – is tasked with moving beyond the simplistic, though relevant, accusation of 'greenwashing'. The central pedagogical task is to reconcile these two seemingly irreconcilable realities. How can a corporation be both a sustainability accounting leader – demonstrating best-practice measurement and reporting in areas like water – and an ecological laggard – demonstrating a persistent and worsening negative impact in areas like plastic waste?

This case requires the student to apply the theoretical lenses from Chapter 10 to diagnose this paradox not as simple hypocrisy, but as the logical and predictable outcome of 'strategising sustainability' within the existing capitalistic, neoliberal framework.

Upon successful completion of this case study, students will be able to:

1. Apply the four-dimensional sustainability framework (Economy, Polity, Society, Ecology) from Section 10.2 to dissect a corporation's business model and identify its fundamental, inherent contradictions.
2. Critically evaluate a company's strategic and management accounting responses to sustainability (e.g., ESG integration, Sustainable Balanced Scorecards, Value Chain analysis) using the frameworks from Sections 10.4, 10.5, and 10.6.
3. Analyse how specific management accounting techniques (e.g., environmental costing, SBSC 'finalities') function to 'privilege the financial over sustainability'.
4. Deconstruct corporate lobbying and reporting not merely as public relations, but as a form of 'biopolitical' governance that attempts to shape the 'polity', thereby resolving the apparent paradox of Friedman's critique.
5. Use the chapter's central thesis of 'overcoding' and 'proxification' to explain how and why genuine, broad sustainability goals are translated, transformed, obscured, or ultimately abandoned by the 'capitalist axiomatic' of organisational logic.

Part 2: 'Strategising sustainability' (chapter 10, section 10.5)

This part details Coca-Cola's formal sustainability strategy. It provides the empirical data that constructs the corporate narrative, positioning the firm as both a 'suspect and prospect' in neoliberal governance, as discussed in Section 10.4.

2.1 Envisioning sustainability: from CSV to a 'world without waste'

Coca-Cola's corporate discourse frames sustainability not as a compliance cost or a constraint, but as a core strategic imperative for long-term value creation. This narrative aligns perfectly with the 'Creating Shared Value' (CSV) model popularised by Porter and Kramer and discussed in Chapter 10. The CSV logic posits that corporations can 'do well by doing good', creating a "win-win" scenario.

A flagship example is Coca-Cola's 'Coletivo' initiative in Brazil. The programme is lauded in the CSV literature for its dual purpose: it increases the 'employability of low income youth' while simultaneously 'strengthening the company's retail distribution channels and brand strength'. This "win-win" logic is the central rationale underpinning its broader sustainability strategy, including the 'World Without Waste' initiative launched in 2018. The company's 2022 Sustainability Report explicitly states that its goals are to build 'long-term business resilience' and 'earn our social license to operate'.

This corporate framing provides a powerful empirical example of the 'rationalisation of the oxymoron' discussed in Section 10.3. When corporate social responsibility (CSR) first emerged, neoclassical economists like Milton Friedman decried it as 'pure and unadulterated socialism'. Coca-Cola's CSV strategy demonstrates the resolution of this apparent paradox. It is not socialism; rather, it is an advanced neoliberal rationalisation.

By applying the Foucauldian perspective introduced in Section 10.3 , this strategy can be understood as a form of 'biopolitical' governance. The firm 'governs' the 'life of populations' (e.g., low-income youth in Brazil) not primarily for social ends, but as a means to enhance its own economic apparatus (e.g., stronger distribution channels). This is a textbook example of the 'Economy' dimension (efficiency, profit) co-opting and instrumentalising the 'Society' dimension (social solidarity, eco-justice) as defined in Figure 10.1.

2.2 Top leadership commitment: ESG and executive compensation

Section 10.5 identifies Environmental, Social, and Governance (ESG) indices as a 'market database-driven analytical framework' that exerts institutional pressure on top management. Coca-Cola's corporate disclosures reflect a clear response to this pressure. The company explicitly notes the prioritisation of ESG practices and, in its 2022 report, stated that it had incorporated ESG goals into executive compensation.

Specifically, the Talent and Compensation Committee approved linking the long-term incentive (LTI) plan for its executive leadership team to a metric related to 'water replenishment in Leadership Locations'. This directly connects top-level managerial remuneration to a stated sustainability outcome.

However, other analyses observe that Coca-Cola has not followed the growing trend of robustly or comprehensively 'incorporating environmental, social, and governance (ESG) metrics into compensation programs'. This apparent contradiction reveals a critical insight into the 'proxification' process discussed in Section 10.7. The choice of which ESG metric to link to executive pay is a strategic act of management accounting. The question is not if ESG is included, but what is included and what is omitted.

The decision to link compensation to 'water replenishment' – and not to a metric like 'virgin plastic reduction' or 'reusable packaging implementation' – is a deliberate one.

1. Controllability and Measurability: As Part 3 will detail, Coca-Cola has invested heavily in developing a sophisticated, proprietary accounting methodology (Volumetric Water Benefit Accounting). This methodology allows it to quantify and achieve a 'win' in water (e.g., 159% replenished). This provides a positive, auditable, and seemingly impressive number, which is ideal for the 'rating games' that influence ESG scores.
2. Conflict with the Core Business Model: Conversely, a metric for reducing virgin plastic or increasing reuse would be in direct conflict with the company's core profit engine, which is predicated on the high-volume, low-cost sale of beverages in single-use PET bottles.
3. The 'Proxification' Act: Therefore, the ESG framework does not, in this instance, drive holistic sustainability. It drives measurement. In response, the firm 'proxifies' its most fundamental, intractable, and business-model-defining sustainability challenge (plastic waste) with a metric it has managerially and technically 'solved' (water). The 'water' metric stands in for 'sustainability' in the compensation plan, 'overcoding' the more significant, unresolved problem of plastic.

Part 3: 'Operationalising sustainability' (chapter 10, section 10.6)

This part examines the specific management accounting techniques that enable and enact Coca-Cola's strategy. These tools provide the technical, 'objective' infrastructure that performs the work of 'overcoding' and 'proxification' identified in Chapter 10.

3.1 Costing sustainability i: the 'proxification' of water

Section 10.6 discusses 'materials flow accounting' and the 'eco-balance' (input-output analysis) as a key method for costing sustainability. Coca-Cola's 'water replenishment' methodology is a world-class and highly illustrative example of this practice.

The company's headline claim is that it returned 159% of the water used in its 2022 finished products. This figure is not the result of a simple 1:1 replacement (i.e., putting 1.59 litres back into the specific aquifer from which 1 litre was drawn). Instead, it is the result of a complex, de-contextualised accounting calculation.

In partnership with The Nature Conservancy (TNC) and the consultancy LimnoTech, the company developed a methodology known as 'Volumetric Water Benefit Accounting (VWBA)'. This methodology estimates the 'annual volumetric water benefit' that is 'yielded' by a 'global portfolio of water replenishment projects'. These projects include watershed protection, improved water access and sanitation, and support for water for productive use (e.g., agriculture). This accounting framework allows the company to 'quantify and measure' the ecosystem benefits of these disparate projects, aggregate them into a single 'volume' of water, and then offset this manufactured 'asset' against its 'liability' of global water consumption.

This VWBA methodology is a perfect, technical manifestation of 'proxification'.

1. The 'Ecology'/'Polity' Problem: The actual sustainability problem with water is (a) ecological (the depletion of a specific, local aquifer) and (b) political (the "tragedy of the commons" where a bottling plant's water extraction creates conflict with local communities and farmers). This represents a fundamental contradiction between the 'Economy' (the plant's need for a low-cost input) and the 'Ecology' and 'Society' (the local community's right to that resource).
2. The Accounting 'Solution': The VWBA methodology 'overcodes' this 'political' and local problem. It de-links the site of impact (the local aquifer from which water was taken) from the site of 'replenishment' (a global portfolio of projects, such as a sanitation project in a different country).
3. The 'Proxified' Metric: The resulting metric, '159% replenished', is an 'eco-balance' that exists only on paper. It is a financialised construct, analogous to a carbon offset, that allows the firm to present a 'solved' problem in its sustainability report. It successfully 'overcodes' the "Polity" (local protests) and "Ecology" (local aquifers) dimensions by translating them into a single, manageable 'Economy' metric that can be audited and celebrated.

3.2 Performance management: the sustainable balanced scorecard (SBSC)

Section 10.6 discusses the adaptation of the Balanced Scorecard (BSC) for sustainability, noting that its top-down structure, which deduces measures from strategy, ensures alignment. Coca-Cola confirms its use of the BSC framework.

The company's public sustainability Key Performance Indicators (KPIs) – such as water use reduction, recycled material content, and emissions reduction – can be mapped to an SBSC, as discussed in Chapter 10.

The critical analysis of the SBSC presented in Section 10.6, however, centres on its reliance on 'causal links' or 'finalities' (Nørreklit 2003) to justify sustainability initiatives. This critique provides a powerful tool for explaining Coca-Cola's central paradox: the abandonment of its reusability goal in 2024.

1. The SBSC 'Story' (2018–2023): The 'strategy map' for the 2018 'World Without Waste' initiative would have contained the following 'finality' (or causal logic):
    - (Customer Perspective): Consumers and regulators increasingly demand sustainable packaging.
    - (Internal Process Perspective): To meet this demand, we will invest in a portfolio of solutions: 100% recyclability, 50% recycled content (rPET), and 25% reusable/refillable packaging.
    - (Learning & Growth Perspective): This will build our brand reputation, stakeholder trust, and 'social license to operate'.
    - (Financial Perspective): This enhanced brand value and social license will drive sales, mitigate regulatory risk, and ensure long-term, sustainable financial value.
2. The SBSC 'Failure' (2024): The abandonment of the reusability goal in 2024 demonstrates exactly where this 'finality' broke down. The 25% reusability target proved to be in direct conflict with the financial perspective. Reusability is not a simple material substitution; it requires a new, capital-intensive business model of reverse logistics, bottle-washing infrastructure, and retailer cooperation. In Scotland, for example, the associated Deposit Return Scheme (DRS) was criticised for its high costs.
3. The 'Rational' Decision: The corporation's internal management accounting analysis likely showed that reusability lacked a 'demonstrable positive causality' to short- or medium-term profit. As predicted by the chapter's critique, the SBSC framework, by its very nature of 'privileging the financial over sustainability', rationally forces the abandonment of the most ecologically significant solution (reuse) in favour of the proxified one (single-use 'recyclable' bottles), which remains highly profitable. The abandonment of the reuse goal is the ultimate proof of the SBSC's "capitalistic" logic in action.

Part 4: The 'overcoding' of sustainability: a critical analysis (section 10.7)

This part synthesises the case, directly applying the book's central thesis from Section 10.7: that management accounting's response to sustainability is a process of 'overcoding' and 'proxification'. This process translates the broad, multi-dimensional, and political concept of sustainability into a narrow, manageable, and financialised set of corporate metrics.

4.1 The 'ecology' vs. 'economy' contradiction: the 'evolution' of waste

The fundamental contradiction for Coca-Cola lies between its 'Ecology' dimension (the planet's finite capacity to absorb waste) and its 'Economy' dimension (a business model that profits from creating that waste).

- The Corporate Claim: The company's 'World Without Waste' initiative and its 2024 sustainability statements present a narrative of responsible management.
- The Ecological Reality: This narrative is contradicted by its status as the six-time #1 plastic polluter. In 2023, 33,820 branded plastic items were collected in global audits. Critically, the company's total virgin plastic use increased in 2024 to 2.94 million metric tons, up from 2.83 million metric tons in 2023.

The 'overcoding' event occurred in December 2024, when Coca-Cola announced it was 'evolving' its environmental goals. This 'evolution' is the central exhibit of the case, as it provides a transparent, auditable trail of 'proxification' in action. The changes are detailed in Table 1.

4.2 The 'polity' contradiction: biopolitical governance in action

The final contradiction to analyse is the 'Polity', defined in Chapter 10 as the system of political accountability and governance. Coca-Cola's actions in this sphere are a textbook example of the 'biopolitical' governance model, where the firm acts like a state and on the state.

The company's strategy is coherent but contradictory:

1. (Action 1) Governing Globally (Engaging 'Politics'): The company engages at the highest level of global 'politics' (the institutional arrangements). It sponsored the UN Climate Conference (COP27) and is a key corporate participant in the UN Plastics Treaty negotiations.
2. (Action 2) Resisting Locally (Blocking 'Politics'): Simultaneously, the company and its proxies have historically lobbied against state-level 'politics'

Table 1: The 'overcoding' of Coca-Cola's packaging goals (2018–2024)

Purpose of Table: This table provides the core evidence for the case study. It operationalises the 'overcoding' thesis by demonstrating how a genuine ecological concept ('reuse') is eliminated and other goals ('collection', 'recycled content') are 'proxified' and weakened when they conflict with the 'capitalist axiomatic' of profit from single-use plastics.

Goal Category	2018 'World Without Waste' Pledge	2024 'Evolved' Goal (Announced Dec 2024)	Critical Analysis: The 'Overcoding' & 'Proxification'
Reuse / Refill	25% of all packaging to be reusable or refillable by 2030.	Goal abandoned. The target "disappeared" from the company website. No new reuse target was set.	Overcoding (Elimination): The most ecologically significant goal—one that would require reducing single-use production—is eliminated entirely because it conflicts directly with the core business model.
Recycled Content	50% recycled material (rPET) in packaging by 2030.	30%–35% recycled plastic by 2035.	Proxification (Weakening & Delaying): The target is quantitatively reduced (from 50% to ~32.5%) and the deadline is temporally extended (from 2030 to 2035).
Collection	Collect and recycle 100% of bottles and cans sold by 2030.	"Help ensure collection" of 70%–75% of bottles and cans by 2035.	Proxification (Obscuring Responsibility): The language is 'overcoded'. Accountability is transferred from a direct, absolute "Collect 100%" to a vague, shared "Help ensure 70%–75%".

Source: Synthesised from.
https://www.coca-colacompany.com/media-center/the-coca-cola-company-evolves-voluntary-environmental-goals
https://www.theguardian.com/environment/2024/dec/03/coca-cola-accused-dropping-reusable-packaging-target
https://www.plasticpollutioncoalition.org/blog/2024/12/12/coca-cola-quietly-drops-reuse-targets
https://www.packagingdive.com/news/coca-cola-new-packaging-sustainability-goals-2035/734379/

that would effectively solve the plastic problem, such as Deposit Return Schemes (DRS). This lobbying creates a 'shaky peg' for effective regulation and protects its core business model.

3. (Action 3) The 'Polity' Fights Back: In response, 'Polity' actors are challenging the company's legitimacy. Lawsuits have been filed by government bodies (e.g., Los Angeles County) and environmental groups (e.g., Earth Island Institute), accusing the company of deceptive marketing and 'greenwashing'.

This behaviour, when viewed through the lens of Chapter 10, is not hypocrisy; it is a coherent strategy for 'Empire'.

1. First, sponsoring COP and the Plastics Treaty talks allows the firm to co-create the global 'politics' of sustainability. It ensures that 'solutions' are defined as "market-based," voluntary, and recycling-focused (like its 'World Without Waste' initiative) rather than regulatory and production-focused (e.g., mandatory reuse quotas or production caps).
2. Second, lobbying against state-level DRS protects its 'Economy' model from costly state intervention.
3. Third, its management accounting systems (the VWBA for water, the SBSC for performance) create the technical, apolitical-sounding justification for this entire biopolitical strategy. The accounting 'proxifies' the 'political' problem into a 'managerial' one, perfectly illustrating the 'overcoding' of sustainability.

Case questions and seminar tasks

This section is designed for advanced seminar discussion or as a final examination case. Students are expected to synthesise the case data (Parts 1–4) with the theoretical concepts from Chapter 10.

Discussion questions

1. The 'Overcoding' Thesis (Section 10.7):

   Using the concepts of 'overcoding' and 'proxification', critically analyse the evidence presented in Table 1. Explain why, from a mainstream management accounting perspective (e.g., SBSC logic), Coca-Cola's 2024 'evolution' of its packaging goals could be seen as a 'rational' and 'strategic' decision. How does this decision demonstrate the chapter's critique of 'privileging the financial over sustainability'?

2. Costing Sustainability and 'Proxification' (Sections 10.6 & 10.7):

   Critically evaluate Coca-Cola's 'water replenishment' accounting methodology (Volumetric Water Benefit Accounting or VWBA).

   a. How does this accounting practice 'overcode' the political (local community conflict23) and ecological (local aquifer depletion) dimensions of water use as defined in Figure 10?
   b. Using the logic of the Sustainable Balanced Scorecard, explain the likely 'finality' (causal link to financial performance) that this '159% replenished' metric 5 is designed to demonstrate.
   c. What material realities does this 'proxified' metric successfully obscure from stakeholders and ESG rating agencies?

3. The 'Polity' and Biopolitical Governance (Sections 10.2 & 10.3):

   Chapter 10 presents a 'biopolitical' reframing of CSR, where corporations act as 'governing' bodies. Analyse Coca-Cola's contradictory 'Polity' strategy: (a) sponsoring global governance institutions like COP27 34 and the UN Plastics Treaty negotiations 36, whilst (b) simultaneously lobbying against effective state-level regulations like Deposit Return Schemes (DRS).

   a. How does this dual strategy resolve the apparent paradox of Friedman's critique that CSR is 'socialism'?
   b. How does it illustrate the fundamental, 'agonistic' conflict between the 'Economy' dimension (profit efficiency) and the 'Polity' dimension (democratic accountability)?

4. Mapping the Four Contradictions (Section 10.2):

   Map the core business model of Coca-Cola onto the four structural categories presented in Figure 10.1.

   a. Provide a specific corporate action, policy, or metric from the case study that primarily operates within each of the four dimensions.
   b. Explain how the logic of the 'Economy' (efficiency, profit, financialisation) is used to 'overcode' and 'proxify' the demands of the 'Ecology', 'Society', and 'Polity'.
   c. In your view, do Coca-Cola's management accounting systems (VWBA, SBSC) resolve these fundamental contradictions, or merely obscure them? Justify your answer using case evidence.

5. The Final Critique (Section 10.7):

   Revisit Milne's (1996) assertion, cited in Section 10.7, that 'sustainability is not an organizational concept, and to apply it at the (capitalistic) organizational level is either very complex or very stupid'.

   Write a 1,000-word response to your (hypothetical) CEO. Using the Coca-Cola case study as your sole body of evidence, you must either support or refute Milne's claim. Your response must demonstrate a mastery of the theoretical concepts from Chapter 10.

Chapter review questions

Part 1: Progress-testing question bank (multiple-choice questions)

Section 1: The Political and politics of sustainability (sections 10.1–10.2)

1. As introduced in Section 10.2, the Brundtland Commission's (1987) definition of sustainable development immediately highlights which fundamental conflict?

    a. The conflict between neoliberal economic logic and socialist ideologies.
    b. The conflict between the 'eco-efficiency' and 'eco-justice' aspects of resource allocation.
    c. The inter-generational conflict between the needs of the present and the ability of future generations to meet their own needs.
    d. The intra-generational conflict between developed and developing economies over carbon emissions.

2. The chapter draws on the political theorist Chantal Mouffe (Section 10.2) to distinguish between 'the political' and 'politics'. Which of the following statements correctly encapsulates this distinction?

    a. 'The political' refers to institutional arrangements like the UN SDGs, whilst 'politics' refers to the underlying, fundamental conflicts in human society.
    b. 'The political' is the ontological dimension of fundamental antagonisms and conflicts, whilst 'politics' is the ontic set of institutional practices that create order.
    c. 'The political' is the domain of corporate strategy and market-based solutions, whilst 'politics' is the domain of government and legislative functions.
    d. 'The political' and 'politics' are treated as synonymous terms, both referring to the democratic process of reconciling interests.

3. Section 10.2 and Figure 10.1 present four fundamental structural categories of sustainability. Which of the following correctly matches a category with its primary driver or logic?

    a. The Economy: driven by the logic of social solidarity.
    b. The Polity: driven by the logic of eco-justice.
    c. The Society: driven by the logic of social solidarity and eco-justice.
    d. The Ecology: driven by the logic of efficiency.

4. When discussing the 'Ecology' dimension in Section 10.2, the chapter differentiates between 'eco-efficiency' and 'eco-justice'. Which of the following statements best describes their relationship?

a. Eco-efficiency and eco-justice are identical concepts, both focusing on minimising the environmental footprint.
b. Eco-justice is a subset of eco-efficiency, as it deals with the efficient allocation of social resources.
c. Eco-efficiency is a sufficient and necessary condition for sustainable development, making eco-justice a secondary concern.
d. Eco-efficiency (minimising environmental impact) is necessary but not sufficient for sustainable development, as it must be paired with eco-justice (equitable distribution).

5. How does the chapter (Section 10.2) use the work of Gray et al. (1996) to define a 'sustainable business' at a minimum?

a. A business that invests heavily in renewable energy and carbon offsetting.
b. A business that leaves the environment no worse off at the end of the accounting period than it was at the beginning.
c. A business that achieves a positive correlation between its financial performance and its ESG score.
d. A business that complies with all government regulations regarding pollution and waste.

Section 2: The neoliberal logic and its biopolitical evolution (section 10.3)

6. What was the core argument of Milton Friedman's (1970) critique of corporate social responsibility (CSR), as cited in Section 10.3?

a. That CSR was a necessary cost of doing business in a modern, free-enterprise system.
b. That corporate managers were 'unwitting puppets' preaching' pure and unadulterated socialism' by engaging in CSR.
c. That CSR was beneficial, but only if it could be directly and immediately linked to an increase in quarterly profits.
d. That corporations should work closely with the government, acting as legislators and jurists to impose taxes for social ends.

7. Beyond the general critique, what was Friedman's specific 'political principle' argument against corporate managers engaging in social responsibility?

a. He argued that managers lack the necessary technical expertise to solve complex social problems like pollution.
b. He argued that engaging in social responsibility was an 'epistemic strategy' to rebrand their firms.
c. He argued that managers, as self-selected agents of stockholders, would be

undemocratically wielding a 'taxing' power and acting simultaneously as 'legislator, executive and jurist'.

d. He argued that social responsibility was a biopolitical strategy to manage the lives of populations, which he supported.

8. According to Section 10.3, academic studies (e.g., Al-Tuwaijri et al. 2004) emerged to 'test' the relationship between CSR and financial performance. What does the chapter identify as the 'crucial aspect' and underlying normative principle of these studies?

   a. They proved conclusively that a positive, causal relationship exists, thus resolving the 'oxymoron'.
   b. Their methodology and principles implied that the rationale for sustainability is derived from its contribution to financial performance, thus prioritising economic criteria.
   c. They focused primarily on the 'Polity' dimension, correcting its omission in corporate discourse.
   d. They revealed that the 'anatomico-politics of the human body' was the primary driver of corporate profit.

9. The chapter offers a Foucauldian perspective (Section 10.3) to explain the evolution of corporate governance. It contrasts 'anatomico-politics' with 'biopolitics of security'. What does this shift represent?

   a. A shift from managing the life of populations ('biopolitics') to managing the disciplinary politics of the individual human body ('anatomico-politics').
   b. A shift from managing the disciplinary politics of the human body ('anatomico-politics') to the management of the life of populations ('biopolitics of security').
   c. A shift from focusing on shareholder wealth (biopolitics) to focusing on stakeholder influence (anatomico-politics).
   d. A shift from state-led socialism (anatomico-politics) to free-market capitalism (biopolitics of security).

10. How does the 'biopolitics of security' perspective (Section 10.3) provide a 'neoliberal reasoning' for the rise of CSR, paradoxically refuting Friedman's initial fears?

   a. It argues that Friedman was correct and that CSR remains a socialist threat to capital accumulation.
   b. It suggests that corporations are forced into CSR by powerful state governments, which exercise disciplinary power.
   c. It reframes CSR as a neoliberal enhancement of governmentality, where pri-

vate capital (the 'empire') assumes state-like governance functions (managing 'life') to enhance its capacity for accumulation.

d. It argues that CSR is a temporary marketing fad that has no real connection to the underlying governance structures of neoliberalism.

Section 3: Management accounting and strategic rationalisation (sections 10.4–10.5)

11. Section 10.4 distinguishes the role of mainstream management accounting from that of economics in rationalising sustainability. What is this key distinction?

    a. Management accounting' tests' the causality between sustainability and financial performance, whilst economics 'creates' it.
    b. Management accounting 'creates' (rather than 'tests') a positive correlation, or 'finality', between sustainability and financial performance by developing strategic frameworks.
    c. Management accounting focuses only on 'eco-justice', whilst economics focuses only on 'eco-efficiency'.
    d. Management accounting is concerned with external reporting, whilst economics is concerned with internal decision-making.

12. According to Section 10.4, the rise of corporate accountability and sustainability reporting is underpinned by a 'neoliberal paradox' of the firm. What is this paradox?

    a. That corporations are 'too big to fail', meaning their failures are shareholder losses, but also political-economic catastrophes.
    b. That corporations are 'suspects and prospects'; they are simultaneously venues where life is profitably sustained and spaces where life is endangered.
    c. That the concept of 'ownership' has been diluted, whilst the concept of 'stake' has become more important.
    d. All of the above.

13. Section 10.4 argues that the concept of 'stake' has become more crucial than legal ownership. How does the chapter redefine 'stake' in this biopolitical context, contrasting it with popular stakeholder theory?

    a. 'Stake' is defined as the capacity of stakeholders to influence the firm.
    b. 'Stake' is defined as the legal, financial share owned by an investor in the corporation.
    c. 'Stake' is defined as the firm's capacity to influence collective and individual life, reflecting its power as a biopolitical governor.
    d. 'Stake' is defined as the contractual obligations a firm has to its employees, suppliers, and customers.

14. Section 10.5 discusses Environmental, Social, and Governance (ESG) indices. How does the chapter primarily define the function of ESG?

    a. As a set of legally binding international laws that force corporations to be sustainable.
    b. As a marketing tool used only for product labelling to attract premium prices.
    c. As a "market database-driven analytical framework" that assesses corporate investment risk, thereby pressuring top management to incorporate ESG elements.
    d. As a comprehensive measure of a corporation's true contribution to the four dimensions of sustainability (Economy, Polity, Society, Ecology).

15. In the discussion on 'envisioning sustainability' (Section 10.5), what does the chapter identify as a primary motivator for corporations to revise their vision and mission statements?

    a. A genuine, internally-driven desire to solve the planet's ecological crises, as documented in their internal audits.
    b. The reporting mandates of accrediting bodies like the Global Reporting Initiative (GRI) and the desire to engage in 'rating games' for legitimisation.
    c. Milton Friedman's 1970 essay, which encouraged corporations to adopt a 'social conscience'.
    d. The technical requirements of Activity-Based Costing, which demand a clear strategic vision for cost allocation.

16. According to Nielsen's 2015 Global Sustainability Report (cited in Section 10.5), what did the survey data reveal about consumer behaviour and corporate marketing tactics?

    a. Consumers were unwilling to pay more for sustainable brands, and most companies (65%) used 'Claim Only' on their labels.
    b. 66% of consumers were willing to pay more for sustainable brands, and the most dominant corporate tactic (65%) was 'Marketing Only' (using websites, news, etc.).
    c. Consumers were confused about sustainability, leading 90% of companies to use a 'Claim + Marketing' combination.
    d. 43% of consumers were willing to pay more, but this was driven only by environmental friendliness, not social value.

Section 4: Operationalizing Sustainability: frameworks and decisions (section 10.6)

17. What was a key finding from Vesty's (2011) survey of Australian CFOs regarding sustainability in capital investment decisions (Section 10.6)?

    a. That 100% of CFOs rejected any project with a negative net present value (NPV), regardless of sustainability benefits.
    b. That enhancing corporate reputation was a key motivator, and 40% of CFO respondents would not automatically reject negative NPV projects if sustainability benefits were identified.
    c. That sustainability managers played no role in the capital investment appraisal process.
    d. That CFOs only considered quantitative data and 'downplayed' or 'ignored' all qualitative narratives about sustainability.

18. Section 10.6 discusses Porter and Kramer's (2006) 'insertion' of sustainability into the value chain. According to Table 10.1, 'Emissions and waste', 'worker safety', and 'hazardous materials' are examples of sustainability considerations for which value chain element?

    a. Inbound Logistics.
    b. Operations.
    c. Marketing and Sales.
    d. After-Sales Service.

19. What is the chapter's critical interpretation (Section 10.6) of the attempts by experts like Porter and Kramer (2006) to integrate sustainability into existing frameworks like the value chain?

    a. It views these as genuine, revolutionary breakthroughs that solve the fundamental contradictions of sustainability.
    b. It views these as a technical failure, as the 'diamond framework' (Table 10.2) is incompatible with sustainability.
    c. It views these as a form of 'epistemic strategy' or 'remarketing strategy' for their existing models in an evolving market, lacking a genuinely sustainable approach.
    d. It praises these attempts for prioritising the 'Polity' and 'Society' dimensions over the 'Economy'.

20. According to Figge et al. (2002), as discussed in Section 10.6, which of the following is one of the three primary approaches for integrating sustainability into the Balanced Scorecard (BSC)?

    a. Removing the 'Financial' perspective and replacing it with a 'Sustainability' perspective.

b. Introducing an additional fifth 'non-market' perspective to house environmental and social aspects.
c. Creating a 'Sustainability Strategy Map' that links all four perspectives directly to shareholder wealth, ignoring non-financial links.
d. Focusing exclusively on eco-justice issues whilst ignoring all eco-efficiency measures.

21. What is the chapter's fundamental ideological critique of integrating sustainability into the Balanced Scorecard and value chain analysis frameworks (Section 10.6)?

    a. That these frameworks are too complex for managers to use effectively.
    b. That these frameworks "privilege the financial over sustainability", limiting action to initiatives with a demonstrable positive causality to shareholder wealth.
    c. That these frameworks, by focusing on 'finalities' (causal links), fail to provide quantifiable key performance indicators (KPIs).
    d. That these frameworks are 'unadulterated socialism' and undermine the free market, just as Friedman warned.

22. According to Section 10.6, how do frameworks like the Sustainable BSC paradoxically compare to the critiques of economists like Friedman and Daly?

    a. They prove Friedman and Daly correct by demonstrating that sustainability is always unprofitable.
    b. They are 'veiled efforts to obscure this inherent contradiction' (between profit and sustainability) that Friedman and Daly openly acknowledged.
    c. They adopt Friedman's ideology by focusing exclusively on shareholder wealth and rejecting all social responsibility.
    d. They adopt Daly's ideology by rejecting 'sustainable growth' and focusing only on 'eco-justice'.

Section 5: Operationalizing sustainability: costing and systems (section 10.6)

23. Section 10.6 describes the foundation of sustainability costing. What is the system theory, also known as 'materials balance' or 'eco-balance', that underpins the tracing of physical flows?

    a. That all physical inputs are eventually sold as products, with zero waste or emissions.
    b. That all physical inputs eventually become outputs—either as products or as waste and emissions—requiring a balance between inputs and outputs.
    c. That monetary flows are the most important factor, and physical flows are only relevant if they have a direct financial cost.

d. That only non-renewable resources need to be tracked, as renewable resources are self-balancing.

24. According to Figure 10.4 (Section 10.6), how is Activity-Based Costing (ABC) considered appropriate for environmental costing?

    a. It exclusively uses a 'cost assignment view' to allocate all environmental costs to a single overhead pool.
    b. It has a dual utility: a 'cost assignment view' (tracing resource costs to activities) and a 'process view' (analysing cost drivers and performance).
    c. It bypasses the need for physical flow accounting by focusing only on monetary values.
    d. It is only used for tracking 'Social' and 'Governance' costs, not 'Environmental' costs.

25. The UN Division of Sustainable Development (2001) framework (Table 10.3) provides an environmental activity-cost classification scheme. Which of the following is one of the four main cost/expenditure categories listed?

    a. Shareholder dividends and executive compensation.
    b. Marketing and advertising costs for green products.
    c. Material purchase value of non-product output.
    d. Research and development for new financial products.

26. Based on the definitions and Figure 10.5 in Section 10.6, what is the primary distinction between Life Cycle Costing (LCC) and Whole Life Costing (WLC)?

    a. LCC and WLC are identical, interchangeable terms for carbon costing.
    b. LCC is a broad framework, whilst WLC is a subset of LCC focusing only on construction.
    c. LCC comprises investment, operational, maintenance, and disposal costs, whilst WLC is a broader concept that includes LCC plus client/user costs and other external costs.
    d. LCC focuses on financial costs, whilst WLC focuses only on non-financial 'externalities' like global warming.

27. The GHG Protocol, discussed in Section 10.6, categorises emissions into three scopes. Which of the following correctly defines these scopes?

    a. Scope 1: Indirect (value chain); Scope 2: Indirect (purchased energy); Scope 3: Direct (owned).
    b. Scope 1: Direct (owned/controlled); Scope 2: Indirect (purchased electricity, heat, or steam); Scope 3: All other indirect (value chain).
    c. Scope 1: Direct (owned/controlled); Scope 2: All other indirect (value chain); Scope 3: Indirect (purchased electricity).

  d. Scope 1: Indirect (purchased energy); Scope 2: Direct (owned/controlled); Scope 3: Indirect (value chain).

28. As described in Section 10.6, what is the primary function of an Environmental Management System (EMS)?

    a. An organisation's formal structure for planning, executing, managing, controlling, and reporting its environmental policies.
    b. A specific costing technique, identical to LCC, for tracking carbon emissions.
    c. A marketing system for promoting a brand's sustainable image to consumers.
    d. A set of government regulations, identical to the GHG Protocol.

Section 6: The critical conclusion: 'overcoding' and 'proxification' (section 10.7)

29. What is the chapter's overarching critical conclusion (Section 10.7) regarding management accounting's response to the sustainability agenda?

    a. That management accounting has successfully solved the sustainability crisis by developing innovative tools like the SBSC and Environmental ABC.
    b. That management accounting's efforts, whilst genuine, fail to recognise and acknowledge the fundamental political contradictions (Economy, Polity, Society, Ecology) that underpin unsustainability.
    c. That management accounting's only failure is its lack of alignment with Friedman's neoclassical economic principles.
    d. That management accounting has focused too much on 'eco-justice' and 'polity', and must now return its focus to 'eco-efficiency' and 'economy'.

30. The chapter (Section 10.7) employs the concept of 'overcoding' from Deleuze and Guattari (1987). What is 'overcoding' in this context?

    a. The process of allowing diverse, agonistic political contradictions to coexist.
    b. A technical error in programming an Environmental Management System (EMS).
    c. The expression of the capitalist axiomatic, resulting in 'phenomena of centering, unification, totalization, integration, hierarchization, and finalization'.
    d. The act of creating new, radical accounting practices that challenge the dominance of financial reporting.

31. According to Section 10.7, what is the result of this 'overcoding' process in management accounting?

    a. The 'proxification' of sustainability, where its broader meaning is lost and translated into narrow, economic, market variables like ESG scores.

b. The successful integration of all four political contradictions into a single, unified, and truly sustainable corporate strategy.
c. The total rejection of sustainability by corporations, who now openly follow Friedman's 1970 advice.
d. The replacement of 'eco-efficiency' with 'eco-justice' as the primary driver of corporate profit.

32. How does the chapter (Section 10.7) use the work of Prahalad (2005) and Roy (2010) to illustrate the dangerous consequences of this 'proxification'?

a. It shows that by 'overcoding' sustainability, accountants can now accurately measure 'poverty capital' and solve global poverty.
b. It argues that by translating sustainability into market variables, strategists do not see poverty; instead, they see corporate 'fortunes at the bottom of the pyramid' or new ecosystems for 'poverty capital'.
c. It praises Prahalad and Roy for developing the key frameworks that allow management accounting to integrate eco-justice into the value chain.
d. It suggests that 'proxification' is a necessary first step towards developing a genuine understanding of poverty and social justice.

33. The chapter concludes (Section 10.7) with Milne's (1996) assertion that applying sustainability at the '(capitalistic) organizational level is either very complex or very stupid'. What is the critical implication of this statement in the context of the chapter's argument?

a. That sustainability is a simple concept that managers are deliberately making complex.
b. That sustainability is not an organizational-level, managerial, or technical concept, but a political one rooted in fundamental contradictions that capitalism cannot solve, only 'overcode'.
c. That the UN and other advocates have failed to provide a clear business case for sustainability, making it 'stupid' for corporations to attempt it.
d. That with more complex models (like WLC and SBSC), the 'stupid' and 'complex' aspects of sustainability can be eliminated.

Comprehension questions

1. List the four fundamental contradictory categories that underpin (un)sustainability and explain the fundamental structural logics according to which or towards which they operate.
2. Explain Chantal Mouffe's differentiation between 'the political' and 'politics'.
3. Explain what you mean by the terms' eco-efficiency' and 'eco-justice'. Which of these would hold the ideas of socio-political justice and ecological justice?
4. Briefly explain the grounds on which Milton Friedman propagated his critique of corporate leaders investing in corporate social responsibility projects.
5. Briefly explain this chapter's 'neoliberal reasoning' for corporate engagement in social responsibility and sustainability projects.
6. Critique the mainstream economic objection to corporate leaders investing in corporate social responsibility projects using the 'neoliberal reasoning' outlined above.
7. Explain why there was an upsurge in 'testing' the correlation between corporate financial performance and corporate social responsibility engagements.
8. List and briefly explain the different levels at which management accounting integration of sustainability takes place.
9. Briefly explain the neoliberal paradox of corporations that underpins the necessity of environmental, social, and governance (ESG) initiatives.
10. List the six key themes or levels of integrating sustainability into corporate management and accounting practices.
11. Briefly describe what you mean by ESG. Briefly explain how ESG may motivate corporations to become more environmentally and socially responsible.
12. With some examples, explain how and why corporate strategic statements such as vision and mission are refined to incorporate sustainability.
13. Using Nielsen's (2015) survey data mentioned in this chapter as an example, explain why and how companies mobilise sustainability as an element of 'market positioning'.
14. Using Vesty's (2011) Australian survey data as an example, briefly explain the manner in which sustainability concerns can influence capital investment decisions.
15. Briefly explain how Porter and Kramer suggest extending the value chain analysis and industry analysis frameworks to integrate sustainability concerns.
16. Using the study of Figge et al. (2002) as an example, explain the different ways that the BSC framework is refined to consider sustainability issues.
17. Briefly explain how the causalities, or 'finalities', that a sustainable BSC embeds could be problematic.

18. Explain the use of activity-based analysis and costing in relation to:

    a. Tracing the physical flow
    b. Tracing the monetary flow

19. Using the United Nations Division of Sustainable Development (2001) framework as a basis, list the cost categories into which environmental activity costs should be classified.
20. Briefly explain life cycle cost (LCC) and whole life cost (WLC) and their interrelationship in relation to sustainability.
21. List and briefly explain the principal elements of an Environmental Management System (EMS).

Explore further

1. Read the following paper to explore the broader meaning of sustainable development:

   Bebbington, J. (2001). Sustainable development: a review of the international development, business and accounting literature. Accounting Forum, 25(2), 128-157. https://doi.org/doi:10.1111/1467-6303.00059

2. Visit the UN SDGs to explore the overall global institutional infrastructure within which the UN operationalises its sustainability goals. Pay special attention to the importance of the corporate sector in that global project.
3. Read the book Capitalism: As If the World Matters by Jonathan Porritt. The author is an influential policy thinker; therefore, this book was influential in policy circles. Think of the ideas this book promotes regarding how managerialist and Western-centric they are.
4. Visit one of the following websites of ESG indices: MSCI ESG Leaders Indices, the FTSE4Good Index Series, or the Dow Jones Sustainability Indices. Explore the methodology it follows in indexing sustainability. Critically evaluate the normative/ideological basis for this indexing exercise and how well the index captures sustainability's broader meaning.

Develop your critical argumentation skills.

1. Write an argumentative essay on the following theme:

   'Sustainability is not an organizational concept, and to apply it at the (capitalistic) organizational level is either very complex or very stupid.'

2. Write an argumentative essay on the following theme:

   'Sustainability involves offering organizations a new set of strategic visions, competitive strategies, and operational tactics.'

3. Write an argumentative essay on the following theme:

   'When I hear businessmen speak eloquently about the "social responsibilities of business in a free-enterprise system,"... they are—or would be if they or anyone else took them seriously—preaching pure and unadulterated socialism. Businessmen who talk this way are unwitting puppets of the intellectual forces that have been undermining the basis of a free society these past decades.' (Milton Friedman 1970)

   Your essay should critically evaluate this statement, first by articulating Friedman's economic arguments against corporate leaders investing in social responsibility-related matters, and secondly by offering a critique drawing on alternative theoretical explanations of why corporations increasingly engage in sustainability matters.

References

Al-Tuwaijri, S. A., T. E. Christensen, and K. E. Hughes. 2004. The relations among environmental disclosure, environmental performance, and economic performance: a simultaneous equations approach. Accounting, Organizations and Society 29 (5-6):447-471.

Alawattage, C., and S. Fernando. 2017. Postcoloniality in corporate social and environmental accountability. Accounting, Organizations and Society 60 (Supplement C):1-20.

Alawattage, C., and D. Wickramasinghe. 2019. Strategizing Management Accounting: Liberal Origins and Neoliberal Trends. London: Routledge.

———. 2022. Strategising management accounting: liberal origins and neoliberal trends. Accounting, Auditing & Accountability Journal 35 (2):518-546.

Alexander, G. J., and R. A. Buchholz. 1978. Corporate Social Responsibility and Stock Market Performance. The Academy of Management Journal 21 (3):479-486.

Artiach, T., D. Lee, D. Nelson, and J. Walker. 2010. The determinants of corporate sustainability performance. Accounting & Finance 50 (1):31-51.

Barnett, M. L., and R. M. Salomon. 2012. Does it pay to be really good? addressing the shape of the relationship between social and financial performance. Strategic Management Journal 33 (11):1304-1320.

Bebbington, J. 2001. Sustainable development: a review of the international development, business and accounting literature. Accounting Forum 25 (2):128-157.

Bebbington, J., C. Larrinaga-González, and J. M. Moneva-Abadía. 2008. Legitimating reputation/the reputation of legitimacy theory. Accounting, Auditing & Accountability Journal 21 (3).

Campbell, D. J. 2000. Legitimacy Theory or Managerial Reality Construction? Corporate Social Disclosure in Marks and Spencer Plc Corporate Reports, 1969-1997. Accounting Forum 24 (1):80-100.

Cho, C. H., and D. M. Patten. 2007. The role of environmental disclosures as tools of legitimacy: A research note. Accounting, Organizations and Society 32 (7-8):639-647.

Cooper, C. 2015. Entrepreneurs of the self: The development of management control since 1976. Accounting, Organizations and Society 47:14-24.

Daly, H. E. 1993. Sustainable growth: an impossible theorem. In Valuing the Earth: Economics, Ecology, Ethics, edited by H. E. Daly and K. N. Townsend. Ma: MIT Press, 267-274.

Deleuze, G., and F. Guattari. 1987. A Thousand Plateaus: Capitalism and Schizophrenia. Minnesota: University of Minnesota Press.

Dragos, D., and B. Neamtu. 2013. Life Cycle Costing (LCC) in the New EU Directive Proposal. EPPPL 1:19-30.

Figge, F., T. Hahn, S. Schaltegger, and M. Wagner. 2002. The Sustainability Balanced Scorecard linking sustainability management to business strategy. Business Strategy and the Environment 11 (5):269-284.

Foucault, M. 1995. Discipline and punish: the birth of the prison. 2nd Vintage Books. ed. New York: Vintage Books.

Friedman, M. 1970. The Social Responsibility of Business is to Increase its Profits. The New York Times Magazine.

Gladwin, T. N., T.-S. Krause, and J. J. Kennelly. 1995. Beyond eco-efficiency: Towards socially sustainable business. Sustainable Development 3 (1):35-43.

Gray, R. 2010. Is accounting for sustainability actually accounting for sustainability...and how would we know? An exploration of narratives of organisations and the planet. Accounting, Organizations and Society 35 (1):47-62.

Gray, R., C. A. Adams, and D. Owen. 2014. Accountability, social responsibility, and sustainability: accounting for society and the environment. Harlow, Essex: Pearson Education Limited.

Gray, R., and J. Bebbington. 2001. Accounting for the Environment: Second Edition: SAGE Publications.

Gray, R., J. Bebbington, and D. Walters. 1993. Accounting for the Environment: Paul Chapman [for] ACCA, Chartered Association of Certified Accountants.

Gray, R., D. Owen, and C. A. Adams. 1996. Accounting & accountability: changes and challenges in corporate social and environmental reporting. London: Financial Times/Prentice Hall.

Gros, F. 2014. The Fourth Age of Security. In The Government of Life: Foucault, Biopolitics, and Neoliberalism, edited by V. Lemm and M. Vatter. New York: Fordham University Press, 17-28.

Hardt, M., and A. Negri. 2000. Empire. Cambridge, Mass.; London: Harvard University Press.

Holmes, B. 2007. Escape the overcode. In Continental drift: the other side of neoliberal globalisation. https://brianholmes.wordpress.com/2007/07/20/escape-the-overcode/.

Hopper, T., and N. Macintosh. 1993. Management accounting as disciplinary practice: the case of ITT under Harold Geneen. Management Accounting Research 4 (3):181-216.

International Federation of Accountants. 2005. Environmental Management Accounting: international guidance document. New York: International Federation of Accountants.

Kaplan, R. S., and D. McMillan. 2021. Reimagining the Balanced Scorecard for the ESG Era. In Harvard Business Review, 1-12.

Lamberton, G. 2005. Sustainability accounting--a brief history and conceptual framework. Accounting Forum 29 (1):7-26.

Langdon, D. 2007. Life cycle costing (LCC) as a contribution to sustainable construction: Guidance on the use of the LCC Methodology and its application in public procurement. Brussels: Davis Langdon Management Consulting.

Lemon, M., and A. Pember. 2014. Environmental Sustainability: Activity-based costing/management. Toronto: Chartered Professional Accountants of Canada.

Lubin, D. A., and D. C. Esty. 2010. The Sustainability Imperative. Harvard Business Review 2010 (May):2-9.

Milne, M. J. 1996. On sustainability; the environment and management accounting. Management Accounting Research 7 (1):135-161.

Mouffe, C. 1993. The return of the political. London: Verso.

———. 1999. Deliberative democracy or agonistic pluralism? Social Research 66 (3):745-758.

———. 2000. The democratic paradox. London: Verso.

———. 2005. On the political. Abingdon; Routledge.

———. 2013. Agonistics: thinking the world politically. London: Verso.

Munro, I. 2012. The Management of Circulations: Biopolitical Variations after Foucault. International Journal of Management Reviews 14 (3):345-362.

Nørreklit, H. 2000. The balance on the balanced scorecard a critical analysis of some of its assumptions. Management Accounting Research 11 (1):65-88.

———. 2003. The Balanced Scorecard: what is the score? A rhetorical analysis of the Balanced Scorecard. Accounting, Organizations and Society 28 (6):591-619.

Porter, M. E., and M. R. Kramer. 2006. Strategy and society: the link between competitive advantage and corporate social responsibility. Harvard Business Review 2006 (December):1-15.

Prahalad, C. K. 2005. The Fortune at the Bottom of the Pyramid: eradicating poverty through profits, enabling dignity and choice through markets. New Jersey: Wharton School Publishing.

Roy, A. 2010. Poverty Capital: Microfinance and the Making of Development: Taylor & Francis.

Thomson, I. 2007. Mapping the terrain of sustainability accounting. In Sustainability accounting and accountability, edited by J. Unerman, J. Bebbington and B. O'Dwyer. London: Routledge, 19-36.

United Nations Division of Sustainable Development. 2001. Environmental Management Accounting Procedures and Principles. New York: United Nations.

United Nations World Commission on Environment and Development. 1987. Our common future (The Brundtland Report). Oxford: Oxford University Press.

Vesty, G. 2011. The influence and impact of sustainability issues on capital investment decisions. Southbank: CPA Australia.

Index

Symbols

A

B

D

E

H

I

J

K

L

M

N

Q

R

S

www.ingramcontent.com/pod-product-compliance
Lightning Source LLC
LaVergne TN
LVHW070845210926
848482LV00016B/872